Social Network Theory and Educational Change

Social Network Theory and Educational Change

Edited by

Alan J. Daly

HARVARD EDUCATION PRESS

CAMBRIDGE, MASSACHUSETTS

Library of Congress Control Number 2010931410

Paperback ISBN 978-1-934742-80-8
Library Edition ISBN 978-1-934742-81-5

Published by Harvard Education Press,
an imprint of the Harvard Education Publishing Group

Harvard Education Press
8 Story Street
Cambridge, MA 02138

Cover Design: Sarah Henderson

The typefaces used in this book are ITC Stone Serif for text and ITC Stone Sans for display.

For my family, my first social network.

Contents

Acknowledgments

Over the course of my career in public education I have been fortunate enough to have had the opportunity to occupy multiple positions in education. (It should be noted that this was of my doing, not that I couldn't manage to keep a job!) As I reflect on my different positions, although they were in a variety of contexts and serving different populations, there was always one constant—the importance of relationships.

During my years as a teacher, I was always amazed at the potential of influencing a student just by building a relationship. The act of creating and nurturing relations with students was something I held dear. I prided myself on connecting with the "most difficult" students, trying to find ways to build bridges over chasms that had been deepened from years of low expectations, self-fulfilling prophecies, and systems bent on sorting and selecting. I observed the transformative power of the relationship in my own students, as well as the slow decay when relations were strained by misunderstanding, miscommunication, misinformation, or outright ignorance.

The power and potential of the relationship was further brought home to me in my work as a psychologist, where again I would see the results of harmful relations and the potential and promise of when relationships held restorative and transformative power. As an administrator working in an underperforming large urban junior high school, I witnessed excellent interventions—well grounded in research and supported through professional development—fail as an informal, highly central school leader publicly stated her disapproval and decided "her" kids would not participate. I saw how others with strong ties to this teacher felt the tension of balancing the force of the informal social network and external formal demands for change, how their resistance trapped them between the informal and formal worlds that simultaneously exist in all human systems. On the flip side, I also watched with amazement those leaders in formal positions who drew on their informal "network," bringing additional resources to the children and families of the community.

Now, at the academy, I realize those skills I honed in junior high (in my professional career; as a junior high youth I was officially central in the nerd network) of being able to access and leverage an informal network of relations are invaluable. In fact, this volume has been an exercise in building, nurturing, and most of all leveraging my informal social network in academia. I am indebted to the contributors, all of whom gave of themselves and in doing so have produced a collection of work representing some of the best, most current thinking in social network theory and educational change. I am equally appreciative of the assistance of my colleagues who were gracious enough to read early drafts of the work—an instrument of torture if there ever was one.

I also am indebted to the faculty and students in education studies at the University of California, San Diego, who have also been extremely supportive of the work—and at this point would like to see the book already. In addition, I would like to offer my appreciation to the William T. Grant and Spencer Foundations, which helped support my research and nurture my development. A book does not come together without wonderful support from the publisher. The staff at Harvard Education Press have been wonderful. Special thanks to Caroline Chauncey, whose patience, graciousness, and care made all the difference in making this work come alive.

Finally, I offer my sincere gratitude to my family near and far, who have always provided love, support, and a good kick in the pants when I was stuck, stressed, whining, or all three. I am truly thankful they are in my life, and now finally my appreciation is in writing.

I am proud to be associated with this work and am deeply indebted to all who assisted in making this book come to fruition. It represents the dream of a working-class Irish kid from Boston who moved beyond his social network to create the ties that matter.

Foreword

Social relationships loom large in portraits of educational change. For decades, explanations for the success or failure of change at multiple levels—from comprehensive reform initiatives to more bounded curricular and instructional innovations—have rested in part on the fabric and dynamics of social relations. Whether in research archives or in accumulated practical lore, the relational aspects of change occupy a prominent place. One might reasonably ask, then: What's new? What does social network theory have to offer that yields new insight and promises new tools for action? The answer is: a great deal. As a field, education has been relatively slow to capitalize on the theoretical, methodological and practical advances represented by social network theory and by methods of social network analysis. This volume does just that, offering a combination of conceptual overviews, empirical studies, and methodological guidance, while also inspiring readers to consider the advances yet to be made.

The rise of social network analysis in education research signals certain key shifts in perspective. In the effort to understand the conditions and processes that propel or inhibit change, researchers have moved steadily from a rather singular focus on the school as the unit of change to a more sophisticated conception of nested organizational relationships. Yet much of this research continues to give primacy to discrete organizational levels and boundaries. With the introduction of social network theory, we find a shift in gaze from formal organizational entities—the school, the district, the intermediary organization—to the network of actors engaged with one another in various ways and degrees. Social network theorists suspend or challenge assumptions about the meaningfulness of organizational boundaries and forms, asking instead how patterns of stability and change might be explained by the web of relations through which ideas, information, resources, and influence flow. Indeed, one might conceive of social network theory as subordinating or even eliminating the organization as an object of interest. However, the concerted focus on social networks in this volume does not leave the organization behind. Rather, the included chapters establish the significance of organizational contexts and actions for network formation and trajectories, as well as the contribution of network dynamics to organizational functions and fortunes.

A second and related shift takes us from a long-standing distinction between formal and informal to an appreciation for the complex interplay between formal *structures* and informal *patterns* of interaction within and across organizations. How are formally designated leaders positioned in relationship to informal networks of information sharing, advice-giving and problem-solving? How are these networks constituted to afford access to ideas, resources, and influence? What is the intersection of formally defined units—grade levels, departments, committees—and the meaningful, informal subgroups where interaction comes to be concentrated? It is in this shift especially that one begins to grasp the potential practical utility of social network analysis for those engaged in the work of educational improvement. The image of "social networks" resonates with a common sense understanding of life inside and outside organizations—we have an intuitive and experiential grasp of their presence and importance—but absent the kinds of mapping tools associated with network analysis, a network's shape and substance seem likely to remain elusive.

Finally, social network analysis offers a new set of tools for illuminating the on-the-ground work of the organization, and it is in that ongoing work that change is legitimated (or not), ideas given meaning, relationships built, broken or changed, and practice sustained or transformed. In prior research, such investigations have been the province of ethnographic studies—often small-scale, intensive microethnographies of situated interaction, typically in defined groups or settings. Social network theory and methods supply new strategic possibilities for embedding the study of interaction in a more systematic understanding of social structure in and across organizations. With its focus on the relative density of ties and centrality of actors, for example, network analysis supplies some needed specificity to the growing discourses on distributed forms of leadership and on professional community. Network structures and dynamics emerge as a key mechanism in the complicated interplay of broad (macro-level) institutional and social developments and the situated (or micro-level) practice of change work at every level of the system, from classroom to statehouse. Admittedly, empirical studies of social networks have granted more attention to mapping the nature of the social ties, or who is connected to whom, than to uncovering what flows through those ties in the way of information, advice, problem solving, material resources, interpretation, and influence. Yet in principle, the growing conceptual sophistication and methodological precision of social network theory afford a vehicle for delving more fully into the conditions, processes, and outcomes of educational change.

Of course, no theory embraces all relevant questions, and social network theory does not purport to account fully for the trajectories and dynamics of educational change. The shifts associated with social network theory might properly be seen as a broadening of perspective that helps to multiply advances that have accumulated elsewhere. Over the past three decades, the field has gone some considerable distance in specifying the conditions conducive to learning and improvement in schools and districts. For example, a sizable body of work points to the power of particular norms, practices, and structures in shaping a school's capacity for improvement. Across studies, evidence confirms the importance of collective responsibility for learning, relational trust, a shared orientation toward innovation, access to expertise, and leadership. Researchers have honed reliable measures of these and other relevant dimensions of school improvement. These gains are fully evident in this volume, where the contribution of social network theory occurs in fruitful combination with related theoretical perspectives and methods associated with research on change. In effect, the growing enthusiasm for social network theory and analysis reflects an appreciation for the added purchase it gives in understanding change trajectories.

Readers will find in this volume a persuasive case for the contributions made by social network theory to the study and practical pursuit of educational change, as well as careful attention to the conceptual and methodological challenges entailed in social network analysis. The papers speak to one another in generative and provocative ways, a cross-cutting conversation aided both by the range of theoretical questions they surface and by the sheer variety of the settings they investigate: the large-scale implementation of new curricula; the turn-around challenge in low performing schools; the introduction of instructional coaching as a dominant model of professional development; the formation of leadership cadres in emerging school systems.

In combination, the papers stimulate new questions about some of the most enduring problems of change. How do network relations—both existing and new—bear on "scaling up" promising innovations within and across organizations? How does the mapping of network ties and flows deepen our understanding of organizational capacity, including the nature of available expertise? What happens to organizational change trajectories when densely connected individuals leave organizations, potentially taking their network ties with them? Or when they draw on their ties to bridge otherwise disconnected individuals and groups? Similarly, what happens to the quality and reach of networks as organizational attention and resources shift over time? Given the demonstrated importance of leadership to change, how is it that designated leaders (and other change agents) vary so widely with regard to network connections and thus in how well they are positioned to promote and sustain change? With regard to these and other crucial questions, attending closely to the form and processes of social networks helps us to interrupt taken-for-granted assumptions about how educational systems work. In this important volume, we have a worthy foundation for the next generation of work on educational change and school improvement.

Judith Warren Little
Dean of the Graduate School of Education
University of California, Berkeley

CHAPTER 1

Mapping the Terrain

Social Network Theory and Educational Change

Alan J. Daly

> *In organizations, real power and energy is generated through relationships.*
> *The patterns of relationships and the capacities to form them are more*
> *important than tasks, functions, roles, and positions.*
>
> *—Margaret Wheatley*

Margaret Wheatley's words focus us the importance of relations in social systems. These words remind me of a key element of leading efforts at reform—the potential of relationships and the importance of others in the work of change. Unfortunately, this issue often becomes lost in the din of legislative mandates and the seemingly constant press for technical reforms, which are typically enacted using a variety of formal structures, processes, and accountability levers to improve performance. However, while such approaches to improving education are important and have been well documented, what is missing in the change equation is attention to the relational linkages between educators through which these change efforts flow.

Recent research suggests that relationships and collegial support are central for the retention, increased professionalism, and depth of engagement of educators.[1] The stronger the professional network, the more likely educators—at all levels—are to stay in the profession, feel a greater sense of efficacy, and engage in deeper levels of conversation around teaching and learning.[2] Thus the building and supporting professional relationships and networks is a critical way to sustain the work of teaching and learning and ultimately of change. This scholarship, coupled with the intuitive sense that relationships are central, raises important questions related to the association between relations, network structure, and efforts at change. Framed more broadly, this book explores the question: *In what ways do social networks support or constrain efforts at change at multiple levels?* It is under this broad question that the studies contained herein provide insight.

RELATIONS IN REFORM

Focusing on the primacy of social networks means challenging a nearly ubiquitous—but often flawed—belief about change: if individuals are provided with overwhelming evidence from an external expert as to how to engage in reform, educators at every level of the system will in fact change. However, what happens in practice is often quite different. A wonderful idea is presented, a few passionate individuals champion that effort, and then the strategy fails to be sustained, becoming yet another layer of sediment in the sea of change. Not surprisingly, in the ever-shifting tides, a strategy once long buried may resurface, under a different name and propounded by a different expert.

How do we begin to understand the processes of change from a more social and relational vantage point? In answering this question we must adopt a more relational perspective that acknowledges what we intuitively know and a growing body of network research suggests: relationships within a system matter in enacting change.[3] Change strategies, no matter how well-thought-out or useful, are more likely to be adopted from a trusted colleague than from an unfamiliar expert.[4] This implies that successful change requires not only attending to the important formal structures, but also to the informal networks of social relations that create webs of understanding, influence, and knowledge prior to, during, and after the implementation of a change strategy.

All too often, knowledge transfer is assumed to move in a rational and predictable manner through formal professional development experiences, trainings, or some form of professional community. However, in the network paradigm, the importance of social structure, position, and the quality of ties has a direct influence on the types of knowledge and information an individual receives.[5] This perspective shifts the emphasis of the old maxim, "It's not what you know, but who you know" to "*Who you know defines what you know.*"[6]

Social network research suggests that informal webs of relationships are often the chief determinants of how well and quickly change efforts take hold, diffuse, and sustain. Focusing on the structure of the relationship network first represents a shift in the way we approach change. Usually, a change effort begins with an overall articulation of the strategy, including the components of the effort, necessary resources, assessment tools, timelines, and personnel. In the best situations these elements are integrated, but more typically they are layered onto existing efforts without systematic attention to the structure of the underlying informal network or established relationships.

For example, a school or district may decide to adopt a new research-based reading program to promote reading achievement. This comprehensive program may require training, adherence to a specific curriculum, regular assessments, and collaboration between vertical and horizontal teams. This strategy assumes teachers will have equal curricular ability prior to and after the training as well as the skills and knowledge in working with, and in, different teams. Coaching may be of assistance to mediate differences in skill sets; however, as suggested above, it is equally likely that an educator will obtain information from trusted colleague—who may or may not be as well versed in the program—as the coach. Relying strictly on formal mechanisms to diffuse information and knowledge may thus leave critical practice gaps in the organization, potentially leading to a lack of depth and fidelity to the curriculum or even threatening the sustainability of the effort.

In terms of collaboration or professional learning communities, merely providing time and directives to "work together" does not necessarily result in meaningful collaboration between vertical and horizontal teams. In fact, forced collaboration may create a "rock and hard place" situation for a teacher who is attempting to balance a strong informal social pressure not to collaborate and equally strong formal pressure to support an initiative; in other words, resistance by a teacher in this sense may not reflect some clash of belief systems, but rather that she is caught between two powerful and opposing forces. A network theory approach provides insights into the motives of resisters to change, spheres of social influence, and the multiple social worlds that must be negotiated when change is enacted.

The idea of examining informal networks prior to engaging change efforts is built on the assumption that change in organizations is often socially constructed.[7] Therefore, attempts to create greater collaboration, distributed leadership, and participative decision making often require changing existing social relationships. It is this interdependence of action and social ties that ultimately may moderate, influence, and even determine the direction, speed, and depth of a planned change. Scholars have argued that change processes emerge and are maintained through interpersonal relationships and that lasting change "does not result from plans, blueprints, and events. Rather change occurs through the interaction of participants."[8] Therefore, a careful exploration and analysis of the network of social relations in an organization may be an important first step in determining an appropriate change strategy as well as identifying the potential for acceptance or resistance. However, this step cannot consist simply of a change agent plotting down who interacts with whom: the research suggests individuals are only about 30 percent accurate in detailing all the complex professional relationships that exist in a system.[9] Examining the informal networks requires a more systematic approach that draws on social network theory and methods.

A network is a group of actors who are connected to one another through a set of different relations or ties. Communication, knowledge, innovation, or any number of resources can flow through channels between actors. Social network methods can reveal the underlying structures through which resources are exchanged between individuals in an organization. Moreover, that knowledge may be used to develop and engage a change strategy. While the network perspective has been well established in sociology, anthropology, and management, it is also gaining momentum in education.

Interest in social networks is indeed one of the major trends in social science research today. According to scientific databases, the number of publications in social sciences using the word "social network(s)" in the title, keywords, or abstract has increased exponentially over the last two decades.[10] Figure 1-1, based in part on a recent analysis, provides evidence of the increasing trend of the use of social networks and education over the last fifty years.[11]

One of the basic conceptual foundations in understanding social networks is the concept of social capital. A number of theorists have written on this subject; each foregrounding a different aspect and offering a nuanced understanding of the concept.[12] Nan Lin notes that the common denominator in all major social network theories is the understanding that social capital consists of "the resources embedded in social relations and social structure which can be mobilized when an actor wishes to increase the likelihood of success in purposive action."[13] Social capital is therefore an investment in a system's social relations through which the resources of other individuals can be accessed, borrowed, or leveraged. This differentiates social capital from human capital, which refers to investments in training, development, or certifications of individuals, or physical capital that is contained in infrastructure and equipment.[14]

Social capital can be operationalized as the resources embedded in social systems, as well as accessed and used by actors. It is therefore concerned with the resources that exist in social relations (sometimes referred to as *ties*) between individuals as opposed to the resources of a specific individual. Thus actors must be aware of the assets in their network and take action through social ties to access these resources.[15] It is the quality of those ties in a social system that creates the structure that ultimately determines opportunities for social capital transactions and access to resources.[16]

Understanding the quality and strength of ties is critical to understanding the larger network. The ties an individual has to others may support or constrain opportunities for resources (information, knowledge, innovation, etc.) to be shared and diffused throughout a system. *Strong* ties support the transfer of tacit, nonroutine, and complex knowledge; joint problem solving; and the development of coordinated approaches.[17] In contrast, less dense

FIGURE 1-1   Social network publications in education

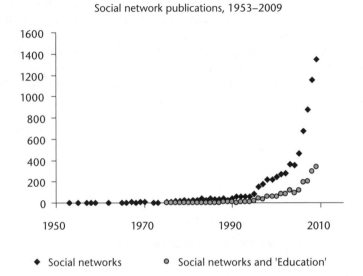

Social network publications, 1953–2009

◆ Social networks   ◉ Social networks and 'Education'

networks, or those with fewer ties, are better suited for the transfer of simple, routine information and providing access to more novel information afforded by opportunities to bridge between disconnected others.[18]

Social capital and social network theory provide useful frames and specific methods for researchers and educators to use in answering such questions as to the extent to which information is diffused throughout an organization; who is sharing information with whom, and at what frequency; or to what degree is there congruence between formal and informal systems. The network perspective can also be helpful in better understanding where funds of knowledge reside in the organization and how to leverage often untapped expertise.

To access such information, a social network survey or interview protocol is developed and asks such questions such as "To whom do you turn for work-related information?" or "With whom do you collaborate regarding instructional issues?" or "How often does your interaction with a colleague increase your energy level?" Respondents can range from a single individual and his or her relations with others, referred to as an *ego* network, to a larger network, typically comprising those people who are important to the intended focus of the study. For example, it might be useful to survey or interview all the teachers in a school who would be engaged in a change effort, or it might be more appropriate seek out only a few key high-performing teachers to better understand their practice.

Responses to the surveys are collected and analyzed at the *whole* (also referred to as *full* or *complete*) network or *ego* (or *personal* or *individual*) level using social network analysis software such as UCINET.[19] This popular program can provide both statistical and visual representations of the different networks in a system or of a single ego network. In addition, network data may be analyzed using qualitative methods, which provides powerful insights into relational patterns.

Once the data are analyzed they can be shared with the respondent group in the form of a network map. Because such maps provide a visualization of relationships, they tend to generate a great deal of excitement and eagerness on the part of respondents to better understand their social system. The next section will outline a longitudinal research study completed with leaders in one school district as a way to illustrate some basic concepts of a social network analysis.

SOCIAL NETWORK ANALYSIS IN PRACTICE

The research study I will use as an exemplar was conducted to examine the informal network of relationships between leaders in a school district that serves sixteen thousand diverse students. Response to the survey was extremely high—98 percent of the site-level (principals/assistant principals) and central office (superintendents/assistant superintendents/directors/supervisors) leaders. Participants answered questions related to the frequency of their collaboration, information sharing, innovation diffusion, and knowledge transfer. Figure 1-2 is a visualization created by NetDraw (a network visualization software) of the collaboration network between site- and district-level administrators.[20]

The first elements of the network map are the lines, or "edges," and arrows. The edges indicate the ties between individuals and may indicate the strength of the tie or the frequency of interaction between individuals. In a directed network (a network that is focused on the directional flow of resources) the arrows indicate the direction a resource flows from one individual to another. For example, in figure 1-2, the arrow labeled *Lines/Arrows* points to a tie from one site administrator to another. The direction of flow in this example is one-way; in other words, site administrator A collaborates with principal B, but B does not perceive a collaborative relationship with A. This is considered an asymmetrical relationship; the flow of resources is not reciprocal. Arrows pointing in both directions denote symmetrical relations, in which resources flow in both ways. This distinction is important because it can reveal from whom and to whom information, knowledge, innovation, and the like move, thus enabling the tracking of resource flows.

Central actors are those who have the most ties with other actors in the organization. These individuals usually have more access to information,

FIGURE 1-2   Collaboration network, pre-intervention

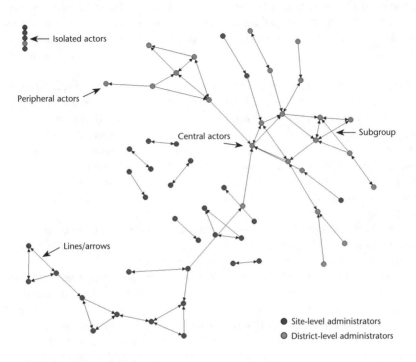

knowledge, and communication than others in the system and therefore may have a disproportionate influence over the larger organization. Central actors may provide cohesion to a network by bridging two different groups, as demonstrated in figure 1-2, or, alternatively, may create a bottleneck that slows the information flow between parts of the network. Highly central individuals are often considered *superhubs*; these actors are able to send and receive information to large segments of the network, thus potentially making the network more effective and efficient—or narrowing the range of relational resources available.

Peripheral actors are connected to the system by limited ties. Their positions in the network structure may mean that he organization may not be effectively using their knowledge resources. In addition, the one person connecting the peripheral actor to the larger network is in effect "controlling" what resources that peripheral individual receives. If that connecting individual is moved out of the network, the peripheral actor may potentially become an isolate.

Isolated actors are individuals who indicated they did not collaborate with anyone else and were not identified as collaborators by other individuals.

Isolated individuals do not have the opportunity to provide any additional resources to the system and therefore it is difficult to leverage their knowledge to better support the goals of the larger organization. Moreover, in terms of a sense of belonging, these individuals may be professionally disconnected and require differentiated levels of support to reconnect them to the larger system.

Subgroups within the larger network are important to the functioning of the organization, since they can lend support or inhibit overall strategies. Subgroups often work in similar areas and have more densely connected relations. Intragroup connections are important for overall specific group functioning. However, at the same time these groups can become so focused on their specific efforts that they limit their connection to the larger network. For example, a content-area team in a school may become so focused on its field of specialization that it misses opportunities for more interdisciplinary interactions.

These four components represent some of the most basic elements of an informal network. They are useful for describing and analyzing the network as well as understanding potential avenues for change.

Figure 1-2 illustrates the original, pre-intervention, structure of collaboration between site and central office administrators in the study. Figure 1-3 shows the same network one year later, after a formal change strategy focused on building collaborative opportunities. These strategies were collectively determined by the administrative team using the data from the original analysis to guide its work. Although the team could have instituted a collaborative intervention without a network map, the visualization provided insight as to where collaboration needed to be specifically supported and allowed the recipients of the change strategy to co-create the efforts and collectively share both responsibility and success. Use of a network map represents a powerful shift in creating reform.

Figure 1-4 provides a map of the knowledge network from the same study after three years of implementation. The first round of data clearly indicated a dense amount of information sharing between the central office administrators and limited information exchange between site administrators. This dense core of connections by one main group (central office) surrounded by less-connected actors from another group (site principals) represents what is termed a *core/periphery* model. This network structure is very effective at transferring routine, noncomplex information like schedules or policy changes. However, the core/periphery structure is less effective at diffusing more complex information and innovative practices that may be necessary to meet increasing accountability demands.

Figure 1-5 represents the same network one year later (after four years). Note that the core is still very much in place, but the previously peripheral site administrators are more densely connected to one another and the core.

FIGURE 1-3   Collaboration network, post-intervention—after one year

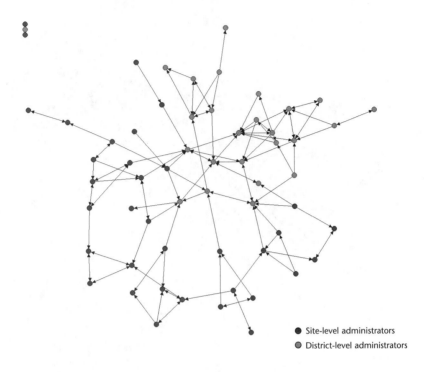

This increase in ties was a result of creating specific structures and opportunities for site administrators to share best practices and diffuse innovative approaches. In fact, the actual membership of these groups was intentionally created to ensure that more "central" administrators were part of every cluster group.

These network maps reflect structures that are common to many organizations. This introduction is meant to provide the reader with some basics of social network theory through an illustrative case; the following chapters will present a collection of much more sophisticated applications of social network theory and methods to a variety of educational settings at different levels.

MAPPING THE BOOK'S TERRAIN

This book represents the intersection of empirical research and theory by some of the leading scholars in the field who are drawing on social network theory as applied to educational change. The collection provides insight into the use of social network scholarship and application in education as well as

Figure 1-4   Information network, post-intervention—after three years

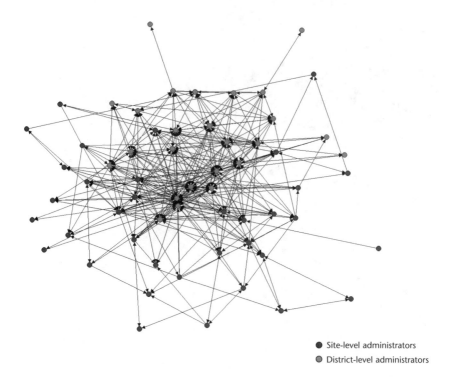

● Site-level administrators
◐ District-level administrators

thoughtful implications for critical areas of practice, including policy, reform, teaching and learning, and leadership. Its contributors bridge the divide between social network theory and practice and provide the reader with an overview of the field, implications for change, as well as future directions.

The volume is organized into an introductory section and three specific content sections. The chapters do not have to be read in any particular order. Although those within a specific section are connected, each stands on its own.

Introductory Chapters

Chapter 1, whose basic overview you have at this point successfully nego-tiated, situates network theory in the broad sphere of educational change while providing some very basic ideas exemplified through a sample study. Chapter 2, by Borgatti and Ofem, provides a more in-depth introduction into social network theory as well as a focus on the common theoretical concepts at differing levels of analysis. For readers new to the field, these chapters offer

FIGURE 1-5   Information network, post-intervention—after four years

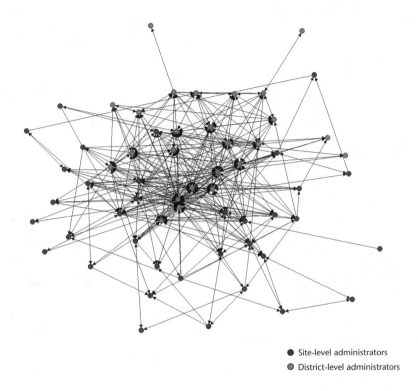

● Site-level administrators
◐ District-level administrators

a general understanding of the network perspective and its potential to illuminate a variety of phenomena in social systems. Readers well versed in network theory will value the typology of network research by domain and level of analysis presented in chapter 2 as a way to consider ongoing work in the field. The introductory chapters set up the three core parts of the text.

Part I: Teacher Networks

Part I focuses on the relationship between teachers, reform, and social networks. The authors in this section build on the increasing body of literature on the relationship between the quality of teacher interactions to educational change. The pieces draw on social network research that suggests the nature and quality of relations within a network is associated with a host of outcomes related to organizational improvement. In addition, the work presented in this section extends the current literature by exploring different levels of analysis, temporal influence, attitude, innovation, and professional development.

In chapter 3, Coburn, Choi, Mata thoughtfully explore how the social ties of elementary teachers changed over time in response to the implementation of a districtwide mathematics reform, following the development and dissolution of ties over the course of a three-year reform effort. The authors examine the impact of the dynamic nature of ties on the social as well as organizational context and the exchange of expertise, and show how shifts in relations had significant consequences for the type and quality of exchanges within the larger social networks. Beyond its substantive contributions, this article is unique in its use of longitudinal egocentric network analysis drawn from carefully collected and analyzed qualitative data.

The study presented by Atteberry and Bryk in chapter 4 examines the implementation of a large-scale elementary reform effort over time. The authors provide insight into the socio-organizational influence on the reform effort suggesting that the "base-state" of social relations before the start of the reform foreshadowed the depth and success of the change effort. Another significant contribution of this work is the close examination of the changing social network position of literacy coaches who are part of the reform. This piece, like chapter 3, also suggests the potential of formal structures to affect informal relations and how the preexisting social relations impact the depth of the intervention.

Chapter 5, by Cole and Weinbaum, moves the reform focus from the elementary to the high school level and from reform-related behaviors to attitudes about reform. This is one of the few studies that specifically examines the influence of attitude. The authors argue that teacher social interactions have a direct influence on the way colleagues view reform. This work also provides a unique lens for understanding some of the "unseen" elements that help to explain variation in reform outcomes.

These three chapters as a group point to the influence of the larger organizational structures, base states of relations, and smaller subgroups on access to expertise and attitude toward reform. They also suggest both the importance of social networks to the enactment of reforms and highlight the tension between the persistence of existing ties and how amenable those ties are to change through formal structures.

The chapters that follow move out of a specific reform context, but continue to focus on relations between teachers. These contributions examine the critical area of teacher trust and innovation, and the learning that occurs between teachers in professional settings. In chapter 6, Moolenaar and Sleegers present the results of a large-scale study of elementary schools in one school district in the Netherlands. Their research provides insights into the mechanisms that underlie educational change and improvement by exploring the intersection between social networks, trust, and support for an innovative climate. The empirical evidence shows that dense work-related relationships support the development and maintenance of an innovative climate. Moreover, high levels of trust within these densely connected social networks enhance the opportunities for teachers to learn together, share innovative ideas, and take risks on novel instructional practices. This work offers a unique perspective on the very current topic of innovation through connecting social relations and the quality of ties, using a sophisticated multilevel modeling approach to network data.

Baker-Doyle and Yoon take a different vantage point on teacher networks in chapter 7. Building on a rich literature, the authors posit that teacher professional development programs must move from more static, passive models to those that embrace and leverage the social capital teachers bring to their learning. Engaging educators as co-constructors and collaborators in developing their professional knowledge, this chapter suggests, requires a better understanding of social networks within a development program. Baker-Doyle and Yoon convincingly argue that, to develop effective and sustainable opportunities for teacher learning, professional developers must incorporate within-group expertise as well as create formal opportunities for knowledge exchange. This renewed emphasis on the knowledge that teachers bring to the work must also be made explicit as well as shared throughout the group. To enhance teacher learning, the authors used a variety of social network methods, including making group expertise explicit, evaluating the effectiveness of the program, and reforming the development sessions to better enhance teacher learning. This chapter illuminates the utility of social networks as both theory and method for supporting and enacting change as well as refining programs. Of particular use to change agents is the way these authors directly applied social network analysis as a diagnostic tool.

These studies in part I focus on networks of teaching centered on innovation and development. Underlying each of these studies is the idea of teacher learning. In the Moolenaar and Sleegers study, the opportunity to learn and innovate comes from residing in densely connected, trusting, work-related networks. In the professional development research, learning happens through the explicit process of surfacing and exchanging expertise and knowledge. On balance, these chapters underline the importance of social network theory in understanding how to enhance the opportunities for learning between and among teachers.

Part II: Leadership and Social Networks

The relationship between networks and leadership is a relatively understudied area in education, and the chapters in part II represent some of the latest work in the area. In chapter 8, Spillane, Healey, and Kim examine the relations of formal and informal leaders in an urban district's reform efforts. The authors explore the social network of instructional advice with individuals who have formal leadership roles as well as those who are often sought out for advice or information and thus can be conceptualized as informal leaders.

This dual lens of formal and informal provides a nuanced window into leadership and the enactment of change. The authors also examine the potential influence of subgroups, suggesting the value of ties between subgroups as a way to access novel information. Their work notes the considerable variation in the congruence of formal and informal leadership structure as well as the role that part-time formally designated leaders play in representing the formal organization across subgroups. This work is particularly useful as a way to conceptualize the roles formal and informal leaders play in change as well as suggest the importance of network maps and measures as reflective tools.

Chapter 9, by Penuel, Frank, and Krause, examines the distributed nature of leadership in twenty-one schools engaged in reform efforts. The authors argue that the implementation of a change effort is at least in part explained by collegial interactions supported through distributed leadership practice. This work illustrates the way in which social networks can support or constrain the distribution of resources and expertise in systems that are enacting change. Their results indicate that when there is limited access to formal professional development, it is important to have more formal and informal leaders within the school network connected to the reform. One of the unique contributions of this work is its emphasis on the importance of subgroups and the value of cross-group interaction in supporting the distribution of knowledge connected to efforts at reform. Moreover, as in chapter 7, these authors draw on the utility of network maps as a tool to illuminate informal relations.

In chapter 10, Finnigan and I focus on the networks of relations between leaders who occupy formal leadership position in a large urban school district. Using this unique data set, we argue that efforts to improve underperforming schools require a broader district perspective and that the linkages between district office leaders and site administrators in the most underperforming schools are critical in improving outcomes. Our study of leaders reveals a highly centralized network structure in which principals, while facing similar issues related to improvement, have very few relations to each other. This lack of connections leads to an uneven distribution of resources as well as reduced opportunities for the exchange of reform-related relational resources. The network structure of relations in this district appears to work against complex efforts at change and may inhibit the progress of schools and the overall system.

The study presented by Hite, Hite, Mugimu, and Nsubuga in chapter 11 is conducted in Uganda, yet many of the issues related to leadership, networks, and change are applicable in any number of settings. Like many nations, Uganda is in the process of implementing changes to increase the availability of high-quality education. The Ugandan education context is becoming increasingly market driven, so schools must compete for resources, prompting their leaders to become more entrepreneurial—a situation not dissimilar to the increasingly market-driven approach in the United States. The context has striking implications for evolving network structure. Leaders (*headteachers*), who are better able to attract students have done so by drawing on their social networks. This interesting case highlights the importance of informal ties in emerging systems by showing how densely connected personal relations were the primary conduits through which leaders accessed otherwise inaccessible resources. As in chapter 10, the piece also notes that these ties were often unequally distributed. In addition, Hite and colleagues suggest the importance of developing school-to-school as well as leader-to-leader ties, since when a highly connected leader left, the school was often essentially "penalized" by losing its ties to resources. Creating interdependent systems within a larger organization is one of the important messages from this work.

The studies in part II suggest the importance of the effect of both informal and formal leaders on the larger system in which they reside. This section further explores the ways in which leadership may be distributed across formal and informal leaders and its relationship to change. Moreover, like the work presented in previous sections, these chapters underscore the importance of both macro and micro lenses of analysis in understanding change from a leadership perspective as well as the potential of network maps and measures as reflective and evaluative tools in the change process.

Part III: Surveying the Terrain Ahead: Social Network Theory and Educational Change

Part III moves to models, methods, and lessons learned around social networks and educational change. Chapter 12, by Frank, Kim, and Belman, pushes the field of social networks in education to suggest the importance of more sophisticated methods and models for the theory, analysis, and reporting of social network data. Their unique piece examines social network data from an underlying theory of utility in an effort to understand the intersection of individual attribute and relational data. This important work represents an increasing area of interest for social network scholars who are exploring the dynamic impact of social selection and social influence. The authors also note advances in social network theory involving longitudinal and agent-based modeling of network data that hold promise for answering important social science questions such as the differential impact of network structure and social influence on outcomes.

In chapter 13, Ávila de Lima provides a general overview of important methodological issues facing the collection and preparation of network data. He illustrates how network methods require a shift from traditional social science approaches, which focus on statistical independence, to recognizing the interdependence of actors in social systems, and explores the limitations and advantages of methods used in collecting network data and the increasing importance of gathering that data through multiple methods from a variety of sources. This chapter provides the lay reader and network scholar alike with important points to consider when collecting and preparing network data.

These two chapters provide approaches for advanced theorizing and modeling of network data that represent some of the latest advances in the field, as well as general ideas and considerations on the collection and analysis of social network data. The methods and sophisticated modeling of this data are quickly expanding to match a growing interest and exploration of a variety of research questions, and the work presented by these authors provides both guidance and a push to expand existing theoretical and methodological boundaries.

The book concludes with chapter 14, which I have written as a survey of the lessons learned. This summing-up also considers promising future directions. In the end, this book is about the importance of relationships and the explicit and subtle ways in which they influence us and the people with whom we interact. Better understanding of our complex social world provides insights and opportunities in developing and leveraging social capital, which may better enable change agents and the systems they serve to meet the increasing demand for educational change.

CHAPTER 2

Overview

Social Network Theory and Analysis

Stephen P. Borgatti and Brandon Ofem

While intellectual forerunners of social network analysis can be found as far back as the ancient Greeks, modern social network analysis is typically seen as beginning in the 1930s with the work of Jacob Moreno.[1] Moreno called the nascent field *sociometry*. It involved graphical mapping of people's subjective feelings about one another. In an early study, Moreno noticed that runaways at a school for girls tended to occur in clumps. He argued that the social links between the girls served as channels for the flow of ideas. In a way that even the girls themselves may not have been conscious of, it was their location in the social network that determined whether and when they ran away. This fundamental insight—that positions in a social structure have consequences for the people occupying them—became a key tenet of the field and led the way for future research.

In the 1940s and '50s, social psychologists used matrix algebra and graph theory to formalize in network terms fundamental social-psychological concepts such as groups and social circles, making it possible to objectively discover emergent groups in network data.[2] During the same period, a team of researchers at MIT under the leadership of Alex Bavelas began studying the effects of different communication network structures on the ability of groups to solve problems.[3] Their study demonstrated that the structure of relations matters, and it captured the imagination of researchers in a number of fields, including anthropology, political science, sociology, and economics. By the 1980s, social network analysis (SNA) had become an established field within the social sciences, with a professional organization (International Network for Social Network Analysis, or INSNA), an annual conference (Sunbelt), specialized software (e.g., UCINET), and its own journal (*Social Networks*). In the 1990s, network analysis expanded into many more fields, including physics and biology. It was also adopted by several applied areas such as management consulting, public health, and crime/war fighting.[4]

The explosive growth of the field might be due in part to a couple of distinguishing features of the network paradigm itself. First, it is amenable to multiple levels of analysis. The network lens can be applied to individuals, teams, and organizations, making it possible to examine nearly any type of social system characterized by relations between entities. Second, network analysis can combine quantitative, qualitative, and graphical data, allowing for fuller descriptions of the social world that are both ethnographically grounded and quantitatively rigorous. In this chapter, we attempt to provide an overview of the core elements of the SNA field, both in terms of theory and methodology. The theory section begins with a description of the network perspective and presents a typology for thinking about different types of relationships. We then discuss the primary domains of inquiry, the levels of analysis that can be examined in each domain, the key social network concepts associated with each level, and a description of studies utilizing those concepts. In the methodology section we discuss two fundamental approaches to studying networks (*whole network analysis*, also known as *full* or *complete* network analysis, and *egocentric* network analysis, or *ego* network analysis), and within each of those approaches we discuss issues of data collection and analysis.

THEORY

In the network perspective, relationships between actors (such as individuals or firms) are the central focus. This differs from the attribute-based approach of traditional social science. For example, in traditional social science we might explain differences in the performance of organizations by highlighting the distinguishing characteristics of the most successful organizations (e.g., resource advantage).[5] According to such a view, the best organizations have the best technology, or people, or organizational structure, or mission, and so on. The explanatory mechanisms focus on the qualities or attributes of the organizations that allow them to outperform others. Similarly, at the individual level, traditional social science approaches explain individual outcomes as functions of individual attributes. For example, a person's success in life is explained as a function of his or her human capital, which includes such things as education, looks, social class, and so on.

In contrast, the network view takes into account the web of relationships in which actors are embedded that both constrain and provide opportunities. This view is strongly focused on an entity's environment, which is conceptualized as consisting of other entities and the relationships between them. So, in explaining organizational performance, network theorists would not only examine characteristics of the organizations, but also the relationships they have with other organizations. In explaining individual achievement,

TABLE 2-1
Typology of relations studied in social network analysis.

Types of relations	Examples
Similarities	
• Location	Same spatial and temporal space
• Membership	Same clubs; same events
• Attribute	Same gender; same attitude
Social relations	
• Kinship	Mother of; sibling of
• Other role	Friend of; boss of; student of; competitor
Mental relations	
• Affective	Likes; hates
• Cognitive	Knows; knows about; sees as happy
Interactions	Talked to; advised; helped; harmed
Flows	Information; beliefs; money

network theorists would not only examine attributes of the individuals, but also the relationships that constrain their choices and actions and/or provide opportunities for achievement.

What really makes SNA distinctive, however, is not simply a relational orientation, but the fundamental concept of the *network*. A network consists of a set of nodes or actors, along with a set of ties of a single type that connect the nodes.[6] The nodes can be persons, teams, departments, organizations, industries, or any other type of entity that is capable of having some sort of relationship with another entity. Ties can be of a wide variety of types, such as friendships between individuals, communication patterns between departments, alliances between organizations, exchange between industries, or conflicts between nation-states. Table 2-1 presents a typology that divides relations into five basic types: similarities, social relations, mental relations, interactions, and flows.

Similarities include spatial and temporal proximity as well as co-membership in groups and events and sharing of socially significant attributes, such as race or class. Similarities are typically not thought of as social ties in themselves, but as providing the relational conditions that facilitate or inhibit social ties. *Social relations* are ongoing ties such as kinship and friendship. Social relations typically have institutionalized rights and obligations associated with them, and have a sense of intersubjective reality. *Mental relations* are perceptions of and attitudes toward others, such as recognizing who someone is, or liking or disliking them. In contrast with social relations, these are more often private and unobservable. *Interactions* are typically conceptualized as discrete events that can be counted over a period of time. We typically view interactions as being facilitated by and occurring in the context of social or mental relations (and vice versa). For example, friends (social relation) give each other advice (interaction). At the same time, through interactions, social relations may evolve (e.g., friends can become business partners). *Flows* are those tangible and intangible things that are transmitted through interactions. Ideas are transmitted through communication, viruses and material resources are transmitted through physical contact, and so on. Flows are typically not measured but rather inferred from interactional and relational data. For example, in studies examining alliances between organizations, it is often assumed that knowledge and expertise flow between them.[7]

An important aspect of the network concept is that ties between nodes are not treated in isolation. Rather, they link up to form paths, thereby providing a mechanism through which nodes may affect one another indirectly. In many cases, these paths can be thought of as pipes through which information, resources, and the like can flow.[8] In addition, the set of paths forms a structure in which each node occupies a particular position. A fundamental tenet of SNA is the idea that a node's structural position in a network determines in part the opportunities and constraints it will encounter. Some nodes will receive more flows than others. Other nodes may be in a position to control such flows, extracting rents for sending them along.[9] Structural positions, therefore, can influence nodal outcomes. Similarly, at the level of a network as a whole, structure is seen as an important determinant of what happens to the network. Thus, a team's success is not only a function of the individual talents of the team members, but of the way they are connected to one other. For example, different communication network structures have been shown to affect the speed and accuracy of a group's problem solving.[10]

Research on social networks can be divided into two broad domains of inquiry based on whether they examine the antecedents or the consequences of network variables. We refer to studies examining antecedents as belonging to the *theory of networks* domain, since they seek to explain why networks or nodes within them have the structure or positions they do. Research in the theory of networks domain is essentially about network evolution. We refer to studies examining the consequences of network structure as belonging to the *network theory* domain, since they seek to explain various outcomes as a function of network properties. Research in the network theory domain is a form of structuralism that is founded on the premise that how a system is put together is as determinative of the system's behavior and outcomes as the composition of its elements. For example, a bicycle has properties that are impossible to predict if one has available only a list of its parts—one needs to know how the parts are connected to understand what the bicycle can do.

In each domain, theorizing takes place at three levels of analysis: the dyad, the node, and the network as a whole. The *dyad* level considers only properties of pairs of actors. Network data is always at the dyadic level, but other dyadic constructs exist as well, such as the geodesic distance between pairs of nodes (i.e., the number of links in the shortest path from one to the other), and structural equivalence (i.e., the extent to which a pair of nodes has ties— and does not have ties—to the same third parties). The *node* level involves characterizing how and where a node is connected in the network. For example, we may measure network size (i.e., the number of other nodes a node is directly connected to), structural holes (the number of nodes that a focal node is connected to that are not connected to each other), and centrality (the family of concepts describing the position of the node in the network, such as betweenness, which measures how often the shortest path between two other nodes passes through the focal node). The highest level of analysis is the *group*, which can include the network as a whole. Typical concepts at the group level include density (the proportion of all pairs of nodes in the group that have a tie with each other) and centralization (the degree to which the network revolves around a single node).

Combining the three levels of analysis with the two domains previously outlined gives us six prototypical types of research studies. Table 2-2 provides examples of each of the six types, along with a generic label for that kind of study.

In type 1 studies, labeled *partner selection*, the goal is usually to explain the relationship between pairs of nodes (i.e., the formation or dissolution of ties). One of the best-known results in this area is the principle of homophily—the tendency for people to form (positive) ties with people who are like themselves on socially significant attributes.[11] For example, Marsden found that Americans are significantly more likely to discuss confidential matters with others of the same gender, race, age, and education level.[12] Another well-known result is the power of propinquity. Specifically, people who are physically close are more likely to have various kinds of ties. For example, empirical evidence suggests that the probability of communication between individuals within an organization is a function of their geographic distance.[13] At the organizational level, studies within this category seek to explain why some organizations form alliances, partnerships, and other types of ties with other organizations. For example, one finding in this research stream is that social networks of prior alliances play an important role in shaping future alliance formation.[14] Such networks serve as conduits of information that allow organizations to learn about opportunities to form new ties and strengthen their existing ones.

TABLE 2-2
Typology of network research organized by domain and level of analysis.

Level of analysis	Theory of networks domain (antecedents)	Network theory domain (consequences)
Dyad level	Type 1. Partner selection	Type 2. Contagion/diffusion
• Strength of tie • Geodesic distance • Structural equivalence	*Example:* Explaining friendships among school children as a function of being the same gender.[a]	*Example:* Explaining similarity of attitudes as a function of interaction among friends.[b]
Node level	Type 3. Positional achievement	Type 4. Individual social capital
• Network size • Structural holes • Centrality (e.g. betweenness)	*Example:* Explaining centrality as a function of personality characteristics.[c]	*Example:* Predicting actor rewards as a function of structural holes.[d]
Group/network level	Type 5. Network structuring	Type 6. Group social capital.
• Density • Centralization	*Example:* Explaining why some organizations are more centralized than others.[e]	*Example:* Explaining teams' ability to solve problems rapidly as a function of the shape of their communication networks.[f]

a. Miller McPherson, Lynn Smith-Lovin, and James M. Cook, "Birds of a Feather: Homophily in Social Networks," *Annual Review of Sociology* 27 (2001): 415–444.

b. Bonnie Erickson, "The Relational Basis of Attitudes," in *Social Structures: A Network Approach*. eds. Barry Wellman and Stephen D. Berkowitz (New York: Cambridge University Press, 1988), 99–121.

c. Ajay Mehra, Martin Kilduff, and Daniel Brass, "The Social Networks of High and Low Self-Monitors: Implications for Workplace Performance," *Administrative Science Quarterly* 46, (2001): 121–146.

d. Ronald S. Burt, *Structural Holes: The Social Structure of Competition*, (Cambridge, MA: Harvard University Press, 1992).

e. Jefffrey C. Johnson, James S. Boster, and Lawrence A. Palinkas, "Social Roles and the Evolution of Networks in Isolated and Extreme Environments," *Journal of Mathematical Sociology* 27 (2003): 89–122.

f. Alex Bavelas, "Communication Patterns in Task-Oriented Groups," *Journal of the Acoustical Society of America* 22 (1950): 725–730.

Type 2 studies, labeled *contagion/diffusion*, include research in which social ties between pairs of nodes are used to explain such outcomes as similar political attitudes or, for organizations, similar structural features. For example, one study showed that just as similar individuals are more likely to interact, interaction between them is likely to make them even more similar.[15] Through interaction individuals share ideas, beliefs, and experiences that tend to make them more similar with respect to how they perceive the world. One of the first studies in this category was conducted by Solomon Asch, one of the pioneers of social psychology.[16] In his famous experiment, he found that subjects were more likely to make an incorrect judgment on a simple task if everyone in their group made the same incorrect judgment first. Hence the behavior of the individual was affected by the apparent views of others. Other studies have used this contagion process to explain the diffusion of the "poison pill" in board interlocks, adoption of tetracycline among physicians, and similarity in perceptions about organizational justice among employees.[17]

Type 3 studies, labeled *positional achievement*, try to explain a node's structural properties, such as the number of structural holes (i.e., the number of nodes within an actor's set of contacts that are not directly tied to each other) or betweenness (i.e., the property of being along the shortest paths in the network). Some individuals have characteristics that make them more likely to reach certain structural positions within a network. For example, in a work setting, high self-monitors (individuals adept at shifting their expressive behavior in ways suited for different social settings) were more likely to be in structural positions that spanned structural holes. Also, since they were connected to more people, they were more likely to be central in workflow networks. Low self-monitors, on the other hand, tended to remain in more cohesive friendship groups.[18] Another study found several personality characteristics associated with centrality in friendship, advice, and adversarial networks.[19] At the organizational level, studies within this category might seek to explain why some organizations become central in a particular network (e.g., research collaboration) as a function of characteristics of the organization (e.g., having many brilliant scientists).

Type 4 studies, labeled *individual social capital*, are concerned with the consequences of occupying different structural positions. For example, having many structural holes is thought to afford control benefits (in the sense of being able to play contacts off each other), as well as information benefits, such as receiving more nonredundant input from others (since they are not connected to each other). Much of the network literature today falls in this domain, with studies showing position to be an important determinant of a wide variety of outcomes, such as the performance of employees in complex jobs, employee perceptions, MBA student satisfaction, and organizational performance, to name a few.[20]

Type 5 studies, labeled *network structuring*, attempt to explain characteristics of entire networks, such as the density of ties within teams. Research in this category is concerned with how and why different structures form. For example, a well-known area of investigation is the emergence of "scale-free" networks, meaning networks in which a few nodes have massive numbers of ties while most nodes have very few. The theory of preferential attachment argues that scale-free networks emerge from a simple process of tie formation in which new nodes arriving on a social scene tend to form ties with nodes that already have many ties, a process that leads to increasing inequality in centrality.[21]

Type 6 studies, labeled *group social capital*, seek to examine the consequences of different network structures. They try to explain group outcomes (such as the performance of teams within organizations) as functions of the cohesion or shape of each group's network structure. The premise behind these studies is that some networks will be better suited to achieve particular objectives than others. For example, teams with greater cohesion (a denser positive affect network) might have greater team satisfaction and, in turn, greater team viability. On the other hand, a team with less density might reap the benefits from a greater heterogeneity of ideas. It could be that sparser team networks promote independent thinking, so that each member of the team is not as influenced by the perspectives of the others.

METHODOLOGY

Just as the network perspective offers a different lens through which we can generate theory, it also requires different empirical methods. Since relationships are the main focus in SNA, it is relationships between entities that must be captured in measurement and data collection. Two major strategies have been developed to capture those relations. The first of these is *whole* (or *full*) *network analysis*, which is the approach most people think of when they hear the term *social network analysis*. In this approach, we select a set of nodes and then measure ties between all nodes in the sample. The second approach is *egocentric analysis* (or *ego network analysis*). In this approach a set of focal nodes (*egos*) is selected from a population, and then we ask the individual egos to give us the names and characteristics of the people in their lives, along with details of the relationship with each one. As a general rule, the whole network approach collects just a few kinds of ties among many pairs of nodes, while the egocentric approach collects many kinds of ties involving just a few focal nodes. Each approach has advantages and disadvantages, as well as different methodological requirements. The choice of strategy depends on the nature of the research question under investigation, as well as the resources available for carrying out the research. We discuss each in turn.

Whole Network Analysis

In the whole network approach the researcher selects a set of nodes to serve as the population for study. Then a small number of types of ties are systematically measured for each pair of nodes in the population. For example, we might choose a classroom of children, and for each pair of children, determine whether they are friends, and whether one seeks help from the other. In this approach, the population of nodes typically corresponds to some kind of group, whether a self-identified group, such as a gang, or an externally determined group, such as all students in a given high school. In general, in this approach we do not sample in the sense of drawing a small number of respondents from a large population, such as taking a random sampling of, say, one hundred Americans. However, this does not mean that a network collected using the whole network approach is necessarily connected (i.e., that there is a path from every node to every other). Instead, it can easily happen that the network is fragmented into multiple components across which there are no ties of the type measured in the study.

The result of a survey administered to a population is a set of ties between all respondents, which can be represented as a series of person-by-person matrices, one for each kind of tie measured. Typically, these matrices— known as *adjacency matrices*—contain 1s and 0s, indicating the presence or absence of a given type of tie. However, it is also possible to measure dimensions of ties, such as their strength and duration (for ties of the social relation type) and frequency (for ties of the interaction type), in which case the adjacency matrices contain values other than 1s and 0s. When ties do not have direction, as in types of ties like "had a meeting with", the adjacency matrices are symmetric, meaning that $x_{ij} = x_{ji}$, for all possible pairs i and j. However, when ties do have direction, as in "gives advice to," then it is possible for a given pair i and j, that $x_{ij} \neq x_{ji}$ (e.g., A gives advice to B, but B does not give advice to A).

One issue that arises in whole network analysis is missing data. For example, if surveys are administered on a certain day and some nodes in the population are absent, their rows in the resulting adjacency matrices will be missing. Note that treating the missing values as 0s would imply that these respondents don't have ties, which may or may not be correct. If we then compute metrics on these data, such as measures of centrality, we are likely to get distorted values. One way to deal with this problem is to infer the missing values from the responses of others. For example, if the type of tie is romantic involvement, it may be reasonably safe to assume that if B lists A as a romantic partner, then, had A answered the survey, A would have listed B. This imputation of ties works well when the type of tie is logically undirected or symmetric. However, for types of tie that are directed, this technique doesn't work. For example, if A claims to go to B for advice, it cannot be assumed that B also goes to A for advice. A preemptive technique to deal with such possible missing data for nonsymmetric relations like advice is to ask the advice question in two ways: "From whom do you get advice?" and "To whom do you give advice?" This provides two estimates, one from each node, of both the (A,B) advice tie and the (B,A) advice tie. If A doesn't fill out the survey, we can estimate whether A gives advice to B by looking to see if B reports getting advice from A. Similarly, we can estimate whether A gets advice from B by seeing if B claims to give advice to A. Despite such solutions to the potential missing data problem, the highest possible response rate should still be sought. Principles of survey design for achieving such high response rates can be found in the survey methods literature and are very useful for network research.[22] Rules of thumb to keep in mind are (a) to build as much rapport as possible with the respondents, (b) let respondents know the value of their participation, and (c) follow up persistently with nonrespondents.[23]

Once network data have been collected, analysis usually begins with the creation of a graphical representation of the network. This allows the network analyst to qualitatively look for patterns in the structure of the network. This can be done through visualization tools such as NetDraw, which is embedded in the UCINET network analysis package.[24] For example, figure 2-1 shows a social network in which the ties indicate who has spent a lot of time with whom, and nodes are colored by gender. It is evident in the figure that nodes tend to have ties with others of the same gender, indicating homophily. After making this observation, the network analyst would then test this pattern statistically. Thus, visualization enables the researcher to make qualitative observations which can then be tested quantitatively. Visualization can also help the researcher to spot possible errors in the data. For example, the node in the far left of figure 2-1 appears to have ties only with people of the opposite gender. This may be the case, but it is also possible that the person's gender was simply miscoded.

Much of the quantitative part of social network analysis consists of measuring the constructs—at all three levels of analysis—mentioned in our discussion of network theorizing. For example, at the node level we might measure various kinds of centrality, while at the group level we might measure such things as density or the extent to which a network has a core/periphery structure.[25] Once such metrics are calculated, they then become variables in the researcher's database and can be used to test hypotheses regarding the antecedents and/or consequences of the social network concepts associated with each variable. Such testing of hypotheses proceeds, in a very general sense, as it does in any social science study. For example, we might theorize that students who are very central in a classroom's friendship network get lower grades because their need to excel in something has already been filled. To test this, the researcher could use *ordinary least squares regression* (OLS) to relate classroom performance to friendship centrality. As another example, if we hypothesize that more friendships within teams are associated with higher levels of overall team satisfaction, we can test this by studying a sample of, say, one hundred teams and, for each one, measuring the density of the team friendship network and the average satisfaction level. We then correlate these two variables across teams.

A few caveats should be observed when analyzing relational data. In some cases, the data violate assumptions that many inferential statistical techniques require. For example, suppose we believe that friendship facilitates knowledge sharing within an organization. To test this, we would want to correlate friendship ties with information-sharing ties. But, the observations

FIGURE 2-1   Network diagram in which node color indicates gender

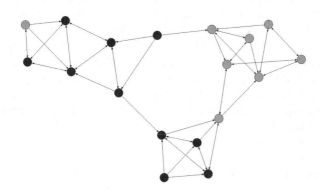

(which are dyads) are not independent because a given node is part of many dyads. Thus, if a node happens to be sociopathic, it affects every dyad in which it is involved. One way to deal with such autocorrelation is with the use of the quadratic assignment procedure (QAP) family of methods.[26] A QAP regression yields the same parameter estimates as OLS, but uses randomization or permutation tests to assess statistical significance. The QAP approach constructs the distribution of test statistics under the null hypothesis from the data itself (similar to jackknifing and bootstrapping techniques), thus ensuring that special characteristics of the data, such as autocorrelation, are taken account of.

Ego Network Analysis

The egocentric approach is in many ways simpler to execute than the whole network approach. In ego network analysis, we begin by selecting a sample of respondents (egos). Since a complete network will not be generated, we are free to take a random sample of egos from a large population, such as selecting fifteen hundred respondents from the population of 300 million Americans. The egos are then interviewed in a two-stage process. First, we apply what is known as a *name generator*. This consists of a battery of network questions such as "What are the names of some of the people you work with?" and "Whom do you tend to socialize with on weekends?" These are typically open-ended questions and provide multiple opportunities for the names of individuals in a person's life (known as *alters*) to emerge. As the respondent answers the questions, the interviewer (or a computer) develops a list or roster of distinct names that were generated. It should be noted that respondents are free to maintain the privacy of their alters by giving pseudonyms, nicknames, or the like.

This roster then forms the basis for the second stage of questioning, known as the *name interpreter*. In this stage, the individual respondents are systematically asked about the nature of their relationship with each person on the roster. For example, they are asked "Is this a friend?" "Is this a coworker?" and so on. Some of the questions at this stage may be the same questions that were asked in an open-ended way in the name-generator phase. The purpose of this dual-stage approach is to deal with the tendency of respondents to forget names when asked in an open-ended format. This way, names are given multiple opportunities to surface, and then the relationship to each named person is systematically explored.

In the name-interpreter phase, the respondent is also asked about the characteristics of each alter, such as gender, age, attitudes, and so on. In addition, in some studies the respondent is asked about the relationships between the alters. For example, the respondent may be asked, for each pair of alters, whether they know each other. This allows the researcher to estimate quantities such as the number of structural holes that a given ego has. Of course, the respondent may be wrong about the relationships between the alters, but in some theoretical frameworks this is not an issue: the behavior of egos is conditioned by their *perception* of the social world around them, rather than the reality.[27]

The analysis of ego network data often focuses on the composition of alters in each ego's personal network. For example, we can obtain, for each ego, the proportion of alters who are women, who are lawyers, who have served in the military, and so on. Each of these proportions is a variable in itself that may be theorized to have certain outcomes. For example, we might hypothesize that people with gay family members would be more positive toward gays in general than people without such ties. In addition, we can construct other metrics, such as the degree of heterogeneity in a person's ego network. For example, we can measure the extent to which a person's ego network is dominated by one gender or a handful of occupations. We can also measure autocorrelation—the tendency for egos to have ties with alters who are similar to themselves with respect to an attribute. This is used to test hypotheses of homophily, such as the tendency for people to interact with others with the same attributes (for example, race).

The egocentric approach can be thought of as combining elements of both traditional attribute-based social science and relation-based social network science. Once measures are constructed that characterize each ego's personal network, the data are no longer dyadic and are indistinguishable methodologically from the attributes collected in traditional social science. However, the data are interpreted using a network-based theoretical framework. Thus, ego network analysis combines the perspective of network analysis with the data of mainstream social science. It is limited in that it does not capture structural features of entire networks that might be important in explaining some types of outcomes. However, it does simplify data collection, especially in dealing with large populations. In addition, it allows researchers to use probability sampling, which enhances the generalizability of findings.

CONCLUSION

This chapter has attempted to provide a brief introduction to the field of social network analysis. We discussed the two primary domains of inquiry and the common theoretical concepts at three levels of analysis. We then provided an overview of the methodology involved in collecting, measuring, and analyzing network data. Although this was only an introduction, it is also a call for analyzing educational settings from a network point of view. What has captured the imagination of scientists and researchers over the past few decades is the ability of network thinking to illuminate a tremendous range of social phenomena. Organizations are inherently relational. They are social systems consisting of people with differing interests, goals, and preferences, interacting, communicating, and making decisions. These individuals are embedded in patterns of relations that have consequences for their own actions as well as for those around them. In addition, the organizations themselves are also enmeshed in networks with other organizations that have implications for their future. The network paradigm offers a powerful lens and methodology with which to model these complex systems. Its beauty lies in its versatility in capturing many of the relationships that comprise our complicated social world. And as we better understand the pattern of relationships between individuals within, between, and among educational institutions, we will be in a better position to effect change.

PART I

Teacher Networks

CHAPTER 3

"I Would Go to Her Because Her Mind Is Math"

Network Formation in the Context of a District-Based Mathematics Reform

Cynthia E. Coburn, Linda Choi, and Willow Mata

There is accumulating evidence that teachers' social networks are an important part of the school improvement puzzle. Researchers have provided evidence that the nature and quality of social networks are associated with a myriad of outcomes that are central to instructional change and school improvement. Social networks with strong ties can facilitate diffusion of innovation, transfer of complex information, and increased problem solving.[1] Strong social networks are also associated with increased individual and organizational performance.[2]

While there is emerging consensus that social networks are important, we know little about how they form or how they change over time.[3] There is a small body of research that investigates the factors that predict the development of the individual ties that form networks. This research highlights the importance of proximity, perception of expertise, and the perception that others are similar to you on some consequential dimension (*homophily*).[4] But these studies focus mainly on characteristics of the individuals or the tie, paying little attention to the social and organizational context within which ties are established and maintained.[5] Furthermore, the vast majority of research on tie formation is cross-sectional.[6] Thus, we know little about how the dynamics of tie formation shift over time. Absent attention to the dynamics of network formation and change, there is little information about how to encourage the development of strong social networks when they do not exist or how to sustain them when they do. Thus, policy makers and school leaders have little guidance about points of leverage for encouraging network development and sustainability in schools.

We address these limitations here. Drawing on three years of social network data from a study of districtwide implementation of mathematics curricula, we investigate the dynamics of tie formation and change among teachers in four elementary schools. We argue that teachers' reasons for reaching out and forming ties shift over time, and that these shifts can be attributed, at least in part, to features of the social and organizational context. We also provide evidence that shifts in teachers' reasons for seeking out individuals with whom to discuss mathematics have important consequences for the nature and quality of their social networks as a whole.

THE DYNAMICS OF NETWORK FORMATION: WHY INDIVIDUALS REACH OUT TO OTHERS

Social networks are an emergent phenomenon. They form as individuals opt into relationships with one another, creating ties. As individuals enter into relationships and, as those with whom they have relationships form ties with others, a social network takes shape. The resulting social networks may vary greatly in size, diversity, the extent to which a person's ties are connected to each other, and other key dimensions.

Researchers have spent a great deal of time investigating how different dimensions of social networks are associated with valued outcomes. For example, researchers have found evidence that networks with strong ties facilitate the transfer of tacit, sensitive, or complex knowledge, joint problem solving, and the development of coordinated solutions.[7] At the same time, weak ties have been found to play an important role in the diffusion of ideas and public information.[8] Diversity of ties, or ties that span across multiple knowledge pools or structural holes (the gaps between two networks that are not otherwise linked) facilitate access to information not immediately available in the proximal environment and, in corporate settings, contribute to competitive advantage.[9] Alternatively, Coleman provides evidence that networks with a high degree of closure, or the extent to which a person's ties are also connected to each other, create social obligations between network members that facilitate their ability to get work done.[10]

However, while there is a rich and growing knowledge base on the consequences of the structure of social networks, there has been far less attention paid to how networks come to have such structure in the first place. Absent this understanding, as Small points out, we do not know why some individuals have larger, more diverse, or stronger networks than others.[11] Furthermore, individuals and organizations are left with few clues about how to build networks more effectively.

There has been some research on predictors of tie formation, which has identified a number of reasons that individuals reach out to others to form ties. First, multiple studies have found evidence that *homophily*, "the principle that a contact between similar people occurs at a higher rate than [between] dissimilar people," plays an important role.[12] In workplace settings, homophily often expresses itself as individuals reaching out to others who hold similar structural positions in the organization.[13]

Second, other scholars have identified physical proximity as a strong predictor of tie formation.[14] *Proximity* is the physical distance separating people in the workplace, and the likelihood they will overlap and communicate about their work.[15] Early research on communication within organizations provides evidence that the physical and perceived distance between members of an organization is directly related to the probability they will talk and form workplace ties.[16]

Third, researchers argue that individuals reach out to others for information when they perceive that those others have expertise.[17] Forming a tie based on perception of expertise requires that the individual knows that the other person has certain knowledge, positively values that knowledge, and has access to that other person. For this reason, knowing and valuing others' expertise mediates the effect of proximity in tie formation.[18]

The research on tie formation has tended to focus on characteristics of the person or the tie. There has been less attention to how features of the social and organizational context might shape these individual choices. Small attempts to address this issue by introducing what he calls an organizational embeddedness approach to social networks.[19] Small provides evidence that organizations (in this case, child-care centers) broker social ties both purposely and nonpurposely to the degree that they provide opportunities for regular, long-lasting interaction and provide a minimally competitive and maximally cooperative environment. Organizations also foster ties through their interorganizational linkages and by creating or enacting norms that promote interaction or brokering as part of the work or professional obligation. In education, there is also evidence that public schools shape interaction via the structure of their subunits. Grade levels in elementary school, subject matter departments in high schools, and organizational units in school district central offices influence patterns of social interaction, which, in turn, shape the configuration of social networks.[20]

However, we know little about how organizational contexts, broadly conceived, interact with individual factors that influence tie formation highlighted in earlier research. Furthermore, the vast majority of research on network formation is cross-sectional.[21] Thus, we know little about when and under what conditions particular factors matter in the tie formation process.

METHODS

To investigate formation and change in social networks, we draw on data from an National Science Foundation–funded longitudinal study of the interaction between district reform strategies, human and social capital, and the implementation of ambitious mathematics curricula in two urban school districts. For this paper, we draw on data from one district for which we have complete social network data over the full three years of the study. The district in question, which we call Greene School District, is a midsize urban school district that was in the first year of its efforts to implement a new mathematics curriculum. The district adopted the innovative mathematics curriculum *Investigations in Data, Numbers, and Space* districtwide in the 2003–2004 school year after piloting select units the year before. In fall 2003, it also launched a comprehensive initiative to support teachers in learning the new curriculum that included the creation of school-based instructional coaches along with multiple opportunities for teachers to meet with others to talk about mathematics.

Consistent with the exploratory, theory-building purpose of our study, we used purposive sampling to select four elementary schools in the district with varying levels of professional community and teachers' expertise. The selection was based on recommendations from the district directors of mathematics.[22] In each school, we selected six focal teachers to represent the full range of grades and attitudes toward the new curriculum, based on recommendations from the principal. We wanted to ensure that the teachers we selected held a range of attitudes toward the adopted curriculum because we thought it possible that those who were supportive might have different kinds of interaction in their social network than those who were not, which might impact the nature and configuration of their networks.

We conducted two interviews and three classroom observations per focal teacher in year 1. We then expanded our data collection in years 2 and 3, collecting five interviews and six classroom observations per focal teacher. We supplemented work with the focal teachers with one to two interviews a year with the mathematics coaches; two interviews per year with the school principal; one interview a year with six additional teachers (whom we called nonfocal teachers); as well as observations of three to five occasions in each school per year on which teachers interacted on matters of mathematics instruction (professional development, grade-level meetings, coaching sessions, etc.).

A subset of this data collection was designed specifically to investigate focal teachers' advice networks. We took an egocentric approach to social network analysis. In this approach, the analyst maps networks that are centered around an individual or social unit (the *ego*).[23] To do this, we interviewed each focal teacher using questions designed to find out who the teacher talked with about mathematics instruction, the frequency and content of these interactions, and why they talked with some people and not others. We then analyzed this data and selected an additional six teachers to interview in each school (nonfocal teachers) who were part of focal teachers' social networks. During the subsequent visits to the school, we interviewed these nonfocal teachers using the same battery of social network questions supplemented with questions on their use of curriculum and background in mathematics. This approach allowed us to investigate in more depth the qualities of focal teachers' networks, including the location of expertise and content of interaction. We also devoted part of our interviews with school coaches and school principals to the same battery of social network questions that we asked teachers. We then supplemented the interviews by observing occasions on which focal teachers interacted with colleagues identified in their social network interviews.

Finally, to understand the role of the district—in particular, the ways in which district leaders envisioned and enacted professional development and structures to encourage teachers' social interaction—we conducted seventeen interviews with thirteen key district leaders, observed twenty professional development sessions for teachers and coaches, and collected and analyzed relevant district documents.

We experienced 50 percent turnover in focal teachers across the three years of our study. For this chapter, we draw on the twelve teachers for whom we have three years of data. We conducted analysis that compared our sample of twelve teachers to the entire sample of teachers in year 2 of the analysis, when we had the most teachers in our sample. We conducted t-tests and found no statistically significant difference between measures of congruence, depth, or access to expertise between the twelve teachers for whom we have data for three years and the broader sample of teachers in the study.[24] Because of the relatively small number of teachers per school and because the patterns we uncovered were quite similar across schools, we refrain from school-level analysis in this chapter, instead reporting patterns across our twelve-teacher sample.

To analyze the data, we mapped each of the twelve focal teachers' social networks for each of the three years. We then analyzed the information we gathered about why teachers formed ties to particular individuals in their network. We used a hybrid approach to coding.[25] That is, we started with a priori codes suggested by existing research (for example, a code for proximity, homophily, and expertise), but then added additional codes that emerged inductively from the data, including reform activities, friendship, shared values, and prior professional relationship. (See the appendix to this chapter for definitions used in coding.) We then charted how teachers' reasons for forming ties changed over each year of the study.

To understand how teachers' choices about whom to seek out for advice influenced the structure of their social network, we also analyzed two dimensions of the structure of the networks: size of network and diversity of ties. To analyze *size*, we simply counted the number of ties in each teacher's network and tracked how that changed over time. To analyze the *diversity of ties*, we mapped each teacher's individual social network and analyzed the degree to which it spanned functional areas, including grade level, cross-grade level, school administrators, coaches, and those outside the school.

Finally, when it became clear that there were interesting patterns in the degree to which teachers sought out others related to perceived expertise, we analyzed the actual expertise in teachers' networks. To do this, we assessed the degree to which individuals in a teacher's social network had participated in prior professional learning opportunities related to mathematics. (See the appendix for definitions of low, moderate, and high expertise.) We then investigated the relationship between teachers' perceptions of others' expertise and our assessment of their tie's expertise, and how that changed over time.

FINDINGS

In fall 2003, the teachers in Greene School District were faced with a new and challenging mathematics curriculum to implement in their classroom. They sought each other out to learn how to use the new curriculum, to discuss their experimentation with new practices, to share materials, and to share how their students seemed to be doing. However, they did not reach out to each other at random. Rather, teachers often gave very specific reasons for why they formed ties with some people inside and outside the school and not others. Furthermore, their reasons for reaching out were not static. Across the three years in our study, teachers' reasons for forming ties with some people but not others shifted considerably.

In the sections that follow, we argue that teachers' reasons for reaching out to others to discuss mathematics were influenced by the organizational context, and that the organizational context, in turn, was influenced by changes in district policy associated with the mathematics initiative. Finally, we show how shifting dynamics of tie formation resulted in social networks with quite different configurations across the years. We close with a discussion of the implications of these findings for research and practice.

Year 1

In the first year of our study, the district embarked on a new mathematics initiative. It adopted a brand-new mathematics curriculum and designed a series of activities to enable teachers to learn from their colleagues how to deepen their implementation. First, it created the role of a school-based mathematics coach. Each school had a minimum of two half-time coaches/half-time teachers who worked with teachers one-on-one and in groups to support their learning. Second, the district instituted weekly grade-level meetings to facilitate joint planning and school-based professional development every two weeks, the latter facilitated by the coach. A district-level

FIGURE 3-1   Teachers' reasons for forming ties over time

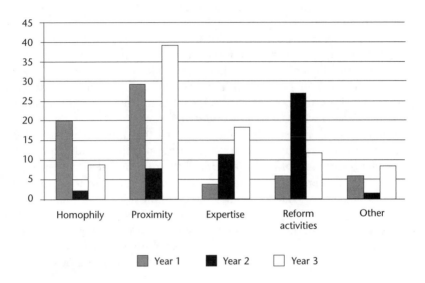

team supported coaches, providing them with monthly professional development, and observing them in action once a month. Finally, the district provided professional development in the summer and intersession to teachers seeking to deepen their knowledge of the curriculum and/or become a mathematics coach. Thus, as part of the mathematics initiative, the district initiated a range of structures that required teachers to interact with new people in new ways around mathematics instruction.

During the year that the district initiative was getting off the ground, focal teachers' reasons for reaching out to others to talk about mathematics were quite consistent with the pre-existing research on tie formation. As can be seen in figure 3-1, the two main reasons that teachers reached out to others were proximity and homophily. Teachers formed 29 percent of ties across their networks (fifteen ties) for reasons of proximity. For example, one teacher commented that she reached out to her colleague to discuss mathematics because "she's next door to me, so she is really easy to talk to." Another teacher asked a colleague for advice about mathematics because she ran into her at the copy machine: "You see someone and you're, like, 'What are you doing? It looks interesting.'"

Homophily was also important in year 1, accounting for 20 percent of all ties. We coded homophily when teachers talked of others as being "like" themselves in some respect. Most teachers sought out others who taught children of a similar age or demographic background. For example, one teacher explained: "Basically, both of our classes are on the same page. We're doing the same things . . . She's my team. She's a colleague in my same grade level . . . Her class is a mimic of mine. Mine is a mimic of hers. We're working on the same thing."

For this reason, when teachers went to others for reasons of homophily, they tended to choose their grade-level colleagues. Two ties to coaches were also for reasons of homophily; teachers noted that the coaches had experience teaching in their grade level. For example, one second-grade teacher reported that she sought out one of the coaches in the school "because I do have a math coach who is also a second-grade teacher."

It is important to note that in spite of the fact that the district was investing heavily in new reform activities—coaching, meetings, and professional development—teachers only chose three of their ties in the first year (6 percent) because of their participation in reform activities. All of these ties were to coaches, suggesting that the creation of this new role did influence teachers' patterns of social interaction, but to a limited degree. Furthermore, it is interesting to note that teachers rarely sought out others to talk about mathematics instruction because they saw them as having expertise. Only two of the teachers' ties (4 percent) were chosen for that reason, both of which were coaches.

Perhaps as a result of the pattern of these choices, especially the fact that teachers focused so heavily on homophily and proximity—which pointed teachers toward their grade-level colleagues—teachers' mathematics networks during the first year were quite small, with an average size of four ties. Also for reasons of proximity and homophily, teachers' networks were not terribly diverse. In year 1, 51 percent of teachers' ties were to grade-level colleagues, and nearly half of all teachers had social networks that were made up entirely of grade-level colleagues and coaches. Furthermore, networks were not very expert. Although ten out of twelve teachers had at least one person in their network who had moderate or high expertise according to our assessment, almost always the coach, for eight teachers, the coach was the only person in their network with expertise.

Year 2

In the second year of the study, the mathematics initiative really took off. The district offered more professional development to teachers, both in on-site and cross-district settings. Increasingly, the school-level professional development shifted from grade-level to cross-grade-level configurations. Importantly, it also became more focused on substantive questions about mathematics pedagogy and student learning, with more discussions about how students learn, the nature of math, and how to solve actual math problems. The district continued to provide intensive professional development to the on-site mathematics coaches, increasing their mathematics expertise. The district also initiated leadership teams—including the principal, coach, and a lead teacher in the school—and conducted intensive professional development with the teams, which brought the school leadership into the initiative in substantive ways.

As the mathematics initiative gained momentum, teachers' reasons for reaching out to others became more focused on mathematics and the mathematics initiative and less focused on other factors. As can be seen in figure 3-1, the activities that are part of the mathematics initiative began to influence whom teachers sought out for advice about mathematics. We coded reform activities when teachers referenced talking to others because of change made as part of the reform: grade-level meetings, biweekly school professional development, district professional development, or coaching. For example, when asked if there was anyone in the school she sought out to talk with about mathematics, one teacher responded: "Yes, actually we have the coaching system in our school, which is phenomenal." Reform activities became the most prevalent reason that teachers sought out others in year 2, accounting for thirty-five ties (27 percent), an enormous increase from year 1.

There was also an increase in the degree to which teachers formed ties with others because they saw them as having expertise in mathematics teaching and learning. The number of ties gained because of perception of expertise went from two in year 1 (4 percent) to fifteen in year 2 (12 percent of total ties). For example, one teacher explained why she went to a colleague in the following way:

> She's just very knowledgeable, very good with the kids, very patient, always willing to try new things, will go that extra mile for kids. After school, she's always there rather late doing her little groups with kids. She just puts forth a great effort every day, and I've seen her in action and she is really good at strategizing, really good at having kids think the processes out before they just do them or speak them. So I think she's qualified in those areas, for sure.

Another discussed why she went to the coach for advice:

> I can count on her. I mean she has a solid foundation. She has a solid mathematics background and she is very familiar with *Investigations* because . . . she has worked in so many different classrooms. I mean, she has worked in the kindergarten, the first grade, the second grade. She is familiar with where the students have come from in kindergarten and where they are going and what they will be working on in second grade. So I know that I can get good advice from her.

Most ties formed in year 2 because of a perception of expertise were with members of focal teachers' grade level, followed by coaches. Only one teacher sought out a colleague in another grade level because she saw her as having expertise.

At the same time that there was an increase in teachers reaching out to others for mathematics-focused reasons, there was also a substantial decrease in other reasons for forming ties. Most notably, there was a sharp decrease in the number of times that teachers went to others for reasons of homophily (down to three ties, or 2 percent of total ties) and proximity (down to ten ties, or 8 percent of total ties). Interestingly, there was also a shift in whom teachers went to for reasons of proximity. While they were most likely to go to teachers in their grade level for reasons of proximity in year 1, in year 2 they were most likely to go to teachers in other grades (six ties), followed by those in their grade level (three ties) and the coach (one tie).

Taken together, this suggests that in year 2, the organizational changes associated with the mathematics initiative began to influence individual teachers' choices about whom to seek out to discuss mathematics. The increase in structures to enable teachers to talk with one another about mathematics, and the fact that these structures were more focused on mathematics teaching and learning, created more opportunities for teachers to interact with one another in mathematics-meaningful ways. And, indeed, teachers reported that they were seeking out others because of these opportunities to a much greater extent than in year 1. Furthermore, the fact that the meetings were often configured so that teachers would interact across grade levels enabled teachers to interact with others beyond their grade-level colleagues in a more regular and sustained fashion than in the prior year. Perhaps for that reason, there was a sharp increase in the degree to which teachers sought out teachers in other grade levels for reasons of proximity in year 2.

It is also clear that teachers increasingly valued mathematics expertise. This may be because the focus on substantive activities related to mathematics teaching and learning enabled teachers to not only see who in the school actually had expertise in mathematics, but also see the benefits of working with them.

As a result of these shifts, teachers' mathematics networks changed dramatically from year 1 to year 2. They expanded greatly, increasing in size from an average of four to an average of eleven as teachers reached beyond their grade-level colleagues to others in the school. Teachers' ties were also more diverse. While 51 percent of teachers' ties in year 1 were with grade-level colleagues, this declined to 43 percent of ties in year 2. Furthermore, teachers' non-grade-level ties diversified. In year 1, 56 percent of teachers' non-grade-level ties were coaches. By year 2, coaches represented only 30 percent of non-grade-level ties. Instead, teachers' networks included many more colleagues from other grades (36 percent of non-grade-level ties in year 2, compared with 8 percent in year 1), administrators (8 percent in year 2, compared with 4 percent in year 1), and those outside the school (26 percent in year 2, compared with 32 percent in year 1).

Year 3

In year 3 of the initiative, the district began to shift its priorities and with-draw support from the mathematics initiative. The initiative had become somewhat controversial, with some in the district arguing that the curric-ulum was not appropriate for English Language Learners (ELL students) because it was too language-intensive. When the superintendent retired, the new superintendent decided that the main priority for the district was going to be the education of ELL students. To that end, he decided to enforce a preexisting agreement with the Office of Civil Rights that required that all teachers in the district teach thirty minutes a day of English Language Devel-opment (ELD) strategies. To make room for this time, he cut back mathemat-ics instruction from ninety minutes a day to sixty minutes a day. At the same time, the state passed new legislation that required all teachers to have a "Structured English Immersion Endorsement" certifying their knowledge of strategies for meeting the needs of ELL students. This endorsement required fifteen hours of professional development on ELL strategies for all teachers across the state. To meet these demands, the district redirected its profes-sional development resources toward ELL instruction.

The superintendent also rolled budget and staffing decisions down to schools in year 3 and ended the district stipend that teachers received if they took on coaching duties, leaving it up to school budgets to fund coaches. In response to greater budgetary autonomy, principals in three of the four schools cut back to a single coach to meet the mathematics needs in their schools. (The fourth school cut back to two coaches from three; however, the second coach left midyear to assume district responsibilities.) At the school level, principals also redirected professional development resources. The dis-trict's new emphasis and the need to provide professional development on ELD instruction meant that many of the biweekly professional development sessions that had previously been devoted to mathematics were redirected to ELL issues. Thus, many of the structures that fostered interaction around mathematics—the weekly grade-level meetings, the biweekly professional development in mathematics, coaches, district professional development—were eliminated or greatly curtailed.

These changes were reflected in teachers' reasons for seeking out others to discuss mathematics. As elements of the initiative were scaled back, reform activities as a reason for reaching out to colleagues declined substantially. As you can see in figure 3-1, teachers sought out only 12 percent of the people in their network (eleven ties) because they interacted with them in grade-level meetings, mathematics professional development, or other structures associated with the mathematics initiative. At the same time, in the absence of structured opportunities to interact, proximity once again increased as the most common reason for selecting others to discuss mathematics, accounting for nearly 40 percent of teachers' ties. In contrast with year 2, when teachers sought out teachers in other grades because of the proximity created by cross-grade meetings, after the meetings were cut in year 3, proximity drove teachers back to grade-level colleagues and coaches.

In spite of the decline in the mathematics initiative, however, teachers' inclination to form ties with others because they saw them as having mathematics expertise increased for the second year in a row, accounting for 18 percent of teachers' ties in year 3 (seventeen ties). For example, one teacher explained that: "I would go to her because . . . her mind is math." And while teachers had previously identified only their grade-level colleagues and the coaches as having expertise, by year 3, they also identified teachers in other grade levels for this reason. In fact, expertise was the main reason that teachers sought out their non-grade-level colleagues to be in their network that year. Finally, after declining substantially from year 1 to year 2, homophily increased slightly in year 3.

Taken together, these data suggest that the district's shift in priorities and the consequent removal of structural supports for interaction influenced teachers' reasons for seeking out others to discuss mathematics. In the absence of structured opportunities to meet, teachers no longer made ties because they interacted with others during meetings. Given limited time during the day when they were not directly responsible for children, teachers had to make do with those nearby if they had a question, needed support, or simply wanted to talk with someone else about mathematics instruction.

At the same time, the appetite for expertise that was nurtured in year 2 by substantive meetings focused on mathematics persisted and grew in year 3, even as these meetings waned. It also appears that opportunities to interact with a wider range of people in year 2 on matters of mathematics teaching and learning enabled focal teachers to learn where the expertise in mathematics was located in the school. Indeed, across the three years, teachers got better at identifying those in the school with expertise. When teachers told us that they went to others because they were knowledgeable or had expertise, this was based on their perceptions of the expertise of others. At the same time, we also independently analyzed teachers' and coaches' expertise based on their experience with and training in reform mathematics (see the appendix for our criteria for determining expertise). Across the three years in our study, focal teachers' perceptions of expertise of the people in their network got progressively closer to our assessment.

There are two ways to show this pattern. First, we assessed the degree to which the individuals whom focal teachers perceived to be expert actually had expertise according to our metric. As you can see in table 3-1, there is an increase in the percentage from year 2 to year 3. (In year 1, teachers only identified two people with expertise, both of whom were coaches. All coaches in our sample had moderate or high expertise.) Second, we assessed the match

TABLE 3-1

Expertise as rated by teachers and researchers

	Year 1	Year 2	Year 3
Number of ties teacher nominated because of expertise	2	15	17
Number of teacher-nominated ties rated as moderate or high expertise on researcher metric	2	9	13
Degree to which teacher-nominated ties were expert on researcher metric	100% (2/2)	60% (9/15)	76% (13/17)
Total number of ties in teachers' network rated as moderate or high expertise on researcher metric	15	33	25
Teacher accuracy in locating expertise in network	13% (2/15)	27% (9/33)	52% (13/25)

between the people focal teachers selected as having expertise and those in their network who actually had expertise according to our metric. As you can see in table 3-1, there is a substantial increase in this percentage across the three years. For example, in year 1, teachers identified two people as having expertise, but there were thirteen other individuals in focal teachers' networks in year 1 whom we considered to have moderate or high expertise. Thus the focal teachers saw only 13 percent of those with expertise in their network as having expertise. In contrast, in year 3, focal teachers identified 52 percent of the individuals in their networks with expertise accurately.

As a result of shifting patterns in the reasons teachers selected others to discuss mathematics, teachers' networks were smaller, less diverse, but more expert in year 3 than in year 2. The average size of teachers' networks declined from eleven in year 2 to eight in year 3. The diversity of ties also decreased. While 43 percent of ties were grade level in year 2, that rose to 68 percent in year 3. Teachers no longer had regular and easy interaction with those in other grades across the school, and the number of teachers in other grades in teachers' networks plummeted.

However, at the same time that the networks contracted in size, they actually became more expert in year 3 because teachers increasingly sought out others because of their expertise and because they got more skilled at identifying this expertise. In year 2, for example, we judged that 43 percent of teachers' ties had moderate or high expertise. By year 3, this had increased to 66 percent. This pattern was even more pronounced for those in teachers' networks who were not at their grade level. In year 2, 78 percent of focal teaches' ties with people outside of their grade level had moderate or high expertise. That rose to 95 percent in year 3. Thus, even though teachers were reaching out to fewer people outside their grade in year 3, those they reached out to were more likely to have moderate or high expertise. This suggests that in year 3, faced with less time and fewer structured opportunities to meet, teachers were able to draw on a more robust understanding of what others in the school actually knew about mathematics to make more strategic choices about where to seek advice about mathematics instruction.[26]

DISCUSSION

Over the three-year course of the study, teachers' reasons for seeking others out to discuss mathematics, and the social networks that resulted, changed dramatically. An early emphasis on homophily and proximity led to social networks that were small, homogenous, and largely focused on grade-level colleagues. As the mathematics initiative expanded and reform activities became more regular, sustained, and mathematics-focused, teachers' decisions were increasingly shaped by the structure of the meetings and a new desire to interact with those with expertise. As a result, networks became larger, more diverse, and more expert. Finally, as support for the mathematics initiative waned and activities to encourage regular interaction were curtailed, proximity once again became the prime reason teachers sought each other out. At the same time, however, teachers' desire for expertise continued to grow and their expanding knowledge of where that expertise was located led to networks that, while smaller and less diverse, were increasingly expert.

These findings have implications for both research and practice. Taken together, the results provide additional evidence for the importance of the organizational embeddedness approach to social network research.[27] Social network researchers have historically paid little attention to the role of formal bureaucratic mechanisms such as organizational structure or social policy in influencing informal social relations.[28] Researchers tend to emphasize the emergent character of social networks, focusing on the choices individuals make as they seek out others with whom to interact. But they often neglect the social arrangements and organizational conditions that shape individual choice. We show that tie formation—the foundation of social networks—can be influenced in profound ways by existing organizational norms, structures, and practices. Furthermore, these norms, structures, and practices can and do change over time, affecting the dynamics of network formation in both positive and negative ways.

First, organizational structures and practices influence the degree to which teachers reach out for reasons of proximity in two ways. Organizational context shapes who teachers are proximate with. For example, in this study, cross-grade meetings in year 2 put teachers in greater contact with teachers in other grades on a regular basis, which led to an increase in teachers forming ties with those in other grades for reasons of proximity. However, organizational context also shaped the degree to which teachers reached out to others for reasons of proximity at all. When teachers had time to interact with others in regular and sustained ways—as was the case in year 2 of the initiative—they chose individuals to go to for more substantive reasons, and proximity declined overall as a major reason for forming ties. But when organizational supports for sustained interaction went away, proximity once again became the predominant reason that teachers talked to others about mathematics. This suggests that schools and other organizations can influence whom individuals reach out to by harnessing the power of proximity and creating spaces for interaction.

Second, the organizational context of public schools shapes homophily in the way it structures work practices and roles. In this study, the grade-level structure of schooling and the organization of the curriculum in question fostered teachers' sense that other teachers in their grade level were "like" them in a consequential way. Work roles, such as specific kinds of teachers (e.g., second-grade teacher, special education teacher) are, at root, cognitive categories.[29] These categories shape how individuals interpret their world and the social interaction within it. Here, we show that the social organization of work roles influences how teachers understand themselves in relation to others, thus guiding whom they go to when they seek out others like themselves. This suggests that homophily is much more than an individual psychological predisposition, as early research on homophily maintains, but is influenced in important ways by the organizational and institutional context.

Organizational context also matters for the degree to which individuals reach out to others for reasons of expertise. It does so in two ways. First, the organization can influence whether or not teachers and others value expertise in the first place. In this study, teachers learned by working with others on substantive issues related to mathematics. This, in turn, was fostered by the development of well-constructed activities that teachers did with one another during formal meetings in year 2.[30] Thus, teachers went from hardly ever seeking out others with expertise in year 1 to using this as a key reason for talking with others nearly 20 percent of the time in year 3.

But beyond fostering an appetite for expertise, organizations can also influence the degree to which teachers know where expertise is located in their environment. Perceptions of others are formed through direct interaction, observation, and third-party commentary.[31] Because teachers usually work alone in their classrooms and because of the well-documented norms of privacy and autonomy in teaching, many teachers have only indirect and often imperfect information about what other teachers actually do in their classrooms and their areas of expertise, even when those teachers are in their grade level.[32] In this study, the district created multiple opportunities for teachers to interact with one another that, by year 2 of the study, were focused on substantive issues. This created a mechanism for teachers to learn more about what individuals in the school actually knew about mathematics instruction. Teachers then used this knowledge to be much more strategic about whom they sought out to discuss mathematics.

That organizations can create conditions to encourage the development of knowledge of others' expertise is significant. Research on organizational learning has provided evidence that this capacity, which some refer to as *transactive memory*, is a key component of collective problem solving, coordination, and group performance. [33] This research shows that it is not enough to have expertise in one's team. One must also know who has that expertise and be able to access and coordinate it.[34] This is especially true in dynamic environments, like those in public schools.[35] Here, we show that knowledge of existing expertise can be a key component in network formation as well, resulting in networks that not only have increased expertise but also the potential to strategically access this expertise to enhance individual and organizational performance.

Finally, this study extends the organizational embeddedness approach to social networks by providing evidence that the tie formation process is amenable to policy intervention. District policy can influence social networks by creating structures, requirements, and focus that impact the creation of ties. Prior research on social networks suggests that ties form when there are opportunities for regular, long-lasting interaction that are maximally cooperative and minimally competitive.[36] This study suggests that social policy can create these kinds of conditions. Indeed, we saw that when district policy increased the opportunities for teachers to meet regularly to talk about mathematics, there was a substantial increase in the degree to which teachers sought out others because they interacted and became acquainted with them in reform activities. This in turn facilitated the expansion and increase in the diversity of teachers' social networks. But this study also shows that district policy can create the conditions for the dissolution of ties as well by interrupting existing relationships, removing supportive structures, and making it difficult for individuals to have the frequent interaction that nurtures longevity in ties.

This study also has implications for school leaders and policy makers because it provides insight into points of leverage for encouraging network development and sustainability. At root, this study suggests that the process of tie formation and the social networks that result *can* be influenced. School leaders and policy makers can influence tie formation through the creation of opportunities for teachers to interact in regular and long-lasting ways. These meetings create conditions of proximity for teachers, which foster the development of ties. How the meetings are configured—whether teachers are meeting in grade-level groups, cross-grade-level groups, or regularly with those outside of the school—influences whom teachers come into contact with, thus affecting the diversity of teachers' social networks.

But this study also suggests that proximity is a first step, not an end in itself. If the goal is to foster ties that enable mathematically meaningful interaction to facilitate learning and joint problem solving, teachers' networks must include others with expertise in mathematics teaching and learning. The district in this study took several fairly common approaches to foster this goal. It hired and trained coaches to work with teachers to bring expertise into the school site, and it provided professional development to teachers to build their expertise directly. However, this approach can work only if teachers (a) know where the expertise is; and (b) make the effort to access it, thus forming a tie.

Our findings suggest that leaders and policy makers can foster the development of the desire for expertise *and* the knowledge of where it is located by ensuring that teachers are engaged in generative tasks focused on teaching and learning during structured meetings. Too often, teachers find themselves in meetings that either have little to do with teaching and learning or have assigned poorly designed tasks.[37] In this study, it was when teachers were engaged in mathematically meaningful tasks that they had the opportunity to actually learn who in their school was knowledgeable about the mathematics curriculum. These opportunities appear to be critical if teachers are to move toward more mathematically meaningful reasons for reaching out to others to discuss mathematics.

We know that robust social networks can facilitate diffusion of knowledge, increased problem solving, and individual and organizational performance. It is time for both researchers and practitioners to pay greater attention to the social and organizational conditions that facilitate the development of these robust social networks in schools.

This work was supported from a grant from the National Science Foundation (IERI Grant REC- 0228343). The content or opinions expressed herein do not necessarily reflect the views of the National Science Foundation or any other agency of the U.S. government. We wish to thank Marc Chun, Teresa McCaffrey, Rebecca McGraw, Chris Nelson, Laurie Rubel, Marcia Seeley, Jaime Smith, Sarah Spencer, Stephanie Sutherland, Mikyung Wolf, and Bahadir Yanik for help with data collection. We would also like to thank Kristine Acosta, Tara Amin, Grotius Hugo, Darlene Poluan, Jennifer Russell, Jaime Smith, and Stephanie Sutherland for help with data analysis. Special thanks to Wanda Nieters for her invaluable contributions to data analysis for this chapter, Mary Kay Stein for ongoing conversations about the project, and Corrie Park for administrative assistance. Finally, we extend our gratitude to all the participants in this study for allowing us into their schools and offices and permitting us to interview and observe them engaged in their reform efforts.

APPENDIX

Definitions Used in Coding

Dimension	Definition
Reasons for forming ties	
Homophily	Teachers form ties with others because they perceive them to be like themselves in some manner. Examples of reasons for homophily include grade level, type of school, or gender. Teachers must identify a person as like themselves on a given dimension to be considered homophily.
Proximity	Teachers form ties with others because they are physically near each other; for example, work on the same floor or hall, run into each other on the playground, or see each other in the hall/workroom/ at lunch.
Reform activities	Teachers form ties with others because they are brought together by aspects of the reform strategy; for example, coaching, grade-level meetings, or professional development.
Perception of expertise	Teachers form ties with others because they perceive them to have expertise; for example, many years of teaching experience, or training and knowledge of mathematics.
Other	Teachers form ties for other reasons; for example, because they perceive similar values about appropriate instruction, because they are friends or "get along," or because they have a shared professional history.
Researcher assessment of expertise	
High	High expertise is defined as: (1) four or more intensive professional development experiences or (2) a math major in undergraduate or specialization in mathematics education in graduate work accompanied by two or more intensive professional development experiences.
Moderate	Moderate expertise is defined as: (1) two or three intensive professional development experiences or (2) mathematics major as an undergraduate or specialization in mathematics in graduate school accompanied by at least some opportunity to learn about pedagogical approaches consistent with the *Investigations* curriculum.
Low	Low expertise is defined as (1) one or fewer intensive professional development experiences and (2) no formal mathematics training in undergraduate or graduate school, or a mathematics major or specialization in mathematics absent at least some opportunity to learn about pedagogical approaches consistent with the *Investigations* curriculum.

CHAPTER 4

Centrality, Connection, and Commitment

The Role of Social Networks in a School-Based Literacy Initiative

Allison Atteberry and Anthony S. Bryk

In an era of increased accountability, public schools face pressure to improve their instruction on an accelerated timeline. As more schools seek to improve the quality of their instruction, school and district leaders look to other schools for strategies that have been effective elsewhere. Yet efforts to identify school interventions that work in varied school contexts has proven challenging.

The remarkable variability in school cultures and contexts implies that a given strategy that appears successful in one school may not take hold in another.[1] Such school-specific factors can determine the ultimate fate of any school change efforts.[2] In large-scale quantitative research involving many school sites, researchers often consider these socio-organizational conditions as unmeasurable or outside the scope of formal analysis.[3] In this chapter, we present findings from one research project that utilizes social network analysis to bring this important information into explanations of how interventions "as intended" interact with local school contexts.

The programmatic context for this research is the Literacy Collaborative model (LC). The cornerstone of the LC program is long-term teacher professional development coordinated by an on-site coach. The success of one-on-one coaching by a "more expert" colleague is likely to hinge on the relational dynamics among teachers. Moreover, the introduction of this new role and a new professional development framework may challenge traditional work norms in schools. As a consequence, insight into the social networks of teachers may account for some of the observed variability in program implementation.

This chapter develops an empirically grounded framework about how network characteristics interact with change efforts aimed at instructional improvement. We begin by presenting evidence across fifteen schools about how the networks among teachers reshape during the course of the LC intervention. Second, we explore how preexisting social networks at the onset of the intervention shaped uptake of the reform and how these networks changed as LC implementation deepened. We consider this question by taking a closer look at two school cases in depth, to illustrate the explanatory power of social network analysis and how it might be used in future work.

BACKGROUND

Literacy Collaborative Program

The Literacy Collaborative (LC) program seeks to improve children's literacy achievement in elementary schools by introducing a comprehensive literacy framework and supporting teachers to develop expertise in its classroom enactment. The LC program is organized around a theoretical foundation explicated by Fountas and Pinnell, who drew on seminal work of Clay and others.[4] For many teachers, the LC program represents a profound intervention into their work. It seeks to change the basic components, procedures, and social routines of teaching. Even more fundamentally, it poses a challenge to basic normative conceptions about how individual teachers think about their work and relations to colleagues.

In a typical implementation, a school selects one of its teachers to take on the role of a literacy coach. These individuals are trained over the course of a full school year while still teaching in their schools. The LC training for coaches focuses on: (1) deepening understanding of literacy theory and content, (2) enhancing coaches' own expertise in implementing the LC model, and (3) supporting other teachers as they encounter this new framework and engage in inquiry about their practice. After the training year, the literacy coaches assume responsibility for school-based literacy professional development for all kindergarten through second grade teachers at the school, regardless of the school's size.

According to program guidelines, all teachers should ideally receive two coaching session per month extending over multiple years. Given the constraints on the available time, however, coaches must exercise discretion as to whom to coach. Considerable variation in exposure to coaching may result. In addition, individual teacher considerations play a role as well. The intensity of a coach's work with any individual teacher may depend on the teacher's openness to this relationship and the likelihood of advancing instructional improvement in a particular classroom.

The Larger Study

The research described in this chapter is part of a larger project that sought to examine the efficacy of the LC program. The linkage between LC activities and changes in student learning is predicated on a set of causal connections that we herein refer to as a *causal cascade*. First, a coach must establish relationships with her school-based colleagues and initiate work routines organized around her new role as a school-based professional developer. Second, teachers must regularly participate in the professional development activities that the coach initiates. Third, this participation must result in changes in teachers' classroom practice. Finally, assuming desired changes in instruction occur, improvements in student learning are expected. Each of these causal connections has been examined in other work, summarized briefly below. In the current chapter, we hypothesize that many of these linkages are facilitated when the preexisting network characteristics support the type of work LC embodies. Moreover, successful engagement in LC is likely to reshape the networks over the course of the study.

Relevant Study Findings

The research already completed on the larger project has indicated a great deal of variability in LC engagement across school sites. Atteberry and Bryk uncovered notable variation in the amount of coaching received among teachers and across schools.[5] Similarly, Hough et al. found considerable variability in the changes in teacher practices.[6] Finally, Biancarosa and Bryk modeled the value added of LC in each school over time as evidence of the extent to which the introduction of LC caused growth in student outcomes.[7] That study also uncovered marked variability in the contribution of LC to student learning across schools. Together, this evidence makes clear that, despite overall positive effects of LC, some schools engaged LC more deeply and successfully. The variability across schools in terms of engagement in coaching is depicted in figure 4-1, which plots the average number of coaching sessions accumulated per teacher within each school. We seek herein to explore this variability through the lens of social network theory and analysis.

CONCEPTUAL FRAMEWORK

The Nature of Teacher Work

The LC perspective on teacher work is an ambitious one. Teachers are viewed as problem solvers who need guidance across a developmental trajectory for their practice. This requires a network of human relationships that supports communication, develops professional knowledge, and makes it possible for peers to agree on and hold each other accountable to common standards of practice. Teachers work on identified instructional problems and systemati-

FIGURE 4-1   **Average number of coaching sessions accumulated per teacher across the 17 schools over time**

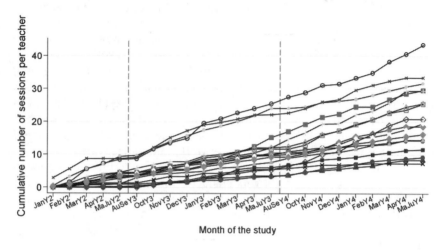

Note: Each line represents 1 of the 17 schools in the study

cally examine evidence about their practice. Structured professional development sessions, individual coaching, and informal support are routine.

Thus, LC seeks to create a community of learners within each school. It aims to deeply embed itself in the life of a school and over time fundamentally change how teaching occurs. LC hypothesizes that the intervention is best supported when a school develops a professional community that values a common body of professional knowledge and skills and shares a collective commitment to advancing student learning.[8] It emphasizes the importance of common practices enacted within a social learning context.[9]

The Key Role of a School's Social Network

According to Frank, Zhao, and Borman, informal social networks act as sources of help and social pressure that can influence a teacher's engagement with any new program.[10] Once initial adopters (in this case a coach) are trained and come to value a new social practice such as LC, they return to their school to share this new approach with their colleagues. When these exchanges go well, the intervention is likely to spread and take root.

However, a countervailing force of resistance may also develop, depending on the base social structure of the school.[11] If the social network is divided or there is little interaction among teachers, diffusion of practices may be slowed or confined to subgroups. Thus, in any given school, the base social network may either hinder or foment change.

A rich understanding of a school's base state necessitates information about the form of its social network at the start of the intervention.[12] Are there existing avenues of communication through which information can flow? How interconnected are teachers within the school? Additionally, because each coach was first a classroom teacher within the school, it is crucial to understand her initial location in the social network. According to the LC model, the coach acts as a trusted resource for fellow teachers as they take on the difficult task of deepening their practice. The extent to which the coach meets this ideal at least partially depends on her peers' preexisting evaluations of her—both in terms of her relational skill and her expertise in literacy teaching and learning. For example, a coach who is not particularly central to her school network at the outset may struggle to engage others in the work.

The data collected by the larger project allow us to examine a set of initial network characteristics that are hypothesized to be of particular importance in program enactment.

Network Density. Through a combination of both structural and normative factors, organizations develop norms around the density of interconnections among its members. A measure of network density provides a sense of how many individuals in an organization interact with one another and how often. What patterns of social connectivity do we expect to find in schools? A common belief among teachers is that good teaching develops primarily through trial and error in their own classroom.[13] The individualist orientation that undergirds these views is supported by a traditional school organization, where teachers work in isolation, experience little task interdependence, and have few structured opportunities for professional collaboration. Teachers who see their work in this way tend to rely heavily on personal opinions when making instructional decisions and are less likely to turn to their colleagues for critical advice. Furthermore, the insights and ideas colleagues offer tend to be mainly of the form of "tricks of the trade" rather than socially agreed-on conceptions of expert practice. In schools where the majority of teachers have such an orientation, one would expect to observe low levels of organizational density.

In contrast, the LC model envisions teachers as members of a school-based professional community. In this role conception, colleagues are not merely a source of helpful hints shared in informal conversations, but are a genuine professional resource for practice improvement. Such a teacher understands that she can improve her practice by engaging in critical dialogue with others around common problems confronted in their classrooms. Network density should be stronger in schools where such norms prevail.

Coach Centrality. Another key consideration is the centrality of the coach-to-be within her school's network as the LC program begins. Is she already viewed as a resource on issues of literacy teaching and learning and already able to work effectively with her colleagues? Or was she more peripheral to other faculty at program initiation?

Disconnectedness. Teacher isolation is common in schools. The uncertainty that teachers feel in their daily work provides one way of understanding why such isolation is normative. In his foundational 1975 study, Lortie asked teachers to describe how they assess whether they are teaching their students well. To his surprise, Lortie found that large numbers of teachers found it difficult to even answer. The anxiety-producing uncertainty surrounding the "How am I doing?" question stood out as the most emotional part of his interviews. On this matter, he states, "a seemingly simple question on problems of evaluating progress unleashed a torrent of feeling and frustration; one finds a self-blame, a sense of inadequacy, the bitter taste of failure, and anger at the students, despair, and other dark emotions."[14]

Such emotions, when embedded deeply within the work task, may dispose teachers to resist others' attempts to gain access to their classrooms, for fear that someone will "find out" that they are not sure about their performance. Yet observing teachers' work and discussing personal strengths and weaknesses in a public setting is central to the LC framework. In schools where trust among colleagues is weak, teachers may not view their colleagues as safe resources for improving practice.[15] When a high proportion of staff in a school is disconnected from one another, it is likely to undermine the diffusion of any new model that rests on collaboration.

In summary, several aspects of social networks in schools are hypothesized to interact with an intervention like LC. Network density, coach centrality, and isolation among the teaching staff are likely to play a key role both at the onset of school change efforts, but they are also likely to be themselves transformed when deep change takes place.

DATA COLLECTION, MEASURES, AND METHODS

Study Timeline and Data Collection

The larger study of LC examined seventeen schools over four years. Coaches were trained during the first year of the study (school year 2004–2005), and data collected during this year of nonimplementation from teachers and students provides baseline information for each school. During this first year, teachers completed surveys on their general background characteristics, their work behaviors and orientations, and the people to whom they turned for advice about their work.

Coaches began working with kindergarten through second-grade teachers during the second year. Throughout all four years, students' literacy skills were measured in the fall and spring in order to estimate the causal contribution of LC to student learning. Coaches maintained online logs of all coaching activities and completed rubrics on the development of teacher practice for every teacher with whom they worked. In the final year of the study, teachers again completed surveys on their work behaviors, orientations, and the people to whom they now turned for advice about literacy.

Social Network Data and Network Measures

The base year and end-of-study surveys asked all kindergarten through third-grade teachers to list up to seven people with whom they most often discussed literacy teaching and learning. Survey respondents indicated how often they talked to each person they listed (less than once a month; two to three times a month, once or twice a week; almost daily), as well as where each listed colleagues worked (in the same building or elsewhere).

We use this information in two ways. First, we construct graphic visualizations of the schools both before the introduction of LC and after three years of implementation. Second, we use the data to create quantitative measures of the key network characteristics identified in the conceptual framework. These measures summarize key aspects of a network in order to enable comparisons across schools and over time. The creation of these measures is described below.

Measure of network density. The density of a network is measured by dividing the total number of ties that individuals report by the total number of possible ties. When many of the potential ties are realized, a network is characterized as *dense* and we conclude that its members interact a great deal. Social network analysts point out that this network density measure is related to the overall size of the network—a point we also explore later in the chapter.[16] Given the relationship between size and density, any analysis that uses density as a potential explanatory variable should somehow control for school size.

Measure of coach centrality. A person's centrality is typically captured by the proportion of possible ties with others that are *realized* (i.e., the relationship is reported in the social network surveys). For nonsymmetric data—in which individuals might name someone who does not name them in return—a person's normalized *in-degree* centrality equals the proportion of possible ties that person could *receive* that were realized. Throughout this paper, we use in-degree centrality of the coach, because we seek to capture the extent to which coaches are sought out by their colleagues to discuss literacy. In addition, since the data from this study is valued (i.e., the frequency of contact is recorded), in-degree centrality is a weighted average of the values of the received ties.

The centrality measure can be used in several ways. One may rank all the teachers within the same school in terms of their centrality in order to determine whether the teacher who becomes the coach was already the most central actor in her school network before the LC initiative began. One can also examine whether coaches subsequently become the most central actor after three years in their new role. In addition, one can standardize the centrality of coaches across schools to compare the relative centrality of coaches across sites.

Measure of network fragmentation. We calculate what proportion of the staff is disconnected from the literacy teaching and learning network. That is, what percentage of the surveyed teachers report that they turn to no one in the school to discuss literacy practice, and in return no one refers to them? When the proportion of such individuals is high, one can characterize the network as fragmented.

Methods of Inquiry

In the following section, we analyze the school social networks in two ways. First, we use the network characteristics to examine whether teacher networks reshaped during the implementation of LC, especially in regard to the teacher who becomes the coach in year two. Second, we examine two schools in more depth using a combination of the network visuals, their summary network characteristics, and other evidence about whether LC took hold according to observable outcomes. These two schools were selected for in-depth examination because they each experienced a different development of LC, though they shared some common characteristics of their networks in the base state.

RESULTS

Changes Across Schools over Time

Fifteen schools in the study had sufficient network data to conduct a comparison of the network characteristics before and after three years of LC implementation. For the many reasons discussed in the conceptual framework, we would expect that engagement in LC activities might challenge traditional organizational features of schools. Herein we posit a series of questions about changes in school networks that relate to the concepts delineated in the conceptual framework. These questions include:

1. Was the coach-to-be chosen because she was already considered a resource for advice on literacy instruction?
2. Do the coaches become more central in their networks once LC is implemented?
3. How many teachers consider the coach a resource before versus after LC?

4. Do the networks become more dense during LC implementation?
5. If the coach-to-be started out more central, does she coach more?

1. Was the coach-to-be chosen because she was already considered a resource for advice on literacy instruction? According to LC, the principal is primarily in charge of selecting a teacher from his or her staff to assume the new coach role. Presumably, it makes sense to choose a teacher who has shown some indications that she might execute the new coach role with skill. That is, the coach-to-be may have demonstrated expertise in issues related to childhood literacy instruction (or at least strong potential in this area). In addition, a strong candidate for the coach role would have some experience working as an adult educator. If the chosen teacher possesses some balance of these qualities, it is likely that her colleagues already view her as a valuable resource when it comes to literacy practice, even before LC begins.

At the time of the pre-intervention survey, nine of the fifteen teachers (60 percent) who were selected to become the coaches were already the most "central" actor of the K–3 staff in their school in terms of the literacy teaching and learning network. This suggests that in over half of the schools, the coach was likely selected based on some skillfulness that her fellow teachers acknowledged. Table 4-1 displays the rank of all coaches at the end of the nonimplementation base year (spring 2005).

For the six teachers who were not initially the most central actor, we can see from table 4-1 that five of them were actually among the *least* central actors in their respective schools. Perhaps coaches in these schools were not selected on the criteria one might have anticipated. It is possible, for instance, that principals made strategic use of the new coach role to remove ineffective teachers from the classroom. It is certainly possible that these coaches were selected because of some positive characteristics that neither the other teachers in the school nor the researchers were aware of. For instance, perhaps the selected teacher was relatively new to the school and not well known by her colleagues, but had expressed a strong interest in becoming a literacy coach.

We might anticipate that a coach-to-be who is already considered an approachable resource by her colleagues will more easily penetrate classrooms in her new role as a coach, and over half of the coaches already exhibited this quality. That said, all coaches underwent an intensive year of LC training and may have developed skills they did not initially posses. It is possible that even a teacher who was not initially often cited by her colleagues might ultimately come to be seen as a trusted resource through her new role coordinating LC activities.

2. Do the coaches become more central in their networks once LC is implemented? Presumably, we would expect the LC coach to be quite central after coordinating all literacy professional development—including staffwide work-

TABLE 4-1
Pre-implementation in-degree centrality ranks of coach-to-be

School pseudonym	Coach-to-be's rank	Total # of teachers
Arlington Elementary	1	6
Baxter Elementary	1	17
Clairborn Elementary	21	23
D.R. Lewis	1	14
Egan Primary	1	5
Huffman Elementary	1	15
Jefferson Elementary	3	9
Larkspur Hills	1	11
Lawndale Elementary	1	6
Newberry Academy	1	18
Riverside Elementary	18	18
Rogers Park Elementary	12	13
Rosemead Elementary	1	7
Tyson William Elementary	14	15
Wilson Elementary	14	17

Table 4-1 indicates the ranking of each teacher in her own school in terms of centrality to the literacy teaching and learning network as of spring 2005. Centrality is measured in terms of valued, normalized in-degree centrality. Implementation of LC activities did not begin until the following school year. Therefore table 4-1 indicates the base-state centrality of each coach before her new role was implemented.

shops and one-on-one coaching sessions—for three school years. By spring 2008, all fifteen (100 percent) of the coaches were indeed the most central actor in their respective schools. This suggests that there is some degree of reorientation of these work networks around the coaches. Over the course of three years, they all become the most-often-cited teacher among their fellow teachers.

3. How many teachers consider the coach a resource before versus after LC? It is important to keep in mind that identifying the *most* central (i.e., highest-ranked) individual in terms of centrality does not provide a context for the overall level of discussion of literacy practice. For instance, it is possible that in some schools very little conversation about literacy is taking place at all. In such a school, a coach might be the most oft-cited person but only in comparison with teachers who are cited rarely or not at all. Hence, the coach could appear to be the most central actor, but be mentioned only by a small proportion of her staff. Therefore, figure 4-2 depicts the proportion of K–2 staff in each school that refers to the coach in his or her network survey, both before and after implementation of LC.

As the figure shows, in the majority of schools—twelve of the fifteen— the proportion of K–2 teachers who refer to the coach increases (and in one school it remains the same). In only two schools—Huffman and Larkspur Hills—does this percentage decrease over the time period. This could be an indication that LC was less successful in these schools. In a subsequent section, we look more closely at Huffman Elementary to examine whether there is any other evidence of difficulties implementing LC and any possible explanations based on the social network.

4. Do the networks become more dense during LC implementation?   Figure 4-3 depicts the overall density among K–3 staff in these fifteen schools before and after LC implementation. In seven of the fifteen schools, overall density increases, and density remains about the same in an additional three schools. In schools with increased density, more conversations are occurring among the teachers about issues of literacy instruction. This may indicate the development of a professional community, since members of professional communities seek to improve practice by engaging in critical dialogue with others around common problems confronted in their classrooms. Increased network density may be an indicator that critical dialogue is growing.

In five schools, density actually decreased over the time period—that is, there are fewer reported literacy connections among the teaching staff by the end of the study. It is interesting to note that two of those five schools are also the two schools that showed a decrease in proportion of staff referring to the coach (Huffman and Larkspur Hills). Overall, however, most schools experienced growth in density of ties during the three years of LC implementation studied here.

5. If the coach-to-be started out more central, does she coach more?   In the conceptual framework, we hypothesized that a coach-to-be who was more central in her network in the base year might find it easier to access her colleagues' classrooms and initiate the personal work of one-on-one coaching. Therefore, we tested whether there was any association between the initial in-degree centrality of each coach and the average amount of coaching sessions teachers in her school received.[17] It is necessary to control for school size, because school size is both associated with measures of centrality and with the amount of coaching that each teacher receives. By including faculty size in the model, we effectively only examine the association between coach centrality and amount of coaching within schools of the same size. This simple model estimates the difference in number of coaching sessions per

FIGURE 4-2   Percent of staff who refer to coach (2005–2008) across study schools

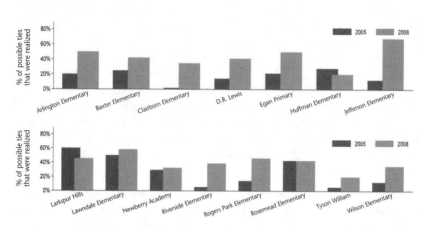

teacher associated with a one standard deviation positive difference in centrality, controlling for school size. Table 4-2 contains the results.

Table 4-2 indicates that a one standard deviation increase in coach centrality across schools is associated, on average, with a 3.23 positive difference in the number of coaching sessions received per teacher, holding constant staff size (significant at the $\alpha = .05$ level). Among these fifteen schools, the more central the coach-to-be was before the onset of LC, the more coaching she conducted per teacher over the following three years. This observed relationship suggests that the coach's position in her network may be a supportive condition for increased coaching, though of course this correlational evidence cannot necessarily be interpreted causally.

In sum, there is evidence that these school networks reshape as the coach-to-be carries out LC activities. In about half the schools, the coach-to-be was already viewed by her colleagues as a resource on early literacy instruction. In all schools, the coach became the most central character in these networks by the end of the study. Furthermore, in about half of the schools, we observed an increasing proportion of the staff turning to the coach for advice about literacy instruction. Finally, most of the networks became more dense after three years of implementation. Increased density implies that more teachers are turning to one another for advice about teaching literacy, suggesting perhaps a stronger set of community norms around sharing practice and learning from one another. Taken together, this evidence suggests that the degree to which these networks may have reshaped in response to LC varies a great deal.

FIGURE 4-3   Comparing density of networks (2005–2008) across study schools

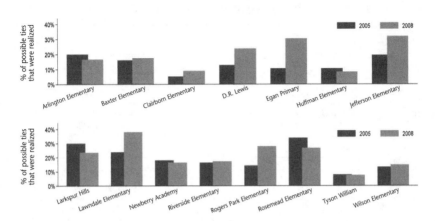

A Closer Examination of Two Schools

In this section, we introduce two example schools, each presenting a unique illustration of the role of social networks in school change efforts. In each case, we begin by examining the social network in the spring before LC implementation began. We consider whether the base state appears supportive of engagement in reform activities such as those prescribed by LC. We also bring to bear key measures of teachers' orientations toward their work and one another, which were measured simultaneously. A combination of base state social network characteristics, alongside knowledge of teachers' attitudes and school climate may help predict where interventions are likely to succeed. We probe this question by subsequently presenting data that together indicate the degree to which the intervention was successful in each school. Indicators of a strong intervention include: (1) teachers receive coaching more often, (2) teachers report a high-quality relationship with the coach at the end of the study, (3) teachers have high "value added" (that is, their students gain more, on average, as a result of LC than their students did before LC began), and (4) teachers report feeling more efficacious in their work. We will follow this same format for each of the two schools.

Baxter Elementary

The upper left panel of figure 4-4 contains the network visualization for Baxter Elementary in spring 2005 (left panel). Each shape represents one teacher, and the lines connecting them represent the ties reported in their pre-intervention surveys. The thickness of each line represents the reported frequency

TABLE 4-2

Amount of coaching, as a function of initial coach centrality in 2005

Coefficient	Beta	Standard error
Intercept, β_0	17.470***	(–1.816)
Coach centrality (standardized), β_1	3.231*	(–1.493)
K–3rd staff size (centered at 12), β_2	–0.451	(–0.320)
R^2	0.563	
N	15	

Coach centrality is measured as the valued and normalized centrality of each coach, standardized around the 2005 mean. It is standardized in order to give the coefficients more meaning by translating observed associations into standard deviation units. K–3 staff size is centered around 12, because this represents the average size of K–3 faculty in this study. Doing so allows the intercept to be interpreted more meaningfully.

of contact. The first letter of the pseudonym indicates grade level (e.g., *K*en teaches *k*indergarten, *F*rank teaches *f*irst grade, *S*andra teaches *s*econd grade, *T*helma teaches *t*hird grade, and *C*laire is the teacher who will become the *c*oach). Node size provides a rough indication of how much coaching each teacher received during the study, and the number in parentheses provides the exact number of coaching sessions each teacher received per year, on average (third-grade teachers are not eligible to receive coaching). In some rare cases, teachers are represented with upside-down triangles, rather than a square (e.g., Simon). This indicates that we did not receive social network data from this individual, though others may still refer to that person.

What can a close examination Baxter's social network diagram in the upper left panel of figure 4-4 reveal about this school just before LC began? First, staff size is one structural attribute of a social network that must be considered in describing the base state of its professional network. Baxter is a relatively large school, with seventeen teachers in kindergarten through third-grade classrooms. Recall that the LC model asks coaches to conduct about two coaching sessions per K–2 teacher per month. Therefore, this goal is much more ambitious than in a small school.

The next consideration is evidence of isolation among the staff. When high proportions of the teaching staff report being disconnected—that is, there is no one in the school they consider a resource for issues of literacy teaching and learning—we might expect this to undermine the diffusion of any new professional development model that rests upon collaboration. At Baxter, we see very little evidence of such isolation, since none of the K–3 teachers are completely disconnected from the literacy teaching network.

FIGURE 4-4   Baxter Elementary, spring 2005 (base state) versus spring 2008

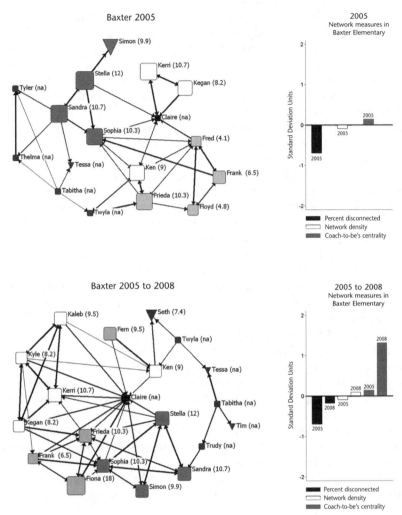

The diagram also illustrates the density of ties in Baxter's network. Recall that network density speaks to whether there are already ties across teachers through which new information about literacy can flow. Density signals whether some dialogue around literacy instruction already occurs. Baxter Elementary already appears to have some density of ties in its network pre-intervention (note the number of lines connecting nodes). That said, there is certainly room for increased density; the second-grade teachers in particular report limited interaction with one another, and there is very little cross-grade conversation about literacy.

Finally, we examine the location of the coach-to-be ("Claire") within the 2005 network diagram. She appears to be a teacher to whom many of her colleagues already turn to discuss issues of teaching literacy (note the many arrows directed toward Claire). In Baxter, we observe a teacher who, even *before* becoming the coach, was central in her network. The fact that her colleagues already view Claire as a resource may facilitate her attempts to initiate coaching relationships in the following years.

It is useful to summarize these observations into measures that allow comparison of these factors both across school sites and over time. The bar graph to the right of Baxter's 2005 network diagram accomplishes this task (upper right panel of figure 4-4). Each bar represents Baxter in 2005 and compares its network characteristics with an average school in the study. The measures have each been standardized around the 2005 school mean, so that the horizontal line at $Y = 0$ represents the average level of each measure across schools in 2005, and the changes in these measures have been translated to the more interpretable standard deviation units. (All following bar graphs of this type will be standardized in this same way.) These measures appear to capture the observations made above: the bar graph illustrates that Baxter exhibits a relatively lower level of disconnectedness than the average study school. Baxter's network density is about average in comparison with the other schools in 2005. In addition, the bar graph confirms that this coach-to-be is already quite central in her network before assuming her new role.

In sum, Baxter appears to have some preexisting advantages and some challenges in terms of its network structure in 2005. On the one hand, the K–2 staff is large, making the goal of coaching all teachers more daunting. On the other hand, there is already some degree of density in this school and no evidence of isolation among the staff. Perhaps most importantly, the coach is already well regarded by her peers as someone to whom they often turn for advice on literacy instruction.

The lower panel of figure 4-4 juxtaposes Baxter's 2005 network diagram against its 2008 diagram, thus allowing one to see the changes that occurred after LC implementation. A comparison of the two diagrams indicates that potentially supportive changes have occurred in this network over time. We observe an increased density among the teachers in this school (i.e., more lines connecting nodes), meaning that there are more connections between the teachers around literacy instruction than were present in the base year. Perhaps most striking is the extent to which the coach has become the absolute center of this professional network: Virtually *all* K–2 teachers report that they now discuss literacy instruction with Claire. These changes in network characteristics at Baxter are summarized in the bar chart to the right of

Baxter's 2008 network diagram. In particular, note the dramatic increase in the coach's centrality. As of spring 2008, this coach is far above average in terms of centrality when compared with the other coaches in the study. Both the base-state characteristics of this school's network as well as the observed changes to its network across the duration of the intervention suggest an environment where LC might be successful.

This portrait of Baxter is incomplete without some information about the *quality* of relations and the overall school climate at the onset of the study. The larger research team on this project constructed some measures of teacher orientations toward one another and their work using items from the base-year surveys. We identified four such measures that we hypothesized might play a role in teachers' responses to the LC initiative. These include:

1. *Willingness to deprivatize practice.* Survey items ask teachers about the frequency of activities that display a willingness to expose their practice to critique. A high score on this measure indicates that the teacher has made her/his practice open to others.
2. *Orientations toward innovation.* This set of questions captures teachers' perceptions of whether or not they are continually learning and seeking new ideas and are encouraged to try new ideas in their teaching. High levels indicate that there is a strong orientation toward improvement and a willingness to be part of an active learning environment.
3. *School commitment.* Questions ask teachers if they look forward to going to work, would rather work somewhere else, and if they would recommend the school to parents. High levels indicate teachers are deeply committed to the school.
4. *Trust levels among teachers.* These questions measure the extent to which teachers feel they have mutual respect for each other, feel comfortable discussing their feelings and worries, and really care about each other. High levels indicate teachers trust and respect each other.[18]

Together, these measures add an additional level of depth to the social network analysis by providing more insight into the social climate in the school just before the intervention began.

In figure 4-5, these four base year measures (middle panel) are placed alongside the changing network characteristics for Baxter Elementary from figure 4-4 (replicated in the left panel of figure 4-5 to facilitate direct comparison). Teachers at Baxter in 2005 were willing to deprivatize their practice and also expressed strong commitment to the school and its improvement efforts. These positive orientations likely made teachers at Baxter more open to the kinds of activities LC prescribes. As discussed previously, LC most strongly challenges traditional school norms by asking teachers to allow a coach to enter their classrooms, and in addition asking them to share their classroom experiences with fellow teachers. The fact that norms around shared practice already existed at Baxter may, in conjunction with the observed strengthening of the network during the study, support school change efforts. On the other hand, teachers at Baxter expressed some hesitation about innovations in practice, and the coach would likely need to address the slightly below-average levels of trust among teachers. The combination of a supportive base-state network characteristics, the four base-state measures of teachers' orientations, and the positive changes to the network over the course of the study might lead one to predict that this is a school where LC was more likely to be successful.

Thus, in the right panel of figure 4-5, we also incorporate available evidence about the success of the intervention at Baxter. Because no single measure of successful school change exists, we present four different indicators that real improvements took place during LC implementation.

The right panel of figure 4-5 shows that, by 2008, the K–2 teachers at Baxter Elementary were receiving more coaching than teachers in other study schools (i.e., above the Y = 0 line). This indicates that this coach was able to penetrate her colleagues' classrooms to a higher degree than coaches in other schools.

In addition, the end-of-study survey asked all teachers about the quality of their working relationship with the coach. The items concern teachers' level of comfort with the coach, their perceptions of coach's intentions, whether they feel respected by the coach, and whether they believe the coach works hard to help teachers improve their practice. Positive feedback from teachers about the coach is one source of evidence about the success of LC. Teachers at Baxter reported a quality of relationship with the coach at about the study average (note the height of the second bar is very close to the horizontal line at Y = 0, which represents the study average). Substantively, the study average is between 3 and 4, where 3 indicates that teachers "agree" with positive items about the coach, and 4 indicates that teachers "strongly agree" with positive items. Therefore, teachers at Baxter appear to report a positive evaluation of the coach.

In addition, evidence of successful LC engagement comes from the value-added estimates constructed in a companion study by Biancarosa and Bryk.[19] Those estimates are constructed using a quasi-experimental research method based on an accelerated multicohort design. The achievement of students prior to LC implementation serves as a nontreatment comparison against which the contribution of LC can be gauged. These school-level value-added estimates are intended to be interpreted causally (for a complete discussion of the construction, see the original paper). Like all other measures presented in the bar graphs, the value-added estimates have been standardized around the average school value added, so that zero represents the average value added across the study schools and the height of the bars are in standard

FIGURE 4-5   Summary of network measures, social, environment, and evidence of successful engagement, Baxter Elementary

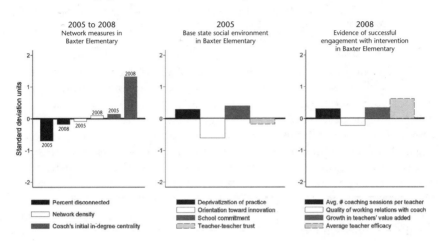

Y = 0 represents 2005 averages across sample.

deviation units. Figure 4-5 shows that the estimated value added of Baxter teachers is relatively high. In other words, it appears that the introduction of LC caused impressive growth in student outcomes at Baxter—perhaps the most direct measure of successful LC implementation.

We also included a measure of teachers' perceived self-efficacy in their work. A high score on this measure indicates a teacher believes that she/he is able to motivate students to engage in learning. In comparison with the 2005 average level of teacher efficacy in study schools, by 2008 Baxter teachers reported a strong sense that they know how to teach well. It is possible that the professional development activities stipulated by LC and introduced to teachers via the coach helped teachers grapple with Lortie's anxiety-producing "How am I doing?" question discussed in the conceptual framework. Taken together, these four indicators suggest that engagement in LC was particularly successful at Baxter Elementary. Teachers were exposed to a large amount of coaching, and they generally reported that interactions with the coach were of a high quality. Furthermore, students at Baxter learned more during LC implementation years, and teachers reported a stronger sense of self-efficacy in their work.

Overall, Baxter Elementary is a case where the socio-organizational context may have facilitated efforts to improve teacher practice and school outcomes. Baxter appears to have had some predispositions toward supporting deep change efforts, such as a centrally located coach and some degree of density among teachers who reported they were generally willing to share their practice and were committed to the school's improvement. Furthermore, all indicators of successful LC engagement suggest that Baxter may have capitalized on these supportive preexisting conditions in order to undergo meaningful change over the course of three years.

Huffman Elementary

Next, we examine a second example school of similar size but with a markedly different trajectory of development over the course of the study. All network diagrams and measures for Huffman Elementary are presented in figure 4-6. As in Baxter, the coach-to-be in Huffman Elementary appears to be quite central among her colleagues for matters related to literacy, even before LC began. However, Huffman differs in two important ways. First, there is some evidence of isolation among the teaching staff: several second-grade teachers are not tied to anyone within the school (e.g., Stacy). In addition, density is lower in the base year at Huffman than was observed in Baxter. Recall from figure 4-3 that Huffman exhibited one of the lowest initial densities among the fifteen study schools.

These observations are captured in the bar graph of network characteristics to the right of Huffman's 2005 diagram: a school with comparatively high levels of disconnectedness and low levels of density, but a coach-to-be who is referred to by many of her colleagues. Though the coach appears to have some capital with her fellow teachers before the onset of the study, the other network characteristics in the base state may describe a school where teachers rarely engage in dialogue about literacy instruction (low density), nor feel comfortable turning to one another for advice about literacy instruction (high isolation).

The lower left panel of figure 4-6 illustrates Huffman Elementary three years later. The 2008 diagram depicts a school that has deteriorated in terms of its social network around literacy instruction. For instance, there continue to be teachers who are completely disconnected from all other teachers. That is, they felt that there was *no one*—not even the coach—to whom they would turn to discuss literacy instruction. Network density, which was low even in the base state, has also decreased dramatically. Very little conversation is taking place between teachers at Huffman by spring of 2008. Note in particular that Suzy reports talking to six colleagues; however, aside from Suzy, surprisingly few ties exist. Furthermore, it is interesting to note that *none* of the first-grade teachers reported discussing literacy with one another by the end of the intervention.

There is also a drop in the centrality of the coach in Huffman. While she is still the most central figure in her school, the number of K–2 staff who do not mention her is greater than those who do. Furthermore, recall from figure 4-3 that Huffman was one of the only two schools in which the per-

FIGURE 4-6   Huffman Elementary, spring 2005 (base state) versus spring 2008

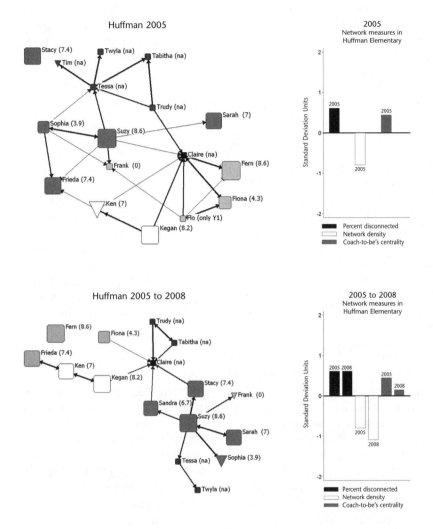

centage of staff referring to the coach decreases after three years of LC implementation. Despite the fact that these teachers were coached over the course of several years, many report *never* turning to the coach to discuss issues of literacy teaching in learning. The bar graph to the right of the 2008 Huffman diagram reflects the deterioration of this school network, as well. It shows no change in the level of isolation, and indicates decreased network density and coach centrality.

Overall, these dramatic changes in the network from before to after LC implementation might lead one to anticipate that very little improvement in teaching or learning occurred at Huffman as a result of LC. While there were some "warning signs" in the base networks, such as a somewhat low preexisting density and some isolation among staff, Huffman was not so different from Baxter just before LC was introduced. Both had large schools with a coach-to-be who was seen as a resource for issues of literacy teaching and learning. Why do we see such a different trajectory for the Huffman network over the course of the study?

Huffman's base state measures of teachers' orientations toward their work and one another help fill in missing gaps in this story. As in Baxter, figure 4-7 incorporates the four measures that we hypothesized might play a role in teachers' responses to the LC initiative (middle panel).

Though Huffman's school network had some positive characteristics in the base year, the teachers nested within that network were not prepared to engage in the deep change efforts proposed by LC. The middle panel of figure 4-7 depicts a school in which teachers are unwilling to open their classrooms to fellow teachers, where commitment to the school is low, and—perhaps most importantly—teacher trust is lacking. When school reforms require a significant reconceptualization of the nature of the work activity, but the impetus to invest the necessary time and energy is absent, the intervention is unlikely to be a success.

Indeed, three of the four indicators of successful reform found in the right panel of figure 4-7 corroborate this story. The one slightly positive indicator shows that Huffman teachers continued to add value to their students' learning at about the study average during LC implementation. On the other hand, the Huffman coach struggled to engage her colleagues in coaching, and when the teachers were asked about the quality of their interactions with the coach, their evaluations were significantly below the average across schools. Unlike Baxter, where *every* teacher agreed with positive statements about the coach, upward of 20 to 25 percent of the Huffman faculty disagreed or strongly disagreed with those survey items. This suggests that, at least for some teachers, the coach failed to execute her new role in a manner that supported the development of teacher practice.

Given the evidence about the low frequency and quality of coaching in Huffman, it is unsurprising that teachers also reported low levels of self-efficacy in their work (right panel of figure 4-7). Since Huffman teachers reported an unwillingness to deprivatize their practice and low trust, they likely struggled to improve their practice in isolation from one another. Such conditions often lead teachers to experience a psychological state of anxiety-producing uncertainty about the quality of their instruction; research suggests that people who doubt their capabilities shy away from difficult tasks, have low aspirations, and weak commitment to the goals they choose to pursue.[20]

FIGURE 4-7   Summary of network measures, social, environment, and evidence of successful engagement, Huffman Elementary

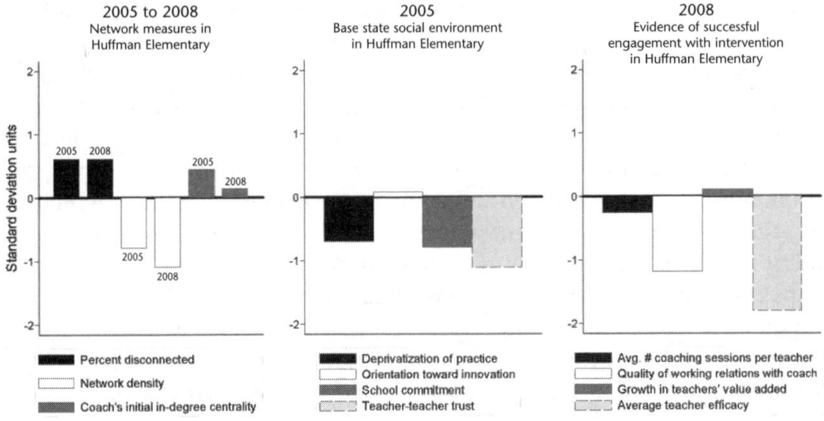

Y = 0 represents 2005 averages across sample

In summary, Huffman provides a stark contrast to the process of school change evident at Baxter. In both cases, given the information about the base-state network structure as well as the orientations of the individuals in each school toward their work and one another, one might have predicted with some accuracy the extent to which LC was implemented with success. This close examination of two schools illustrates the insight that social network analysis might afford those who wish to engage schools in deep reforms such as LC.

CONCLUSIONS AND FUTURE WORK

This study analyzes the introduction of an intensive school reform intervention, Literacy Collaborative, in fifteen schools across the United States. The social network data collected as a part of that study revealed considerable variability in schools' social structures just before the intervention began. Preliminary evidence suggests that this variability may account for some of the subsequent diversity of engagement across school sites. Furthermore, the in-depth examination of two example schools suggests that social networks play a key role in understanding the degree of success schools experience in terms of improvements for teachers and students. We conclude that, as schools attempt ambitious school reform (such as LC), it may be important to consider the preexisting state of the working relations in the school.

When schools already exhibit patterns of interaction that are likely to support the intervention efforts, the proposed changes may be met with less resistance. When the base state indicates some potential weaknesses, concerted efforts may be necessary to address these issues before the intervention gets under way.

In addition, it appears that interventions that successfully challenge school norms around teacher work may fundamentally restructure the professional network. LC, for example, seeks to create a community of learners among teachers, guided by a "more expert" coach. The intervention prescribes one-on-one interactions with the coach inside classrooms, which led to coaches becoming quite central in their schools by the end of the study. In addition, the coach coordinates a series of professional development workshops through which teachers interact with *one another*, and these activities may have led to increased density of the networks over time. This finding also suggests that the diffusion of new practices travels not only through the direct dyadic interaction of coaches with teachers, but perhaps also through the increased density of the overall network among teachers themselves.

Finally, the two example schools illustrate another way in which social network analysis might be useful in the study of school change. In those schools, the reshaping of the network that occurred during the intervention appeared to foreshadow each school's response to the intervention. Baxter Elementary possessed a moderately strong base state in many ways (some degree of density, a central coach-to-be, little isolation) and whose teachers expressed positive orientations toward their school and one another. By spring 2008, not only did Baxter exhibit positive indicators of LC engagement, but its network became stronger as well: almost every teacher considered the coach a resource for discussing issues of literacy teaching and learning, and the school developed greater density of ties among the K–2 teachers. On the other hand, Huffman Elementary's staff exhibited some isolation and low density in 2005, along with low levels of trust, school commitment, and willingness to open up their classrooms for critique. By 2008, the network had visibly deteriorated, indicating that teachers did not discuss literacy instruction as a collective, nor did they consider the coach a strong resource. In this way, the health of the network may also be indicative of the success of school reform efforts. Future work should examine whether the patterns observed in these study schools holds across a larger sample.

The use of social network analysis may help school and district leaders anticipate whether interventions in struggling schools will be met with challenges from the base state. In addition, practitioners may find the tools produced by social network analysis (e.g., network visualizations and measures) useful for diagnosing barriers to successful school change efforts. Moreover, researchers who are concerned with the sociological process of school change are likely to find that social network analysis provides greater insight into the schools they study. Finally, researchers concerned with estimating the effects of school interventions may also benefit from the fact that social network data may account for the often-mysterious variability in implementation across school sites. This current study demonstrates how social networks can be used both on a micro level to add nuance to the understanding of school improvement in a single school, as well as on a macro level to summarize key characteristics across schools and over time for use in larger studies.

CHAPTER 5

Changes in Attitude

Peer Influence in High School Reform

Russell P. Cole and Elliot H. Weinbaum

Much has been written about schools as complex organizations in which the introduction of change is a slow and difficult process.[1] The loosely coupled nature of school systems and the relative autonomy of teachers in their classrooms, provide school teachers—and high school teachers in particular—with a great deal of discretion in their practice.[2] In contrast to that tradition of teacher autonomy, a host of school improvement programs have been created—by organizations external to schools—with the goal of enhancing teacher practice and student achievement. The introduction of a school reform program is of particular interest as a stimulus for change as ever larger numbers of schools partner with external organizations in search of new and improved practices.[3] Reform programs' approaches to improving both practice and outcomes range from introducing a new curriculum, to providing content- and/or pedagogy-focused professional development directly to teachers, to creating new organizational structures or systems, to a host of other change strategies.

The research conducted for this chapter departs somewhat from much of the previous research on school reform in that it does not focus on the reform-related *behaviors* of teachers, but rather on their reform-related *attitudes*. Though less apparent to the external observer than teacher behavior, attitude about school reform effort may be a necessary precursor for change. Supporting this contention, Supovitz and Turner found that teacher attitude toward reform was one of the most powerful influences on teacher practices.[4] In order to better understand the development of prevailing attitudes about school reform, this chapter investigates the effect of teachers' peers on the changes in teacher attitude that occur in the early years of school reform efforts.

This chapter begins with a theoretical basis for our focus on teachers' attitude, defined as "the degree to which a person has a favorable or unfavorable evaluation of the behavior in question."[5] We argue that implementation of reform efforts is intrinsically tied to teacher attitude about those reforms, and use our data to demonstrate empirically that teacher attitude is a function of the social networks within a school.

ATTITUDE AND IMPLEMENTATION

In spite of a host of school reform efforts, successful stories of school reform at any large scale have been relatively limited.[6] Many evaluations that focus on changes in teacher behavior as well as research that focuses on changes in student performance have shown that the effects of such reform programs are unsatisfactory.[7]

Regardless of their content or objectives, it is clear that policies and programs are enacted differently, depending on how teachers interpret the new material in light of their prior experiences, on their own knowledge and beliefs about the subject at hand, and on the sense that they make of the program in collaboration with peers and colleagues engaged in similar pursuits.[8] While we don't dwell extensively on them, all of these explanations suggest the importance of teachers' attitudes about change efforts.

Two recent studies suggest that teacher attitude toward a reform program is related to the degree of success of future implementation of that program. Programs that were perceived as coherent, aligned with previous practices, or confirming an individual teacher's own perceptions were positively associated with implementation.[9] The effects found by Penuel et al. support the contention that teachers' interpretation of and attitudes about professional development related to school change are as important in changing practice as the program design itself.[10] This chapter seeks to better understand the origins of those attitudes toward reform by establishing that they are influenced not only by the reform effort but by the social environment in which a teacher is located.

Understanding the development of teacher attitude is important to school reform because research has documented the relationship between attitude and subsequent behaviors. In a recent meta-analysis of 128 studies linking attitude and behavior, it was noted that attitudes are a strong predictor of future behavior, especially when frequently expressed.[11] A previous meta-analysis of 88 empirical studies found that attitudes significantly predict future behavior.[12] Though a number of variables have been found to moderate the relationship between attitudes and subsequent behavior, the role of attitude as a precursor to behavior is well established.[13]

This research has been heavily focused on individual attitude formation, while contemporary research has been more limited in its consideration of the social and institutional influences on attitude formation. Much of the work indicating that attitudes are socially constructed is decades old, though interest in this area has recently revived as a result of measurement advances in social network analyses of influence processes.[14] Before describing our study of the social influences on attitude, we briefly review the foundational literature.

SOCIAL CONTEXT AND ATTITUDE FORMATION: A THEORETICAL FRAMEWORK

Individuals develop an attitude or predisposition about something prior to making a choice based on their own individual attributes, experiences, beliefs, and the information and attitudes of others that they can access.[15] The ongoing process of development though which people form attitudes that are sensitive to their relationships and their context has been called *social information processing theory*.[16] This theory seeks to identify the many factors that influence attitude development in social settings.

In exploring the influence of social settings, Ajzen and Madden argue that attitude about change is in a dynamic relationship with what they call the *subjective norm*—the "perceived social pressure to perform or not perform the behavior."[17] This argument is similar to research about how teachers develop shared norms of practice and internal accountability that serve to encourage aligned practices.[18] However, rather than focusing on the behaviors themselves, Ajzen and Madden focus on the development of attitudes as precursors to behaviors.[19]

The mechanism through which the subjective norm exerts pressure on individuals to adjust their attitudes has been described by social psychology researchers as individuals' search for "balance" between themselves and those with whom they have social connections. Balance theory holds that people are likely to seek alignment between their own attitudes and those of their peers either by changing their own attitudes or by choosing to interact with people who share attitudes more similar to their own.[20] Regardless of the way in which balance is achieved, this research suggests tangible effects of pressure exerted by peers in an organization.

Figure 5-1, borrowed from the work of Ajzen and Madden, builds on the theory and research discussed above and illustrates our framework for analyzing the relationship between individual attitude, prevailing norms in the school, teacher intention, and practice.[21] Bold outlines identify the areas on which we focus in this chapter.

We hypothesize that an essential element in shaping teachers' attitudes about reform is the attitudes of their colleagues in the organization. In order to empirically test this theory and the concept of the subjective norm, we use social network analysis to measure social interaction and communication within an organization.[22]

FIGURE 5-1   Theoretical framework

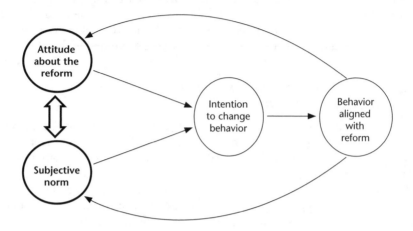

SOCIAL NETWORKS

In schools, there are many formal structures that help to predict communication patterns. Academic departments, administrative titles and positions, and physical arrangements have all been shown to influence teacher communication in high schools.[23] However, in order to examine the social systems in which a teacher is embedded, and thus the peers from whom teachers are most likely to receive pressure, it is necessary to uncover the "organic" networks that exist and emerge between teachers rather than look at formal structural or organizational arrangements. Social network analysis is well-suited to identifying these networks.

Social network theory and methods allow one to identify teachers' networks and to assess the impacts that such networks have on their attitudes.[24] Social network influence models can be used to empirically demonstrate the effects that peer attitudes have on a focal individual in an organization.[25] However, what flows to individuals is not limited to the information that they obtain through direct contact with peers. Attitudes, like information, can be passed or conveyed through individuals and will contribute to the subjective norm of an institution, even if an individual is not in direct communication with many peers.[26] The idea that individuals are influenced by a prevailing norm created by those with whom a person is in contact as well as others in the organization would suggest a correlation between the attitudes of all of the individuals surrounding a particular actor, even those who are connected through an intermediary, and the attitude of that actor.

Information (and attitudes, according to our hypothesis) will tend to be diluted or will contain less of the original message as it passes from peer to peer, much like the children's game of "Telephone." As the number of steps between individuals increases, the amount of information or intensity of attitude is likely to be diminished.[27] Similar findings were noted by Bidwell, Frank, and Quiroz, who found that a greater number of steps between an influential individual and an advice seeker led to a greater distortion of the message sent.[28] Thus, while individuals are affected by information obtained through the subjective norm, this information may be less persuasive than information obtained through direct conversation.

Network Types

In any organization in which people have the opportunity to interact, there are networks of communication that link people one to another. These connections may be forged for multiple reasons. Previous researchers have categorized these networks as *expressive* and *instrumental*.[29] These different types of network ties are associated with carrying unique information and providing different types of support.[30]

Expressive networks are those that are created as a result of non-work-related relationships and generally refer to the natural social and friendship-based affinities that arise between people in an organization. These ties tend to be strong and carry a great deal of social support and influence.[31] However, they do not necessarily facilitate the sharing of workplace information.

Instrumental networks, in contrast, develop for a particular purpose related to the professional context, generally as people seek access to information or other resources they view as necessary for successful completion of their work. These instrumental ties tend to be weak ties, linking advice seekers and perceived experts or resources.[32] Several researchers have argued that the instrumental ties tend to be less durable and trusting than expressive connections.[33]

Regardless of their type or origins, both of these network types offer access to peers and thus have the potential to serve as conduits for conveying or conducting attitudes about reform. While expressive ties tend to carry greater potential for persuasion and influence, both of these access points are likely to serve as avenues through which individuals will feel normative pressure to conform.[34]

These two networks do not exhaust the types of conversation that exist in schools. A shock to the organizational system (such as the introduction of a new school reform) is likely to create new professional dynamics and to stimulate the development of a new communication network of either type mentioned above.[35] As new information or practices are introduced into an organization, new conversation paths will be produced, some of which will be instrumental and some of which will be expressive. However, it is unclear whether or not these new pathways will facilitate the transmission of information in the same ways that the older, more durable networks had in the past.

RESEARCH QUESTIONS

Building on the theoretical framework outlined above and using social network analysis, we investigated the relationship between communication networks (established and new, instrumental and expressive) and teachers' attitudes about these reforms. This research was undertaken as part of an effort to better understand the variables that impact the implementation of reform programs. We were guided by the following primary research question: What is the impact of peers' attitudes on teachers' attitudes about school reform? Secondary questions include: What is the extent of teachers' connections in instrumental and expressive networks? How does each of these different networks impact change in teacher attitude over time? Are teacher attitudes solely affected by the peers with whom they communicate directly, or are teachers also influenced by the normative pressure of a larger set of colleagues?

DATA

In order to answer these questions, data about teacher networks and teacher attitude about reform efforts were collected using written surveys. These surveys were administered as part of a larger two-and-a-half-year investigation by the Consortium for Policy Research in Education (CPRE) into the role of reform in high schools.[36] For the purposes of this research, nine high schools were identified in which sufficient data had been collected to answer the questions posed above. The nine schools were using a variety of externally designed school reform programs, all of which sought significant change in teachers' classroom practice.[37]

All nine of the high schools were completing the first or second year of their reform partnership at the time of our initial survey in the spring of 2005. A second survey was administered to these schools in the spring of 2006. In the first round of surveys, 592 responses were gathered from teachers at the nine schools; response rates ranged from 46 percent to 84 percent, with an average response rate of 64 percent. In our second survey in the spring of 2006, 648 surveys were returned from the nine schools. Response rates ranged from a low of 37 percent to a high of 98 percent, with an average response rate of 74 percent. Across both time points, 392 of the respondents returned surveys.

METHODS

The survey captured information about teachers' attitudes about the reform in their schools. It also asked teachers to identify those teachers with whom they had conversations related to both expressive and instrumental issues.

Measuring Attitude

Ten survey questions were used to measure teachers' attitudes about the reforms. For each of the reforms, the questions were identical except for the name of the reform with which any particular school and teacher were working. These questions asked teachers about the degree to which they felt that the reform effort provided clear guidance and plans for improvement that would be useful in their practice. Individuals were asked to indicate the degree to which they agreed or disagreed (measured on a four-point Likert scale ranging from "strongly disagree" to "strongly agree") with statements that assessed their attitudes with respect to the reform.

Exploratory factor analysis indicated that the attitude items represented a single, unidimensional factor, and precision weighted scale scores were generated according to the item loadings on this attitude construct.[38] Cronbach's coefficients for each reform attitude scale score exhibited a high degree of internal consistency (for each of the five reform attitude scales).[39]

Measuring Change in Attitude

Multiple regression analyses were used to explain the variance in changes in individual teacher attitude over time. In the multiple regression models used, the dependent variable is the change in individual i's attitude (as measured by the precision weighted scale score described above) between the 2005 and 2006 survey administrations. The baseline analysis (model 1) used to estimate changes in attitude incorporated predictor variables for department membership, department chair status, and years of teaching experience. These predictors were included to understand the relationship between organizational position and attitude change. We also incorporated a school-level residual term to appropriately adjust for the non-independence of teacher attitude changes across schools.[40]

Measuring Social Context

The survey instrument that was used to obtain data about the school wide communication networks asked teachers to identify their conversational partners by name. Table 5-1 lists the questions used in the survey and names each of the resulting communication networks.

Respondents were prompted to indicate the individuals with whom they communicated in that area (their communicative *alters*). Under each question, there was space on the survey for a respondent to list up to five alters for each network.[41]

Using these individual responses, we combined individual ego networks into a schoolwide social network for each of the three network types in each of the nine schools.[42] These communication networks were generated for both periods of data collection.

TABLE 5–1
Measured communication networks

Network label	Survey question
Instrumental	During this school year, to whom in your school have you gone for help in selecting and planning course content coverage and pacing?
Expressive	During this school year, with whom among your colleagues at this school do you "hang out" and discuss family, home, and/or personal issues?
Reform	Please list the people inside or outside your school to whom you turned for advice in using [reform name] during this school year.

In assessing the impacts of peers' attitudes, we use the subjective norm that individuals access at both survey data collection points. This allows us to incorporate the attitude and network data of all survey respondents at each time point to describe the social networks in a given school and the prevailing attitudes of all potential peers who responded to the survey. However, because our research questions are focused on changes in attitude, our analysis sample is limited to those 392 respondents who completed surveys at both points in time. In the methods section below, we describe how the data from respondents who contributed only to a single round of data were used.

To address the research questions, we had to examine three types of social network data. The method for analyzing each network type is described below.

Measuring Impact of Reform Network

The change in an individual's attitude toward reform is likely impacted by the information that he/she obtains through conversations about reform; we refer to this as the *reform network*. Through advice-seeking activity, teachers can learn about their peers' opinions of the reform. For example, if a teacher talks with peers whose attitudes (on average) are positive, we hypothesize that these conversations would subsequently result in an improvement in the focal teacher's attitude about the reform. To operationalize this, we calculated the average attitude scale scores that each teacher was able to access through conversations about reform during a particular data collection period. We included this *reform peer attitude* variable as a predictor in our multiple regression models, along with a variable that indicated the number of peers involved in reform conversation (model 2). For the purpose of this chapter, we refer to the difference between a focal teacher's attitude and the average of the attitudes to which that teacher is connected through a given network as *<network name> peer deviation*. Thus, *reform peer deviation* refers to average difference in attitude scores between a focal actor and those with whom that focal actor communicates through the reform network. For example, consider a teacher i who converses with three other teachers through the reform network. If, for the sake of the example, teacher i had an attitude score of 2 and the other three teachers had attitude scores of 2, 3, and 4, then the average attitude of i's peers would be 3; the reform peer deviation would be the difference between the peer teacher attitude and teacher i's score, which would be 1 in this example.[43]

Measuring the Impact of Instrumental and Expressive Networks

There is little doubt that the introduction of a reform into schools creates new opportunities and needs for conversation. However, many communication networks existed in schools prior to the introduction of the reform. These existing instrumental and expressive networks are possible conduits of information. In order to compare these three information channels, additional parameters were examined in the analytic model.

As with the reform peer deviation variable, two similar variables were created for the existing expressive and instrumental networks to explore the role of peers on change in attitude. The *expressive peer deviation* variable indicates the difference between a focal teacher's attitude and the average attitude score of those teachers with whom that teacher is in conversation using the expressive network. Similarly, the *instrumental peer deviation* variable indicates the differences in attitudes between focal teachers and those teachers with whom they were engaged in conversations using the instrumental network. These predictor variables were included in our multiple regression analyses in model 3.

Measuring Impact of Indirect Information

Teachers can gain access to information about reform through an intermediary, or a series of intermediaries; these are each links in the path between individuals. This information obtained indirectly is filtered at every step along the communicative path. As discussed above, the amount of information obtained is indirectly related to the length of the path between the sender and the receiver of the information.

If there is a communicative link between individuals i and j, and a link between individuals j and k, but no link between i and k, individual i still has access to information from k, as k is reachable in two steps. It is expected that as information passes through intermediaries, the quality of the original information is diminished with each link. To operationalize the reduced impact of information or attitude from individuals at some distance from the focal individual, an inverse weighting scheme was used to calculate the average attitude scores of indirect peers. In the example above, individual i was two links away from individual k, and therefore the inverse weight of this link would be one-half.[44] The information obtained through indirect information was calculated as the weighted average (where the inverse of the number of links between teachers was used as the weight) of the attitudes of teachers accessible through a given network. As with the original <network> peer deviation variables, the indirect <network> peer deviation variables are an indicator of the difference between the focal teacher's attitude and the weighted average attitude of indirect peers for a particular network.[45] For the purposes of this chapter, indirect <network> peer deviation variables were calculated for each of the three communication networks, and included as predictors in the final multiple regression analysis (model 4).

RESULTS

As stated above, 392 respondents were available to provide data at both time points about their changes in attitude. Tables 5-2 and 5-3 contain descriptive statistics for this sample of individuals. There was great variability in teaching experience in this sample, ranging from teachers with only 1 year of experience to veterans with 38 years of experience, with the average experience level at 9.57 years.

The analysis sample included teachers from more than 8 different departments, and 36 department chairs (9.2 percent) from the nine different schools responded to the survey at both time points.

The outcome of primary interest—change in teacher attitude about reform—is relatively stable over time, with average individuals improving their attitudes about their particular reform by only .003 standard deviation units between years. While on average, teachers did not appear to change their attitudes over time, there was variability in attitude changes noted in the sample (standard deviation of attitude change = .93). As a result, the variance in attitude change can be meaningfully explored using the multiple regression approach described earlier.

Individuals were relatively limited with respect to *direct* communication regarding the reform in their school, as the average ego network size was 1.35 (i.e., on average, respondents asked for advice about reform from only 1.35 individuals between 2005 and 2006). There was more conversation about instrumental and expressive issues. On average, teachers asked for help about course content and planning (instrumental network) from 2.40 individuals, and indicated that they had 4.25 connections to friends with whom they discussed more personal information (expressive network).

With respect to the information about the reform that could be obtained through direct ties, individuals found that their peers in the reform network had positive attitudes (mean peer attitude score was .13 standard deviations higher than the average attitudes of the analysis sample). When individuals

TABLE 5– 2
Departmental memberships and chairpersons

Special education	15.3%
English	14.8%
Math	13.5%
Science	11.7%
Vocational education	11.0%
Social studies/history	10.7%
Foreign language	6.1%
Other department*	16.8%
Department chair	9.2%

Note: n = 392.
*These teachers taught a variety of general electives or a combination of health/physical education classes

turned to their instrumental or expressive networks, however, their peers' attitudes were generally more negative (peer attitude scores were .05 and .06 standard deviations below the attitude scores of the analysis sample).

While teachers did demonstrate some similarity in their expressive and instrumental networks, the data show that most communication ties are unique. Phi correlation coefficients were calculated to compare individual responses across the three networks. The correlations between the three networks ranged between .22 and .34. This indicates that while teachers do have some overlap in their networks, much of the communication is distinct, and thus, each network represents connections to a different set of peers in the organization.

On average, teachers were *indirectly* connected with far more "friends" (46.15) than people with whom they discussed curricular (3.64) or reform (2.01) issues. These are unique indirect alters and represent different sources of information than direct alters. The large number of indirect connections in the expressive network was owing to the fact that there were far more ties in the expressive network than in the others. It was also the network in which the greatest amount of reciprocity in conversation was evident. Forty-eight percent of teachers who were identified as friends reciprocated the friendship nomination. In the sparse reform conversation network, only 12.4 percent of advice requests were reciprocated. Because individuals were connected with friends who shared friends, teachers were able to access a much larger indirect teacher population through their expressive networks.

TABLE 5-3
Sample descriptive statistics

	Variable	Mean	STD
Dependent variable	Attitude change	.00	.97
Network information (direct)	Reform attitude deviation	.13	.81
	Reform alters	1.35	1.76
	Expressive attitude deviation	− .05	.97
	Expressive alters	4.25	2.73
	Instrumental attitude deviation	− .06	.90
	Instrumental alters	2.41	2.02
Network information (indirect)	Reform attitude deviation	.01	.58
	Reform alters	2.01	3.62
	Expressive attitude deviation	− .02	.89
	Expressive alters	46.15	41.55
	Instrumental attitude deviation	− .07	.72
	Instrumental alters	3.64	5.22

Note: n = 392.

Change in Teacher Attitude

Table 5-4 summarizes our findings from the multiple regression analyses for models 1–4. In examining teacher attributes in model 1, we found evidence that general teacher characteristics were not significantly related to attitude change. The parameter estimates in the table can be interpreted in terms of how they relate to the outcome of interest. For example, the parameter estimate for years of teaching (.08) indicates that each additional year of experience for a teacher is associated with a .08 standard deviation change in teacher attitude. In other words, the results suggest that teachers with greater experience are associated with increased positive attitude changes towards reform. However, years of experience and formal leadership roles (e.g., designation as a department chair) were not statistically significantly related to attitude change, and thus these parameter estimates should not be interpreted as indicating a meaningful result. Furthermore, with the exception of membership in a vocational education department (which was positively associated with attitude change), we found that department membership was not significantly related to attitude change. This generally supports the

TABLE 5-4
Multiple regression analyses on attitude change

		Model 1	Model 2	Model 3	Model 4
Indicator independent variables	English	.10 (.18)	−.05 (.17)	.05 (.18)	.16 (.16)
	Foreign language	.03 (.23)	−.05 (.22)	.00 (.21)	.12 (.20)
	Math	−.03 (.19)	−.12 (.18)	−.11 (.18)	−.03 (.16)
	Other department	.22 (.18)	.01 (.17)	.09 (.17)	.20 (.16)
	Social studies	−.00 (.20)	−.18 (.18)	−.22 (.18)	−.22 (.18)
	Special education	.07 (.18)	−.11 (.17)	−.03 (.17)	.07 (.16)
	Science	.00 (.20)	−.07 (.18)	−.02 (.18)	.03 (.17)
	Vocational education	.54** (.20)	.44* (.19)	.43* (.19)	.49** (.18)
	Department chair	.00 (.17)	−.01 (.16)	.11 (.15)	.08 (.15)
Continuous independent variables	Years teaching	.08 (.05)	.01 (.01)	.01 (.01)	.04 (.04)
Network information (direct)	Reform attitude deviation		.39*** (.06)	.11+ (.06)	.04 (.06)
	Reform alters		−.02 (.03)	.02 (.03)	.09 (.06)
	Expressive attitude deviation			.30** (.06)	.14+ (.08)
	Expressive alters			−.00 (.02)	−.01 (.06)
	Instrumental attitude deviation			.21** (.06)	.13* (.06)
	Instrumental alters			−.00 (.03)	−.03 (.06)
Network information (indirect)	Reform attitude deviation				.07 (.06)
	Reform alters				−.05 (.06)
	Expressive attitude deviation				.21* (.09)
	Expressive alters				.02 (.08)
	Instrumental attitude deviation				.04 (.07)
	Instrumental alters				.05 (.05)

Note: N = 392. Standard Errors in Parentheses. +p < .10, *p < .05, **p < .01, ***p < .001

theory that stable attributes by themselves do not play a role in whether or not teachers are likely to change their attitudes over the course of time.

Impact of the Reform Network

As seen in model 2, the attitudes that were directly accessible in the reform network were positively related to attitude change. A teacher with peers whose average attitude toward reform is one standard deviation higher than his/her own attitude was associated with a .39 standard deviation increase in his/her attitude change over the course of the year, after controlling for all of the other variables in the model ($p < .001$). The directionality of the peer deviation is captured in this model. If a teacher's peers have attitude scores one standard deviation *below* his/her own, then his/her attitude change is expected to *decrease* by .39 standard deviation units. As the parameter estimate for the influence of peer attitude deviation is positive and significant, there is support for the attitude balance theory. Teachers do tend to change their attitudes based on the attitudes of their communicative peers. However, in this network the *number* of reform advice requests was unrelated to attitude change. Peer *attitudes* appeared to be influential, whether a teacher had many connected peers or just a few (though in this network most teachers had only a few).

Impact of the Instrumental and Expressive Networks

Model 3 illustrates the relative contribution of each of the three networks toward individual attitude change. While the effect of one's reform network peers was statistically significant when the reform network was the only avenue of peer influence included in the statistical model, the reform network's effect is diminished once the effects of the instrumental and expressive networks are included. When all three networks are considered, the effect of the reform network is only marginally significant ($p < .01$). The influence of peers' attitudes accessed through the expressive and instrumental network were statistically significant at the $p < .05$ level. As in model 2, the contribution of additional conversational partners was not significantly related to attitude change, in any of the three networks.

Impact of Indirect Communication

Flow of attitude parameters was estimated in the final model, model 4, to better assess the relationship between the attitudes of indirect peers and any given teacher's attitude. Essentially, this model examines the additional influence exerted on a teacher's attitude by individuals who are two or more links away from the individual in a communication network; this is the impact of people with whom the individual does not directly converse but whom that individual could "reach" by playing a game of "Telephone."

Our findings indicate that the only new contribution to attitude change (above and beyond that contributed by direct conversational partners) from indirect peers can be found in the expressive network. The parameter estimate for the effect of communication with indirect peers in the expressive network is positive and statistically significant. This indicates that individuals are influenced by the larger connected community of friends, even those with whom they are not in direct communication. The role of information from indirect peer communication in both the instrumental and reform networks was not significantly related to individual attitude change.

It is worth noting the diminished relative impact of the influence of direct ties in the instrumental and expressive networks in this final model. The parameter estimate for the influence of direct expressive ties is now only marginally significant ($p < .10$ level)). The parameter estimates for the influence of direct instrumental and expressive ties were not significantly different from each other, nor were they different from the estimate for the information accessible indirectly through friendship ties. Thus, these three sources of information—direct instrumental ties, direct expressive ties, and indirect expressive ties—appear to contribute equally to teachers' changes in attitude about their schools' reform programs.

Using only the individual attributes in model 1 as predictors, 15.5 percent of the variation in attitude change is explained. However, in model 4, where both indirect and direct sources of information are included, fully 40.4 percent of the variance in attitude change is explained. This relatively large R^2 value (for social science research) indicates that the final model does indeed uncover a significant portion of the factors that determine teacher attitude change. Furthermore, this finding illustrates that the proportion of variance explained using the network data is greater than the variance explained through more traditional regression analysis of teacher attributes.

LIMITATIONS

There are a number of limitations to this study that may affect the generalizability of our findings. We argue that teacher attitude about reform is both a precursor to and a result of behavior aligned with the reform. In this study, we did not actually observe whether or not teacher attitude did eventually influence behavior. However, we are convinced by the cited extant research that teacher attitude is in fact a correlate of subsequent behavior.[46]

The survey data for this study were collected from high school teachers whose schools had recently brought in a new reform. Given the different nature of the reform programs, we initially analyzed different types of reforms (whole school, literacy, and data analysis) independently to determine whether or not the influence mechanisms we observed were particular to one type of reform over another. However, the analyses of subsets of our data did not reveal any explanations for variation in attitude. Additionally, we did not have measures of teacher expertise or teaching philosophies. It is possible that these preexisting individual characteristics could be operating and influencing teacher attitude in addition to the social network data that we collected. More research in this area is necessary to uncover the ways that different reforms and teacher characteristics can change communication pathways and how these new pathways promote change in attitude and practice.

DISCUSSION

This study illustrates the importance of a network perspective in research on schools as institutions by providing an existence proof of a quantifiable measure of attitude change and reasons for it. Though changes in teacher attitude about reform were minimal over the course of a year, the influences of peers played a greater role in explaining variation among teachers than traditional school-based factors (experience, departments, formal titles). Teachers' attitudes were significantly "pulled" toward the attitudes of their conversational peers. The multiple networks explored in this chapter provided unique information, with some of these networks being related to individual attitude change. The unique nature of the networks and their relationships to attitude changes indicate the active role that teachers play in selecting sources of advice for different issues and the ways in which these choices may influence their attitudes and eventual behaviors.

When a reform is introduced into a school, new conversation pathways are created about that reform. However, when one considers all of the communication networks in which teachers are involved, these new networks do not appear to be as influential as existing instrumental and expressive networks in terms of influencing teachers' attitudes related to the reform. Furthermore, with respect to direct communication, teachers were significantly influenced by their expressive and instrumental peers, but not by those with whom they only discussed the reform. This finding is compelling, as it illustrates how certain relationships, manifested here by network connections, are more salient for influence than others.[47] While a new reform does indeed alter the social fabric of an organization, it appears that the enduring qualities of the original social structure are more important for influencing the predisposition of teachers toward a new reform.

Ibarra and Andrews note that there are differences in instrumental and expressive networks with respect to the ways that peers affect perceptions of the workplace.[48] In our study, we observe that these two networks do facilitate change. The influence of instrumental peers is limited to those in direct contact, while the influence of expressive peers can be found across those in both direct and indirect contact. Teachers are affected by the friends of their friends (indirect expressive peers), and this influence is as strong as the influence of their direct peers. These findings support the theory put forth at the beginning of this chapter—that attitude as part of a subjective norm within the network based on friendship affinities has a clear influence on individual attitude. This appears to be true even if one considers the subjective norm to be a sort of organizational zeitgeist to which *all* organizational members contribute, either through direct or indirect pathways. Thus, both immediate and indirect peer influences will impact the ways that teachers feel about reform.

This work also makes clear the additional information that can be gained by using social network theory and analysis to gain a better understanding of how schools work. Education researchers continue to study why improvement programs in schools have such variable impacts on teachers' work.[49] The significant influence that peers have on each other's attitudes (and likely their behaviors) helps us to understand the variation that has been so well documented. It is one piece of the implementation puzzle.

IMPLICATIONS

Significant research has been done about how a new *practice* spreads through an organization including innovations in schools.[50] Much less work has been done examining the relationship of teacher *attitude* and how that is related to individual attributes and interpersonal connections. This chapter illustrates a relationship between teacher attitude and social structure that is consistent with the central tenets of social information processing theory. We find significant evidence for the influence of social ties on attitude development among teachers. Because successful implementation of innovation depends on (among other factors) the extent to which employees develop a positive attitude about the innovation, we feel that this finding has significant implications for education research and practice.[51]

In the realm of practice, our research would argue that a small (but well-connected) clique of individuals can, through communicating with peers, easily influence teacher attitudes about (and subsequent implementation of) a reform. Because of the influence of attitude on intention and behavior, our findings indicate the power of the subjective norms in a school to influence teachers apart from (and potentially preceding) their demonstration of particular behaviors and practices. This helps to explain the variability in reform program implementation by shedding light on prevailing school attitudes. This result has been seen in previous research on school reform; reforms that make extensive use of teacher collaboration are particularly successful in promoting implementation, given that these reforms gain authority when they are embraced by peer teachers.[52]

Furthermore, this research illustrates that existing configurations of the social structure within schools plays a key role in the ways that teachers will gain access to new ideas and information. These networks are often defined by teachers and do not appear to be significantly influenced by formal school structures and organizational features. The considerable influence found in the established instrumental and expressive networks in shaping teacher opinion (in comparison with the reform network) illustrates the power of relationships that predate the introduction of reform to influence the change process. Though a new reform network was created by teachers in our study, and may become established over time, at the early stage in the reform effort (when we were collecting data) these new relationships were a weaker sibling to the other networks. In order for a new reform to be accepted and implemented within schools, practitioners must consider the existing configurations of individual social support and information access to help grow the reform into a tangible component of the school culture. For reforms targeted at anything from school restructuring to remedial reading, this means that school leaders will have to pay close attention to the "organic" networks that exist among their teaching staff. Utilizing these networks appears to have great potential in influencing the attitudes about a reform program among teaching staff.

For school leaders and those wishing to create fertile ground for school change, this research suggests that convincing particularly popular teachers that a planned reform is a good thing is likely to have a significant effect on many teachers' predisposition toward the reform. In order for these positive attitudes to spread efficiently, teachers with social ties to peers that predate the reform effort must be targeted. Fortunately, because our study indicates that indirect ties are also influential, leaders need not reach every teacher directly, but can work to create a significant cadre of teachers who will sway others in a positive direction. How one can go about sowing the seeds of positivity among teachers likely to have the largest influence is a question for further research. However, it seems that top-down organizational strategies are unlikely to create influential networks, at least in the short term.

Even when school reforms attempt to redirect relationships by reconfiguring teachers into small learning communities or other collaborative settings (two of the reforms in this study utilized this strategy), established relationships persist. Our findings show that teachers continue to be much more strongly influenced by the traditional relationships in their schools. More than their own individual attributes (given those that we were able to measure) and more than the new structures and materials that a reform may bring to the school, teachers are influenced by the peers with whom they have formed relationships over time. Granovetter recognized this phenomenon in his argument regarding the strength of weak ties; the strong social ties we observed in the instrumental and expressive networks of teachers may be keeping teachers from embracing ideas from other groups (e.g., reform groups), which may limit the implementation of these changes.[53] Any reform that seeks to change attitudes, and subsequently teaching behaviors, has to recognize this reality.

Finally, this research demonstrates the need for a social network component in future research on teachers. Existing research has demonstrated the importance of professional communities (or lack thereof) in influencing teachers' practice, and this study contributes to that line of work and argues that *personal* communities—those peer groups selected and identified by individual teachers—are at least as important as externally imposed professional communities.[54] The value added by this study is the illustration that interaction with teaching peers imparts a significant and measurable influence on teachers. This influence has implications both for changing teacher practice as well as for broadening our conceptions of, and research about, school improvement efforts. The case is clear: future school research must consider the impact of teachers' social networks and the individuals and organizations that shape them.

CHAPTER 6

Social Networks, Trust, and Innovation

The Role of Relationships in Supporting an Innovative Climate in Dutch Schools

Nienke M. Moolenaar and Peter J. C. Sleegers

In educational practice and research around the globe, social relationships between educators are increasingly recognized as an important resource in support of school improvement and educational innovation. The idea behind the potential of social relationships is that a strong informal teacher community benefits from the know-how that is shared among the community members. The sharing of information, knowledge, and expertise increases the likelihood that current knowledge will be retained and multiplied, and new knowledge and practices will be created.[1] In educational research, the importance of strong professional communities for teachers' professional development, collective learning, and educational change is therefore becoming an increasingly important area. In practice, these communities are being increasingly developed to create a climate oriented toward knowledge exchange and shared learning, with the goal to improve instruction and student learning.[2]

Recent educational studies underline the value of strong social networks among teachers for the spread and depth of policy and reform implementation and schools' innovative climate and their capacity to change.[3] Research outside education suggests that formal and informal social relationships between organizational members play a crucial role in organizational learning by stimulating the development of new knowledge and practices.[4] Thus the extent to which organizations are able to innovate depends in part on the social links within and across organizational units, as well as the links outside the organization.[5]

In an effort to understand how social relationships between educators may support school improvement, and to explore ways to target and optimize the potential of these links, educational scholars often build on social capital theory. Social capital theory is concerned with the social embeddedness of individuals in social networks and posits that this embeddedness may support or constrain the opportunity for individuals and organizations to achieve desired goals.[6] While the field of educational research has already been greatly enriched by the discovery of the benefits of relational linkages, there is yet much to learn about potential mechanisms that could explain why strong social networks may elicit these beneficial outcomes. One of the key concepts of social capital theory, trust, is greatly overlooked for its potential to serve as such a mechanism. We therefore explore the role of trust in the relationship between social networks and innovative climate in this chapter. The following research question guides our inquiry: *To what extent do characteristics of educators' social networks affect schools' innovative climate, as mediated by trust?*

In the next section, we will briefly introduce social capital theory and social network theory as our starting point to elaborate the role of social ties in relation to innovation and trust, and then develop hypotheses on the relationships between teachers' individual and school-level social ties, their school's innovative climate, and teacher trust. Using data from 775 teachers and principals of 53 schools in the Netherlands, this study provides a unique contribution to the knowledge base of social networks in education by examining an important mechanism through which social ties among teachers may support school improvement, and eventually, student achievement.

THEORETICAL FRAMEWORK

Schools' Innovative Climate

As in the United States, educational policy in the Netherlands is characterized by a push for innovation in support of school improvement and increased student achievement. In organizational literature, the process of innovation is often described as iterative and cyclic, developed and sustained through social interaction that provides multiple opportunities for refinement.[7] In this view, the development of innovations can be understood as a social process in which innovation "emerges between rather than within people."[8] Critical to the development of innovations is a supportive organizational climate that stimulates opportunities to engage in discussion and collaboration. In an innovation-oriented climate, organizational members are willing to take risks and accept the vulnerability of possible failure.

This chapter focuses on the extent to which the organizational climate is supportive of the development of new knowledge and practices. This stands in contrast to the body of literature that has examined the adoption, diffusion, or implementation of innovations themselves. We define schools' *innovative climate* as the shared perceptions of organizational members concerning the practices, procedures, and behaviors that promote the generation of new knowledge and practices.[9] Key elements underlying this definition are teachers' willingness to adopt an open orientation toward new practices and change and to collectively develop new knowledge, practices, and refinements to meet organizational goals.[10]

In educational research, the continuing governmental push for innovation has been translated into a myriad of studies that focus on change and the development and diffusion of innovation through professional learning communities and social networks. Recent research suggests that dense social networks, in which knowledge and information are created and multiplied, support an innovation-oriented school climate. Interactions with others in dense social networks are associated with a positive attitude toward change, since these networks provide ample opportunity for new knowledge and new practices to develop in a safe environment that promotes risk taking.[11]

Social Networks and Schools' Innovative Climate

To understand the supportive role of social ties for an innovative climate, we draw on the concept of social capital. Several scholars have contributed to the conceptualization of social capital, each offering a nuanced understanding of the concept and emphasizing a different aspect of social capital.[12] As defined by its principal theorists, *social capital* refers to "the sum of the actual and potential resources embedded within, available through, and derived from the network of relationships possessed by an individual or social unit."[13] Social capital thus comprises both the network and the assets that may be mobilized through that network.

From an organizational standpoint, social capital may be conceptualized as an organization's pattern of social relationships through which the resources of individuals can be accessed, borrowed, or leveraged. Studies argue that social capital contributes to organizational goals by facilitating the flow of information between individuals and overcoming problems of coordination.[14] In educational research, social capital has gained interest chiefly in regard to students; for instance, to explain the impact of family or peer social capital on educational outcomes such as student attainment and achievement.[15]

Although views on the dimensions of social capital differ widely, two common threads can be found throughout most social capital literature.[16] The first addresses the pattern of social relationships, and is referred to as the *structural dimension*. Studies into this structural dimension suggest that strong teacher networks enhance the dissemination of information on schoolwide reform efforts, an open orientation toward innovation, and overall school functioning, as well as counteract negative phenomena such as absenteeism and low job satisfaction resulting from teacher isolation.[17]

Social networks can be characterized by the content exchanged within the social relationships. For example, collaboration networks may be built around information and knowledge exchange related to work. Friendship networks may mainly encompass confidential discussions and social support. A distinction is commonly made between instrumental and expressive networks. *Instrumental* social networks describe relationships in which resources are exchanged that can facilitate achieving organizational goals. In contrast, *expressive* social networks most often refer to affective relationships between organizational members that are formed to exchange social resources, such as friendship and social support, that are not directly aimed at achieving organizational goals. In comparison with instrumental relations, expressive relationships tend to be stronger and more durable, but also more difficult and time-consuming to develop.[18]

Common terms to describe the social network characteristics at the organizational level are density and reciprocity. *Density* refers to the existing proportion of ties in a network to possible ties; in a dense network, many people are connected to one another, while in a sparse network, there are fewer connections between the individuals in the network. *Reciprocity* addresses the mutuality of ties; a relationship between two people is reciprocal when both individuals indicate that they are connected to one another. The higher the reciprocity in a network, the more dyadic (one-on-one) relationships are mutual.

The transfer of resources in a social network is dependent on the pattern of the social ties.[19] For example, the extent to which a social network is characterized by density and reciprocity may reflect the network's ability to circulate creative knowledge and materials that can be recombined into new creative materials and ideas.[20] Earlier studies suggest that strong social relationships facilitate joint problem solving and the exchange of tacit, non-routine, or complex knowledge. Moreover, strong ties have been associated with low-conflict organizations. However, when the necessary relationships are lacking or insufficiently accessed, social networks may also constrain the flow of knowledge and information.[21] Dense and reciprocal social networks in schools may hold valuable potential for innovation, because an increase in the cohesion and connectivity of social relationships may facilitate the generation, application, and diffusion of new knowledge and evidence, as well as shape an innovation-oriented climate in which educators are open to change and willing to take risks to enhance school improvement. Moreover, a centralized network structure may facilitate the diffusion of knowledge and practices related to a top-down implementation of innovations, as is often the case in (Dutch) school improvement programs. Therefore, we expect that social network characteristics (density, reciprocity, and centralization) will have a positive effect on teachers' perceptions of their school's innovative climate (*hypothesis 1*).

Trust as a Potential Mechanism

A second component of social capital, the *relational dimension*, addresses the quality of the relationships in social networks. This quality is often described in terms of the norms, values, and expectancies shared by group members. In most social capital literature, trust among organizational members is recognized as an important affective norm that characterizes a community.[22] Trust can be defined as an individual's or group's willingness to be vulnerable to another party based on the confidence that the latter party is benevolent, reliable, competent, honest, and open.[23] As such, trust may be a critical ingredient in all human learning. Research has indicated that trust has positive effects on teacher motivation and learning. Moreover, trust is important for both teachers' individual and collective sense of efficacy, which is in turn associated with the improvement of classroom practice and student achievement[24].

In social capital literature, trust and social interaction are often mentioned as interrelated elements. Trust is embedded in relationships based on interpersonal interdependence and often associated with group cohesion and collaboration. Trust is believed to facilitate collective action because it allows for collaboration to occur in the absence of sanctions and rewards. Positive experiences in prior social interactions may foster trust by reducing uncertainty about the engagement and involvement of the other party and decreasing the sense of vulnerability between individuals.[25] Thus social ties between educators may prompt a trust-rich environment by offering a blueprint for future interactions, shaping mutual expectations and conveying information about the norms and values of social interaction within the school community.

Although social networks and trust are important elements in social capital theory and literature on school reform, studies into the interrelatedness of social networks and trust as two major constituents of social capital in school organizations is missing. Based on social capital theory, we suggest that having more relationships has a positive effect on teacher trust (*hypothesis 2*).

In turn, we suggest that teacher trust is positively related to schools' innovative climate. Trust allows teachers to be vulnerable, to rely on each other to achieve goals, and to be open to new learning experiences that are central to ongoing teacher development in schools.[26] As a result, improving the quality of education and student learning becomes both an individual and collective enterprise that motivates teachers to engage in instructional change and increases their willingness to take risks to improve instructional quality. A school climate that is infused with trust will provide teachers with an environment in which it is safe to engage in new teaching practices, try new strategies to improve teaching, and collaboratively develop innovative ways to address the changing context of teaching. We hypothesize that trust may be the factor that explains why dense and reciprocal social networks may be

FIGURE 6-1   Path diagram of hypothesized relationships

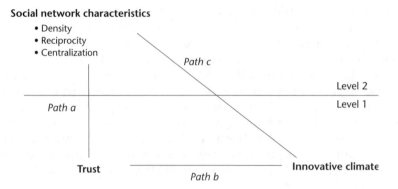

associated with an increased willingness to innovate and an open orientation toward change. We therefore expect that trust will positively mediate the relationship between schools' social network characteristics and schools' innovative climate (*hypothesis 3*). In sum, figure 6-1 shows a path diagram of the hypothesized multilevel relationships under study.

While previous research suggests that teachers' professional relationships foster a climate of trust and a safe environment to engage in innovative behavior and risk taking in reform efforts, empirical evidence on the interplay between social ties, innovative climate, and teacher trust is limited.[27] This study offers a unique contribution to this line of research by exploring the links between social networks and trust in support of schools' innovative climates. In addition, we point out and act on the need for a multilevel approach to the study of social networks by examining the proposed relationships at multiple levels of analysis. In the next section, we will describe a large-scale empirical study of teachers and principals of 53 Dutch elementary schools, designed to address our research question and test our hypotheses.

METHODOLOGY

Data Collection

The data for this study were collected in the Netherlands. As in the United States, the push for educational innovation has coincided with a growing focus on social relationships between teachers to stimulate the exchange of knowledge and expertise in support of school improvement. Our study surveyed 775 educators representing 53 schools that together formed the Avvansa School District.[28] The district coordinated collective resources such

TABLE 6-1
Teacher and school demographics (n = 775)

		#/(%)
Gender	Male	210 teachers/(27.1 %)
	Female	565 teachers /(72.9 %)
Experience at the school	6 months to 3 years	152 teachers/(19.6 %)
	4 to10 years	256 teachers/(33.0 %)
	More than 11 years	367 teachers /(47.4 %)
Team in current formation	6 months to 2 years	20 teams/(37.7 %)
	More than 2 years	33 teams/ (62.3 %)

as financial, IT and personnel support. The sample schools participated in the study as part of a districtwide ongoing school- and teacher-monitoring process around school improvement.

In total, 51 school leaders and 724 teachers participated in the study by filling in a questionnaire, reflecting a total response rate of 96.8 percent. Of the respondents, 72.9 percent were female, 54.5 percent worked full-time (thirty-two hours or more) and 44.1 percent were fifty years or older. All respondents had been working at the school for at least six months, and the school teams had comprised the same members for at least six months. Additional sample demographics are presented in tables 6-1 and 6-2.

Instruments

Social Networks. The social networks among the teachers in the sample schools were studied using social network analysis. To capture a diverse palette of teacher relationships, two social network questions were asked:

1. To whom do you turn in order to discuss your work? (Instrumental relationship)
2. Whom do you regard as a friend? (Expressive relationship)

Each survey included a school-specific appendix in which the names of all school team members were represented by a letter combination (e.g., Mrs. Nicole Marsden = AB).[29]

Innovative Climate. To assess schools' innovative climate, we used six items derived from a questionnaire designed by the Consortium on Chicago School Research.[30] The scale taps the degree to which the teachers perceive the organizational climate in their school as innovation-supportive and

TABLE 6-2
Sample characteristics of teachers (n = 775) and schools (N = 53)

	N	Min.	Max.	M	Sd
Teachers					
Age	774	21	63	45.7	10.7
Percentage of working hours (FTE)*	774	.20	1.00	.73	.25
Administrative tasks (no/yes)	724	0	1	.19	.39
Shared Decision-making (SD)	775	1.14	4.00	3.38	.52
Innovative Climate (IC)	775	1.00	4.00	2.95	.55
School					
SES**	53	0.4	47.3	7.9	9.5
Number of students	53	53	545	213	116.6
Team size	53	6	31	14.8	6.8

* E.g., a teacher with 0.40 fte is employed at the school for (a total of) two days per week.

** SES is calculated as the weighted percentage of students for whom the school receives extra financial resources

change-oriented, and assesses the extent to which teachers are willing to try new practices, are continually learning and creating new ideas, and have an open orientation toward change. For example, teachers were asked to evaluate the statement, "In our school, teachers are willing to take risks to make this school better."[31]

Trust. Trust among educators was assessed by a Dutch translation of the "trust in colleagues" scale developed by Hoy and Tschannen-Moran.[32] The scale measured trust as the extent to which teachers feel that they can depend on their colleagues, even in difficult situations, and that their colleagues can be trusted and are open and honest to each other. For example, teachers were asked to respond to the prompt, "I trust my colleagues" . The items were also scored on a four-point scale. Principal component analysis confirmed that the five items loaded highly on a single factor that explained 65.6 percent of the variance (α = .87). Scale scores were composed using the mean score of all trust items. Both "Innovative Climate" and "Trust" items represent teacher perceptions of organizational-level phenomena, and are therefore assessed at the individual level of analysis. The trust and innovative climate items were entered in a single principal component analysis with varimax rotation resulting in a two-factor solution, explaining 62.4 percent of the variance, indicating that the two scales assessed separate constructs. The items and factor loadings of this principal component analysis are presented in table 6-3.

TABLE 6-3
Items and factor loadings of the scales used in the study (n = 775)

	Factor I	Factor II
Trust (α = .87)		
1. I find that my coworkers are open to me	.83	.19
2. Even in difficult situations, I can depend on my coworkers	.81	.23
3. I find that my coworkers are honest to me	.80	.21
4. I trust my coworkers	.78	.21
5. I share personal information with my coworkers	.73	.10
Innovative climate (α = .87)		
1. Teachers are generally willing to try new ideas	.16	.81
2. Teachers are continuously learning and developing new ideas	.15	.80
3. Teachers are constantly trying to improve their teaching	.18	.74
4. Teachers are willing to take risks to make this school better	.18	.73
5. Teachers have a positive 'can-do' attitude	.26	.73
6. Teachers are encouraged to go as far as they can	.13	.69

Demographic Variables. We collected demographic variables to assess the presence of any relationships between demographics and social network characteristics, trust, and innovative climate. In the questionnaire we asked for background demographics of the educators, such as age, gender, additional staff task hours in support of the principal, number of working hours, and number of years of experience teaching and in the school. Information on team size (number of educators), years of experience of the team in its current formation, school size (number of students), socioeconomic status (SES, based on a governmental weighting factor for additional financial support) was collected from the district main office. Additional collective-level demographics were calculated by aggregating individual-level demographics such as average age, gender ratio (percentage of female educators in the team), and average number of working hours.

Data Analysis

Social Network Analysis. To systematically study patterns of social relationships among educators in school teams, we employed social network analysis.[33] We use a whole network approach, which means that we focus on specific network characteristics (e.g., density, reciprocity, and centralization) of the social network of the school team as a whole. Whole social networks comprise a finite number of individuals and relationships between these individuals within a bounded community of people (e.g., class, school team, or district office). In this study, three collective-level social network measures were collected by analyzing individual social network data, namely density, reciprocity, and centralization. For each of the schools' social networks, *density* was calculated as the proportion of existing relationships to the maximum number of relationships possible in the network. *Reciprocity* was calculated as the ratio of the number of observed reciprocated relationships to the total number of relationships in the team. Defined this way, reciprocity can be understood as reflecting the extent to which work discussion or friendship is mutually exchanged in the team. *Centralization* of a social network refers to the difference between one or a few highly central person(s) and other (more peripheral) people in the network. A highly centralized network is one in which all ties run through one or a few nodes, thus decreasing the distance between any pair of nodes.[34]

RESULTS

Descriptive and Correlational Analyses

An examination of the social network characteristics (see table 6-4) indicated that the friendship network tended to be less dense and less centralized than the network around work-related discussion. The amount of reciprocity was similar for both networks. Results from the correlation analyses indicated that on average, the amount of density in the instrumental network is positively related to the density of the expressive network. The same also held for reciprocity in both networks. Moreover, density and reciprocity of both networks were interrelated. Surprisingly, we found a negative association between centralization of the instrumental network and the density of the friendship network; in other words, the more centralized the network on work-related discussion, the less dense the friendship network among educators. In addition, a positive correlation between the density and centralization of the expressive network was evidenced; that is, the more centralized the friendship network in a school, the more dense the network. Furthermore, findings with regard to the instrumental network suggest that density is positively associated with trust, while reciprocity is negatively associated with trust. In addition, the more dense and reciprocal the instrumental network, the more teachers perceive their school's climate to be innovative. In regard to the expressive network, results suggested a positive relationship between the density of the friendship network and schools' innovative climate. Finally, trust and innovative climate are significantly interrelated.

Multilevel Analyses

The intercept-only multilevel model for innovative climate (IC) showed that a statistically significant amount of variance in individual trust scores is

TABLE 6-4

Means, standard deviations, correlations, and internal consistencies (Cronbach's alpha) for the study variables ($N_{schools}$ = 53, $n_{teachers}$ = 775)

	N	Min	Max	M	Sd	1b	1c	2a	2b	2c	3	4
1. Instrumental network												
a. Density	53	.15	.77	.37	.12	**.54****	−.06	**.42****	**.28***	.10	*.08***	*.25***
b. Reciprocity	53	.17	.64	.39	.10		−.09	**.39****	**.36****	.21	*−.08**	*.08**
c. Centralization	53	.04	.64	.34	.11			**−.31***	.17	−.03	*−.01*	*.04*
2. Expressive network												
a. Density	53	.00	.32	.12	.06				.18	**.59****	*.04*	*.10***
b. Reciprocity	53	.00	1.00	.35	.23					.26	*−.01*	*.07*
c. Centralization	53	.00	.44	.18	.09						*−.05*	*.05*
3. Trust	766	1.00	4.00	3.23	.56						*(.87)*	*.44***
4. Innovative climate	775	1.00	4.00	2.95	.55							*(.87)*

Notes: Significant estimates are displayed in **bold** font; *** p < .001, ** p < .01, * p < .05

Correlations in regular font are calculated at the collective level of analysis (N = 53)

Correlations in italics are calculated at the individual level of analysis (n = 775)

attributed to the school level (see table 6-5). The intraclass correlation coefficient (ICC) for IC is .244 (Chi-square (1) = 103.85, p < .001), thus indicating the need to use multilevel analysis techniques to examine the relationship between school-level social network measures and schools' innovative climate. In other words, 24.4 percent of the variability in teachers' climate perceptions occurs between schools, and the remaining 75.6 percent of the variance occurs within schools at the teacher level. The intercept-only multilevel model for trust also confirmed that a statistically significant amount of variance is accounted for at the school level (ICC = .136, Chi-square (1) = 46.98, p < .001). In other words, 13.6 percent of the variability in teachers' perceptions of trust occurs between schools, and the remaining 84.7 percent of the variance occurs within schools at the teacher level.

Demographic Variables, Schools' Innovative Climate, and Trust

Before examining our hypotheses, we examined the relationship between demographic background variables on both innovative climate and trust. In a first step, the multilevel models were conducted including all demographic variables in varying subsets. Findings suggested that gender was the only

TABLE 6-5 Multilevel regression analyses of the effect of social network characteristics and trust on innovative climate and the effect of social network characteristics and trust ($N_{schools}$ = 53, $n_{teachers}$ = 775)

	Innovative climate								Trust					
	Model 1		Model 2a		Model 2b		Model 3		Model 1		Model 2a		Model 2b	
	Est.	S.E.	Est.	S.E.	Est.	S.E.	Est.	S.E.	Est.	S.E.	Est.	S.E.	Est.	S.E.
Intercept	2.97	.04	2.94	.04	2.96	.04	1.72	.11	3.21	.04	3.20	.03	3.21	.03
Individual level														
Gender (male/female)	.02	.02	.02	.02	.02	.02	.00	.02	**.05***	.02	**.05***	.02	.05	.02
Collective level														
Instrumental Network														
Density			**.14***	.04			**.11****	.02			**.08***	.04		
Reciprocity			.00	.04			.03	.04			**-.08***	.04		
Centralization			.04	.04			.05	.03			-.01	.03		
Expressive Network														
Density					.05	.05							.04	.04
Reciprocity					.05	.05							.02	.03
Centralization					-.04	.05							-.08†	.04
Trust							**.38***	.03						
-2*log likelihood	1057.47		1040.54		1054.60		924.31		1097.08		1091.71		1093.64	
	Chi-square$_{DIFF.}$ (1) =1.61, n.s.		Chi-square$_{DIFF.}$ (4) = 18.54 ***		Chi-square$_{DIFF.}$ (4) = 4.48, n.s.		Chi-square$_{DIFF.}$ (5) = 134.67 ***		Chi-square$_{DIFF.}$ (1) = 5.83 *		Chi-square$_{DIFF.}$ (4) = 11.20 *		Chi-square$_{DIFF.}$ (4) = 9.27†	
Explained variance	(total)								(total)					
School	(24.4 %) 0.8%		8.1%		1.9%		25.1%		(13.6 %) 1.0%		2.6%		1.9%	
Teacher	(75.6 %) 0.4%		27.0%		5.9%		52.4%		(86.3 %) 34.5%		39.5%		37.1%	

Notes: Significant estimates are displayed in **bold** font; *** p < .001, ** p < .01, * p < .05, † < .10. *Intercept-only for innovative climate:* Chi-square (3) = 1059.08; ICC_{IC} = .244, Chi-square (1) = 103.85, p < .001. *Intercept-only model for trust:* Chi-square (3) =1102.91, ICC_{SD} = .136, Chi-square (1) = 46.98, p < .001

demographic variable that was associated with trust. Therefore, in the second step, only this demographic variable was included in all subsequent multi-level models. These models showed that female educators display slightly higher levels of trust than male educators. Other demographic variables were excluded from following analyses.

Relationship Between Social Network Characteristics and Schools' Innovative Climate

Hypothesis 1 concerned the extent to which collective-level characteristics of instrumental and expressive social networks (density, reciprocity, and centralization) were associated with increasingly innovative climates in schools. Findings indicated that the density of the network of work-discussion relationships was significantly related to schools' innovative climate. In other words, the more densely connected the school's social networks were around work discussions, the more teachers perceived their school to be characterized by an innovation-oriented climate in which teachers were willing to collectively learn and create new knowledge and practices. Contrary to our hypothesis, reciprocity and centralization were not significantly related to schools' innovative climates. The extent to which relationships were mutual, or distributed across the system, did not appear to affect teachers' perceptions of their school's innovative climate. Moreover, the characteristics of friendship networks were not found to be significantly related to innovative climates in schools. Therefore, these findings provided only partial support for hypothesis 1.

The second hypothesis involved the relationship between advice network structures (density, reciprocity, and centralization) and trust. Results indicated a significant positive relationship between the density of schools' instrumental social network structure and trust. The more teachers were embedded in a densely connected work-discussion network, the more they indicated that they trusted their colleagues and believed their colleagues were honest and open with them. This result was not replicated in the expressive network, indicating that the amount of friendship relationships among teachers did not significantly affect the degree to which they trusted their colleagues. These findings suggest that relationships around work-related discussions may have a more substantial impact on building and nurturing trust among teachers in school teams than friendship relationships. Another striking finding: there is a slightly negative significant relationship between trust and instrumental reciprocity. This means that the more a team is characterized by reciprocal relationships, the less the teachers appear to trust each other. As with the results of the previous analysis, centralization in both networks had no significant association with trust. Thus hypothesis 2 was only partially supported.

Mediating Role of Trust

Hypothesis 3 posited that trust would play a mediating role in the relationship between social network characteristics and schools' innovative climate. To test this hypothesis, additional analyses were conducted[35]. Step one required a significant relationship between social network characteristics and innovative climate (path c in figure 6-1). Findings indicated that reciprocity and centralization were not significantly related to schools' innovative climates. Step two required a significant relationship between social network characteristics and trust (path a). Results showed that only density of the instrumental social network was related to trust. Thus, preconditions for mediation of the relationship between any other social network characteristic and schools' innovative climate were not met. Therefore, we only tested the mediating role of trust in the relationship between density of the instrumental network and schools' innovative climate (see model 3 in table 6-5).

Results showed that teachers' trust influenced their perception of their school's innovative climate significantly, above the prediction of schools' innovative climate by social network characteristics.[36] This suggests that the relationship between density of the instrumental social network and innovative climate is partially explained by trust among teachers. In other words, density of the network around work-related discussion facilitates the creation of new knowledge and builds orientation toward innovation partly because teachers in more densely connected advice networks display higher levels of trust in their colleagues. Being embedded in a dense network of work-related relationships facilitates a more innovation-supportive school climate and increases teacher trust, which in turn also benefits this innovation-supportive school climate. Therefore, results provided partial support for hypothesis 3.

In sum, the relationships between social network characteristics, trust, and schools' innovative climates share an interesting story about the way in which teacher interactions contribute to schools' willingness to innovate and, ultimately, improve school performance. It appears that building and nurturing strong social relationships around the discussion of work-related matters increases teachers' trust in their colleagues, which in turn affects the willingness of teachers to take risks and be vulnerable and open to new practices and knowledge in order to improve school performance. In the next section, we will discuss our findings, provide limitations to the study, and offer implications for research and practice.

CONCLUSIONS AND DISCUSSION

Under increasing pressure to improve and innovate, scholars and practitioners have started to insist on the importance of understanding how initiatives aimed to improve education through social interaction, such as professional learning communities, affect the extent to which schools build capacities for change. While relationships between social interaction, trust, and innovation-supportive climates seem commonsense and are suggested by a few smaller-scale studies within education, the interrelatedness of these concepts has, to our knowledge, not yet been the subject of extensive study. This chapter contributes to the literature around innovation in education by empirically testing the degree to which the resource exchange in work-related and friendship networks affect schools' innovative climates with a large sample of schools.

Building on social network theory, we chose to explore educational innovation in terms of a school's willingness to learn and try new ideas and practices, rather than focus on the implementation of specific innovations that are much more bounded by the school's context. To answer our research questions, we examined the relationship between social network characteristics (density, reciprocity, and centralization) and innovative climate in schools in a large educational system in the Netherlands. We also explored the role of teacher trust as a potential mechanism that may explain the relationship between social network characteristics and schools' innovative climate. In doing so, we provided an important piece of the puzzle with regard to both social network theory and social capital theory. While organizational studies have pointed to the importance of social ties for change, this study is among the first to examine the relationship between social networks and innovation in education. With the global push for innovation to improve schools eminent, this study offers a first outlook on the way in which social relationships between educators may contribute to innovation in schools, namely through the creation and maintenance of innovation-supportive climates. In addition, this chapter contributes to social capital theory by conceptualizing and explicating the relationship between social network characteristics and trust, thereby taking a first step toward connecting social networks (the structural dimension of social capital) with trust (the relational dimension of social capital).

Our findings suggest that teachers in dense school teams perceive their school's climate as more innovative than teachers who have fewer relationships around the discussion of work. These results support the importance of relational links that nurture and stimulate the growth of a schoolwide innovation-supportive climate in which risk taking can occur in a safe environment. It is this willingness to be vulnerable and engage in risk taking with multiple others in the organization that appears important for the creation of new knowledge and practices. According to our findings, dense networks around work-related discussions contribute to trust among educators, which is in turn associated with taking risks to improve the school, creating and fostering an innovation-oriented climate in which educators feel they can experiment with new teaching practices without the fear of failure or ridicule of colleagues, and be open and vulnerable to the new ideas and opinions of others that are exchanged through work-related discussions.

Links with Practice and Policy

In the current educational debate there is a growing emphasis on the need to manage and strategically build social ties in order to redesign the way in which teachers work.[37] Social network theory stipulates that the more an organization provides opportunities for members to enter the stream of social activity, the more actors are exposed to multiple others, and the more likely new ideas can be exchanged and practices created. In this study, we indeed find evidence that dense teacher teams characterized by a common exchange of work-related information and discourse are the cornerstones of organizational climates in which teachers not only trust each other, but also have a "can-do" attitude toward change and innovation, are willing to try new ideas and collectively develop new knowledge, and are continuously working to improve their instructional practice. This being the case, educational practitioners are advised to invest time and energy in building strong teacher teams that focus on work-related discussions.

Through providing resources such as time and creating flexible management arrangements and informal organizational structures, principals can stimulate teachers to rethink their existing practice and share their expertise, know-how, and creativity with the goal of improving teaching and learning. More specifically, principals should provide opportunities for joint staff development events and powerful forms of professional learning within and across teams (e.g., peer coaching, effective induction, dialogical learning) around agendas that can make a contribution to improvements in teaching and learning. This will create commitment at different levels within schools, build dense ties that bind teachers together in social networks within the school, and foster the sharing of responsibilities through forms of distributed leadership. Through focusing on teaching and learning as the core business of schools, providing resources, and creating powerful forms of collaboration, principals can develop strong informal teacher communities that benefit from the expertise, information, and know-how that is exchanged and shared among their members. As our findings suggest, this work-related exchange will encourage trust and teachers' willingness to engage in change-oriented practices, and in turn, increase schools' capacity to adapt to changes and provide opportunities to move practice forward.

There is also a message in this work for educational policy. Current educational policies stress the importance of technical knowledge and subject-specific goals and strategies to improve student achievement. Yet when educational reforms hit the school door, they are modified, socially co-constructed, and assigned collective meaning.[38] It is educators' interaction with others, in combination with educators' willingness to implement and adjust the reform to fit their own classroom, that to a large extent determines the spread and success of the reform.[39] Our findings strongly suggest that, besides the technical elements of reform, policy makers would be advised to also increase attention to the importance of social linkages that may support or constrain the uptake of reform. A key role for educational policy makers, district managers, and local authorities should be to create an overall sense of what the educational reforms should look like that can help schools to focus their improvement efforts, generate their own goals, and set their priorities. In this way, policy makers can help foster ownership and commitment at different levels within schools, a greater capacity for managing change, and a common language of practice that will facilitate social learning processes.

Social Networks, Trust, and Innovation

Educational policy and practice around the globe treat educational innovation as the key to success in improving education. Yet the social interactions between educators that lie at the heart of every collective effort to improve schools are largely overlooked as a valuable resource to support the implementation of reforms. In this chapter we suggest that to unlock schools' capacity to effectively develop and implement educational innovations, it is vital to understand how social relationships support innovative climates in which teachers feel free to experiment and collectively invent new teaching strategies that meet the needs of their students. Through building and fostering relationships that nurture trust and shape an innovation-supportive climate, practitioners and policy makers can tap into the vast potential of collective action and collaborative invention that is often locked inside a single creative teacher or shared among only handful of resourceful teachers. It is through these links with trust and innovation that the creation of new educational innovations flow and hold the promise of sustained school improvement and increased student achievement.

TECHNICAL APPENDIX

Testing the Hypotheses

To account for the nested characteristics of our data (teachers in schools), we applied multilevel analysis (hierarchical linear modeling). Separate analyses were conducted for the instrumental and expressive social networks. For comparing the multilevel models, we used maximum likelihood estimation in the Statistical Package for the Social Sciences version 16.0.

There is a methodological challenge in conducting regressions using network measures, which is that violations to the basic assumption of independence underlying regression analysis may occur.[a] Individuals in a social network are by definition interdependent because they share the same network. Along the same lines, the instrumental and expressive networks refer to the same set of individuals. As such, the social network measures of our two network types cannot be considered independent and using similar network measures in the same regression equation (e.g., density of instrumental *and* expressive network) would challenge the assumption of independence of the data. We avoid this methodological challenge by comparing the work-discussion and friendship networks and contrasting their respective impact on schools' innovative climate, as mediated by trust.

a. See David A. Kenny, Deborah A. Kashy, and Niall Bolger, "Data Analysis in Social Psychology," in *Handbook of Social Psychology*, vol. 1, 4th ed., eds. Daniel Gilbert, Susan T. Fiske, and Garder Lindzey (New York: McGraw-Hill, 1998), 233–265.

CHAPTER 7

Making Expertise Transparent

Using Technology to Strengthen Social Networks in Teacher Professional Development

Kira J. Baker-Doyle and Susan A. Yoon

Over the last quarter century in the United States, the perceptions and expectations of the role of teachers in professional development programs have undergone a dramatic shift. The traditional notion of teachers as passive recipients has been largely rejected for a more active conception of teachers as co-constructors and contributors to the pedagogical knowledge base.[1] Today, most in-service professional development activities are geared toward engaging teachers in collaborative work and inquiry so that they can continue their professional learning beyond a particular workshop or course. This approach values the knowledge that teachers bring from previous experiences and their social networks, and fosters the development of social capital (the knowledge and resources that exist in a social network) through collaborative practices. Despite this shift in practice, there are few evaluative tools that reveal how teachers develop their social capital within professional development programs.

In this chapter, we argue that, for contemporary professional development programs to be effective and sustainable, we need to help teachers learn to recognize and access their social capital. In particular, we advocate for programs to develop participants' *expertise transparency*—knowledge of the distribution of content knowledge expertise within the social networks of program participants. Social network analysis (SNA) methods can reveal this information. Program facilitators can use SNA as an evaluative tool to develop strategic approaches for developing expertise transparency in the group.

To illustrate our argument and give specific suggestions for practice in this chapter, we offer an example of our social network research project. Over the course of two years we studied the social networks of twenty-nine urban public high school teachers in a science professional development program. In year 1 (2008) our findings revealed surprising patterns of content knowledge and resource exchange in teachers' informal advice networks. We used this information to reform aspects of the program for year 2 (2009) to enhance teachers' exchange of social capital. The initial results of our interventions are promising and support our claim that expertise transparency is a key element of effective professional development.

PROFESSIONAL DEVELOPMENT IN THE TWENTY-FIRST CENTURY: CHANGES AND CHALLENGES

Beginning in the mid-1980s, the notion of teacher professionalism began to take hold as an essential element of school reform. In the late years of the twentieth century, reforms focused on the teacher as an individual and on measuring his or her success in implementing a particular curriculum. By the early 2000s, this perspective was challenged by scholars who argued that teachers' capacities for implementing and sustaining curricular reforms were directly tied to their relationships with their peers, and that to improve professional development there must be a fundamental change in the individualistic norms of teaching.[2] Researchers found that teachers' professional community is one of the primary factors that influence their interpretation and implementation of new policy and changes.[3] In response to these findings, many professional development leaders and administrators reshaped professional support programs to focus on creating communities of practice and fostering collaborative or mentor-mentee relationships between participants.[4] Formally organized teacher networks have come to be of particular interest in the last decade of research on professional development and teacher support because they have been found to positively affect teachers' motivation and capacity for change.[5]

Today, instead of independent practice, collaboration is encouraged and long-term situated learning is valued over one-shot workshops. Teachers' background knowledge is recognized and valued.[6] Furthermore, these conceptual developments emerged, in part, because of an urgent need to help teachers learn about new technology and information management practices. Workforce pressures have increased with the emphasis on developing twenty-first-century and cyberinfrastructure-enabled scientific skills. Thus, learning from and using digital technologies for developing conceptual knowledge and process skills now figure prominently in education.[7] Despite the growing emphasis on cyberlearning, schools struggle to provide instruction in these kinds of knowledge work and complex processes.[8] Many well-documented constraints arise with the incorporation of innovative or progressive technology programs in classrooms.[9]

To respond to these needs, researchers in the learning sciences and STEM (science, technology, engineering and mathematics) education have focused attention on making innovative science- and technology-reform-oriented programs sustainable. Investigation and discussion have centered on what mechanisms and variables are required to create the conditions for success and how success may be evaluated.[10] One theme that resonates through much of this research is the challenge reformers face in adapting their programs to specific contexts.[11] Elmore writes about the difficulties experienced by nested clusters of innovation in educational settings, noting that, historically, failures in generating successful large-scale reforms can be attributed to an "absence of practical theory that takes account of the institutional complexities that operate on changes in practice."[12] Similarly, Fishman et al. point out that those designing for improvement need to account for the multiple embedded levels of stakeholders who must actively support the reform if it is to succeed.[13] Coburn reinforces the idea that educational reform and improvement are matters of complexity, highlighting the inability of research to address the inherent multidimensionality between and within educational constituents.[14]

Collaboration, teacher knowledge, and community have become valued elements of professional development and school reform as a result of changing perspectives on teachers' roles in professional development, new research on teacher learning, and growing pressures to help teachers adapt to technological advances in communication and science. These elements are difficult to study because of the complexity of human relationships and interactions. To evaluate and understand the effectiveness of these practices and create sustainable professional development programs, we need new methodological approaches that reveal complex patterns of socialization and information exchange. This chapter offers an example of one approach—using social network analysis to develop expertise transparency by revealing the informal advice networks of teachers in a professional development program.

EXAMINING TEACHERS' SOCIAL NETWORKS

The use of SNA in studies on teacher networks and collaboration has grown alongside the reconceptualizations of professional development. SNA research on teacher leadership and socially mediated reform began to emerge in the early 2000s.[15] Toward the latter half of the decade, SNA studies focused on early career teachers and whole-school networks.[16] The studies revealed the strong influence of informal networks on teacher practice: informal networks shape teachers' attitudes toward reform, abilities to understand and implement new practices, information-sharing patterns, and commitment to ideas or practices.

These studies, in addition to other SNA workplace research, illustrate trends in networking characteristics that can help to inform and predict how teachers develop their informal networks. First, individuals tend to seek advice from people with whom they share demographic similarities and equal work status.[17] Secondly, individuals who develop diverse networks tend to demonstrate more innovation and have higher levels of social capital.[18] Finally, in dense close-knit networks, tacit knowledge and personal support are frequently exchanged, whereas in open networks, new information and ideas are often exchanged.[19]

These trends and findings were uncovered through a range of SNA approaches. For example, SNA studies can be *egocentric*, focusing on a social network reported by one person, or *whole network*, taking into account the ties reported by members of a group. SNA studies can examine different types of networks, such as friendship, advice, or status networks. Elsewhere we have used one approach to SNA that is particular to research on teachers—a measure of the practitioner-based social capital (PBSC) of teachers, which is defined as the resources, information, and support for effective teaching available through a teacher's social network.[20] PBSC focuses specifically on social capital related to teaching (such as years of experience, content knowledge or specification, and leadership experience), which helps to narrow the focus in examining teacher collaboration through networks.

Investigating PBSC can reveal the distribution of content knowledge in a network of teachers. These patterns of interaction in a group can determine the success or failure of a particular program or reform. For example, if teachers with high levels of content knowledge or expertise form an isolated clique in an advice network, other teachers will not have access to them for advice, which will decrease PBSC for many in the group. The goal in this case would not be to have the teachers with high content knowledge deluged by advice seekers (which would cause stress and overcentralization), but rather to find a balance in the network so that teachers seek advice from diverse others.

Teachers and program administrators develop expertise transparency when PBSC is revealed, examined, and strategically facilitated. Expertise transparency can be developed in three ways: (1) presenting the background and expert knowledge of the teachers to the group, (2) giving teachers strategies and opportunities to collaborate and learn about each other's expertise, and (3) discussing PBSC and explicitly encouraging collaboration with individuals who have different backgrounds or experiences. In the following research case description, we will describe how we investigated teachers' PBSC and implemented an intervention to develop teachers' expertise transparency.

THE ITEST-NANO TEACHER NETWORK STUDY

We used SNA to study the advice networks of urban high school teachers in a science professional development program. Our aim in the beginning of the study was simply to examine the PBSC and to see if we could use the information to help make the program more sustainable in year 2. We were surprised to learn that in year 1 many of the teachers with expert science knowledge were isolated from others in the informal advice networks. In year 2, we decided that we wanted teachers to have a clearer picture of each other's science expertise (i.e., develop expertise transparency) and more opportunities to share information. We implemented an intervention based on these principles using Ning (a Web-based social network software platform similar to Facebook, but accessible only by group members). Preliminary results are promising—collaboration (particularly online) increased in year 2. Below, we briefly describe the context, research design, intervention, and findings of the study.

Program Description

Our study is part of a comprehensive large-scale National Science Foundation–funded project under the program title Innovative Technology Experiences for Students and Teachers (ITEST). The ITEST program is designed to increase opportunities for students and teachers in underserved schools to learn and apply information technology concepts and skills in the STEM content areas. Our project, entitled "Nanotechnology and Bioengineering in Philadelphia Public Schools" (ITEST-Nano) aims to achieve the broader ITEST goals through a curriculum and instruction framework premised on five component variables addressing content knowledge, pedagogical content knowledge and workforce development goals: (1) real-world science and engineering applications, (2) educational technologies to build content knowledge, (3) information technologies for communication, community building and dissemination, (4) cognitively rich pedagogical strategies, and (5) STEM education and careers investigations.

In addition to the central curriculum and instruction goals, another major goal of the project is to build teaching capacities and self-directed interests toward program sustainability through communities of practice structures. These include working with groups of teachers from the same school, implementing an online comprehensive professional development database for peer-to-peer interaction, and requiring teachers from different schools to construct units collaboratively.

There were two parts to the scope and sequence of project activities, which entailed a three-week, seventy-five-hour teacher professional development workshop in the summer, during which teachers learned to construct and pilot curricular units based on the five component variables of the ITEST-Nano curriculum and instruction framework. These units were also aligned with school district standards for ninth-grade physical science and tenth-grade biology. The summer workshop was followed by school-year implementation of these units in teachers' classrooms.

During week 1 of the 2008 summer workshop, teachers attended workshops facilitated by experts in the five component variables of the program.

In week 2, teachers worked collaboratively to develop pilot modules of curricula. In week 3, teachers co-taught their pilot curricula with their collaborating partners. During year 1, we selected Google Groups to be the platform for online teacher collaboration. During year 2, teachers used a Ning network for this purpose.

The population of teachers were drawn from the School District of Philadelphia, a large urban district that serves 215,000 students, of whom 80 percent qualify for free or reduced-price lunch and 71 percent live in households under the federal poverty level. It is a racially diverse district, with African American students forming the majority (65.5 percent), followed by Hispanic students (14.5 percent), white students (14.2 percent), and Asian students (5.3 percent).

Data

To collect data on the teachers' social networks, we asked participants to complete a social network survey at the end of the summer workshop. The survey required participants to identify the people from whom they sought content-related advice (selecting from a list of the names of the other program participants). For each person listed, they were required to characterize the topic of advice, frequency and time period of request(s), mode of communication, and the main reason(s) for their choices (on the basis of a relationship type, knowledge, and/or social circumstances). Participants also described how well they knew the other participants in the program and the type of relationship they had or were forming (collegial, mentor, mentee, friendship, or other). In addition to the social network survey, we conducted pre-and postprogram content knowledge assessments, gathered observational data, conducted focus groups with the teacher participants, and analyzed online activities.

In order to examine the PBSC, first we calculated teachers' teaching characteristics index (TCI) scores, which gave a measure of the teachers' expertise in the variables most applicable to the goals of the ITEST-Nano curriculum and instruction framework. Accordingly, the TCI measure included number of years of teaching experience; amount of pedagogical content knowledge as determined by the kind of advanced postsecondary educational degree; formal leadership roles within their schools; generalized versus specialized subjects taught (e.g., eighth-grade general science versus eleventh-grade chemistry); experience with information and educational technologies (both self-reported and observed); initial understanding of nano content; and previous workshop experience in nanotechnology.[21] See table 7-1 for TCI scores of our year 1 cohort of teachers.

Next, we used survey data to measure teachers' perceived mentorship qualities (based on other teachers' reports on whether they seemed mentorlike). Together, these measures gave us a picture of teachers' expertise and their

TABLE 7-1
Scores for the Teaching Characteristics Index (TCI)

For each of the characteristics, teachers were assigned a numerical value of 0 or 1. Teaching experience (TE): less than 10 years = 0; equal to or more than 10 years = 1; advanced degree (AD): 0 = no or 1 = yes; leadership role (LR): 0 = no or 1 = yes; general or specialized subject (GS): 0 = general or 1 = specialized; self-reported technology use (Ts): 0 = low or 1 = high; the observed technology skills in the workshop (To): 0 = low or 1 = high; initial nano content knowledge (NC): 0 = low or 1 = high; previous workshop experience (WE) in nanotechnology: 0 = no or 1 = yes. Aggregate mean = 4, standard deviation = 1.30.

	TE	AD	LR	GS	T(s)	T(o)	NC	WS	Aggregate
Dana	1	0	1	1	1	1	0	0	5
Angela	1	1	0	1	1	1	0	0	5
Randy	0	0	1	0	1	1	0	0	3
Henry	1	0	0	1	1	0	1	1	5
Jane	1	0	0	0	1	0	0	0	2
Cindy	1	0	0	1	0	1	0	1	4
Lucy	1	0	1	1	1	1	0	0	5
Frank	1	0	0	1	1	1	0	0	4
Perry	1	0	1	1	1	1	1	1	7
Manny	0	0	1	1	1	1	0	1	5
Jake	0	0	0	0	0	1	1	1	3
Jerry	1	0	0	1	0	0	0	1	3
Andy	0	0	0	1	1	1	0	0	3
Zane	0	0	0	1	1	1	0	0	3

perceived accessibility. Finally, we used SNA data to find the in-degree scores of each teacher (how many people sought that person for help), which we used to map the distribution of TCI and mentorship qualities based on network ties. Our SNA data therefore focused on the in-degree advice network of the whole group. We used background data such as observations, online activity, and additional survey data to provide specific examples and explanations for networking activities.

Year 1

In year 1 sixteen teachers, ten male and six female, participated in the summer workshop from ten high schools and one middle school in the district. Cohort 1 was racially/ethnically diverse: seven teachers were white, six were

African American, and three were Asian. Courses taught ranged from grades 8 to 12 in the content areas of physical science, biology, chemistry, and physics. Teaching experience ranged from 1 to 39 years, with an average of s 15.8 years..

Although the number of participants was too low to analyze for statistical significance, the networking patterns of the group did give us a picture of what was occurring in the informal advice networks. As summarized in table 7-2, two patterns emerged. First, individuals with high TCI (expertise) scores were more isolated in the group than others in that they had the lowest in-degree scores.[22] For example, the top three teachers who had the lowest mentoring and in-degree scores (Manny, Perry, and Angela) had among the highest TCI scores. Second, individuals with higher mentorship qualities were most often sought for content-related advice, even if they had low TCI scores. In the first column of the table, Randy, who was perceived to have high mentoring qualities, had a relatively low TCI score.

These findings surprised us. We had organized the professional development workshop to provide opportunities for collaboration, and teachers *were* collaborating; however, the experts in the group were isolated. The group was not maximizing its potential PBSC.

The Intervention

Upon analysis of SNA data, observational data, focus group conversations, anecdotal conversations, and reflective remarks made by teachers about the curricular units, we found that teachers did not have a strong awareness of who had science content expertise. For example, on at least two occasions, a teacher expressed surprise that another teacher knew about some advanced concept being demonstrated in their unit. In addition, during focus group interviews several teachers stated that they wished there were more opportunities to share teaching experiences and STEM teaching strategies. There were several reasons that teachers may have had difficulty accessing information on expertise in the group. First, this information was never explicitly offered to the teachers. Second, teachers were not strongly encouraged to seek out a diverse range of opinion and advice; many tended to work closely with only one or two other individuals. For example, Angela, who had a doctorate in science education, communicated mostly with her unit construction partner throughout the three-week workshop; and a similar pattern of interaction—working solely with one other individual in the group—was observed for Perry (TCI score of 7), although our surveys revealed that he felt he had reached out to other teachers during the workshop. Therefore, we constructed an intervention for year 2 based on these assumptions. Our plan was to actively and explicitly reveal teachers' expertise and encourage teachers to seek each other for their expertise.

TABLE 7-2

In-degree scores of teachers grouped by in mentoring and TCI ranks

High mentoring Average in-degree score: 2.8		High TCI Average in-degree score: 2.0	
Cindy	2	Manny	0
Lucy	2	Perry	1
Mark	3	Angela	1
Dana	3	Lucy	2
Randy	4	Mark	3
		Dana	3
		Henry	4

Low mentoring Average in-degree score: 1.8		Low TCI Average in-degree score: 2.2	
Manny	0	Nancy	2
Perry	1	Jane	2
Angela	1	Jake	2
Andy	1	Zane	2
Zane	2	Jerry	2
Jerry	2	Randy	4
Nancy	2	Andy	1
Jane	2	Frank	3
Jake	2	Cindy	2
Henry	4		

We decided that a technological tool, the Ning platform, would work to support this plan. In year 1, teachers had the opportunity to use Google Groups, which allowed them to post and share information. However, they were unable to view each other's specific background knowledge and expertise through this software. The Ning network, however, was similar in design to social network sites, and included a profile page, a status bar, the ability to "friend" others and start or join groups, as well offering resource-sharing features like Google Groups. Four organizational parameters informed the intervention: (1) switch from Google Groups to Ning to allow for more collaboration and self-organizing, (2) require teachers to post information about their expertise and background on their profile pages, (3) assign Ning activities as part of summer workshop lessons, and (4) hold periodic "check-ins" during the workshop to discuss Ning participation and collaboration strategies.

Year 2

In year 2, seventeen cohort 2 teachers from thirteen high schools participated in the summer workshop. This was also a racially/ethnically diverse group: nine teachers were African American, six were white, and two were Asian. Courses taught ranged from grades 9 to 12 in the content areas of biology, chemistry, physical science, and Earth science. The average amount of teaching experience was 18.6 years, with a range of 4 to 33 years' experience.

While data continues to be collected and is yet to be comprehensively analyzed, initial results from year 2 are encouraging. Participants used the Ning site more frequently than Google Groups during the summer workshop. In year 1, with Google Groups, there were a total of six conversations (i.e., more than one person participating), and twenty-five broadcasts (posts made only by one individual). Comparatively, in year 2, there were twenty-nine conversations and eighty-nine broadcasts on Ning. Further, there was a greater diversity of topics in year 2, and teachers shared more than twice as much content-related information on Ning than on Google Groups. There is also evidence showing that teachers have communicated with each other more frequently on the Ning network during the school year to share resources, request directed help from peers for both curricular and technological instruction, and connect about difficulties experienced in implementation efforts. The language of communication is also notably different. Teachers appear to be using a more colloquial and collegial tone that indicates knowledge sharing rather than knowledge telling. We hypothesize that the shifts observed in their online professional development activities are a result of our efforts to increase expertise transparency as discussed below.

A NETWORK CONCEPTION OF COLLABORATION

Our study shows how SNA can be used as an effective evaluative tool for developing expertise transparency for program administrators and teachers. Drawing on our initial findings, we believe that expertise transparency is a professional development quality that should be actively cultivated. This can be done by revealing social network patterns by analyzing our measure of PBSC, having teachers share expertise and background knowledge, and offering teachers strategies and opportunities to seek advice and support from people with new or different ideas. Such activities are challenging and can be achieved only by changing the culture or conceptualization of collaboration itself. This network conception considers diversity of ideas and experiences as an asset; the alternative values commonality. When teachers develop expertise transparency, they come closer to realizing this network conception of collaboration.

As we continue into the third year of our professional development program, we are influenced by this new conceptualization. While we value self-organization into collaborative groups, we have learned from this study that self-organization should not mean unexamined organization—without explicit discussion and examination of teacher networks and backgrounds prior to and during collaborative activities, participants are likely to pay more attention to surface similarities than to valuable differences. We have also learned more about how technology can play a role in developing expertise transparency. The components of the Ning platform that allowed teachers to view each other's expertise and collaborate in a collegial online environment were important factors in developing expertise transparency and extending collaboration beyond the program.

The steps we took in developing expertise transparency supported our goal of program sustainability. Teachers in cohort 2 were presented with a new conceptualization of collaboration and strategic networking tools that encouraged them to access knowledgeable peers beyond the boundaries of the summer workshop. Further, SNA was a valuable tool in revealing complexities of the teacher community and the ways in which the participants collaborated. The additional dimension that SNA brought to our understanding of program effectiveness improved our practices as program facilitators. These research outcomes changed our long-term approach to program implementation. We are committed to developing expertise transparency in order to use what we know about participants' advice networks to improve the program structure and teacher collaborative learning.

CONCLUSION

This research offers a unique tool and perspective for examining reforms in professional development. In 1995, Lieberman called for a "radical rethinking" of conventional teacher professional development.[23] Since that time, professional development has undergone some reform and now reflects a more teacher-centered perspective. Although our field is moving toward embracing teacher knowledge and collaboration in professional development practices, we must not do so blindly, but rather with clear theoretical and empirical understanding of how teachers learn with others. To do so, we need to have tools and strategies that reveal what is happening under the surface, in the informal networks, as teachers collaborate and exchange knowledge. One such strategy is to develop expertise transparency among program participants and facilitators. This and other strategies that focus on social capital are valuable for researchers, administrators, and teachers, and can offer guidance or propel change, as they have done for us in our ongoing professional development efforts.

From a broader perspective, our study also contributes to social network theory and SNA. Kilduff and Krackhardt argued that perceptions of network ties have more impact on individuals' beliefs about other network members' social status than actual network structures.[24] Their research challenged the structuralist perspective that individual psychology should not be considered in SNA. Our research continues this line of research—looking not only at individuals' perceptions of ties, but also their awareness of others' expertise. While an awareness of "who knows what" by network members is valued by SNA scholars, this research places an explicit focus on expertise and highlights the role of this knowledge within a network that is primarily focused on knowledge sharing and creation.[25]

In research on schools, a central element of successful reform has been found to be teachers' capacity to cope with change.[26] Further, teachers' ability to change is heavily influenced by the social mechanisms that frame their interpretations and adjustments of policies.[27] These social mechanisms are often hidden in traditional research, but made visible through SNA. Our SNA research has attempted to use our knowledge of the informal social mechanisms to inform the development of our contemporary science professional development program.

PART 2

Leadership and Social Networks

CHAPTER 8

Leading and Managing Instruction

Formal and Informal Aspects of the Elementary School Organization

James P. Spillane, Kaleen Healey, and Chong Min Kim

Teacher knowledge is especially critical to instructional innovation.[1] To successfully implement reforms that advance new instructional strategies, many teachers will have to unlearn and relearn a great deal about what they teach and how they teach it.[2] Changing core dimensions of teaching, such as the knowledge represented in classroom tasks and classroom discourse patterns, is arduous and complex and depends on teachers developing new knowledge about instruction. As a result, successful instructional reform ultimately depends on the actions and interactions—or what many might label as work practice—of schoolhouse actors. School leaders, formal and informal, and classroom teachers determine the fate of reform initiatives, whether homegrown or initiated from outside the school. The available evidence also suggests that school leadership and management matters with respect to valued school outcomes such as student achievement. What seems especially critical vis-à-vis student achievement is school leaders' attention to matters of instruction.[3] A key dimension of leading and managing instruction involves knowledge development or, more specifically, the building blocks of knowledge—advice and information.

As organizational scholars have long recognized, efforts to understand organizational leadership and management must attend to formal and informal aspects of the organization.[4] The *formal* aspect refers to the organization as represented in official accounts and documents, which identify, among other things, formally designated leaders and their positions, responsibilities, committee memberships, and formal organizational routines. The dimension of the formal organization of interest in this chapter is formally designated leadership positions such as school principals, assistant principals, and instructional coaches. The *informal* aspect of an organization refers to the organization as lived by organizational members in their day-to-day work life: it is the organization as experienced by school staff. Attending to the informal organization, we expand our focus beyond formally designated school leaders in a school's advice networks to also include those individuals who are key advice givers but who have no formal leadership designation in their school—informal leaders. Taking a distributed perspective to school leadership and management, we attend to both formal and informal aspects of the school organization, exploring the role in instructional advice networks of both formally designated school leaders and school staff with no formal leadership designation.[5] Recent empirical work suggests that this sort of attention to a variety of schoolhouse actors is critical in any effort to understand school leadership and management.[6]

Social network theory and methods provide useful conceptual and methodological tools for examining how advice and information—the key ingredients of knowledge development—flow in organizations. Social network analysis allows us to tap into the role of formally designated leaders in instructional advice networks as experienced by school staff, rather than relying solely on formal accounts. Further, network methods enable us to identify informal leaders.[7] In this way, network analysis allows us to attend to relations between the formal and informal organization by examining the prominence of formally designated school leaders relative to informal leaders in advice giving. Social network theory also provides a set of core constructs and measures that form the basis for our efforts to theorize and empirically investigate relations between the formal and informal organization.[8] Two basic network measures—in-degree centrality and betweenness—provide us with a window into the role of key advice givers in a school's instructional advice network. Whereas *in-degree centrality* captures the number of people who go directly to a particular individual for advice, *betweenness* gives us another measure of how central a person is in an advice network by taking account of his or her direct as well as indirect ties to others in that network. Moving beyond a focus on individual measures, we use a network clustering algorithm to identify cohesive subgroups in advice networks in order to examine the role of formal and informal leaders at the subgroup level.[9] Further, in order to theorize about and measure the role of informal leaders in advice networks, we use social network theory on triadic relationships.[10] While these various measures and constructs have their limitations, they provide a valuable launching point for our efforts to theorize about relations between the formal and informal organization in school leadership and management.

In this chapter we examine the work of leading and managing instruction, focusing on the role of formally designated school leaders and informal leaders in their schools' instructional advice and information network. The term *formally designated leader* refers to a school staff member with a formal leadership position such as principal, assistant principal, or mentor teacher, whereas *informal leader* refers to a staff member with no formal leadership position but who occupies an influential position in the school's advice network. Our account is part of a larger initiative to develop study operations and measures that frame investigations of school leadership and management within a distributed perspective. Such work is essential in order to build and test theory on school leadership and management. Confining our analysis to the core elementary school subjects, mathematics and language arts, we draw on data from twenty-eight elementary schools in a midsized urban school district. After detailing our research methods, we describe the formal positions in schools for leading and managing instruction. We then consider how these positions figure in the informal organization as captured in the instructional advice and information networks in each school. We document considerable variation between schools in the congruence between the formal and informal organization. Next, we examine informal leaders. Focusing on two schools in our sample, we attempt to tease apart differences in formal and informal congruence. Turning our attention to subgroups, we examine the roles of formal leaders and informal leaders in the flow of advice and information within and between subgroups.

RESEARCH METHODOLOGY

We use data from twenty-eight elementary schools in one midsized urban school district in the United States that we call Cloverville. For the purpose of this chapter, we focus on our second round of survey data with school staff in these elementary schools that was collected in spring 2007.

Study Site and Participants

Data for this analysis are drawn from a larger study of school leadership and management in one public school district in the southeastern United States. In the 2006–2007 school year, the Cloverville district served 33,156 students, including 16,214 at its thirty elementary schools.

Data Collection

Staff members at each of Cloverville's schools completed a school staff questionnaire (SSQ) in the spring of 2007.[11] Of the 1,436 elementary school staff members in the sample, 1,194 completed the survey (an 83 percent response rate), though the response rate ranged from 63 to 100 percent by school. Two schools with response rates of less than 70 percent were dropped for this analysis, leaving us with twenty-eight schools and 1,123 respondents. See table 8-1 for demographic information about these schools.

Included in the SSQ were two sociometric questions regarding respondent's instructional advice-seeking behavior. Specifically, the questions ask,

TABLE 8-1
Elementary school descriptive statistics for the 2006-2007 academic year, n=28

	Mean	SD
Number of students	531.8	131.4
Number of faculty members	41.1	9.8
Percent free and reduced-price lunch eligible students	63.8	23.1
Percent white students	27.4	25.1
Percent African American students	63.4	29.6
Percent Hispanic students	4.2	5.0

"To whom do you turn in this school for advice or information about mathematics instruction?" and, "To whom do you turn in this school for advice or information about language arts or English instruction?" Participants could write the names of up to seven colleagues in spaces provided, and were also instructed that it was not necessary to fill in all seven open spaces.

Additionally, the SSQ asked participants about any formally designated leadership positions to which they were assigned, which permitted us to distinguish formally designated leaders from those without a formally designated leadership position. School staff were also asked to indicate their appointment and teaching responsibilities, which allowed us to differentiate formally designated leaders whose primary responsibility was classroom teaching from those whose primary responsibility was leading and managing. We consider those formally designated leaders who were *not* the primary instructor for any classes during a typical school day as full-time formally designated leaders, indicating that their primary responsibility was administration rather than teaching. Formally designated leaders who also had teaching responsibilities are considered part-time formal leaders.

Data Analysis

In this analysis we rely on several network measures to examine the alignment of the formal school structure with the informal advice-seeking networks that facilitate the flow of instructional information throughout the school. We acknowledge that other aspects of the formal structure, such as formal organizational routines, are also important considerations but beyond the scope of this chapter.

Using the sociometric data provided on the SSQ, we first calculated degree centrality measures for each staff member. *Degree centrality* is the simplest way of determining which actors are most central in a network and is measured in two ways: in-degree centrality and out-degree centrality. For both measures, centrality is simply a count of the total number of relations an actor has. Using an individual's in-degree centrality, which captures the number of coworkers who seek that individual out for instructional advice in either math or language arts, we identified key advice givers in the school. Given the potential for influence that is present in triadic relationships, individuals with an in-degree of two or greater were considered key advice givers.[12] Further, we delineated key advice givers who held a formally designated leadership position from those who held no such position. We consider individuals who have an in-degree of two or greater, but no formal leadership designation, as *informal leaders* in their school.

To further examine the role of formally designated leaders in the networks, we consider the *betweenness* scores of these individuals. These scores can only be calculated for nondirectional data, so the data is symmetrized as having a relation if either actor cites the other. Betweenness measures the probability that a path from any two actors takes a particular path, assuming that all lines have equal weight and that the shortest path will be taken. To measure the betweenness of actor i, we calculate the total number of geodesics (the shortest path), g, between all other actors that include i. We remove all of those that connect any two actors j and k that are longer than the shortest path, and then count together all of those that include i. We divide this by the number of paths using i. This accounts for the extent to which an actor lies between other actors.[13]

However, we can see that this does not control for the size of the network, so we control for this by dividing by the total number of possible pairs.[14]

Additionally, to identify nonoverlapping within-school subgroups, we used combined sociometric data regarding teacher's mathematics and language arts instruction and used Frank's network clustering algorithm, which has been employed in the natural sciences as well as social sciences.[15] In this clustering algorithm, staff members were assigned to subgroups in order to maximize the increase in the odds that a relationship occurs between a pair of actors if they are in the same subgroup relative to the odds of a relationship occurring if they are in different subgroups. Ultimately, we identified 121 subgroups across twenty-seven schools.[16]

SCHOOL LEADERSHIP AND MANAGEMENT:
FORMAL AND INFORMAL ASPECTS

While formal and informal aspects of the organization are related, they are not mirror images of one another.[17] We might think about aspects of the formal organization such as organizational charts and job descriptions as broad scripts or guides that more or less inform the work of organizational members. Still, these formal accounts are often weak road maps for how things actually get done from one day to the next in organizations.[18] For example, while the job description of a school principal might center on leading and managing instruction—and principals themselves might describe their responsibilities as focused on instruction in the actual enactment of the job—instruction might be marginalized relative to other responsibilities. The chains of command documented in organizational charts don't always reflect or capture what actually happens on the ground when decisions are made.

Differences between formal and informal aspects of an organization are not a result of duplicity on the part of organizational members or intentional subversion of organizational designs on their part. Formal accounts and descriptions are general and often abstract scripts about work; such abstractions are essential so that the formal entity can inform practice in different situations.[19] Further, the formal aspects can be used to give an account of how the organization works to external stakeholders and in this way lend legitimacy to the organization even if they do not reflect what organizational members actually do.[20]

Acknowledging differences between the formal and informal aspects of organizations does not mean rejecting one in favor of the other in investigating leadership and management arrangements. Indeed, attending to both formal and informal aspects and understanding relations among them is important.[21] Recent work presses for attention to both the formal and informal in efforts to understand leadership and management. A distributed perspective, for example, foregrounds formal and informal aspects of the school organization; it attends to those in formally designated leadership positions while also allowing for the possibility that school staff with no leadership designation may take responsibility for the work.[22] Further, by foregrounding practice and defining it in terms of interactions between school staff as mediated by aspects of their situation, a distributed perspective argues for investigating formal and informal aspects of the school organization in tandem.

The Formal Organization

Various studies document that formally designated leaders other than the school principal also have responsibility for leading and managing schools, though their responsibilities differ depending on their position.[23] A study of more than one hundred geographically dispersed U.S. elementary schools, for example, found that responsibility for leadership functions was typically distributed across three to seven formally designated leadership positions per elementary school.[24] Such positions included principals, assistant principals, program coordinators or facilitators, subject area coordinators or facilitators, mentors, master teachers, teacher consultants, and other "auxiliary" professional staff, such as family outreach workers.

Including the school principal, the average school in our sample had approximately thirteen formally designated leaders, though the number

TABLE 8-2
Formally designated leaders per school, n=28

	Mean	SD	Min.	Max.
Number of staff per school with formally designated leadership role	12.6	3.4	6.0	19.0
Percent of staff with formally designated leadership role	31.2	7.8	16.2	50.0
Ratio of formally designated leaders to all other staff	0.47	0.17	0.19	1.00
Number of staff with full-time formally designated leadership role	3.5	1.5	1.0	8.0
Percent of staff with full-time formally designated leadership role	8.6	3.8	3.0	19.0
Ratio of full-time formally designated leaders to all other staff	0.10	0.05	0.03	0.24

ranged from six to nineteen depending on the school. Roughly 31 percent of respondents in our study reported having a formally designated leadership role in their school (see table 8-2). Formally designated leadership positions included assistant principal, math coordinator, language arts coordinator, mentor teacher, school improvement coach, special program coordinator, and teacher consultant. Approximately 28 percent of these formally designated leaders were full-time, meaning that they were not the primary instructor for any class during a typical day and reported having at least one formally designated position. Including the school principal, the average number of full-time formally designated leaders per school was 3.5, with approximately 9 percent of the professional staff in the average school having a full-time formally designated leadership position (see table 8-2).[25]

As one would expect, the number of formally designated leaders was partially driven by school size, as indicated by a Pearson's correlation of .474 ($p<.05$). As schools vary tremendously in size, a better metric for formally designated leaders in a school is the ratio of formally designated leaders to school staff.[26] Our analysis suggests substantial between-school variation in the number of formally designated leaders for each staff member. The formally designated leader/all other staff ratio ranged from 1:5.2 to 1:1. So, while one school had one formally designated leader for nearly every other staff member, another had roughly one formally designated leader for every 5 staff members.

The full-time formally designated leader to all other staff (including other formally designated leaders who are not full-time) ratio ranged from roughly 1:35 to 1:4.2. While two schools had approximately one full-time formally designated leader for every 4 staff members, another had just one full-time formally designated leader for every 35 staff members. Examining the distribution of our 28 elementary schools, we see that the modal ratio of full-time formally designated leader to other staff is 1:12, or roughly one full-time formally designated leader for every 12 other staff members. Again, there is considerable variation across the sample schools (see figure 8-1).

Focusing for a moment on those formally designated positions that were specific to mathematics or language arts, we find that the average school had approximately 2.0 formally designated language arts coordinators and approximately 1.9 formally designated mathematics coordinators. The number ranged from 0 to 7 for language arts coordinators and from 0 to 5 for mathematics coordinators, depending on the school. Our analysis also reveals 12 full-time language arts coordinators and 6 full-time mathematics coordinators, signaling that it is somewhat rare for these formal leadership designations to be assigned to individuals who do not also teach at least one class in a typical day. In order to take into account the prevalence of these subject area coordinators among the rest of the school staff, we again consider the ratios. The ratio of language arts coordinators to all other staff ranged from 0:33 to 1:5.4, while the ratio for mathematics coordinators to all other staff ranged from 0:37.7 to 1:7.9. We acknowledge that these are likely conservative estimates of the support available for mathematics and language arts in that other formally designated leadership positions such as mentor teacher or teacher consultant very likely also had responsibility for mathematics and language arts instruction.

The Informal Organization

While respondents' self-reports of their positions gives us a sense of the organization in terms of formally designated leadership positions, we must also attend to the informal. The informal organization refers to the organization as experienced by school staff in their daily work. As noted earlier, while these two aspects of the organization are related, they are not mirror images.[27] Formally designated leaders don't always behave as the titles of their positions suggest. How did formally designated leaders figure in the instructional advice and information networks for language arts and mathematics, the two subjects that consume the bulk of the elementary school curriculum?

We examine this issue using social network data to construct two different measures of the congruence between the formal and informal organization.[28] First, we examine the percentage of the advice- and information-seeking ties that were directed toward formally designated leaders. We then consider another measure of the congruence between the formal and informal organization, turning our attention to the frequency with which formally designated leaders are also key advice givers in their school.

FIGURE 8-1   Ratio of full-time formally designated leaders to all other staff

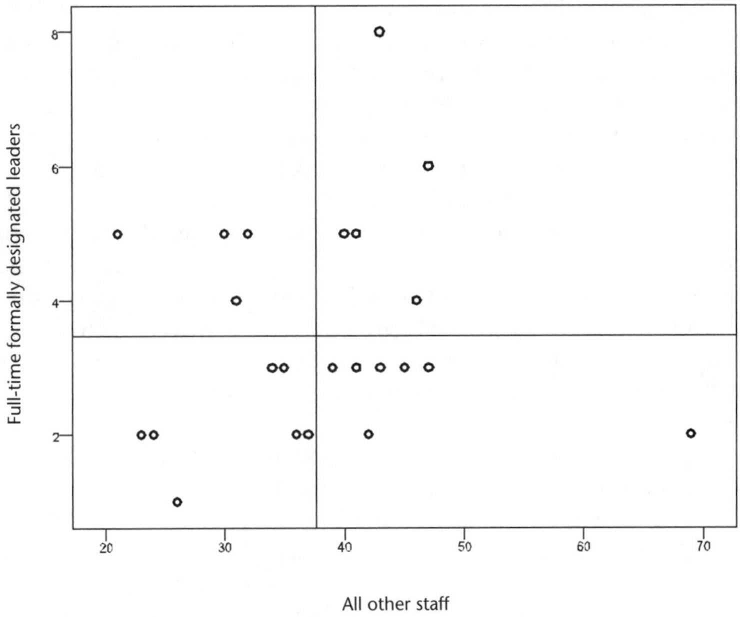

All other staff

The horizontal and vertical lines represent the mean number of full-time formally designated leaders and other staff, respectively.

Formally Designated Leaders in Advice and Information Networks

Examining the percentage of advice- and information-seeking relations about mathematics and language arts directed toward formally designated leaders, we find that on average, 57 percent of all mathematics advice interactions and 55 percent of all language arts advice interactions are directed toward formally designated leaders in any position. In just under half of the advice-seeking interactions, staff members with no formal leadership designation are sought out for advice or information about instruction. The mean values mask substantial variation between schools: the range of advice-seeking ties directed toward formally designated leaders for mathematics is from 17 percent to 86 percent and from 19.7 percent to 100 percent for language arts. Hence, in one school all the advice- and information-seeking interactions about language arts are directed toward formally designated leaders, whereas in another just one-fifth of those interactions are directed toward such leaders.

Though school principals accounted for just 1.9 percent of all language arts ties and 1.8 percent of all math ties in the average school, other full-time formal leaders figured prominently, particularly in language arts. In the average school, full-time formally designated leaders accounted for 26 percent of all language arts ties and 11 percent of all math ties. One might expect that mathematics coordinators would play a large role in the mathematics networks, but on average only 22 percent of all mathematics advice relationships are directed toward mathematics coordinators.[29] The prominence of math coordinators, however, varied widely across schools, with 0 to 59 percent of mathematics advice relations directed toward math coordinators at the schools in our sample. Similarly, on average, language arts coordinators account for only 21 percent of advice relationships in the language arts networks.[30] Again, this varied widely across schools, as 0 to 68 percent of language arts ties were directed toward language arts coordinators. We might expect these patterns in organizations with more organic, as distinct from mechanistic, structures.[31]

To take a closer look at the role of formally designated leaders in the advice and information networks, we defined anyone with two or more individuals seeking them out for advice as a key advice giver, regardless of their position. We designated such individuals as key advice givers because triadic relations are thought to be the basis for informal influence in organizations: relations embedded in triads are more durable and produce more pressure for conformity to group norms and behavior.[32] Using this definition, we identified 304 individuals as key advice givers, including 201 key advice givers in math and 226 in language arts.[33] On average, schools had 8.1 key advice givers for language arts and 7.1 for mathematics, but this ranged from 1 in one school to 18 in another for math, and from 1 in one school to 23 in another for language arts. Of those individuals identified as key advice givers in either subject, 49 percent had a formally designated leadership position. In other words, roughly half of the key advice givers for language arts or mathematics had no formal leadership designation. Again, this varies across schools, with over half of the formally designated leaders in 18 schools not serving as key advice givers in either math or language arts (see figure 8-2).

Against these two measures, principals and assistant principals do not play a large role in giving advice about mathematics and language arts instruction. Three principals emerge as key advice givers in mathematics, and three emerge as key advice givers in language arts. Assistant principals are slightly more prominent: 5 were identified as key advice givers in math and 9 in language arts. More striking, only 51 percent of the 57 language arts coordinators in our sample were identified by school staff as key advice givers for language arts, and of the 54 mathematics coordinators, only 57 percent were identified by their colleagues as key providers of instructional advice and information for mathematics (see table 8-3).

FIGURE 8-2   Frequency distribution of the proportion of formally designated leaders who are not key advice givers

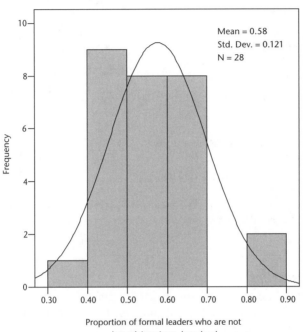

Mean = 0.58
Std. Dev. = 0.121
N = 28

Proportion of formal leaders who are not
key advice givers, by school

Our account to date has dwelled mostly on formally designated school leaders. Still, in analyzing the roles of formally designated school leaders in the instructional advice and information networks for mathematics and language arts, we have uncovered another group of individuals whom we label *informal leaders*. As noted above, we define informal leaders as those individuals who have two or more colleagues seeking them out for advice or information about mathematics or language arts but *who do not have* a formally designated leadership position. These individuals have the potential to exercise influence over their colleagues by virtue of being sought out to provide advice and information.

We identified 155 informal leaders in our sample, including 122 informal language arts leaders and 98 informal math leaders.[34] On average, schools had 4.4 informal language arts leaders, though this ranged from 0 to 19 informal leaders. Similarly, the average school had 3.5 informal math leaders, though this ranged from 0 to 16 (see table 8-4).

TABLE 8-3
Key advice givers per school, n=28

	Mean	SD	Min	Max
Key advice givers	10.9	5.4	2.0	28.0
Percent of formally designated leaders who are key advice givers	42.4	12.1	13.3	66.7
Key math advice givers	7.2	4.1	1.0	18.0
Percent of formally designated leaders who are key math advice givers	29.1	12.8	6.7	58.3
Key language arts advice givers	8.1	4.8	1.0	23.0
Percent of formally designated leaders who are key language arts advice givers	28.7	12.3	0.0	58.3
Percent of math advice seeking ties directed toward formally designated leaders	57.3	17.0	17.2	85.7
Percent of language arts advice seeking ties directed toward formally designated leaders	55.4	21.3	19.7	100.0

Formal-Informal Congruence Across Schools

Schools vary in the extent to which their formally designated leaders are sought out for instructional advice. Figure 8-3 shows that in nine of our sample schools, fewer than 50 percent of the math ties are directed toward formally designated leaders. For language arts, less than 50 percent of the ties were directed to formally designated leaders in ten schools (see figure 8-4). This variation suggests that the alignment of the formal and informal organization cannot be taken as a given and that reform efforts that operate solely through formally designated leaders may not be as effective in schools with low congruence.

Of course, formally designated leaders may not be *direct* conveyers of advice and information about mathematics and language arts, but they may still hold positions in the network that enable them influence the advice and information provided to teachers. One way they may do this is by connecting two other individuals in the network who would otherwise not be connected. In other words, the interactions between any two actors may depend on a third actor who connects them, making that third actor prominent in the network. To examine this, we considered another network measure of centrality, betweenness. *Betweenness* is a way of measuring the centrality of an actor that factors in the extent to which he or she provides an important link between other actors. Specifically, it measures the number of geodesic paths between other actors in the network upon which the individual falls as a proportion of the maximum betweenness that is possible in the network.[35]

TABLE 8-4
Informal leaders per school, n=28

	Mean	SD	Min	Max
Informal leaders	5.5	4.7	0.0	23.0
Percent of staff who are informal leaders	12.6	8.7	0.0	34.3
Informal math leaders	3.5	3.5	0.0	16.0
Percent of staff who are informal math leaders	7.9	6.9	0.0	28.6
Informal language arts leaders	4.4	4.0	0.0	19.0
Percent of staff who are informal language arts leaders	9.8	7.5	0.0	26.8

In the twenty-eight schools in our sample, formally designated leaders had significantly higher betweenness scores in both language arts (formal leaders = 1.22; others = 0.70; $p < .001$) and math (formal leaders = 1.09; others = 0.47; $p < .001$). This indicates that formally designated leaders were more likely than their colleagues without such a designation to connect staff members who weren't otherwise connected, and suggests that formal leaders may serve as intermediaries among school staff.

Contrasting Cases: The Formal and Informal Organization Up Close

To take a more in-depth look at relations between the formal and informal organization we consider cases of two schools in our sample—Jefferson and Roosevelt. Jefferson Elementary has 52 staff members in the SSQ sample, and a 90 percent response rate. Of the 628 students enrolled at Jefferson, 77 percent receive free or reduced-price lunches and approximately 80 percent are African American. Approximately 85 percent of Jefferson's students met or exceeded the state's standards in language arts, and roughly 89 percent did so in math.[36] Roosevelt Elementary has 58 staff members in the SSQ sample, and a 78 percent response rate. The school serves 646 students, 68 percent of whom receive free or reduced-price lunches and approximately 66 percent of whom are African American. At Roosevelt, approximately 78 percent of students met or exceeded the state's standard for language arts while 72 percent did so in math.

The school principals at these two schools have relatively similar characteristics and backgrounds. Jefferson's principal has been an administrator for nine years, three of which have been as principal at Jefferson. Roosevelt's principal has been an administrator for ten years and principal at Roosevelt Elementary for nine years. Both are white women. Jefferson's principal had been a teacher for nineteen years and Roosevelt's principal had taught for fifteen years prior to entering school administration. Both schools made Ade-

FIGURE 8-3   Frequency distribution of the proportion of math ties directed towards formally designated leaders

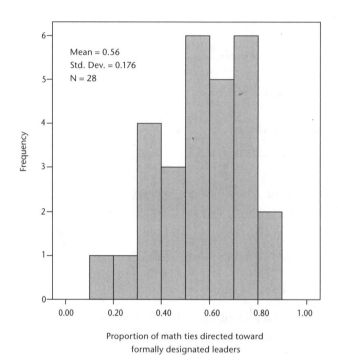

Proportion of math ties directed toward
formally designated leaders

quate Yearly Progress under NCLB in the two years prior to the survey, as well as in the school year in which the survey was administered. We selected these two schools because, even though they are relatively similar in terms of staff size, there were substantial differences between them in terms of the relations between formal and informal aspects of the organization.

Roosevelt had twelve formally designated leaders, including assistant principals, whole school reform coaches, special program (such as Title I) coordinators, language arts coordinators, math coordinators, other subject coordinators, teacher consultants and mentor teachers. Of these twelve formal leaders, seven were part-time and five were full-time. On average, these formally designated leaders had 17.6 years of teaching experience and had worked at Roosevelt for an average of 11.6 years.

At Jefferson, there were eleven formally designated school leaders, including assistant principals, whole school reform coaches, special program coordinators, language arts coordinators, math coordinators, other subject coor-

FIGURE 8-4 Frequency distribution of the proportion of language arts ties directed towards formally designated leaders

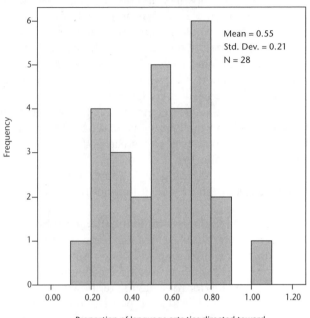

Proportion of language arts ties directed toward
formally designated leaders

dinators, school improvement coordinators, teacher consultants, and mentor teachers. Of these eleven formal leaders, eight were part-time and three were full-time. Jefferson's formally designated leaders had an average of 19.4 years of teaching experience and had worked at the school for 5.4 years.

While the number of formally designated leaders at the two schools was almost identical, there were substantial differences with respect to their prominence in the mathematics and language arts networks. At Roosevelt, 63 percent of the language arts advice-seeking ties were directed toward formally designated leaders, whereas just 29 percent of the advice-seeking interactions about language arts were directed to formally designated leaders at Jefferson. Similarly, at Jefferson just 34 percent of mathematics advice-seeking relationships were directed toward formally designated leaders, while 73 percent of such ties were directed to Roosevelt's formal leaders. Formally designated school leaders were more than twice as prominent in the instructional advice and information networks at Roosevelt than at Jefferson.

These differences are especially puzzling, considering that the schools are relatively similar in terms of staff numbers and formally designated school leaders. Perhaps formally designated leaders at Jefferson still occupied prominent positions in their networks despite not being key advice and information givers. Perhaps they served as go-betweens connecting other staff members who otherwise would not be connected. To explore this issue, we examined the betweenness scores for formally designated leaders in both schools. Formally designated leaders in Roosevelt had higher betweenness scores in the reading/language arts network (Roosevelt = 0.75, Jefferson = 0.32), and Jefferson's formal leaders had higher betweenness scores in the math network (Roosevelt = 1.36, Jefferson = 2.43), but neither difference was significant. Specifically, formally designated school leaders at Jefferson were just as likely as those at Roosevelt to serve as go-betweens, connecting other staff members with one another.

Still, at Roosevelt there was greater formal-informal congruence with respect to instructional advice and information, compared with Jefferson (see table 8-5).

This is all the more puzzling, considering that Jefferson fared significantly better than Roosevelt on those key organizational conditions thought critical for school improvement, including collective responsibility, teacher-teacher trust, principal trust and support, teacher collaboration, and teacher influence (see table 8-5). (Scales for these items are shown in the appendix.)While we cannot infer any causal relationships here, our analysis does call into question suggestions that the relationship between the formal and informal organization is simplistic. Greater congruence—a better match between the formal and informal organization—does not appear to be directly related to the conditions believed to be conducive to school improvement and instructional innovation.

As one might expect, considering differences between the two schools in terms of the prominence of its formal leaders in the advice network, Jefferson has ten informal leaders, whereas Roosevelt has just five informal leaders. At Jefferson, these informal leaders included teachers at each of the school's grade levels (K–5), as well as two special education teachers. The informal leaders at Jefferson had an average of 19.0 years of teaching experience and had spent 9.9 years at Jefferson. At Roosevelt, these informal leaders included a first-grade teacher, two third-grade teachers, and a teacher in the school's early intervention program. Roosevelt's informal leaders had an average of 15.3 years of teaching experience, including 7.8 years teaching at Roosevelt. In summary, Jefferson had informal leaders spread out across each grade level and in special education, whereas Roosevelt's informal leaders were confined to first and third grades and the school's early intervention program.

Our account to this point has centered mostly on individual leaders and their direct and indirect ties to other staff members. However, another impor-

TABLE 8-5
Differences in organizational measures in case study schools

	Roosevelt		Jefferson	
	Mean	SD	Mean	SD
Collective responsibility**	3.28	0.78	4.09	1.40
Teacher-teacher trust**	2.98	1.06	3.61	0.68
Principal trust and support***	2.77	0.71	3.53	0.49
Teacher collaboration*	2.93	0.83	3.32	0.74
Teacher influence***	2.34	0.70	3.11	0.48

*p<.05 **p<.01 ***p<.001

tant component of any network is the subgroup. Individual staff members' access to advice and information may be mediated by colleagues in their immediate circle—their subgroup.[37] Both theoretical and empirical work on social networks in organizations suggests that subgroups are important to the flow of information. Both intra- and inter-subgroup dynamics are important considerations with respect to the creation of knowledge and innovation.[38] Further, ties between subgroups are important in the implementation of reform in schools.[39] We examined the subgroups for both Jefferson and Roosevelt, paying particular attention to the role of formally designated school leaders and informal leaders both within and between subgroups. Our goal here is to try and tease apart the puzzle posed by differences between the schools in formal-informal congruence.

Examining the subgroup patterns for Jefferson and Roosevelt schools, we notice that they have five and three subgroups, respectively (see figures 8-5 and 8-6). While the staff size at the two schools was almost identical, Roosevelt's three subgroups consisted of nineteen staff, whereas Jefferson's five subgroups consisted of thirty staff members. Whereas seventeen staff members did not fall into any cohesive subgroup at Jefferson, at Roosevelt, twenty-eight did not. Indeed, just over 41 percent of the staff at Roosevelt belonged to a subgroup, whereas 64 percent did at Jefferson. One hypothesis, then, is that in schools where fewer staff belong to a subgroup, formally designated leaders may play a more prominent role in the advice and information network. In other words, subgroups may compensate for, or perhaps compete with, formal leadership arrangements. The direction of the relationship between subgroup membership and formal leadership is beyond the scope of the current analysis.

At Roosevelt, there were three subgroups each containing teachers from multiple grades (see figure 8-5; figure 8-7 shows Roosevelt's directed ties).

FIGURE 8-5   Sociogram for Roosevelt school with leader type and grade-taught level

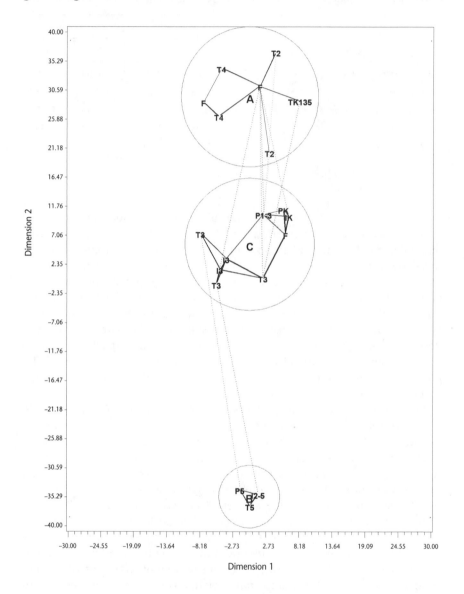

Note: Leader types are *full-time formal leader* (F); *part-time formal leader* (P); *informal leader* (I), and *teacher* (T). Grade levels taught are kindergarten (K) and first through fifth grade (1—5).

FIGURE 8-6   Sociogram for Jefferson school with leader type and grade-taught level

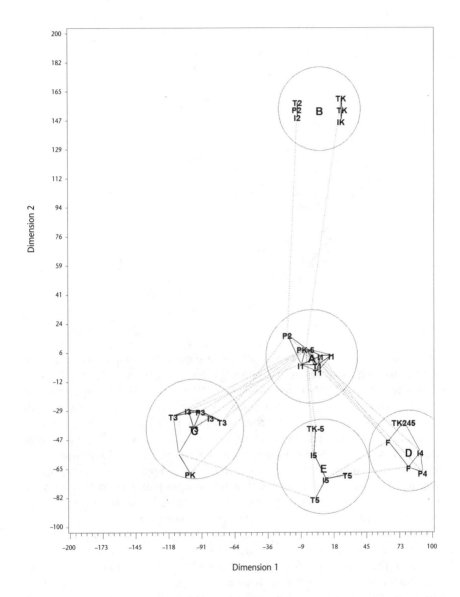

Note: Leader types are *full-time formal leader* (F); *part-time formal leader* (P); *informal leader* (I), and *teacher* (T). There was one missing case in both leader type and grade taught level in the sociogram.

FIGURE 8-7   Sociogram for Roosevelt school with directed ties

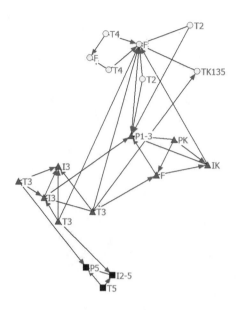

For example, subgroup A has teachers from second and fourth grades as well as a teacher who teaches across kindergarten and grades 1, 3, and 5. With respect to Roosevelt's five full-time formal leaders, their in-degree ranged from zero to eleven. Of these five full-time formal leaders, two holding multiple positions (e.g., mentor teacher, assistant principal) were in subgroup A; one, a special program coordinator, was in subgroup C; and the principal and an assistant principal belonged to no subgroup. One of the full-time formal leaders in subgroup A, who had five leadership positions, was an advice giver for eleven colleagues both within her subgroup and in other subgroups across multiple grade levels. The other two full-time formal leaders were each connected to two others *within* their respective subgroups.

Of the seven part-time formally designated leaders at Roosevelt, their in-degree ranged from zero to seven, and three were found in subgroups B and C. One of these part-time formally designated leaders was a key advice giver within and between subgroups, with an in-degree of seven, while another part-time leader had an in-degree of five. Four of the part-time formal leaders were not sought out by any colleagues for advice or information about instruction.

FIGURE 8-8   Sociogram for Jefferson school with directed ties

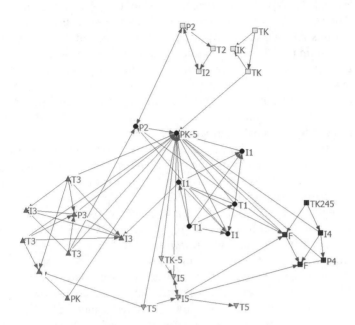

At Roosevelt, there were five informal leaders who had between two and four colleagues seeking them out for advice and information about instruction. Three of these informal leaders—two third-grade teachers and one kindergarten teacher—are in subgroup C. Of these three informal leaders, one had a total of four colleagues seeking him/her out for advice and information while another was sought out by three colleagues within the subgroup. At Roosevelt, the informal leaders appear to exercise influence mostly within subgroups, whereas formally designated leaders exercise influence both within and between subgroups.

At Jefferson, the five subgroups contain teachers from multiple grades, though there are clear concentrations of teachers by grade level in some subgroups (see figure 8-6; figure 8-8 shows Jefferson's directed ties). For example, subgroups C and E are made up primarily of third- and fifth-grade teachers, respectively. The three full-time formally designated leaders had an in-degree ranging from zero to four; two of these full-time formal leaders, both holding multiple formally designated positions, were located in subgroup D. The eight part-time formally designated leaders had an in-degree ranging from zero to twenty-one, with part-time formal leaders spread across four of the five subgroups, the exception being subgroup E, which had no formally designated leaders. One part-time formally designated leader, the mathematics coordinator, had a total of twenty-one advice ties, both within and between subgroups and cutting across grade levels. A second part-time formal leader, a program coordinator for another subject, was a broker of advice and information between subgroups, with four colleagues seeking him/her out for advice and information. The other six part-time formal leaders, some occupying multiple leadership positions, had an in-degree for instructional advice ranging from zero to four. Four of these part-time formal leaders had ties that spanned subgroups, whereas two had no ties.

At Jefferson, there were ten informal leaders, all female and distributed across the five subgroups—including one kindergarten, three first-grade, one second-grade, two third-grade, one fourth-grade, and two fifth-grade teachers—with an in-degree ranging from two to four. One of these informal leaders had an in-degree of four, stemming from third-grade teachers *within* her subgroup. Another informal leader had an in-degree of three, because she was sought out by first-grade teachers *within* her subgroup. These informal leaders were advice givers within their subgroups.

In both schools, most informal leaders were advice givers *only* within their subgroup, while some served as brokers or boundary spanners between subgroups. Also in both schools, some formally designated leaders served as key advice givers within but also between subgroups. Indeed, whereas informal leaders were less likely to be boundary spanners linking different subgroups, formally designated leaders were more likely to play this role. With respect to the distribution of formally designated leaders across subgroups, at Jefferson all but one of the subgroups contained a formally designated school leader, whereas at Roosevelt all three subgroups contained a formally designated school leader. One possibility, then, is that high formal-informal congruence is not so much a function of the overall number of formally designated schools leaders but how these individuals are spread across subgroups.

Situating Formal and Informal Leaders in Subgroups

Our two case schools suggest that subgroups may be important in understanding relations between the formal and informal organization. We constructed subgroups based on ties between school staff for mathematics and language arts in all twenty-seven schools for which we had identified subgroups.[40] Our analysis found 121 subgroups across the twenty-seven schools, ranging from three to seven depending on the school. Ninety-five subgroups (79 percent) had at least one full-time or part-time formally designated leader. Hence, the formal organization was represented in more than three-quarters of the 121 subgroups.

Part-time formally designated leaders were especially important in accounting for the strong presence of the formal organization because 68 subgroups

(57 percent) included part-time formally designated leaders but no full-time formal leaders. Absent these part-time leaders, over half of all subgroups would be without a formally designated leader. Three-quarters of all subgroups had a part-time formally designated leader. At the same time, 68 percent of the subgroups included at least one informal leader suggesting that the informal organization was also well represented among subgroups. At the same time, only 14 percent of all subgroups included an informal leader but no formally designated school leader. Of the 121 subgroups across the twenty-seven schools, 119 (98 percent) had at least one connection to other subgroups within their school.

METHODOLOGICAL CHALLENGES IN USING SOCIAL NETWORKS TO INVESTIGATE SCHOOL LEADERSHIP AND MANAGEMENT

Using social network instruments to study school leadership and management comes with its share of methodological challenges. We focus on two issues here. First, there is the issue of validity; that is, the question of whether these social network survey instruments measure what they purport to measure. How are respondents making sense of the questions we ask them? Second, question-order effects are an important consideration if one acknowledges that the work of leadership is subject-specific and designs instruments that attempt to measure both the multidimensional networks and the validity of the dimensional comparisons (e.g., mathematics compared with language arts advice and information networks).

Validity

To examine the validity of the survey, we conducted two studies. The first involved administration of the SSQ's network questions in twenty-two schools and interviews with a subsample of school staff in six of these schools. The second study involved cognitive interviews in which interviewees were asked to "think aloud" as they completed a revised version of the network questions. Overall, our findings, reported in detail elsewhere, indicate that the SSQ did identify leadership operationalized as social influence interactions related to advice and information.[41] Our analysis of the second study's interview responses indicates that teachers interpreted the question "To whom have you turned for advice or information about teaching [subject X]" as we had intended, describing interactions that were intended to influence their teaching of a particular subject. Several teachers explicitly distinguished advice seeking that was intended to influence teaching from interactions that were not intended to influence teaching. In all cases, as interviewees described the kinds of advice they received from the people they listed, they tied their descriptions back to the particular subject they had been asked about.

Our analysis also suggests some reasons for caution. First, the prevalence of informal interactions over formal interactions is somewhat surprising, and it is difficult to figure out whether it is a function of the SSQ design or the actual interactions engaged in by school staff members. With respect to instrument design, one possibility is that the wording of the question may prompt respondents to focus on informal exchanges and to ignore interactions that occurred as part of formal routines and meetings. Specifically, getting advice or information from people in a meeting may be construed by respondents as not intentionally or actively *seeking out* advice or information from someone. Further, asking "To *whom* have you turned . . ." may predispose respondents to focus on interactions with one other person (dyadic interactions) rather than interactions that involve multiple people. Hence, the current SSQ may be better designed to pick up informal leadership and may underreport on formal leadership. Still, our data might be capturing what school staff actually experience in their daily work. For example, informal interactions are likely much more prevalent than interactions in formal organizational routines and meetings that happen only weekly or monthly.

A second caution concerns directionality, and in particular our method of identifying leaders. Our analysis of interview data suggests that some social influence interactions were bidirectional—a two-way street—though this was not always reflected in the survey responses. Specifically, the SSQ may be a more accurate in identifying the *participants* in social influence interactions than in nominating the advice givers as the *leaders*. At the same time, if multiple individuals identify the same person, then we might conclude that this person is very likely a leader for instruction or has considerable opportunity to lead instruction.

A third caution from our analysis of the "think aloud" interviews is that there were some inconsistencies in what teachers included as *advice* or *information*, particularly when it came to the inclusion of teacher observations and the informal bouncing around of ideas. Three teachers brought up observations in the interview; of these three, two *included* observations, and one *excluded* them. As survey designers, we would like for teachers to consider observations of their colleagues' teaching as potential advice and information-seeking interactions. Not all teachers interpreted the prompt to include observations. One teacher explicitly excluded those she observed, noting "Well . . . there are certain teachers . . . I see what they're doing in their classroom and that might influence (my teaching), like the seventh-grade teacher. And some of these teachers I feel like I didn't even necessarily go to them to ask things; it was just like looking and observing things they do." In some respects, then, the SSQ, because of its suggestions of verbal (or even written) exchanges, may underreport interactions that mostly or exclusively involve observation.

Question-Order Effects

We have explored ways that surveys designed to collect multidimensional social network data are vulnerable to question-order effects, using a split-ballot experiment embedded in an online multiple name-generator survey.[42] Using a randomized experiment embedded in two studies of advice networks among elementary and middle school teachers, we examined the effects of question order on responses to multiple name-generator surveys (e.g., language arts and mathematics advice networks). Specifically, we randomize the order of the math and reading prompts in our online survey with these two samples of teachers.

We found a consistent pattern of question-order effects in the two samples. The reading name generator reveals significant differences between treatment groups in the distribution of out-degree; respondents in the math-first treatment, who received the reading name generator after first answering the math name generator, list an average of 1.33 fewer names than respondents in the reading-first treatment, a decrease of 50 percent in the number of names generated. In contrast, results from the math name generator do not display a significant difference between treatment groups. In the elementary school sample, respondents in the math-first treatment list an average of 0.09 fewer names for mathematics than respondents in the reading-first treatment, a difference that is neither large in magnitude nor statistically significant. In the middle school sample, math-first respondents list even fewer names, on average, than reading-first respondents, though the difference is still not statistically significant.

If the purpose of our research were only to determine whether teachers sought more advice about reading or about math, we would reach opposite conclusions if we looked only at the reading-first treatment or only at the math-first treatment. Data from the reading-first treatment suggest that the average reading out-degree is significantly larger than the average math out-degree. On the other hand, data from the math-first treatment suggest that the difference between reading and math is much smaller and statistically insignificant.

DISCUSSION AND CONCLUSION

The analyses reported here are part of a larger initiative to develop study operations and measures in order to build and test hypotheses about school leadership and management. In this chapter, we focused in on one aspect of this work—the relations between the formal and informal organization related to managing and leading instruction in schools. By drawing on conceptual and methodological tools from social network analysis, we have captured and diced up relations between the formal and informal aspects of the school organization in various ways in order to capture between-school differences. Our account documents considerable between-school variation on numerous study operations and measures intended to capture relations between the formal and informal organization with respect to leading and managing instruction. Further, we report on our preliminary hypotheses using these measures. While formally designated leaders figure prominently in the advice networks of some schools, they figure much less prominently in other schools; our measures of formal and informal congruence pick up on considerable variation between schools. Our preliminary analysis also suggests that subgroups may play a role in mediating relations between the formal and informal organization, and that part-time formally designated leaders may be especially important in representing the formal organization across different subgroups within schools. Our ongoing work here involves combining these measures with measures of other dimensions of school leadership and management (e.g., team diversity) in order to theorize what factors might account for variation in school leadership and management arrangements between schools, *and* on the relations between combinations of these measures and valued school outcomes such as instructional innovation and student achievement.

Our analysis shows how basic social network measures can be combined to develop new study operations and measures for examining relations between formal and informal aspects of the school organization. In particular, our work develops some new study operations and measures for scholars investigating school leadership and management from a distributed perspective—operations and measures that go beyond simply aggregating the number of school leaders—to take account of both formal and informal sources of leadership. Further, we show how analyses that include multiple levels of the school organization simultaneously—individual, subgroup, and organization—provide new insights into relations between formal and informal aspects of the organization. Our account in this chapter suggests that using social network theory and methods provides potentially powerful ways of measuring relations between formal and informal sources of school leadership and management. We are in the early stages of this analysis, but our preliminary work suggests that social network analysis has much to contribute to the field.

Our account also suggests some epistemological and methodological cautions when using social network approaches. Whereas basic network measures offer insights into relations between formal and informal sources of leadership and management in school, in order to realize their full potential we will have to combine these measures in various ways, carefully theorizing about their use to measure school leadership and management. This chapter also captures some basic methodological challenges in designing social network surveys, including how question-order effects can influence staff responses to multiple name generators. Similarly, our account suggests that the wording of network questions is critical in order to generate valid and reliable data across subjects.

With respect to relations between the school organization and classroom instruction, we documented considerable between-school variance within the same school district on various dimensions of formal and informal relations. Our account suggests that formal-informal congruence is neither simply nor linearly related to organizational conditions generally deemed critical for school improvement. Specifically, while it is tempting to argue that formal and informal congruence might be predictive of valued outcomes, our account does not support this conclusion. We suspect that this is the case because we have not included other measures of school leadership and management arrangements. We have relied in this chapter on correlation-based approaches to analysis in examining relations between our measures of relations between the formal and informal organization. This variable centered approach has limitations in that it fails to take into account that causation is typically a function of combinations of factors, what Ragin terms "causal recipes.".[43] Following Ragin's lead, our ongoing work uses fuzzy set theory in mathematics to identify causal recipes that might account for particular leadership and management arrangements in schools *and* that might be predictive of valued school outcomes. Our efforts here are preliminary—hypotheses generating and theory building as a precursor to theory testing work in this domain.

While this chapter focused chiefly on the fruits and follies of using social network approaches in research on school leadership and management, our account does point to the potential uses of social network analysis for school practitioners and policy makers. At one level, our account highlights the potential of social science research using social network theory and methods to generate important insights into school leadership and management arrangements. Beyond this somewhat conventional contribution to the world of practice, our work also suggests that social network data can be especially helpful in engaging school practitioners in reflection on leadership and management arrangements in their schools. First, we have used our social network data to draw school leaders' and teachers' attention to particular dimensions of school leadership and management arrangements for instruction, such as the relations between formal and informal sources of leadership. Second, we have used our social network maps and measures with school leaders to engage them in diagnosing school leadership and management arrangements in particular schools, often their own schools. Using social network maps and measures from actual schools, we have engaged practitioners in diagnosing patterns of instructional advice seeking in schools and encouraged them to consider the implications of their diagnosis for efforts to reform curriculum and instruction in particular school subjects. Our experience with these efforts to date suggest that social network based approaches to researching school leadership and management can have both indirect and direct relevance to practice and policy.[44]

This chapter draws on and extends previous analyses especially Spillane, Hunt, Healey, 2009; Spillane & Healey, 2010.

TECHNICAL APPENDIX

Collective responsibility ($\alpha = .80$)

Number of cases = 92   Number of items = 3

How many teachers in this school do the following?
(1 = never; 2 = less than half; 3 = about half; 4 = most; 5 = nearly all)

- Take responsibility for helping one another do well
- Help maintain positive student behavior in the entire school
- Take responsibility for improving the overall quality of teaching in the school

Teacher trust ($\alpha = .72$)

Number of cases = 92   Number of items = 4

Please indicate the extent to which you agree or disagree with the following statements about the school in which you work. (1 = strongly disagree; 2 = disagree; 3 = agree; 4 = strongly agree)

- Teachers at this school respect colleagues who are expert in their craft
- Teachers in this school trust each other
- Teachers in this school really care about each other
- Teachers respect other teachers who take the lead in school improvement efforts

Principal trust and support ($\alpha = .91$)

Number of cases = 92   Number of items = 7

Please mark the extent to which you disagree or agree with each of the following:
(1 = strongly disagree; 2 = disagree; 3 = agree; 4 = strongly agree)

- I feel respected by the principal
- The principal makes me feel comfortable to try new things in the classroom
- I trust the principal at his or her word
- It's OK in this school to discuss feelings, worries, and frustrations with the principal
- The principal takes a personal interest in the professional development of teachers
- The principal and teachers collaborate to make this school run effectively
- The principal is available when I need to see him/her

Teacher collaboration ($\alpha = .83$)

Number of cases = 92   Number of items = 10

This school year, how often have you had conversations with colleagues about the following topics? (1 = never; 2 = a few times per year; 3 = a few times/month; 4 = 1–2 days per week; 5 = more than 2 days/week)

- What helps students learn the best
- Development of new curriculum
- The goals of this school

- Managing classroom behavior
- Your reading/language arts or English instruction
- Your math instruction
- Content or performance standards in reading/language arts or English
- Content or performance standards in math

This school year, how often did you have scheduled meetings with other teachers in this school to discuss and plan curriculum or teaching approaches? (1 = never; 2 = once or twice a year; 3 = once every other month; 4 = once a month; 5 = 2-3 times a month; 6 = once a week; 7 = more than once a week)

This school year, how often did you have in-depth discussions about your teaching with any of the following? (1 = never; 2 = once or twice a year; 3 = once every other month; 4 = once a month; 5 = 2–3 times a month; 6 = once a week; 7 = more than once a week)

- Another classroom teacher

Teacher influence (α = .81)
Number of cases = 92   Number of items = 7

How much influence do teachers have over school policy in each of the areas below? (none = 1; a little = 2; some = 3; a great deal = 4)

- Hiring professional staff
- Planning how discretionary school funds should be used
- Determining which books and instructional materials are used in classrooms
- Establishing the curriculum and instruction program
- Determining the content of in-service programs
- Setting standards for student behavior
- Determining goals for improving the school

CHAPTER 9

Between Leaders and Teachers

Using Social Network Analysis to Examine the Effects of Distributed Leadership

William R. Penuel, Kenneth A. Frank, and Ann Krause

It is rare today that schools invest responsibility for school change in just one leader. Instead, leadership is spread across a number of actors and settings requiring intensive interactions and among school leaders and between leaders and teachers. A network approach to analyzing those interactions can help scholars assess the effectiveness of distributed leadership for promoting school change by considering how teachers access resources and expertise through interactions. In this chapter, we elaborate on the hypothesis that teachers' implementation of reform practices can be partly explained by collegial interactions of the type fostered within distributed leadership practice.

We provide evidence for the hypothesis that distributed leadership practices can effect meaningful distributions of resources and expertise in schools from a study of twenty-one schools engaged in schoolwide reform efforts. We combine social network analysis with an analysis of changes in teacher practice to show how interactions with more experienced peers and with coaches and mentors in schools that exemplify distributed leadership practices can lead to changes in teacher practice. In contrast with earlier studies of distributed leadership, however, we focus not only on networks of leaders but also on the collegial networks of all school actors responsible for instructional improvement, including classroom teachers.

THE DISTRIBUTED LEADERSHIP PERSPECTIVE

The distributed perspective is a cognitive view of leadership that draws inspiration from the idea that the cognition involved for carrying out most complex activities requires coordination of people, tools, and practices.[1] This perspective deemphasizes individual characteristics in favor of a more interactive perspective on the practice of leadership. In contrast with views of leadership that focus on the characteristics or actions of individuals in positions of authority, a distributed leadership perspective emphasizes that leadership is "stretched over" both people and practices.[2]

Distributed leadership is a promising framework for addressing a fundamental challenge of school reform: ensuring that *all* teachers in a school have access to the resources and expertise they need to implement innovations.[3] Studies of instructional practice show wide variation between classrooms in the same school, even when they are engaged in a common reform effort.[4] Success in improving instruction across all classrooms in a school, then, requires leadership practices that improve the distribution of relevant expertise and resources within that school.[5] The distributed leadership perspective thus leads to the following hypothesis (stated at the school level):

> H_1: The more widely distributed leadership is across people and practices in a school, the more, on average, teachers in that school will implement school reforms.

COLLEGIAL INTERACTIONS AND DISTRIBUTED LEADERSHIP

Distributed leadership is fundamentally an interactional perspective on leadership, emphasizing the way that leadership is constituted in interactions between people within particular situations. To date, research on distributed leadership has given the most attention to studying interactions between leaders and teachers.[6] However, it is teachers who are most directly responsible for enacting instructional reforms in their classrooms, and a critical goal of leadership is to improve teaching and learning.[7] Therefore, to gain a better understanding of distributed leadership and its effects, it is necessary to form a conceptualization of practices of distributed leadership that lead to productive interactions between teachers with respect to matters of instruction and facilitate access to outside resources such as professional development.

HOW INTERACTIONS FACILITATE CHANGE IN PRACTICE: THE ROLE OF SOCIAL CAPITAL

The interactions between teachers constitute a resource in support of teachers' implementation of reforms. This resource, which teachers access through interactions with colleagues, can be considered a form of social capital.[8] Our definition of social capital here is consistent with contemporary sociological theorists' definition in that it differentiates two key components of social capital: relationships and resources.[9] *Relationships* or *social ties* are important to the extent that one can access resources or expertise through them. The value of particular relationships, in turn, depends on the value of the resources exchanged as people interact with one another. The value of those resources is partly a function of the quality of these resources, the social setting, and their affordances for action.[10] Thus, as teachers interact informally, they may share knowledge and expertise, which then affects their ability to adopt new innovations.

For school reforms, one of the critical resources teachers can access is the expertise of their peers. *The subject matters*—in other words, expertise must be conceptualized in terms of the specific knowledge, experience, and skills necessary for implementing particular reforms.[11] For a mathematics reform initiative, a teacher might be an expert relative to her peers, but in a language arts initiative, that same teacher might be considered more of a novice. Therefore, the value of expertise a teacher can access through her ties with others for implementing a reform is likely to be linked closely to the know-how of colleagues with respect to implementation. We would predict:

H_2: A teacher will implement school reforms more the higher the level of implementation (that is, the expertise) of those with whom she interacts.

THE SOCIAL CONTEXTS OF LEADERSHIP

When social capital is defined as above, the focus is primarily on the level of the individual. It is the individual teacher who accesses expertise and the individual teacher who makes a relatively autonomous decision to implement a reform. This focus on the individual helps us to understand the value of particular interactions for facilitating change in practice, but a distributed leadership perspective forces us to consider the broader social context in which these interactions take place. In particular, we must attend to the implications of how people respond to interactions with multiple people over time in different situations.

Our second hypothesis is stated in terms of the *sum* of the expertise of those who surround them, and it is not stated in terms of the social context. But diffusion can occur as teachers' *conform* to the behaviors of those with whom they interact or share a common setting. Thus a teacher who interacts with several others who have extensively implemented a practice may increase her own level of implementation by conforming to colleagues' behavior in order to avoid being ostracized. Conformity in this example is a response to social context; correspondingly, teachers should respond to the *mean* behavior of those around them. Thus a teacher whose social context is defined by two people whose practices have been strongly influenced by a reform should be more likely to implement the reform than a teacher whose social context is defined by ten people whose practices have not been strongly influenced by a reform. This would not necessarily be the case if the individual responded primarily to the resources to which she had access, which could accumulate over several low-level implementers as well as a few high-level implementers. The distinction leads to the following hypothesis:

H_3: Teachers' levels of implementation respond to the mean level of implementation of those in their social contexts.

A second implication of the need to focus on teachers' response to interactions is that it is important to understand how teachers perceive their context. Teachers are likely to respond differently to accessing help from a mentor or colleague in a school in which teaching is viewed as a private matter than in a school in which teachers routinely discuss problems of teaching practice with peers.[12] In the latter type of school, norms of shared responsibility for student learning facilitate instructional improvement because teachers are able to identify strongly with the school's organizational goals.[13] The ability of individuals to place their trust in colleagues can function similarly as a "resource for reform" because it helps to moderate the risk and uncertainty involved in adopting new practices.[14] Relational trust allows leaders and teachers more latitude and discretion in making difficult decisions, creates clearer understandings of role obligations, and sustains commitment to improving student outcomes. Macy and colleagues also argue that perceptions of collective efficacy are a key to collective action—people are more likely to allocate resources to a collective when they perceive that the collective is likely to be effective and that their allocations will contribute to the collective effort.[15] Thus, we hypothesize that:

H_4: Teachers' perceptions that their colleagues are trustworthy and share a common commitment to students make them more likely to implement reforms.

A third and final implication concerns the definition of the social context. Frank and Fahrbach show that the social influence occurs through remarkably different mechanisms, depending on the density of the network.[16] In dense networks, informational resources such as expertise can flow through many indirect as well direct interactions. Thus a teacher can be influenced by expertise in her social context even if she does not interact directly with the source of expertise. In fact, a single source of expertise within a dense network may be sufficient to support a change in behavior, with all other sources being redundant. By implication, a teacher may be only *moderately* influenced by any single interaction that *is* embedded in a dense social network. By contrast, interactions that are not embedded in a dense social network should contain unique and valuable resources.[17] By implication, a teacher may be *strongly* influenced by each interaction that is *not* embedded in a dense social network.

The conditioning of the effect of access to resources on the density of the network suggests that we attend to the relative density of the network in which any given interaction resides. Systemically, this implies that we characterize social structure in terms of cohesive subgroups in which interactions are concentrated. The subgroups may consist of teachers who share a similar assignment (e.g., all the fourth-grade teachers), a common history (e.g., they came to the school at the same time), or a common social or cultural identity. Extant evidence suggests interactions among faculty in a school may well be concentrated within cohesive subgroups.[18]

The structuring of interactions within and between subgroups can help us understand how resources flow and consequently how leadership is distributed within schools. In particular, by locating help provided relative to subgroups, we can explore whether teachers are more influenced by members of their own subgroup or members outside their subgroup. Members of one's own subgroup may define a social context to which teachers are likely to conform—it is difficult to be the only second-grade teacher not employing phonics. On the other hand, members of other subgroups may hold expertise that is less readily available, and therefore more valuable. This suggests the following hypothesis:

H_5: A teacher is equally influenced by members of her subgroup and others outside her subgroup.

METHODOLOGY

Sample

The sample includes 425 school staff from twenty-one schools from a single state in the U.S. Pacific West region. In constructing our sample, we sought to include schools that (1) were engaged in a reform initiative intended to have a *schoolwide* influence on teachers' practice and (2) had distributed leadership across people and practices, evidenced by assignment of responsibility for reform to multiple actors in a school and by allocation of time for teachers to meet regularly to discuss their school's initiative. Our sample included schools that had different foci; in all but one case, the reform was locally defined at the school or district level, rather than following a specified whole-school reform model. Locally defined schoolwide initiatives are the most commonly adopted type of school reform models, and also the most problematic with respect to implementation.[19] Table 9-1 indicates the focus areas of initiatives for the schools in the sample.

There was evidence that schools in our sample did distribute leadership over multiple actors and practices. An average of 2.76 (SD = 1.58) teachers in each school self-identified as "formal" leaders of their school's reform efforts

Table 9-1
Focus of initiatives at schools in the sample

Focus of initiative	Number of schools
Literacy/language acquisition	5
Technology integration	4
Data-based decision making	3
Restructuring the school	3
Fostering students' social development	2
Creating standards-aligned assessments	2
Lesson study (review of lessons and student work)	1
Comprehensive instructional improvement	1

and another 1.86 (SD = 2.08) as informal leaders of their school's initiative. Also, the schools in our sample did share a commitment to fostering teacher collaboration about their school's initiative: teachers reported regularly attending multiple team meetings in which the initiative was the focus.

The school staff we surveyed included regular faculty members in schools, as well as specialized staff whose chief assigned function in their school was to promote the schoolwide initiative. In our research, furthermore, teachers could and did nominate *any member* of the school staff (including the principal) as someone who provided them with expertise or resources to help them implement their school's initiative. Thus, our social network data include so-called "positional" school leaders. Table 9-2 summarizes key characteristics of faculty members in our sample.

On average, teachers in the sample reported having thirteen years of experience in classroom teaching (SD = 10), including 6.7 years (SD = 6.6) at their current school. The median class size was twenty-two students. More than three-quarters of the teachers were female, and the vast majority of faculty members, as the table indicates, held a clear credential. Consistent with the ratio of elementary to secondary schools in the sample, the majority of teachers in the study were elementary-level teachers.

Measures

A questionnaire administered to all staff with responsibilities for classroom teaching in fall 2004 (time 1) and again in spring 2005 (time 2) provided us with data to characterize the social ties between faculty at the school, their perceptions of norms governing collegial interaction at the school, reports about how much the reform had influenced their teaching practice at the beginning of the study and at the end, their roles in the reform, and participation in formal team and committee meetings in which the reform was dis-

TABLE 9-2
Characteristics of faculty members in the sample

	Number	%
Gender		
Male	73	17.2%
Female	352	82.8%
Race/ethnicity		
White	338	79.5%
African American	11	2.6%
Hispanic/Latino	43	10.1%
Asian	18	4.2%
Other/unknown	15	3.5%
Certification status		
Provisional	57	13.4%
Emergency	5	1.2%
Clear	341	80.2%
National board	9	2.1%
Missing	13	3.1%
*Teaching assignment**		
Pre-K	3	0.7%
K	31	7.3%
1	61	14.4%
2	48	11.3%
3	57	13.4%
4	28	6.6%
5	54	12.7%
6	37	8.7%
7	10	2.4%
8	40	9.4%
9	2	0.5%
10	12	2.8%
11	6	1.4%
12	32	7.5%
Other	14	0.9%

* Some teachers listed multiple assignments.

cussed. In addition, the questionnaire provided information on variables we sought to control as part of the study; namely, perceptions of the clarity of reform goals and plans and teachers' backgrounds. The overall response rate to the questionnaires in fall 2004 was 83.6 percent (SD = 8.7%), and in spring 2005 the mean response rate for participating schools was 80.4 percent (SD = 12.9%).

We analyzed data at three levels: individual, subgroup, and school. Below, we present the measures used and levels in the order of our hypotheses:.

Influence of the Initiative on Teachers' Practice (Dependent Variable). Because our study focuses on how interaction change teachers' implementation of reforms, our dependent variable is a measure of how much reforms affected teachers' classroom practices. Thus, we developed an index of the degree to which teachers reported that their school's initiative had influenced different aspects of their practice. The measure was the sum of the different elements teachers reported as having been influenced by the reform; a larger number of elements influenced was taken to indicate a greater, more comprehensive reform effort aimed at multiple aspects of teachers' practice.[20]

We derived this index from a measure used by RAND in its study of whole-school reform initiatives to measure implementation.[21] Aspects of practice queried included influence of the reform on curriculum materials used, instructional strategies and activities used with students, assessment strategies used, standards and topics covered, performance levels expected of students, complexity of work assigned to students, classroom management techniques employed, student grouping methods used, professional development sought out, and roles and relationships in the school. The reliability of the index was $\alpha = .92$.

Role in the Reform (Level 1). Our theory suggests that the more leadership is distributed, the more a reform will be implemented because resources, such as expertise, will be distributed throughout the school (H_1). But it could simply be that those who are engaged in the reform are themselves more likely to implement. Therefore, we asked faculty members to identify themselves as having leadership roles (or not) in their school's reform. We used a self-report approach because the formal organization of schools often does not match the distribution of responsibility and authority for advancing the goals of school reforms. In fact, in schools with extensive distribution of leadership, responsibility is stretched over multiple people through both formal and informal mechanisms.[22]

To identify leaders, then, at time 1,we asked faculty members to identify their role within their school's reform by selecting one of four options with respect to the initiative from a single item on our questionnaire: (1) "I am aware of this schoolwide initiative, and I do what is required of me"; (2) "I am part of the team of teachers who are implementing this schoolwide initiative"; (3) "I have an informal leadership role helping other teachers implement this schoolwide initiative"; or (4) "I have a formal leadership role in the effort to implement this schoolwide initiative." By *formal*, we explained to participants, we meant that they had been allocated time, responsibility, and authority for advancing the school reform efforts.

Participation in Leadership Practice: Committees or Teams Where Reform Is Discussed (Level 1). Another aspect of distributed leadership we measured to test H_1 was participation in practices of distributed leadership. At time 2, we asked teachers to identify how often they participated in eight different committees or teams in which the reform was discussed (0 = not at all, 1 = < 1 time per month, 3 = 2–3 times per month, 4 = at least weekly). We calculated a weighted sum from faculty members' responses to all eight types of meetings to measure their level of participation in formally structured leadership practices related to the reform. The weights for this measure were based on the frequency of meetings.

Number of Self-Identified School Leaders (Level 3). From their responses to the questionnaire, we identified the number of faculty members who nominated themselves as either formal or informal leaders of their school's reform efforts. We used this number as an index of the extent to which leadership was distributed across people in the school in order to test H_1.

Distribution of Discussion of the Reform Across Teams: Matrixing (Level 3). One way we sought to capture the extent to which leadership practice was stretched across activities was to ask teachers to identify different formal opportunities they had for discussing the reform. When teachers participate in multiple groups in a school, we can say that the school is to some degree *matrixed*, in that teachers have both opportunities to interact within grades or subgroups as well as to gain different perspectives on the reform's practice by participating with different combinations of actors in meetings in which the reform is discussed. We used the mean number of meetings, weighted to account for the frequency of those meetings, to model the degree of matrixing in a school and as another measure to use to test H_1.

Access to Colleagues' Expertise (Level 1). To test H_2, we developed a measure of colleagues' expertise. A social capital measure of the flow of resources through a network depends on information regarding both resources and the network. Here, we define *resource* as a teacher's expertise in implementing the reform in her classroom. Therefore, the measure of this resource is a teacher's level of implementation at time 1. The flow of resources to a given teacher is then based on the expertise of the colleagues—including formal and informal leaders in the school—with whom she interacts. In particular, it is the sum of the extent of implementation of the teachers a given teacher nominates as being helpful in implementing reform between time 1 and time 2.

As an example, consider a teacher, Lisa, who at time 2 nominates teachers Sue and Bob as helping her implement a schoolwide initiative between time 1 and time 2. If Sue has high expertise, implementing the reform at time 1 at a level of 8 (out of an arbitrary scale from 1 to 10) and Bob has low expertise, implementing at time 1 at a level of 1, then Lisa accessed 9 (8 + 1 = 9) units of expertise through her interactions between time 1 and time 2. Furthermore, she would have access to less expertise (as a form of social capital) than another teacher who interacted with three high-level experts.

Our actual measure also accounted for the frequency of interaction. Thus total access to expertise is the sum of extent of implementation of the other teachers (*i'*) who helped teacher *i* multiplied by the frequency of interaction in the previous year.[23]

Critical to our theoretical framework here is the structuring of interaction by subgroups boundaries. Thus we created separate measures of access to expertise from members of one's own subgroup and access to expertise obtained from outside one's s ubgroup. In order to obtain comparable metrics within and between subgroups, we divided the total access within the subgroup by the number of others from whom a teacher received help within her subgroup and, similarly, divided the total access outside the subgroup by the number of others from whom a teacher received help from outside her subgroup.

Sum and Mean Level of Expertise Accessed from Other Subgroups by One's Own Subgroup (Level 2). If information flows uniformly within subgroups, then access to external resources may best be measured at the subgroup level. That is, every member of a subgroup may benefit from the expertise that any given member accesses from outside the subgroup. To test this alternative mechanism (H_3), we calculated the sum and mean level of expertise available to faculty in a given subgroup from other subgroups.

Norms for Collegial Interaction (Level 1). To test H_4, we measured faculty members' perceptions of norms governing collegial interaction in the school, using two different scales. One scale included four items from the teacher-teacher trust scale reported in Bryk and Schneider to measure perceptions of trust among faculty at each school.[24] This scale asked teachers to indicate the extent to which they felt trust, respect, and mutual regard for fellow faculty members at the school. The items used a four-point scale from "strongly disagree" to "strongly agree," and the scale in our study had a reliability of $\alpha = .86$, similar to the reliability found in Bryk and Schneider's study ($\alpha = .82$). We also used a five-item measure of collective responsibility.[25] *Collective responsibility* is a measure of teachers' perception that all staff members have a shared commitment to the goals of the school and to fostering student learning. This measure asked teachers to indicate the proportion of teachers in the school who they believed felt a sense of responsibility for different aspects of school functioning. The scale had a reliability of α = .89 in our study, similar to the reliability found in Bryk and Schneider's study (α = .92).

Mean Level of Expertise Available Within Subgroups (Level 2). Our operational definition of social capital is that teachers will benefit by accessing expertise through direct interaction. But the structuring of interaction by subgroups offers an important alternative. It could be that teachers are equally exposed to the expertise of each member of their subgroup via the dense interactions within subgroups, which corresponds to H_5 in our study. Therefore we test this alternative through a measure of the mean level of expertise of subgroup members. This measure does not depend on direct interactions: it is based on subgroup membership.

Control Variable: Access to Outside Professional Development (Level 1). Recognizing that teachers may increase their implantation of a reform because of resources they access from outside the school, at time 2, we asked teachers to rate the value of different forms of professional development they had received from people outside the school on a three-point scale (1 = not valuable, 2 = somewhat valuable, 3 = very valuable) or indicate that they had not received that particular form of professional development. We asked about a range of formats of professional development: workshops, conferences, study groups, teacher networks, mentoring and coaching, and online professional courses and created a scale based on the mean ratings of outside resources (α = .89). From their ratings, we coded "not received" as 0, but included a flag indicating we had done so in our analyses to control for potential misinterpretations of teachers' responses.

Control Variable: Perceptions of Clarity of Reform Goals and Plans: Level of Specification (Level 1). At time 1 and time 2, we asked four attitudinal questions focused on faculty members' judgments about how specific the initiative was as to what it required of them; these were scaled from "strongly agree" to "strongly disagree" using a four-point scale. These are intended to be a broad measure of the reforms' specificity, as viewed from teachers' perspective.[26] The reliability of this scale was α = .87.

Control Variables: Teacher Background (Level 1). At time 1, we asked teachers about their grade-level assignments, number of years' experience teaching and in the school, certification (emergency, provisional, clear, National Board Certified), class size, subjects taught, gender, and ethnicity. We included each of these background variables in our initial models as controls in our study.

Approach to Data Analysis
We specify effects at the individual, subgroup, and school level; therefore, the prologue for our analysis was to identify cohesive subgroups from the sociometric data. First, we determined that subgroups should be based on

stable and enduring relationships between actors.[27] For our purposes we used a sociometric question asking teachers to list their closest professional colleagues. Identifying subgroups across all the schools in our sample then required an algorithm that could objectively and successfully identify within-school subgroups with a minimum of subjective input or interpretation from the researcher (e.g., specification of the number of subgroups, criteria defining subgroups). We used Frank's (1995, 1996) network clustering algorithm for this purpose.[28] Related to network models such as p* and p_2 Frank's algorithm iteratively reassigns actors to subgroups to maximize the increase in odds that a relationship occurs between a pair of actors if they are in the same subgroup relative to the odds of a relationship occurring if they are in different subgroups (see figure 9-1).[29] Thus, the odds ratio is large to the extent that relationships are concentrated within subgroups (as indicated by cells A and D) versus outside of subgroups (cells B and C). This property makes it an ideal quantity to maximize to identify subgroups in which relationships are concentrated. Ultimately, we identified 115 subgroups across 21 schools, with the typical subgroup containing about 3.7 teachers.

Having identified subgroups within each school, we could then analyze our data at three levels: individual, subgroup, and school. Because of the nested structure of the data set, we used hierarchical linear modeling to examine individual interactions, beliefs about the school, exposure to professional development, expertise, and faculty background characteristics (level 1), the effect of access to expertise at the subgroup level (level 2), and the extent to which leadership of the reform was stretched over people and practices (level 3).[30]

Initially, for our single-outcome variable, the extent of the influence of the initiative on teachers' practice, we first conducted an unconditional model to determine the variance structure at each level (table 9-3). We then constructed a model (model 1) that analyzed the effect of having multiple

FIGURE 9-1

Association between membership in the same subgroup and a relationship occurring between a pair of actors

		Relationship occurring	
		No	*Yes*
Same subgroup	*No*	A	B
	Yes	C	D

TABLE 9-3
Variance components:Individual, subgroup, and school levels

Level	Variance	Percent of variance
Individual (level 1)	9.56	92.8%
Subgroup (level 2)	.29	2.8%
School (level 3)	.45	4.4%
Total	10.3	100%

leaders and formal opportunities for interactions about schoolwide initiatives (H_1) and a second model (model 2) that examined how this effect might be mediated by influence of access to expertise within and across subgroups (H_2–H_5). These models are described in the technical appendix. Finally, we examined interaction effects across levels, examining specifically the relationship between distributed leadership and access to informal and formal expertise.

RESULTS

Descriptive Statistics for Variables in Models

Table 9-4 shows descriptive statistics for each of the variables in our models. Overall, the mean level of influence of the reforms on teacher practice changed little from time 1 to time 2. On average, faculty members reported that roughly eleven of sixteen dimensions of practice we queried had been influenced by their school's reform. On the collective responsibility scale, teachers in the sample reported that their school had high overall levels of collective responsibility; on a scale of 1 to 4, the mean rating for their school was 3.08 (SD = .69). About 60 percent reported they taught English; in some respects, this may reflect that our sample consisted primarily of elementary schools in which all teachers taught reading. Class size on average was from fifteen to twenty-four students, typical for early elementary schools in this state. Ratings of how well-specified reforms were in schools were just above average for the 1-to-4 scale we constructed, a finding consistent with locally defined whole-school reform initiatives, in which reform designs do not always provide clear blueprints for implementation. Roughly 17 percent of the sample reported being a formal or informal leader, with each subgroup having an average of just under one leader and each school 4.6 leaders. The mean school influence of reforms on practice was similar to the individual mean: roughly eleven of sixteen elements had been influenced already by time 1.

TABLE 9-4

Descriptive statistics for model variables

Level/variable	N	M	SD
Individual level			
Mean influence of reform at time 2	425	11.59	4.15
Mean influence of reform at time 1	425	11.60	4.67
Collective responsibility	425	3.08	.66
Teach English	425	.62	.49
Class size (scale 1–5)	425	3.37	1.23
Outside professional development	349	6.84	3.23
Reform specification	425	2.86	.64
Male	425	.17	.38
Expertise accessed from outside subgroup	425	1.42	2.33
Role (formal or informal leader)	425	.17	.38
Emergency credential	425	.01	.11
Dummy: Outside professional development	425	6.84	3.23
Subgroup			
Number of leaders in subgroup	115	.80	1.18
Mean influence of reform at time 1	115	11.16	3.23
School			
Number of leaders in school	21	4.62	3.20
Mean level of influence of reform	21	11.16	2.49

Model 1 Results

The unstandardized coefficients and standard errors for each of the variables in model 1 appear in table 9-5. In model 1, the effect of distributed leadership as measured by the number of formal and informal leaders did not achieve significance ($p = .09$), lending no significant support for H_1. The effects of prior implementation at the school and subgroup levels were significant, however. Teachers' perception that others in their school felt a collective responsibility for student learning was a strong predictor of influence of the reform on practice. This finding partially supports H_4: although the effect of trust was not significant, the effect of collective responsibility was.

Access to outside professional development also had a significant effect on practice, but being an informal or informal leader was not significant ($p = .09$). Control variables that had a significant positive effect on practice

TABLE 9-5
Model 1 results

Level/variable	Coefficient	Standard error
Individual level		
Mean influence of reform at time 1	.415***	.047
Collective responsibility	.842***	.226
Teach English	.939**	.311
Class size (scale 1–5)	.362**	.127
Outside professional development	.148**	.049
Reform specification	– .513*	.261
Male	– .833*	.400
Role (formal or informal leader)	.681†	.09
Emergency credential	– 4.34**	1.33
Dummy: Outside professional development	– .202	.502
Subgroup		
Mean influence of reform at time 1	.426***	.088
School		
Intercept	10.70***	.211
Number of leaders in school	.108†	.061
Mean level of influence of reform	.823	.076

†*p* < .10, *p* < .05, **p* < .01, ***p* < .001

were level of influence of the reform on practice at time 1, teaching English, and teaching in a larger class. Control variables with a significant negative effect were level of reform specification, holding an emergency credential, and being male.

We also examined the interaction between leadership and access to outside professional development; the interaction was significant, and we found that the overall effect of leadership was stronger (*p* = .02) when teachers had less access to outside expertise through teacher professional development. In other words, having multiple leaders in a school was more important when access to outside professional development was more limited.

Model 2 Results

The unstandardized coefficients and standard errors for each of the variables in model 2 appear in table 9-6. Note that when the effect of accessing expertise from colleagues was introduced to the model, the effect of leadership was farther from being statistically significant ($p = .16$). The effect of being an informal or formal leader, however, increased and approached significance ($p = .07$), suggesting a refinement to H_1. In particular, it appears that being a leader was more important when considering subgroups than simply being in a school where responsibility for reforms is distributed across multiple actors. Further, when one's own subgroup accessed more expertise from outside that subgroup but within their school, there was a significant positive effect on practice, which supports H_5. The negative effect of being a male was reduced somewhat in model 2. Other variables that were significant in model 1 remained significant in model 2.

Note that the model reports significant effects for the mean of access to expertise within and outside teachers' subgroups. We report the mean because we found the mean of others' levels of implementation to be a significant predictor (H_3) with a coefficient of .0007, standard error of .0003, and t-ratio of 2.5 but not the sum, which had a coefficient of .00005, standard error of .00004, and t-ratio of 1.2.

For model 2, we examined interactions between level of influence of colleagues and access to outside professional development and the initial level of influence on practice at time 1, in order to explore the extent to which already being an expert at the beginning of our study might influence the results. We found that the effect of getting expertise from outside one's subgroup was reduced for those groups that had high levels of influence at time 1. We also found that the effect of outside professional development was stronger for faculty members who began with lower levels of expertise.

DISCUSSION AND CONCLUSIONS

The results of our study suggest that assigning responsibility for reform goals to multiple actors in a school by designating them as either formal or informal leaders can have a positive effect on the implementation of reforms (H_1) when there is limited access to outside professional development. When there was more abundant access to valued opportunities to learn through professional development from outside experts, faculty members reported higher levels of influence on their practice. The interaction with the number of leaders in a school was negative, meaning that when there was less access to professional development, for individuals to change their practice it was important to have more leaders in a school. This finding suggests that in schools where resources for professional development are scarce, the activities principals undertake to distribute authority and responsibility for leading reform efforts are important.

The effect of accessing help from colleagues who are already implementing reforms is significant (H_2), and when it is included as part of the model,

TABLE 9-6
Model 2 results

Level/variable	Coefficient	Standard error
Individual level		
Mean influence of reform at time 1	.414***	.047
Collective responsibility	.855***	.219
Teach English	.878**	.306
Class size (scale 1–5)	.429**	.122
Outside professional development	.146**	.049
Reform specification	– .489*	.253
Male	– .691†	.393
Expertise accessed from outside subgroup	.102	.074
Role (formal or informal leader)	.732†	.398
Emergency credential	– 4.30**	1.31
Dummy: Outside professional development	– .206	.500
Subgroup		
Mean access to expertise from outside group	.394**	.146
Mean influence of reform at time 1	.442***	.080
School		
Intercept	10.67***	.197
Number of leaders in school	.081	.055
Mean level of influence of reform	.737***	.071

†$p < .10$, *$p < .05$, **$p < .01$, ***$p < .001$

the effect of distributing responsibility for advancing reform goals to multiple leaders was smaller. It was the mean, rather than the sum, of access to expertise that was significant in our models (consistent with H_3), and the effect was significant for both the mean level of implementation for teachers' own subgroups and for the other subgroups in the school with which they interacted (H_5). This finding is consistent with the idea that both normative pressures within subgroups and the need for new information sought from outside the subgroup are important aspects of teachers' social capital. On the one hand, dense interactions with members of one's own subgroup may put pressure on teachers to conform to either high or low levels of implementation of their group. At the same time, a desire to change may be facilitated by learning about and accessing expertise from people who are not their closest colleagues.

An alternative explanation for this finding is that the information available to a subgroup from members' ties to other subgroups circulates widely within the subgroups, and is a resource equally accessible to each of the group members, no matter what its original source. This is consistent with the pattern in our data that it is at the subgroup level where the effect on implementation is significant. Future studies might explore which of these explanations is more plausible and in what kinds of situations and school contexts.

The strong effect of collective responsibility in both models for predicting a reform's influence on practice suggests that teachers' perceptions of their context also matter (H_4). Judgments that the faculty as a whole is committed to the goal of improving student achievement for all students and beliefs that faculty members share responsibility for meeting that goal appear to lead teachers to make changes to their practice. Collective responsibility may be a mechanism that leads teachers to develop a much stronger sense of identification with the school and its goals, leading teachers to want to make changes to their practice that align with those goals. This hypothesis would be consistent with other research that has shown identification to be a source of motivation for individuals to embrace organizational goals and align their actions with those goals.[31]

Our principal findings that expertise from both outside and inside subgroups point to the value of a social network approach to analyzing distributed leadership. An important characteristic of social networks in a school is that even though they are structured, they are also permeable, and all actors in a school grapple with the institutional pressures on their school.[32] All teachers are aware to varying degrees of policy demands placed on their schools at the federal, state, and district levels; similarly, many of the resources and expertise to which they have access through formal professional development are shaped by policies set outside the school. Schools' differential access to resources such as textbooks and to expertise in the form of certified teachers is often a deep concern of researchers studying educational equity.[33]

There are some important limitations to this study that limit the generalizability of the findings presented above. First, the sample was a purposive one, intended to include only schools engaged in some form of distributed leadership. Therefore, although the variability in the extent to which distributed leadership was enacted in schools enabled us to analyze how different levels of distribution (in terms of the number of leaders there were in a school) affected outcomes, the study did not have a comparison group. Both the lack of a comparison group and absence of an experimental design make our study results suggestive of a potential effect of distributed leadership but not definitive. Further, because ours was a survey study, we had to rely on a limited, measurable index for distributed leadership. This measure did not take into account how leadership was distributed across practices and situations, a core notion of distributed leadership. It may be that our limited measure was a chief reason why we failed to detect significant overall effects of distributed leadership on reform implementation.

Even with these important limitations, the findings tell us something about how the formal organization of schools can facilitate teachers' access to necessary expertise for implementing reforms. Assigning responsibility to multiple school actors for advancing reform goals can affect both those actors' implementation levels and facilitate implementation of others. Indirectly, and just as important, for the schools in our sample at least, distributed leadership facilitated particular kinds of collegial interactions that helped distribute resources and expertise to those teachers who most needed it. Future research can and should build on this social network approach to understand better how particular interactions can and do facilitate the flow of expertise to advance ambitious school reform goals.

School leaders may benefit from knowing about how collegial interactions are structured, in order to promote the broad distribution of access to resources and expertise needed for reforms. We presented social network graphs showing subgroup-level characteristics to principals in three schools; those graphs had no information that could be used to identify individuals. Still, the graphs pointed out to principals ways in which implementation of reforms was uneven by subgroup, and the graphs showed pictorially the strong link between teachers' perceptions of the social context and implementation. These and other principals have been eager to collect their own network data to better understand how expertise and resources flow within their schools. We caution principals about the potential for harm in making visible interactions that teachers may prefer to remain outside the monitoring of principals. We also believe that some informal leaders who might be identified by the process could prove to be valuable in supporting the spread of reforms in a school, but the trust other faculty have in them may depend on the informality of their roles. Thus, one aspect of our findings, namely that the informal social structure of a school does not map perfectly onto its formal organization, is likely to persist even when leaders intentionally foster specific kinds of collaborative relationships in a school.

This work was supported by National Science Foundation grant #0231981, a project that explored the feasibility and value of applying social network methods to studying the implementation of schoolwide reform initiatives. All opinions expressed herein are the sole responsibility of the authors. We wish to thank core members of the data collection and analysis team for their efforts in making these analyses possible: Christine Korbak, Judi Fusco, Christopher Hoadley, Joel Galbraith, Amy Hafter, Aasha Joshi, Amy Lewis, Margaret Riel, Willow Sussex, and Devin Vodicka.

TECHNICAL APPENDIX

Model 1 as reported in the analyses is specified below as:
For teacher i in subgroup j in school k, we have:

Level 1: Individual

$$Y_{ijk} = \varpi_{0jk} + \varpi_{1jk}(\text{PRIOR IMPLEMENTATION}_{ijk}) + \varpi_{2jk}(\text{COLLECTIVE RESPONSIBILITY}_{ijk})$$
$$+ \varpi_{3jk}(\text{TEACH ENGLISH}_{ijk}) + \varpi_{4jk}(\text{CLASS SIZE}_{ijk}) + \varpi_{5jk}(\text{OUTSIDE PD}_{ijk})$$
$$+ \varpi_{6jk}(\text{REFORM SPECIFICATION}_{ijk}) + \varpi_{7jk}(\text{MALE}_{ijk}) + \varpi_{8jk}(\text{ROLE}_{ijk}) +$$
$$\varpi_{9jk}(\text{EMERGENCY CREDENTIAL}_{ijk}) +$$
$$\varpi_{10jk}(\text{DUMMY: OUTSIDE PD}_{ijk}) + e_{ijk}$$

Level 2: Subgroup

$$\varpi_{0jk} = \beta_{00k} + \beta_{01k}(\text{MEAN PRIOR IMPLEMENTATION}_{jk}) + \rho_{0\,jk}$$
$$\varpi_{1jk} = \beta_{10k}$$
$$\varpi_{2jk} = \beta_{20k}$$
$$\varpi_{3jk} = \beta_{30k}$$
$$\varpi_{4jk} = \beta_{40k}$$
$$\varpi_{5jk} = \beta_{50k}$$
$$\varpi_{6jk} = \beta_{60k}$$
$$\varpi_{7jk} = \beta_{70k}$$
$$\varpi_{8jk} = \beta_{80k}$$
$$\varpi_{9jk} = \beta_{90k}$$
$$\varpi_{10jk} = \beta_{100k}$$

Level 3: School

$$\beta_{00k} = \gamma_{000} + \gamma_{001}(\text{NUMBER OF LEADERS}_k) + \gamma_{002}(\text{MEAN PRIOR IMPLEMENTATION}_k) + u_{00\,k}$$
$$\beta_{01k} = \gamma_{100}$$
$$\beta_{10k} = \gamma_{200}$$
$$\beta_{20k} = \gamma_{300}$$
$$\beta_{30k} = \gamma_{400}$$
$$\beta_{40k} = \gamma_{500}$$
$$\beta_{50k} = \gamma_{600}$$
$$\beta_{70k} = \gamma_{700}$$
$$\beta_{80k} = \gamma_{800}$$
$$\beta_{90k} = \gamma_{900}$$
$$\beta_{100k} = \gamma_{1000}$$

In model 2, we added mediator variables at level 1 and level 2 that correspond to the effect of access to expertise from colleagues. At level 1, the variable MEAN BETWEEN-GROUP INFLUENCE refers to the expertise faculty members accessed from others in their school who were not in their immediate subgroup. At level 2, we have aggregated the scores of between-group expertise of the subgroup to create a subgroup-level variable.

CHAPTER 10

Learning at a System Level

Ties Between Principals of Low-Performing Schools and Central Office Leaders

Kara S. Finnigan and Alan J. Daly

Public education in the United States is at a crossroads. On one hand, we are more aware of inequality in the distribution of schooling in the United States, given the increased attention to the achievement gap between minority and white students, and "in need of improvement" or INI schools that failed to make Adequate Yearly Progress (AYP) under No Child Left Behind. On the other hand, despite attention to these inequities, little consensus exists around how to bring about the complex change that might turn around failing schools and districts. At this critical juncture, policy makers and practitioners have ratcheted up the reform strategies. However, as Fullan argues, few reforms have worked because not enough attention has been paid to the important relationship between leadership and system transformation.[1]

A number of scholars have shifted their focus from the school site to the district as the unit of reform.[2] This line of inquiry suggests that the larger context may have a direct impact on the success of school-level change as district administrators reorient structures and processes to align with reform goals and develop supportive conditions to sustain reform.[3] Furthermore, shared theories of action, mutual sense-making, and consistent communication at the district level result in greater systemic coherence.[4] These studies, in combination, suggest the importance of linkages between central office and site leaders for not only school reform but also districtwide reform to occur. In essence, reform efforts require an interconnected, systems approach to organizational change.[5]

In this chapter, we examine the leadership network of restructuring (the final stage of NCLB sanctions) school principals and central office administrators in La Urbana (a pseudonym), one of the largest urban districts in the United States. By examining the lateral and vertical connections within the larger system, we seek to better understand the flow of organizational resources between and among these low-performing schools and how this may facilitate or hinder improvement. While these restructuring principals play a critical role in La Urbana in terms of school site leadership, it is consideration of the work of the site and central office leaders, in combination, that provides insight into the reform capacity of this district.[6] Given that the district itself has been cited as INI under NCLB and must show signs of improvement or face more severe sanctions, attention not just to these failing schools but to the overall system is critical.

THEORETICAL FRAMEWORK

Our study is grounded in the work of research and theorists who have studied organizational learning as well as the diffusion of innovation and information.[7] Both external and internal networks serve as conduits through which research findings can flow throughout the organization. External ties allow new ideas or approaches to enter organizations, while internal ties provide access to expertise within the organization. As school and district staff search for various sources of evidence that supports the necessary changes and embed these strategies into change processes, they undergo organizational learning.[8] In addition, strong ties within and across the units of an organization are associated with initiating and sustaining large-scale change resulting in positive organizational outcomes, such as organizational performance and innovation.[9]

Social capital can be conceptualized as "the resources embedded in social relations and social structure which can be mobilized when an actor wishes to increase the likelihood of success in purposive action."[10] This concept is foundational to our work, and in this study, we draw heavily on the work of network theorists who argue that social capital research should be rooted in individual interactions and that the quality of ties between individuals in a social system create a structure that determines access to resources.[11] Networks are typically identified by the content or resources that are exchanged between actors, and the structure of these networks varies by the type of resources involved.[12] Dense network structures support the movement of complex knowledge, while less dense structures facilitate the transfer of simple or routine information.[13]

The ties that exist between hierarchical levels within the organization, such as school and central office administrators, are critical to building an organization's capacity for change.[14] At the same time, lateral communication is vital for the diffusion of new ideas and to facilitate knowledge transfer, cooperative relationships, and innovation between subgroups.[15] In fact, informal networks within and between units that have dense ties generally achieve at higher levels than those with sparse connections.[16]

Social network analysis reveals the underlying network structures that must be part of any attempt to understand resource exchanges between individuals in an organization. Thus, social network analysis is an important tool to understanding school improvement under sanction.[17] Beyond facilitating improvement, the underlying relationships within an organization may ultimately determine the direction, speed, and depth of a planned change.[18]

STUDY METHODS

La Urbana is a large urban district in California. During the 2007–2008 school year, seventeen of its two hundred schools were in NCLB restructuring, and many more were in the various stages of program improvement (or PI). This study involved forty-four members of La Urbana's leadership team, including these seventeen restructuring school principals. Our study involved only those in formal district leadership positions, including the superintendent, assistant superintendents, central office directors, and principals. We included only the principals in restructuring schools as a way to understand the flow of information and innovation into and between these low-performing schools under the stress of sanctions. We used a bounded/saturated network approach, meaning that we provided respondents with a list of all leadership team members and asked them to describe each relationship and the frequency of that interaction; this provides a more complete picture of the leadership network and potentially more valid results.[19]

The online survey was administered in spring 2008 and resulted in a 75 percent response rate. As table 10-1 shows, most of the leadership team members in La Urbana were white (71 percent). In addition, nearly one-third of respondents had been at the district for less than four years, while approximately one-third had been in the district more than twenty-five years, suggesting a bifurcated system in terms of district experience. More than half had been administrators for fewer than nine years and nearly two-thirds had been at their current sites for fewer than four years, indicating a great deal of movement within this system.

In order to assess these social networks, we developed a survey instrument that comprised distinct networks and demographic questions. Specifically, we asked respondents to quantitatively assess their relationships with each of the other administrators on an interaction scale ranging from 0 (no interaction) to 4 (1–2 times a week). In developing and validating the social network questions, we drew on the literature regarding district reform processes, previous network studies, and our recent work.[20] We piloted and refined the relational questions with practicing administrators.

Data analysis involved a series of network measures using the UCINET software, including density, centrality, reciprocity, and the external-internal (E-I) index.[21] For interactional ties, strength of tie can be measured either by

TABLE 10-1
Sample demographics

	Percentage of respondents
Ethnicity	
White	71
Latino	16
African American	6
Asian/Pacific Islander	6
Years in district	
25+	34
20–24	9
15–19	13
10–14	6
5–9	6
<4	31
Years as an administrator	
25+	3
20–24	0
15–19	25
10–14	19
5–9	41
<4	13
Years at current site (school/central office)	
25+	3
20–24	0
15–19	6
10–14	9
5–9	19
<4	63

quantity ("How frequently do you interact?") or quality ("How 'good' is the interaction?"). In this study we focus on the quantitative aspects of the interaction measured by frequency. Given the extensive literature on the importance of tie intensity in networks, as well as the higher levels of accuracy and greater stability of these patterns, we dichotomized the data to include only the most frequent ties between actors.[22] In order to be considered a frequent tie, individuals would have, for example, communicated from once every two weeks to a couple of times a week.

RESULTS

In social network research, studies often concentrate on two types of social networks that reflect different content or resources flowing through the ties: instrumental and expressive networks.[23] *Instrumental* social networks are conduits for the circulation of information and resources that pertain to organizational goals. These networks often initially follow patterns of formal hierarchical relationships. *Expressive* social networks reflect patterns of more affect-laden relationships, such as friendships, are more likely to transport and diffuse resources such as social support, trust, and values. These two types of networks tend to overlap and are not mutually exclusive: one type of relationship may possibly even lead to another.[24]

Instrumental/Technical Relationships

As restructuring school principals seek to improve their schools, they must have key information regarding school restructuring under NCLB, as well as information relating to restructuring in La Urbana specifically. In addition, they require more general information on work-related topics, reflecting more technical or instrumental exchanges. Instrumental or technical relationships are important to organizational change as scholars have called for an examination not just of social relationships but of these more technical, information-based relationships to understand "who knows what" within the organization.[25]

As figure 10-1 indicates, La Urbana's restructuring/program improvement (PI) information network is sparse, with few principals turning to other principals or central office leaders for information. In the figure, darker nodes are restructuring principals (labeled with *S* [for "site"] and an identifying number) and lighter nodes are central office leaders (labeled with *D* [for "district"] and an identifying number). All of the nodes in the top left corner of the figure represent individuals in the network who neither seek out nor are sought out by anyone for information on this area. The nodes are sized by in-degree centrality, referring to the number of people who seek out that person.

The network measures indicate that only 2 percent of all possible information exchange ties are present in the most frequent relationships (39 out of a possible 1, 980 ties between individuals exist). Furthermore, eight central office staff and nine restructuring principals are shown as isolates in this network, meaning that they did not seek (nor were sought for) information related to restructuring/PI on a frequent basis. The centrality measures indicate that, on average, leaders at the school and central office levels had ties

FIGURE 10-1   Leadership network: Information on restructuring/program improvement

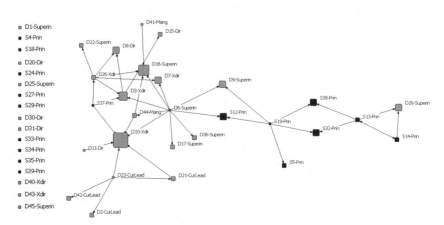

with just over one other district leader (1.689) (SD=2.031; range=0–9), suggesting that the information flow in the network was extremely limited. The overall network tended toward centralization with two district leaders (D10 and D16) serving central roles in the information network. Interestingly, principals did not play central roles in the system, despite the fact that the network was about the exchange of information directly related to program improvement under NCLB.

This information network suggests that there were very few reciprocal relationships (people seeking each other out) compared with one-way information flows. Only 3 percent of the relationships in the existing network were reciprocated. In fact, only two individuals (both principals) had any reciprocal ties, and these were with each other, indicating *one* reciprocal relationship in this entire network. This may not be surprising for information of this sort: the person you seek out for information would tend not to be the same person who seeks you out for information, since that person would in turn seek out someone who has greater knowledge.

In figure 10-1, both hierarchical (central office-school) and lateral (school-school or central office-central office) relationships are rare. Furthermore, the division between central office and school staff in La Urbana is triangulated by findings from the external-internal (E-I) index, which range from –1 (completely internal; meaning within work location) ties to +1 (completely external; between work locations) connections, and was run on an actor's primary work location (central office or school site). The E-I index for this network was –.632, suggesting that this network was more internally than externally connected. In other words, principals went to principals and central office

FIGURE 10-2   Leadership network: Information on work-related topics

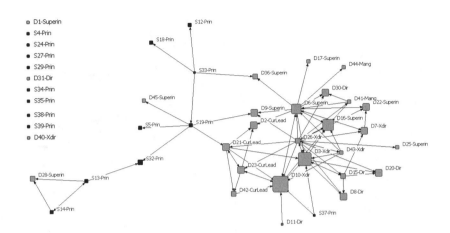

staff went to central office staff, but they did not cross groups for restructuring/PI-related information. In fact, figure 10-1 shows that D9 and S12 play important *bridging* roles, serving as brokers between different parts of the system. On the other hand, S19 plays a *connector* role, seeking out information from both principals and central office leaders.

While this first information network was specifically focused on information regarding restructuring/program improvement, we found a somewhat similar pattern in regard to the more general question about work-related information, as seen in figure 10-2. For instance, a large number of people are isolates, including three district leaders and eight restructuring school principals. Leaders connect, on average, with 3.067 other leaders (SD=3.568; range=0-16) with a centrality measure of 30.76 percent suggesting a more centralized network than the previous more specific information network around restructuring/program improvement. This network is only slightly more dense (4 percent), however, with a total of 78 ties of 1980.

The lateral relationships in figure 10-2 are distinct from figure 10-1, with the subgroup networks of principals even more sparse and subgroup network of central office leaders more dense—D10 and D16 continue to play a key role, with D3 emerging as another central person in the work-related information network. Few information connections exist between restructuring schools and central office staff and the E-I index of –.768 suggests a more internally connected structure than the previous network. Finally, this more general information network has a higher degree of reciprocity (.1304), though it is still quite low, with eleven network members, including nine district leaders and two principals exhibiting reciprocal relationships.

FIGURE 10-3   Leadership network: Input on a work decision

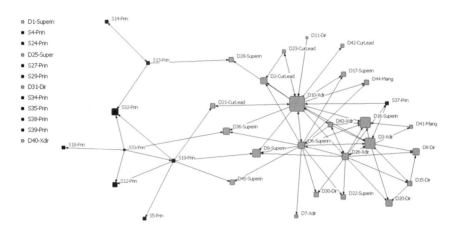

Expressive Relationships

Expressive relationships, as described above, refer to the more supportive social relationships individuals have with one another. One type of expressive relationship involves going to colleagues for advice. We included two different advice networks: one relating to input on an important work decision and the other focused on engaging with someone in work-related problem solving. Figure 10-3 shows the network map for advice on work decisions. This network looks somewhat similar to the instrumental network around general information, with a more dense internal (lateral) network of central office staff compared with relationships between principals. On average, leaders seek out 2.889 other leaders on an important work decision (SD=3.659; range=0-16) in this district. This expressive network shows similar density (4 percent) to the general information network, with a total of 76 of 1, 980 ties, suggesting a sparse network. As the figure illustrates, D10, D16, and D3 play central roles in this advice network, just as they did in the more instrumental relationship of work-related information. A number of actors continue to remain on the periphery with no in-out relationships, meaning they do not go to anyone and no one seeks them for input on an important work decision. In fact, nearly half of the restructuring principals in La Urbana (47 percent) were isolated in this way.

As with the instrumental (information) networks, few hierarchical connections exist between restructuring schools and central office administrators for advice seeking; in addition, the E-I index of −.754 indicates that these networks are primarily internal, with few cross-group ties. The degree of reciprocity is also similar to the network shown in figure 10-2; there are few

FIGURE 10-4   Leadership network: Turn to for best practices

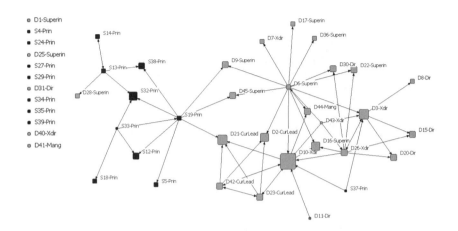

reciprocal relationships (reciprocity = .1692). While we do not include the network map for engaging in work-related problem solving, a very similar network structure exists for this additional advice network.

Two additional expressive networks are linked to advice, but rather than focusing on input or problem solving, these networks targeted best practices and expertise (see figures 10-4 and 10-5). Scholars have called for more attention to be paid to these types of networks to better understand "who knows how" within the organization.[26] The best practices network map (figure 10-4) shows similar patterns to the network maps in figures 10-1 to 10-3, although this network structure is slightly less centralized (25.21 percent; mean=2.4 ties; SD=2.824; range=0-13) and less dense (3 percent or 59 frequent ties exist of the 1, 980 possible ties). In addition, this network map shows greater clustering, with S32 playing an important role in the exchange of best practices between principals. In addition, S19 serves a connector role by turning to central office staff as well as principals for best practices. On the other hand, the hierarchical interconnections are very similar to the previous network maps with mostly internal, rather than cross-group, connections (E-I= –.778). When these connections do occur, it is always a principal seeking out a central office leader regarding best practices, with no central office leaders seeking out restructuring principals. Only 9 percent of the relations in the best practice network are reciprocated.

While best practices and expertise have overlapping structures, as can be seen in figure 10-5, the expertise network is slightly denser (5 percent) than any of the others, although it remains quite sparse. This figure shows the first evidence of at least some lateral linkages between restructuring princi-

FIGURE 10-5 Leadership network: Reliable source of work-related expertise

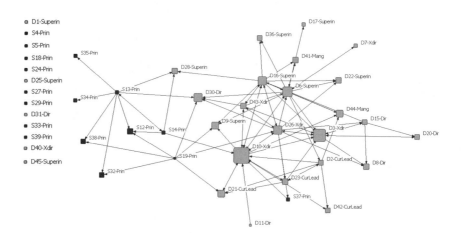

pals. Nevertheless, the interconnections between schools and central office remain rare and one-way (a few schools indicate central office leaders are a reliable source of work-related expertise but no central office leaders report this of school principals). Leaders have more connections around expertise than the other resource areas (e.g., information, best practices) with 3.378 ties to other district leaders, on average (SD=3.860; range=0-14). D30 plays an important role in this network as both central office leaders and principals turn to this administrator as a reliable source of expertise. In addition, many central office leaders and restructuring principals remain on the periphery. However, reciprocal relationships are much higher in this expertise network (reciprocity=24 percent), with nearly a quarter of the existing frequent ties being reciprocal in nature.

While the best practices and expertise-related networks show some promising connections, the expressive network relating to the culture or climate of the organization is less so. This critical, though often overlooked, network relates to whether individuals are recognized for their efforts (see figure 10-6). One key central office leader (D3) in this sparse network stands out as providing recognition to other central office staff (and, in one case, a principal) regarding their work efforts, while D10 and D16 are also central in this network. However, this network map suggests such recognition is quite uncommon, not only between central office staff but between school principals and between school and central office leaders as well. Importantly, more than half (58 percent) of the district leaders had neither received nor given recognition frequently. While recognition is important as a sign of a positive organizational culture, it may also be related to the degree of awareness peo-

FIGURE 10-6   Leadership network: Recognizes me for my work efforts

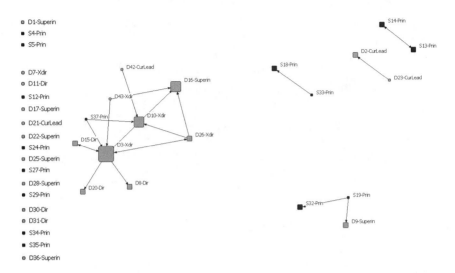

ple have of the practices of individuals within this district. By implication, little awareness of individual work efforts in restructuring schools exists, with slightly more in the central office.

Networks and Organizational Change

A final important consideration regarding these underlying networks is the capacity for complex change. Two areas—innovation and influence— are important to consider in combination with the above instrumental and expressive networks. Innovation is especially important to organizational learning as organizational members search for new ideas through explora- tion and exploitation.[27]

It is important to note that the innovation and influence networks are examined a little differently than the previous networks, as in-degree cen- trality, rather than network structure, is the key analytical tool used here. *In-degree centrality*, in essence, suggests agreement around which leaders are innovative or influential in the district. Since the nodes are sized by cen- trality, the largest nodes in the network maps are the most central, indicat- ing, for example, the individuals in this system whom most people think are innovative. As figure 10-7 shows, the actors who are clearly identified as innovative include four central office (D10, D6, D16, and D9) and three school (S5 and S12) leaders. However, of these innovative leaders, only D10 and D16 have central roles in either the instrumental or the expressive net- works, suggesting that most people do not have access to these "innovators," particularly the school-level innovators (S5 and S12).

FIGURE 10-7 Leadership network: Innovative

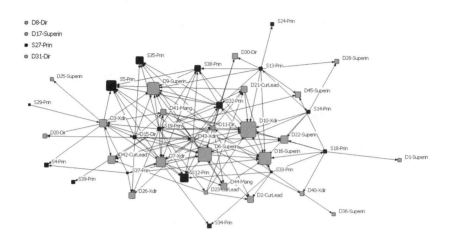

The network map regarding influence (see figure 10-8), referring to who has influence in the district, is also interesting. This map indicates that few restructuring principals have an influential role, with only S12 serving as a central player in this map. In addition five central office leaders (D16, D10, D45, D6, and D9) are central figures in this leadership network, thus indicating high and disproportionate (compared with school leaders) levels of influence in La Urbana.

An important part of this story of relationships and organizational learning is that D10 plays a key role in nearly all of the network maps, as does D16 (though slightly less central). These two individuals, therefore, are in critical positions, as they control much of the flow of resources (information, best practices, etc.) within central office (though not as much between central office and schools given the sparse ties). Overall, these network maps show quite fragmented relationships and sparse network structures.

DISCUSSION

Our data suggest weak underlying relationships of the restructuring leadership team in this urban district. The network maps show sparse and somewhat centralized networks with few reciprocal relationships. Even the more instrumental or information-based relationships are quite limited, particularly across the two groups (central office and school site), suggesting a lack of knowledge sharing around both restructuring/PI information and more general information. Furthermore, the incidence of central office leaders seeking out principals for information or expertise is extremely rare. Finally, a large

Figure 10-8   Leadership network: Individuals with greatest influence

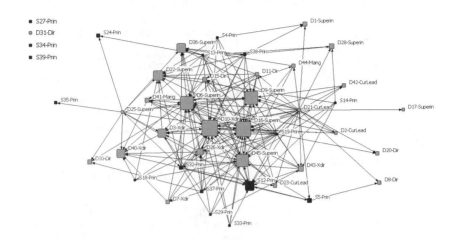

proportion of leaders are isolated from each other, residing on the periphery of these networks or, more commonly, not having any linkages at all.

In the remainder of this section we discuss the cross-cutting themes of the social network analysis of La Urbana's leadership team. First, to bring about complex change in any organization, the underlying relationships of organizational members must be dense enough to allow information and innovation to flow throughout the organization. As indicated in the network maps, La Urbana has a somewhat centralized, tightly connected central office staff but less centralized and loosely connected restructuring site administrators, with few connections across groups and few reciprocal relationships. This type of fragmented system limits district coherence and the ability of central office and school leaders to develop the meaningful partnerships that are necessary for sharing ideas and practices.

Second, the sparse connections between district office and restructuring administrators in La Urbana suggest that organizational change under the stress of sanctions will be challenging. We found similar, disconnected relationships in our study of Dos Mundos and La Estasis (pseudonyms), two other California districts facing NCLB sanctions.[28] Across these three districts, we have found sparse cross-group ties, asymmetric patterns with most resources flowing from central office to school leaders rather than vice versa, and limited systemwide interaction. Like Dos Mundos and La Estasis, the underlying relationships in this district, which are both centralized and internally focused, may be linked to the threat these leaders face from NCLB sanctions. Given that we found greater centralization and homophily (actors seeking out relationships with those most like themselves) over time in our longitudinal study of La Estasis, focused efforts to develop dense ties in La Urbana may be necessary to moderate the response to threat and bring about system-wide change.[29]

Third, the lack of connections in La Urbana, as suggested by the low density measures and number of isolated actors, indicate that the complex information necessary for improvement will be difficult to spread throughout this restructuring leadership network. In fact, across the various networks, only two to three administrators played central roles, thereby limiting the flow of information and other resources throughout the system. In fact, both instrumental (information) and expressive (advice, etc.) networks were centered around these few central office leaders. To limit the overreliance on these leaders and prompt greater access to innovation and expertise within La Urbana, the district should find ways for additional leaders to play central roles in these networks and target innovative principals to be among these key players.[30] This is particularly important because centralized networks with a small number of key players can be unstable when a key player leaves the organization, as occurred after these data were collected. In fact, the departure of one of these central figures can have quite an impact on network structure, disrupting it and sometimes even fragmenting the network into separate components.

Fourth, the sparse network structure suggests that large-scale, complex change will be unlikely, because dense social ties support the development of coordinated solutions to complex problems. In particular, a high proportion of restructuring principals are isolated in both the more technical or instrumental networks and the expressive or more supportive networks. The lack of connection between restructuring principals means that each principal is "starting from scratch" rather than building on the knowledge that resides in this district and sharing strategies with leaders facing similar challenges. These sparse ties restrict the districtwide knowledge base, since these restructuring school principals are not acquiring novel knowledge or ideas, and thus have lower capacity to assimilate and replicate new information. The expertise network showed the most promise in terms of organizational improvement because of greater existence of internal (lateral) networks, although these would not be considered dense by any measure. Without dense lateral connections between different levels (central office or school), there is little ability to exchange information. Investing in a subgroup's ability to take in information from other subgroups (e.g., principals acquiring information from other principals) may lead to that unit releasing additional new information into the larger organization. This suggests the importance of developing dense lateral ties between district leaders as a way to build capacity and support overall organizational goals. In an educational system, the way to increase these types of lateral connections would be through the creation of clusters of schools that interact and share research-based evidence and knowledge, as well as structures like reading circles or book groups among central office leaders. While most of the literature on professional learning communities focuses on the development of these at the school level, districts would also benefit from these types of communities and the relationships that are embedded within them.[31] Through structured time and attention to developing these learning communities, district leaders would have opportunities to develop trust, as well as share information, knowledge, and best practices to encourage the diffusion of innovation districtwide.

Fifth, limited hierarchical connections—or interorganizational interactions between central office administrators and restructuring school principals—exist, suggesting the isolation of schools in restructuring from various types of expertise that reside in the district. A few key principals and central office staff serve as *boundary spanners*, connecting the other restructuring principals and central office staff and in essence serving as filters or conduits for the resources that flow between these two groups; but these types of hierarchical relationships are extremely rare. This may make it difficult for restructuring schools to explore and acquire new ideas and strategies as they attempt to improve under intense sanctions. Furthermore, intraorganizational interaction is critical to the diffusion of new ideas and innovations which are necessary for schools in restructuring. In La Urbana, however, school and central office leaders remained disconnected from each other, with few identifying any individuals in the other group as a reliable source of work-related expertise. To further strengthen the hierarchical networks, cross-group membership in learning communities or cross-group reading circles could allow both groups to learn from each other. In fact, the on-the-ground best practices of site administrators surely warrant further investigation by central office leaders who rarely sought out this type of information.

Finally, leaders in La Urbana had low levels of reciprocity, yet reciprocated communities of relations are important in systems-oriented change.[32] As leaders interact by reciprocally engaging one another, they likely modify their own practices. Reciprocated relationships in this sense are important to organizational learning; however, these relationships are firmly grounded in the broader culture of the organization. They require trusting relationships, since leaders must share both what they know and what they do not know with their colleagues. La Urbana's leaders would benefit from greater opportunities to develop trust districtwide—a challenging task when layoffs are widespread and individuals are constantly worried about losing their jobs, as in the current economic context. Furthermore, organizational learning requires a degree of risk taking, and this will be unlikely in a climate of distrust. La Urbana's leaders should adopt a *learning* orientation toward reform in which the districtwide change effort is seen as a chance to learn, grow, and develop as leaders mutually support each other in their efforts to improve.

CONCLUSION

Our findings suggest that staff in La Urbana should leverage this knowledge of their underlying networks as a way to improve the district's reform potential by finding ways to increase the connectivity between restructuring principals and between restructuring principals and central office staff. This is not to suggest that all individuals need to be connected to each other, but rather that clusters of individuals should be connected to other clusters to ensure that more people have access to the expertise and knowledge that reside in the district. Small clusters or subgroups within the larger network may more readily share information, since they have developed norms for interacting; however, these subgroups can only be leveraged for systemwide change if they are connected to each other in a way that encourages novel information to enter each subgroup (rather than group members relying on past practices). The district must find ways to provide greater opportunities for interaction of individuals in similar (e.g., principals) or different (e.g., principal-central office) positions. By supporting increased two-way (reciprocal) communication, the district will provide greater access to innovation, information, and expertise in its effort to bring about change both districtwide and particularly in these low-performing schools.

While more formal or structural opportunities are necessary to facilitate linkages, what perhaps is even more critical is the development of a culture of trust and risk taking for innovation and change to occur. For novel ideas to enter these low-performing schools, restructuring principals must not only have the opportunity to access innovators, but also be willing to try to new approaches and acquire new ideas and practices from other district leaders. The reauthorization of NCLB and other related policy should focus on districtwide capacity building to leverage both school and district change. In the end, La Urbana will require systemwide attention to school improvement rather than allowing each restructuring school to survive or fail, thereby creating its own destiny. However, any formal support mechanisms developed in La Urbana or similar districts will be pointless without strong informal relationships between district leaders.

While the study involves only one district, it clearly demonstrates the important role that social network analysis has in the understanding of how information and innovation flow between restructuring school principals, and these principals and central office staff, in an underperforming district. SNA can reveal the underlying network structures that are important in understanding resource exchanges between individuals and groups within an organization. The fact that La Urbana has not improved despite a multitude of efforts may be linked to the existing structure of relations throughout this district. Through this type of analysis, districts can see empirically the ways in which their reform efforts are facilitated (or in this case constrained) by the network structures and density. Acquiring this type of knowledge of their underlying networks will increase districts' awareness of the strength of existing ties and allow them to evaluate whether these allow for complex change to occur or whether additional strategies are necessary to strengthen these network ties.

This study is particularly important as districts adapt to meet greater accountability demands. School and district leaders, as well as policy makers, must understand the mechanisms that facilitate organizational learning and improvement (and removal from sanctions). Understanding these network structures may be useful for educational organizations enacting research-based improvement efforts, since they can be leveraged to better create, use, and diffuse knowledge and innovation. Through this type of in-depth examination of underlying social networks and the flow of information and innovation, district administrators and policy makers will better understand whether NCLB restructuring has the potential to spur low-performing schools into learning organizations. In light of the growing list of schools and districts in need of improvement, reauthorization of NCLB, and current juncture in U.S. public education, the timing of this study is critical.[32]

CHAPTER 11

Strategic "Co-opetition"

Headteacher Networking in Uganda's Secondary Schools

*Julie M. Hite, Steven J. Hite, Christopher B. Mugimu,
and Yusuf K. Nsubuga*

Global imperatives to improve education guide the reform and change initiatives under way in many nations. This study examines current challenges regarding educational change in the Ugandan context and highlights how networks can provide critical bridges for collaboration that can enhance the reform efforts. The Ugandan education system is implementing changes at all levels to increase accessibility to quality education for every child. A particular focus of the last ten years in Uganda has been the improvement of the secondary school sector.[1] In Ugandan secondary education, the acquisition and deployment of critical resources to support competitive academic performance have been central strategic concerns.

The micro-level problem for Ugandan schools is that they are balancing two interrelated factors, both of which create strategic challenges for resource acquisition. First, in Uganda's increasingly market-driven educational context, schools compete for scarce financial resources based on school performance: better performance attracts more students who pay school fees. Second, achieving competitive levels of school performance requires resources, which must be obtained in a resource-poor environment. Network theory can clarify how an informal secondary school network in the Mukono District of Uganda facilitates resource acquisition to create and sustain competitive academic performance.

BACKGROUND

Informal school networks, composed of ties between headteachers (equivalent to principals in the United States), appear to be facilitating and enhancing educational change in Uganda. The development and nature of the Ugandan educational settings create and enable the conditions in which these networks have emerged to address critical needs of an expanding number of Ugandan students.

The Ugandan Education System

Formal education was introduced in Uganda during the 1890s by European Christian missionaries. Since that time, a British-style schooling system has emerged that is in a number of ways ahead of many sub-Saharan Africa countries, as evident in global efforts such as the Education for All (EFA) initiatives of Universal Primary Education (UPE) and Universal Secondary Education (USE).[2] For example, Uganda doubled gross enrollment in primary education during the decade of the 1990s, and in 2006 it was the first and remains the only sub-Saharan African country to adopt a policy of free USE.[3]

The commitment of the Ugandan government to UPE in the early 1990s came at a crucial time in Ugandan history. The Idi Amin era (1971–1979) had left the country critically short on resources of all kinds, with too few schools to provide UPE. This context of high demand and low supply of government school facilities quickly gave rise to a system with a high proportion of private schools.

The EFA initiatives are core to the operation of the Ugandan Ministry of Education and Sports (MOES). The organization's commitment to increasing educational quality, equity, and access for all Ugandan children is particularly high. To monitor the quality expectations of EFA, the MOES uses the results of three public examinations: at the end of the seventh year of primary schooling, at the end of the first four years of secondary education, and at the end of the final two years of secondary schooling. While other measures of quality are included in the overall approach of the MOES, the national examination results remain the central measure of school performance.

The MOES moved quickly in the mid to late 1990s to embrace and enable UPE.[4] Financial and human resources were allocated by President Museveni's government to facilitate building schools, training teachers, and enrolling students in the best schooling available. Such efforts significantly increased primary school enrollment, which by the end of the decade approached the UPE access goal of EFA.[5]

Strategic Consequences of UPE

Uganda's success with UPE, however, created a challenge. Doubling gross enrollments in ten years is certainly a significant achievement, but it generated tremendous pressure on the relatively low number of secondary schools in the system. Consequently, the decade of 2000–2009 became focused on consolidating UPE gains while attempting to meet the increasing demands on the overcrowded secondary system.

The market-driven context of secondary school expansion in the 2000s generated a quick period of private school growth. This expansion was followed by market saturation in urban areas creating a surplus of private schools, followed by increased competition among all schools, which led to the demise of a significant number of private schools. The research for this study showed that 26 percent (37) of the private secondary schools in operation in the Mukono District in 2002 were no longer operating in 2008. In the same six-year time period, 181 new schools began operation, 35 percent (64) of which were no longer in operation by 2008. (These schools had either been completely closed or were operating under a different name and different management.) As these statistics show, the 54 percent growth rate of schools in the secondary system of this District (147 to 227) during the 2000s belies an underlying condition of high instability.

The major burden of navigating these volatile conditions falls squarely on the shoulders of secondary school headteachers.[6] The strategic challenges facing headteachers in Uganda changed throughout the 2000s from an initial focus on growth to meet demand to a focus on survival. The consistent pressure for ensuring quality through high performance on national exams shaped the strategic challenges of headteachers, regardless of whether the emphasis was on growth or survival. The demand on headteachers for quality comes from various stakeholder groups: MOES (macro policy need), private school owners (profitability imperative), parents (consumer power), teachers (employment stability), and students (exam performance).[7] While government and private schools are affected differentially, headteachers in both types of schools are impacted significantly by these stakeholder demands.

Resources and Co-opetition

Uganda, like other developing countries, is resource poor. Schools are particularly vulnerable to resource-poor conditions and, consequently, they typically lack necessary resources to produce adequate or desirable levels of performance.[8] The problem of how resource-poor schools in developing countries actually acquire their resources is underresearched, but the strategic answer to meeting demands of performance and stakeholder groups nonetheless rests on those schools acquiring critical resources.[9] Resources can be clustered into four basic groups: financial, physical, human, and information.[10] Effective headteachers use successful strategies to acquire and utilize first the most available and then the most critical of these resources.

Under conditions of low school competition, as in the 1990s and early 2000s when demand for secondary education was high and supply low, social networking between headteachers was a low-cost means for acquiring all types of resources.[11] However, when supply exceeded demand and created competition between schools (as in the late 2000s), a decrease in networking, or at least more limited types of resources shared through network ties, would have been anticipated. But these fluctuating market conditions created instead a context of *co-opetition*, in which school headteachers cooperate for some purposes while competing in others.[12] Under co-opetition, headteachers create cooperative network ties with other headteachers for sharing physical, human, and information resources while at the same time competing with them for students and the financial resources that students provide.[13]

Network Theory

Network theory provides a useful theoretical framework for understanding how headteachers can access resources to support school performance, as it facilitates examining educational networks at multiple levels of analysis.[14] At a micro level, headteachers function as individual network actors representing their schools, and the relationships or dyadic ties between headteachers are the conduits for network content flow (e.g., resources). At the macro level, the headteacher relationships between schools create a whole network structure.[15]

Network Actors and Their Relationships

Network ties between headteachers create pathways for the potential flow of a variety of network content to and from schools, such as strategies, information, and—most important in the Ugandan educational context—the acquisition and sharing of resources.[16] The development of network ties to other headteachers can be useful in acquiring resources to improve school performance, particularly in resource-poor environments.[17] Conversely, absence or inadequacy of headteacher ties can inhibit a school's access to resources and, consequently, its performance. Kitavi and Van Der Westhuizen as well as Herriot et al. promoted networking strategies to help Kenyan headteachers obtain needed resources for their schools.[18] Headteacher relationships both provide "awareness of resources into which one can tap" and the foundation for strong social relationships.[19] Stronger social relationships increase social capital, facilitating access to a wide variety of resources.[20] Three key mechanisms for creating network ties—homophily, geographical proximity, and resource sharing—increase the potential for resource flows:

> *Homophily.* Homophily indicates that "contact between similar people occurs at a higher rate than among dissimilar people."[21] For example, network ties may develop more easily between headteachers of the same gender or tribal affiliation. Similarly, membership in the Mukono Headteacher and Parents Association (MHTPA), first organized in 1996, may also help headteachers become aware of each other, build relationships, and understand where available resources are located. Headteachers may also develop ties to schools with similar strategic characteristics, such as size, type of founding body, and academic performance.

Geographical Proximity. Geographical proximity can contribute to the development of network ties. Barney encourages "a geographically embedded view of relations."[22] Additionally, "network theorists are beginning to more regularly incorporate considerations of geographic space in their research questions and analyses."[23] Close geographical proximity supports tie development between headteachers of schools owing to the number of opportunities for interaction and the likelihood of reaching available resources.[24] In the Ugandan context, Hite et al. found that "measures of distance and proximity can and do predict the existence of 'frequent interaction' network ties—that is, participation in a social network."[25]

Resource Acquisition. In Uganda, better performance attracts students. Consequently, higher-performing schools are likely to obtain more student fees and have greater resource stocks. As headteachers search for resources to improve school performance, they are likely to try to "network up" to headteachers of schools with better performance to acquire a variety of excess or shareable asset-specific resources.[26] Headteachers of established, high-performing schools can "mentor" headteachers at emerging schools, reaching out to provide physical and human resources, knowledge, and social capital. Mentoring emerged as a strong cultural norm of cooperation during the 1990s era of high student demand and low competition. Headteachers at mentoring schools, though not needing ties for resource acquisition, often knew aspiring school owners and were willing to share resources with headteachers at these emerging "sister schools."[27] Thus network ties between headteachers can be developed due to the search for resources and/or to the desire to help emerging schools "come up."

The Structure of the Whole Network

The various ties between headteachers create a structural system of conduits and pathways between schools within the network. This network structure can be described in terms of the connectedness and centrality of schools:

Network Connectedness. As headteachers develop more ties within the network, the connectedness within the network increases, creating more pathways for potential resource acquisition. Higher connectedness facilitates stronger ties, greater trust, and more social capital, all of which enable easier access to information and resources and create greater range and extent of available resources within the network.[28] Connectedness also influences cultural cohesion within the network, which can reinforce shared behavioral norms of resource sharing for school performance.[29] The structural embeddedness of headteachers within this connected network system may affect their strategic co-opetition capabilities for improving school performance.[30] For example, because headteachers are in different network positions, they experience differential access to resources, creating resource sharing asymmetries that enhance or constrain how a school is able to participate in co-opetition.[31]

Network Centrality. Headteachers with more ties are located in the core or center of the network, while headteachers with fewer ties are positioned more peripherally. Headteacher centrality, measured by the number of ties a headteacher has, is a strategic resource for a school, as higher centrality can influence the "flow of assets, information and status, thereby creating resource asymmetries."[32] Central headteachers have greater access to resource flows from the network to their schools and, as a result, can build resource stocks to improve school performance and effectively compete for students.[33] As headteachers create more ties and increase their centrality, they have more influence and visibility within the network, diffuse the school's resource dependencies across more ties, and make the school more attractive for new ties.[34]

Both the MOES and secondary schools have common goals of improved school performance, which can help the MOES accomplish national educational goals and help schools attract students. The problem for secondary schools and their headteachers is how to survive in a market-driven environment and be competitive enough to attract students and the financial resources they bring. Both schools and the MOES will benefit as they better understand the strategic need to develop headteacher networks for resource acquisition. This research focused on the nature of the network of secondary school headteachers in Mukono District, Uganda and its functions in facilitating resource acquisition and school performance.

DATA COLLECTED ON SECONDARY SCHOOLS

The network, geo-spatial, and school performance conditions presented and analyzed in this chapter regarding Mukono District, Uganda, are based on four research projects conducted between 2002 and 2008, as well as on data from the archives of the MOES (table 11-1). The data sampling, collection and analyses are briefly described below.

Network Data: 2002 and 2008

Snowball sampling for the 2002 study began with 10 secondary schools within five kilometers of Mukono Town (the administrative center of Mukono District).[35] Each of the ten initial headteachers named all other headteachers with whom they frequently interacted, resulting in 35 more schools added to the network sample. These new schools indicated an additional 26 schools, for a final sample of 61 network schools. In 2008, the network survey was replicated with headteachers at the 48 schools from the 2002 survey that were still operating. These headteachers identified seventy headteachers with

TABLE 11-1
Research data on secondary schools in Mukono District, Uganda, 2000–2009

Type of data (Year)	Sampling (n)	Instrument	Data Analysis (Package)
Network (2002)	Snowball (n = 61)	Network survey	Network (UCINET) Mapping (NetDraw)
Network (2008)	Replication of 2002 (n = 118[a])	Network survey	Network (UCINET) Mapping (NetDraw)
Geo-spatial (2002)	Mukono Census (n = 143)	GPS location	Mapping (ESRI ArcInfo)
Geo-spatial (2008)	Mukono Census (n = 227)	GPS location	Mapping (ESRI ArcInfo)
School performance (2002 and 2008)	Uganda Census (n = 2,278 schools)	MOES archives	Statistical: Descriptive, correlation, inferential (SPSS)

a. By 2008, thirteen schools (21%) in the 2002 network study had ceased operation leaving forty-eight schools common to both networks.

whom they were frequently interacting. The total 2008 snowball sample included 118 schools. Of these new network schools in 2008, 30 had existed in 2002, and 40 were new schools started after 2002. The network survey, conducted in an interview setting, also collected data for multiple resource sharing relations between these headteachers.

The network data generated five headteacher networks (one frequent interaction and four resource networks). UCINET facilitated analysis of network homophily, connectedness and centrality.[36] Homophily was calculated using UCINET's measures of percentage of homophily (percentage of school's ties similar on a given dimension) and the external-internal (E-I) index (ratio of percentage of ties external and internal to a given dimension). Connectedness was assessed using density—the number of actual ties over the number of potential ties. Centrality was assessed using degree centrality—the number of symmetric ties. NetDraw facilitated the generation of graphical network maps for further display and analyses of size, density, centrality and directionality.[37]

Geo-Spatial Data: 2002 and 2008

Starting with lists provided by the MOES of all secondary schools in the Mukono District, teams of two field researchers geographically located every secondary school in operation in 2002 and 2008, whether or not they were included in the network studies. A total of 147 schools were geo-located in

2002, and 227 were geo-located in 2008. As Tita and Faust indicate that few studies have exact spatial locations for both ego and alters, such geographical data for the network schools provide a rare opportunity for examining the intersection of social and geographical space.[38] The geo-spatial location of each school was collected using handheld global positioning system (GPS) units, in minutes and seconds of latitude and longitude. These data were entered into ESRI's ArcInfo for analysis and mapping.

School Performance: 2002 and 2008

Each year the MOES obtains the annual ordinary level (O-level) national examination data for every student in every school in the country from the Uganda National Examination Board (UNEB). The MOES provided the 2002 and 2008 data for each student and school in the Mukono District. O-level student and school performance data were extracted for the schools involved in the network studies and entered into SPSS for analysis.

School performance was defined categorically as either high, mid, or low.[39] Schools performing one-half standard deviation or more above the mean were labeled as high-performing schools, those between one-half standard deviation above and below the mean were mid-performing schools, and those at or below minus one-half standard deviation were labeled as low-performing schools.

SECONDARY SCHOOL NETWORKS IN MUKONO, UGANDA

In this section, we first address the nature of the network of secondary school headteachers in Mukono, Uganda, including their ties and the larger network structure. The analysis examined five network relations between headteachers: one frequent interaction and four resource-sharing relations.

Frequent Interaction Network

Table 11-2 provides demographic details for the population of schools in the Mukono District and for the headteachers' frequent interaction network. When comparing the schools in the population and in the network between 2002 and 2008, six patterns were evident:

- Growth in the number of network schools (93 percent) outpaced growth in the number of schools in the district (59 percent).
- Network schools reflected the demographics of the larger school population in having a large percentage of private schools.
- Network schools reflected the demographics of the larger school population in having a large percentage of mostly male headteachers.
- Network schools reflected the demographics of the larger school population in having headteachers mostly from the Ganda tribe.

TABLE 11-2

Comparison between all schools and network schools

	All secondary schools in Mukono District			Mukono secondary schools in network		
	2002	2008	% change[a]	2002	2008	% change
Total number of schools	147	227	59%	61	118	93%
Mean number of students	235	360	51%	336	496	48%
Number of private schools[b]	128	206	61%	49	99	102%
Number of government schools	19	21	11%	12	19	58%
Number of urban schools	49	55	12%	27	38	41%
Number of rural schools	98	172	76%	34	80	135%
Number of schools in MHTPA	45	N/A	N/A	39	77	97%
Female headteachers	24	37	54%	15	22	47%
Male headteachers	123	190	55%	46	96	109%
Ganda headteachers	88	148	68%	38	81	113%
Non-Ganda headteachers	59	89	51%	23	27	17%

a. All changes between years were positive.

b. The distinction between private and government schools is based only on whether the founding body was a private entity or the Ugandan government.

- Network schools mirrored the shifts in the larger population toward larger schools and more schools in rural areas.
- Network schools were less likely to cease operation than schools outside the network. Between 2000 and 2008, approximately 33 percent of the secondary schools started in the district closed or "collapsed," while only 20 percent of the 2002 network schools closed.

Network Structure

The "frequent interaction" network represents all ties identified by the headteachers. Figure 11-1 presents the graphical network maps of these networks in 2002 and 2008. Together, these maps illustrate the growth of this network. The 2002 network has 182 ties among 61 headteachers, while the 2008 network has 327 ties among 118 headteachers. The six most central headteachers in each network are indicated on these maps. Two headteachers were among the most central in both 2002 and 2008. The six most central headteachers averaged 15 ties in 2002 and 22 ties in 2008, while the average number of headteacher ties for both years was 5 ties. In 2002, four of the six most central

FIGURE 11-1 2002 and 2008 headteacher frequent interaction networks

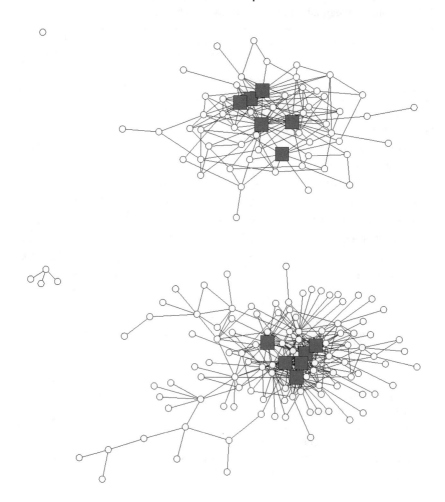

headteachers were at government schools. By 2008, two of these 2002 government schools had new headteachers, who had fewer ties than the previous headteachers, resulting in decreased centrality for these schools. Two other headteachers, also at government schools, rose in centrality to replace them.

Geographical Proximity

Figure 11-2 illustrates the geographical location of headteacher frequent interaction network ties in both 2002 and 2008. In 2002, the distribution of these ties clearly aligned with the tarmac roads, and the distance between

FIGURE 11-2 2002 and 2008 geographical location of headteacher frequent interaction network ties (Maps created by Dr. Patrick R. Wauro)

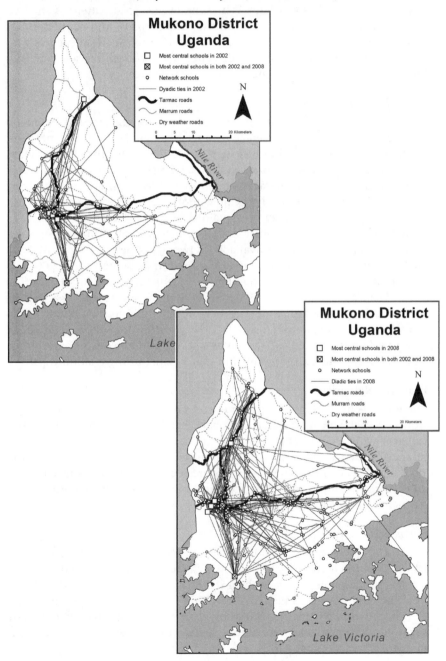

the schools predicted the existence of the ties.[40] By 2008, the growth of the network created a change in the geographical distribution of schools and the ties between their headteachers. While the tarmac road pattern is still evident, network ties expanded beyond the tarmac roads, and connectedness increased for schools in outlying rural areas. Of the two headteachers who were central in both years, one headteacher is still located in a southern outlying rural area well beyond the reach of tarmac roads.

Network Tie Homophily

Homophily patterns of frequent interaction ties were assessed based on schools and headteachers characteristics (see table 11-3). The concept of homophily suggests that headteachers create ties with other headteachers with similar demographics or school characteristics. Across both network years, headteachers did interact frequently with other headteachers of the same gender and at similar types of schools (private versus government). This homophily pattern may be explained by the fact that the majority of network headteachers were male and at private schools. Thus, these headteachers would be the most available network partners. Contrasting with 2002, headteacher ties no longer demonstrated tribal homophily in 2008. No pattern of homophily existed in either year for membership in MHTPA. The network contains two patterns of heterophily, demonstrating diversity of ties in school size and performance. This heterophily indicates that resource relationships were often between smaller, lower-performing schools and larger, better-performing schools. This difference indicates many resource flows were likely asymmetric (one-way) and suggests mentoring relationships.

Resource Networks

The four resource relations are subnetworks of the frequent interaction network. The network survey asked all of the headteachers which of the headteachers with whom they frequently interacted had provided them with financial, physical, human, and information resources. Figures 11-3, 11-4, 11-5, and 11-6 compare these four resource exchange networks in 2002 and 2008. Directional arrows in the graphical maps indicate where each headteacher went for these resources.

Financial Resource Network

Figure 11-3 presents the graphical maps for the financial resource network, which comprised the ties through which headteachers received financial resources. The number of schools in the financial resource network dropped from 28 to 17, losing 18 ties. In 2002 all 6 of the most central schools were in this network, whereas in 2008 only 2 of the most central schools were involved. Both networks were quite sparse, with very few ties relative to the frequent interaction network.

TABLE 11.3
School homophily and heterophily patterns[a]

	Frequent Interaction Network		Patterns and Trends
	2002	2008	
Headteacher gender	.64	.70	Homophily continuing
Headteacher tribe	.64	.48	Some homophily to no pattern
MHTPA	.51	.61	No pattern
School size	.32	.35	Heterophily continuing
Private versus government	.74	.66	Homophily contining
Performance	.27	.37	Heterophily continuing

>a. 1 = complete homophily, 0 = complete heterophily (.40–.60 would indicate no pattern)

Physical Resource Network

Figure 11-4 presents the graphical maps for the physical resource network. These ties represent headteachers' sources of physical resources. Both of these networks are more connected than the financial resource networks, and the 6 most central schools were found in both networks. While the whole frequent interaction 2008 network added 57 more schools, the 2008 physical resource network added only 13 schools—and the number of ties increased by only one. This pattern indicates that the 2008 physical resource network was less connected than that of 2002. However, the 2008 network demonstrated clearer patterns of centrality around the most central headteachers in the frequent interaction network.

Human Resource Network

Figure 11-5 presents the graphical maps for the human resource network, ties that indicate that one school receives help from another school to find teachers. "Sharing" teachers across schools is quite common in Uganda. Many teachers board at one school while also teaching at other schools. The 2008 network was much less connected than the network of 2002. While the number of schools sharing human resources increased from 44 to 66, the number of resource sharing ties actually decreased by 16. The centrality pattern in 2008 included all of the most central headteachers in the 2008 frequent interaction network (compared with five of six in 2002).

Information Resource Network

Figure 11-6 presents the graphical maps for the information resource network, the relationship whereby one headteacher provides information and new ideas to another headteacher. For both years, this resource network most

FIGURE 11-3 2002 and 2008 financial resource networks

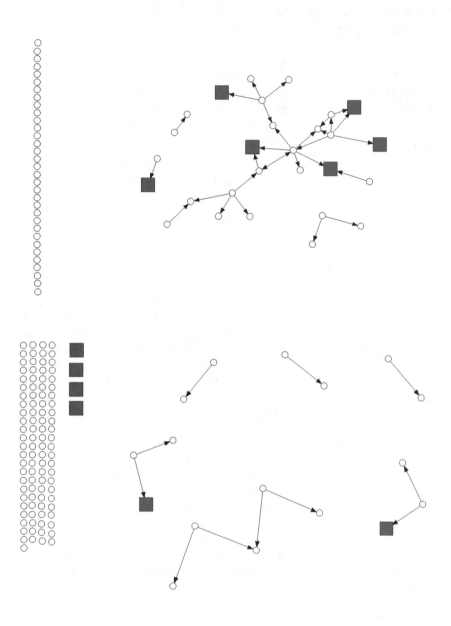

FIGURE 11-4 2002 and 2008 physical resource networks

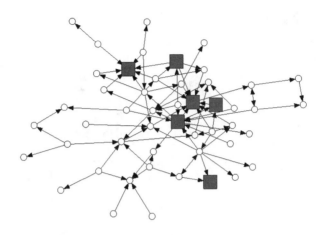

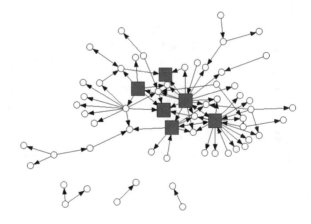

FIGURE 11-5 2002 and 2008 human resource networks

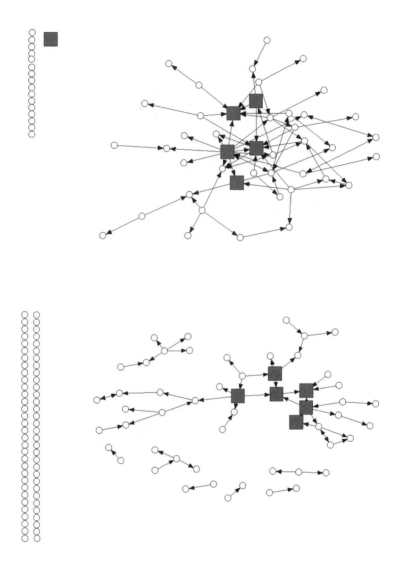

Figure 11-6 2002 and 2008 information resource networks

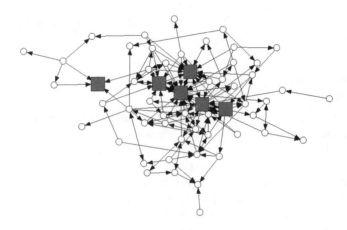

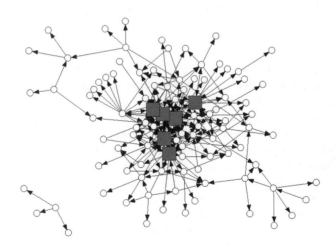

closely resembled the frequent interaction network structure, and all six of the most central headteachers in the frequent interaction were connected in these networks as well. This network had the highest connectedness of all the resource networks in both years, and was the only resource network to have increased in connectedness over the years, even though 42 more schools were involved in 2008. As a result, the information network also had the lowest number of isolate or unconnected headteachers.

FUNCTIONS OF HEADTEACHER NETWORKS FOR SCHOOL PERFORMANCE

Uganda's market-driven educational context provides an interesting setting for the study of school networks. Network theory provides a valuable lens for viewing how the relationships between Ugandan headteachers function to benefit schools and enhance educational performance. The nature of these networks in terms of connectedness, centrality, and homophily (having similar characteristics) highlights four key network functions that, in this context, are associated with the educational change efforts of headteachers: (1) school stability, (2) resource acquisition and exchange, (3) mentoring and learning, and (4) leverage for development of school-level ties. In Uganda, these functions can help secondary schools overcome market-driven educational challenges to enhance performance.

School Stability

Headteacher networks enhance the stability of schools. Market-driven and competitive environments make it difficult for schools to survive, particularly emerging private schools. Emerging organizations rely on their strong network ties to help nurture them through this process.[41] The most obvious change in the school networks over time has been the increase in the number of schools in the network. This increase has outpaced the number of new schools, suggesting that network development has been due not only to the creation of more schools but also to more headteachers reaching out and seeking connections to other schools. As more ties were built, the network developed, and the schools within the network benefited from the stabilizing forces of these headteacher relationships. Network partners can provide a critical infrastructure supporting emerging and struggling schools. For example, increased school stability was evidenced by schools in the 2002 frequent interaction network having a lower collapse rate than schools not in the network.

Headteachers can increase stability for their schools, which translates to their own employment stability, by creating ties with many other headteachers. As headteachers create more ties, the web of connectedness and structural embeddedness develops, pulling some headteachers closer to the network core. Headteachers with more ties are more securely connected to the network than those with only one or two ties, which if lost unlink them entirely from the network. Their ties with headteachers from similar schools (homophily) provide stability through specific support for similar strategic needs. At the same time, their connections to headteachers from schools that differ in size and performance provide stability by reducing reliance on redundant resources, providing access to new types of resources, and building awareness of strategies from larger, better performing schools.

Resource Acquisition and Exchange

Headteacher networks provide conduits and pathways for resource acquisition and exchange. Given the resource-poor context, schools in Uganda must locate and access resources from their environments. As the network becomes increasingly connected, more pathways provide more potential network partners and more potential for the flow of resources within the network. Headteachers with more network ties decrease the school's dependence on any one resource relationship, providing greater security in acquiring vital resources from the environment.

The nature of the different resource networks has changed over time. The financial network was sparse in 2002; it was even sparser in 2008, suggesting that headteachers had shifted where they searched for financial resources. Given that USE provides government funding for some students, even in private schools, schools can look to this government source as a viable option for financial resources.[42]

Schools in 2008 also had fewer human resource network ties, likely due to increased market competition. Headteachers may have become less cooperative about providing or sharing teachers (human resources), as this resource is most directly related to academic performance. Headteachers continued to share physical resources such as desks, lab equipment and vehicles, which have less direct effect on school performance.

However, the information resource network grew dramatically. Information is the most easily shared resource, as sharing it does not deplete it.[43] The information resource network also most closely resembled the frequent interaction network, suggesting that much of the network interaction has involved the sharing of information and ideas. Sharing information resources may be less threatening, as the receiving school may not have the capabilities to use the information competitively. Thus in a competitive environment, information and physical resource sharing create less competitive risk than human resource sharing , yet still allow the schools to participate in the cultural norm of cooperation.

As a headteacher develops more ties and increases centrality in the network, these network partners are also more connected and can more easily broker the headteacher into resource-bearing ties elsewhere in the network.

Note that the most central headteachers in the frequent interaction network each year were also involved, most often centrally, in all of the resource networks except for the financial. Highly central headteachers have increased control over resources in the network, functioning as gatekeepers and brokers to resources that flow across the larger network.

Headteachers can also develop multiple resource flows within one tie, which strengthens the tie, providing an important strategy for the stability of the relationship. Additional resource acquisition can be layered on ties that initially serve other purposes.[44] For example, the similarity between the interaction and information resource network suggests that headteachers may create personal ties and then add other functions such as information sharing. Personal ties may be latent ties that can be activated when and if certain resources are needed.[45]

Mentoring and Learning

As increased competition intensifies a schools' needs for adaptive learning and change, headteacher networks create avenues for essential learning and mentoring.[46] These networks facilitate the flow of information and new ideas between schools, provide strategies for adaptation and improvement, and enable productive co-opetition. A highly connected headteacher has more potential learning partners than a more isolated headteacher. Knowledge within the network flows through network ties, is easy to share, and can enhance a school's capabilities for school improvement.

Many headteachers were involved in mentoring relationships in the network in which headteachers of larger, better performing schools mentored headteachers at smaller, lower performing schools that, often, were struggling to emerge and survive. Historical Ugandan norms of school cooperation had benefited most of these mentor headteachers' schools when they were new and emerging.[47] Surprisingly, cooperative mentoring relationships have continued despite the increase in competition for students. Mentor headteachers were generally at larger, more network-central schools with higher school performance, and thus higher school fees and more resources, than the schools of headteachers they helped. The pattern suggests that headteachers mentored those with whom they did not directly compete for students, and they provided resources that were shareable with low competitive risk. The critical support, information, and ideas received through mentoring enhances the emergence and stability of smaller, lower-performing schools. The finding of diverse school relationships contrasts with expectations of homophily. Headteachers networking up and mentoring down may provide a useful explanation of interaction in the resource networks. This asymmetric networking may facilitate educational change due to isomorphic processes, particularly in this increasingly competitive educational context.[48] Educational strategies and change may be easily diffused from higher-performing schools, allowing lower-performing, more resource-dependent schools to gradually become more like them.

Leverage for Development of School-Level Ties

Headteacher network ties are fundamentally based on personal relationships. Given that headteachers often move to other schools, these personal relationships help ties stay intact.[49] For example, although the study found that that closer geographic distance predicts ties, two of the most central headteachers in the 2002 frequent interaction network worked at the greatest distance from their network partners, having retained personal ties developed when they had previously worked at a centrally located school in Mukono Town. When they both moved further away, their new schools benefitted from these ties, and their network partners easily established relationships with the new schools based on the prior personal connections.

This example also shows that a headteacher's personal ties need to become institutionalized at the school level for the long-term benefit of the school.[50] If headteacher ties do not become school-level ties, the school is at risk when (not if) the headteacher moves to another school. In the above example, the same two headteachers who left these central schools took their personal ties with them. Both schools lost network ties, which decreased their centrality so that they were no longer among the most central schools in 2008. The new headteachers at these schools came from different districts and did not know the headteachers in Mukono. Consequently, these schools lost ties and centrality and thus network conduits for accessing resources.

Headteachers, school directors, and school boards must strategically ensure that these connections, particularly for resource acquisition and exchange, remain intact when the headteacher moves. School-level ties begin with personal relationships between headteachers that create opportunities for interaction between other school administrators. As a rope becomes stronger with multiple threads, ties between schools are stronger when they include a variety of relationships serving multiple purposes.

Theoretical Implications for Network Theory and Education

The theoretical implications of this educational network research for social network theory are twofold. First, the value of integrating both social and geographical space informs how networks can be influenced by their larger contexts, and that social network research needs to account for the influences of these contexts. Second, this network research provides rich insights into network functioning because it directly explores the inherent multiplexity of network ties and content.

This research also informs network theory as it applies to education in at least three ways. First, education processes occur through the interaction and collaboration of educational stakeholders, such as headteachers or principals, as network actors. Second, interaction within educational networks can have critical strategic outcomes for schools, as in the case of these resource networks. Third, educational stakeholders do not operate within a vacuum in education; rather, they must account for the larger social contexts in which they function, as is the case in the market-oriented and highly competitive environment of Ugandan education.

Practical Implications for Educational Leaders

Headteacher networks increase school stability; create critical conduits for acquiring resources, learning, and mentoring; and provide leverage for the development of school-level ties. As a result, school performance can be enhanced, more students can be attracted to the school (providing financial resources), and school survival will be more likely in the market-driven environment. School, district, and national MOES leaders in education, recognizing the value of developing strategic relationships between headteachers and between schools, can proactively promote and support network development.

Headteachers can proactively seek to interact with other headteachers, intentionally building mutually beneficial ties for seeking and sharing information and other resources. As headteachers come together to create formal networks, such as the MHTPA, they build critical infrastructure that contributes to school survival and performance. They can also help to leverage and facilitate the development of multiple ties between their schools.

The MOES and district leaders must support the creation of both formal and informal school networks by providing and supporting formal and informal opportunities for interaction. They can facilitate strategic brokering of headteacher relationships and encourage formal associations for headteacher support, such as the MHTPA. MOES can also create its own network ties to central headteachers to leverage information distribution. In this way, national and district leaders can help ensure school survival and thus help accomplish national educational policies of UPE and USE and international goals of EFA.

Headteacher and school networks can be a strategic stabilizing force in localization and decentralization endeavors critical to UPE, USE and EFA. With formal and informal network infrastructures in place, the MOES can more confidently manage decentralization of critical functions and funding by tapping into information flows that pass through these network-central schools to calibrate the status and progress of localization and decentralization efforts. Headteacher and school networks can also encourage diffusion of new ideas and alleviate enforcement needs that would otherwise require more costly policies and mechanisms.

CONCLUSION

Network theory provides a valuable lens for understanding how the relationships between headteachers and the larger structure of these relationships influence educational processes and outcomes. Network relationships are more than simple lines drawn between schools: These ties have the potential to be rich mediums of critical resource acquisition and exchange. Any effort toward school improvement and positive change requires critical resources. Resource-poor educational contexts, such as Uganda, exist throughout the world. Effective strategies for acquiring school resources are therefore particularly crucial for generating and sustaining effective educational change and improvement. This research indicates that educational leaders need to strategically craft and nurture interschool network relationships, building conduits for the flow of critical resources to support improvements in the quality, equity, and access of education at their schools.

PART 3

New Directions in Social Network Theory and Education

CHAPTER 12

Utility Theory, Social Networks, and Teacher Decision Making

Modeling Networks' Influences on Teacher Attitudes and Practices

Kenneth A. Frank, Chong Min Kim, and Dale Belman

The analysis of social networks has tremendous capacity to inform educational research and policy related to teachers' behavior. But social network analysis is not without its limitations. It is all too easy to simply make attractive pictures and tell stories that could have been told without network data or that do not emerge from a rigorous analysis of the data. As Zuckerman states in the organization theory blog:

> One of the features of social network analysis that is at once a great strength and a great danger is that network diagrams are highly evocative. In teaching and presenting network material, I have found that if I put up a picture of a network and start spinning a story about it, even untutored audiences follow along easily and they tend to accept the network as an accurate characterization of the actors and the social structure they inhabit. This is great, but the problem is that any such presentation tends to bake in all kinds of assumptions that should always be questioned.[1]

Zuckerman's concern is an example of the need to push social network analysis beyond mere graphics and metaphor.[2]

We recognize that graphical representations of data, especially network data, can be helpful in developing theory or expressing data in accessible form, especially of systemic phenomena. Indeed, the first author's introduction to network analysis came primarily through his technique, KliqueFinder, for embedding subgroup boundaries in sociograms.[3] But here we urge educational researchers to move past graphical representations of data to explicitly model effects of network processes. In particular, our goal is to help researchers model how teachers' attitudes or practices are influenced by others in their networks and how teachers select colleagues with whom to interact or to whom to allocate resources (e.g., curricular materials or pedagogical help). Specifying and estimating models of these processes will facilitate an interdisciplinary understanding of teachers' behaviors that can be related to network processes.[4]

Although there are extensive publications and guidelines regarding introductions to network analyses, in this chapter we suggest deriving network models from an underlying theory of a utility.[5] A utility-based theory provides at least three important benefits. First, focusing on teachers' utility reflects the importance of teachers' agency for educational outcomes, and therefore attends to teachers' motives.[6]

Second, as in labor economics, utility may describe the basic trade-offs individuals make in their allocations of time and resources (e.g., how much a teacher will help another teacher versus develop her own curricular materials).[7] As a result, utility functions are well understood as able to formalize the ordering of individuals' preferences for different quantities of nonmonetary goods, facilitating an interdisciplinary understanding of motivation.[8] For example, utility functions can represent the trade-off teachers make between the psychological satisfactions of teaching effectively versus the sociological rewards of fitting into the social organization of the school.

Third, utility functions can be maximized with respect to any given quantity (e.g., effort employed using specific teaching practices) to develop expressions for the pursuit of that quantity at equilibrium. This can also be understood as the minimum amount of a given behavior required to achieve a given utility.[9] Importantly, such reduced-form models and their components lend themselves to estimation using empirical data, as we will show below.

The particular utility we employ here is a function of a teacher's efficacy and her desire to conform to school norms (see technical appendix for details).[10] For example, a teacher who believes that children learn best when taught whole language might immerse her students in reading materials. This would contribute to her utility by increasing her efficacy. On the other hand, if the norm in the teacher's school is to teach phonics, then the teacher may contribute to her utility by emphasizing decoding practices in order to fit into the social organization of her school.

The utility function we develop here reflects two aspects of the school's institutional function in educating students. First the teacher's efficacy represents how well the teacher's own production contributes directly to the school's institutional role to educate students. But the school as an organization also serves as an institution for coordinating behavior.[11] And the teacher's compliance with the norm of others in her school is one aspect of her contribution to this coordinative function.

Consider a first-grade teacher, Ashley, who teaches whole language because she believes this most contributes to the learning of the students in her classroom. Even if Ashley is correct, some of her students may not learn phonics, compromising the efficacy of next year's second-grade teachers, whose pedagogies assume most incoming students can decode words. Thus, by failing to conform to the expectations of the second-grade teachers, Ashley compromises the coordination function of the school. Ashley's deviation from expectation may also make it difficult for her to access others' knowledge, further compromising the coordinative function of the school.

The implications of a teacher's utility for her teaching practices can be understood as a lens for directing inputs from a teacher's social contexts into practices. As shown in figure 12-1, the asymmetric convex lens of utility represents a teacher who assigns a higher value to fitting in with her colleagues than to her own sense of efficacy. Therefore she adopts phonics to align more with her colleagues' norms than to her own sense of the efficacy of whole language. This might apply, for example, to a junior elementary teacher who is uncertain of the efficacy of her own practices and very concerned about her ability to fit in with her colleagues. The figure then shows how a teacher's behaviors create student outcomes that feed back into the teacher's utility either through changes in her beliefs about effective practices or others' expectations.

Figure 12-1 shows how a theory of utility can guide models that can be empirically estimated. A teacher's effort in a particular area can be modeled as a function of the perceived payoffs in student learning versus the conformity to norms of others in her context. This is a basic statistical model (called *regression*, or the *general linear model*). As such, and given longitudinal data, the model can be estimated with ordinary software once one has constructed the term representing exposure to others' behaviors or expectations.[12] These models can also include controls for other characteristics of teachers, especially a measure of prior practice to control for the confounding of the characteristics of interaction partners with prior behaviors. As an example, Frank, Zhao, and Borman estimated a model of the influence of interaction partners' use of technology on a teacher's use of technology, controlling for the teacher's prior use of technology.[13] They found the practices of interaction partners were approximately as influential as the teacher's own perceived value of using technology. This implies that conformity is roughly evenly balanced with efficacy (α in the technical appendix = .5).

The model of influence does not confine the researcher to estimating influence of a single set of actors. For example, Sun et al. model teachers' practices as a function of influences of informal leaders (those listed as a close colleague) versus formal leaders (e.g., coaches, reading specialists, designated mentors), finding that informal leaders influence the core practices of teachers (e.g., pedagogical practices such as decoding) while formal leaders

FIGURE 12-1   Utility as a lens for directing inputs from a teacher's social contexts into practices

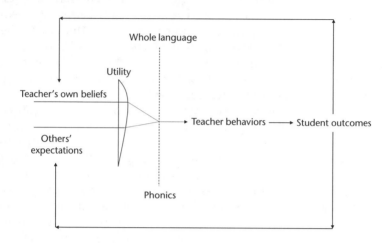

influence peripheral practices (e.g., classroom management).[14] Networks can also be extended beyond direct interactions. For example, Penuel, Frank, and Krause (chapter 9) use multilevel models to estimate the effect of subgroup members' prior implementation of reform on a teacher's practices (where subgroups are defined by application of Frank's 1995 clustering algorithm to network data).[15]

Influence models can be estimated for attitudes as well as behaviors. For example, Cole and Weinbaum (chapter 5) show that an attitude about the value of reform can itself be a function of a normative influence. [16] This model can be written as:[17]

Attitude toward reform at time 2 = β_0
+ ($1-\beta_1$) attitude toward reform at time 1
+ β_1 previous attitude of others in reform network
+ β_2 number of peers in reform network
+ β' covariates,   (1)

where covariates include controls for language taught, formal position, etc.[18] Thus the model represents the trade-off between a teacher's own valuing of the reform, associated with ($1-\beta_1$), versus the normative attitude of others, associated with β_1 (in the technical appendix, we show how the model is analogous to the influence model). Cole and Weinbaum included similar network exposure terms for instrumental (advice-seeking) and expressive (friendship) networks, finding the strongest effects for the instrumental network, with the estimate of β_1 equal to about .3, similar to that of Frank et al.[19]

Utility and the Model of Selecting Others in a Network

Youngs et al.'s utility function can also help us to understand how teachers choose to whom to allocate resources (e.g., provision of help, sharing of curricular materials, providing emotional support). In particular, teacher i invests in j versus j' if there is greater utility for doing so. For example, if Kim, as a second-grade teacher, helps first-grade teacher Ashley, then next year's second-grade students will be more prepared to learn, increasing Kim's efficacy. The same would not apply if Kim helped a third-grade teacher. Thus we would expect teachers to be more inclined to help those who teach lower grades than higher grades (this is consistent with Rothstein's findings that fifth-grade teachers affect the quality of fourth-grade students, compromising the validity of value added models).[20] On the other hand, a teacher may have incentive for helping another teacher if that will raise the provider's status in the school. For example, Kim may distribute help throughout a school if she is recognized by peers and administrators for doing so, especially if Kim identifies strongly with the members of the school as a collective.

Teachers can easily maximize their utility if helping a given other both increases efficacy and status. More interesting is if allocating to one teacher likely increases efficacy while allocating to another increases status. For example, Kim might have to choose between helping an isolated teacher who teaches the preceding grade versus a senior teacher leader who teaches a higher grade level. Helping the isolated teacher contributes more to efficacy, but less to status.

The result in the technical appendix shows that teachers can make their allocation choices based on the same parameter that governs their desire to conform. The greater a teacher's desire to conform, the more likely she will be to help another for increased status. The greater her desire for efficacy, the more likely she will be to help another whose behavior can contribute to her efficacy.

As shown in the technical appendix, the comparison of the utility of helping one versus another teacher has direct implications for empirical models that can be estimated. For example, Hite et al. (chapter 11) estimate a model of how teachers select with whom to interact frequently.[21] Using a homophily index (effect of common attributes on the occurrence of a network relation—birds of a feather flock together), they estimated the effects of each term separately and at two different time points (2002 and 2008). They found strong homophily effects for gender and sector across time points, and heterophily (interacting with others different of different attributes) of school size and performance at both time points. It is worth considering, from a utility perspective, how to interpret their results. For example, teachers might interact frequently with others of the same gender or sector because of greater commonality in language, and thus greater potential for efficacy through knowledge gained, whereas the heterophily effects might be due to the seeking of status among teachers in schools of different sizes or levels of performance.

Spillane et al. (chapter 8) also estimate elements of a selection model, finding that formal leaders provide much of the informal advice in schools.[22] This represents an effect of the type of person who provides help. Following Van Duijn's multilevel framework, this can be modeled as the effect of characteristics of the potential help providers on the likelihood that help will be provided. For example,

$$\text{help provided by } j \text{ to } i = \beta_0 + \beta_1 \text{ formal leader}_j + u_i + v_j \qquad (2)$$

where γ_{01} represents the effect of actor j having a formal leadership role on the likelihood that she provides help to others (the u_i represent any residual effects associated with potential help providers such as unmeasured effects of training or knowledge; and the v_j represents any residual effects associated with potential help receivers). Here one could ask why a teacher would seek advice from formal versus informal leaders. Perhaps the formal leaders possess higher levels of knowledge and thus can contribute to effectiveness. Furthermore, seeking advice from a formal leader may be associated with less stigma and loss of status than seeking advice from an informal leader.[23]

DISCUSSION

There are several advantages to using a formal utility function to generate estimable models of social network effects. First, such functions express a theory about the underlying motivations of teachers. Here we posited that teachers were fundamentally motivated by the pursuit of efficacy as well as the desire to fit into their social contexts. Critically, we recognize that the trade-off between efficacy and conformity does not necessarily create a stark choice. In those situations where a teacher fits well in her school, a single behavior will be effective and satisfy the expectations of others around her. Correspondingly, our model is more informative when the practices a teacher believes are effective are *different from* those expected by others in her school—when a teacher does not fit well in her school. We also recognize that teachers will prioritize the practices they think are effective versus conformity to different degrees. A junior teacher with anxiety about fitting in and a low sense of efficacy may prioritize conformity more than a senior teacher close to retirement who is confident in her own abilities. In each case, the utility function helps us to specify models for empirical testing that can provide information about the conditions under which a teacher will prioritize practices consistent with her own perceived efficacy versus conforming to others' expectations.

Second, one can examine the theoretical implications of maximizing with respect to a specific quantity such as effort. Here, maximizing with respect to effort generates models consistent with standard models of influence in the network literature. Thus the utility function is not an empirical model in and of itself. What it does is provide a unifying framework grounded in individual motivation for empirical models, in this case those including social network components. This facilitates integration across contexts; for example, allowing us to compare the relative magnitudes of influence in Cole and Weinbaum versus Frank, Zhao, and Borman.[24]

Third, we were able to use a single utility function to generate models of influence through a network as well as selection of network partners. Thus the parameter governing the influence of network members on one's behavior is the same as the parameter governing choice of network partners. Compare for example with Frank and Fahrbach, who integrated models of influence and selection, but who did not recognize the potential for common parameters derived from a single utility function.[25]

Implications for Policy

Conspicuously absent from our utility function is the value of monetary rewards. We note this exclusion is consistent with recent findings from a recent large teacher survey, where teachers listed support from leadership and opportunities to collaborate as more important for retaining good teachers than factors associated with salary.[26] Yet it is an open question as to how much monetary rewards figure into teachers' utilities. In particular, given the findings mentioned in this paragraph, we suspect that teachers will not be strongly influenced by modest changes in monetary compensation versus the other rewards of efficacy and fitting in socially. Importantly, the utility function presented in this chapter and the models of influence and selection generated from it allow one to specify and test the importance of monetary rewards relative to the other components in the function.

Emphasizing the nonmonetary rewards offers a new take on measuring the value a teacher adds to her school. Teachers who add value to a school by coordinating and sharing knowledge with others may not be recognized by current formulas that are primarily functions of the achievement gains of the students in a teacher's own classroom. The implication is that if teachers incorporate value-added incentives (such as merit pay) into their utility they may reduce levels of coordination and knowledge sharing.

Implications for Change Agents

Our analysis suggests that change agents should consider the rationality of the teacher as she responds to external demands for change within the social organization of her school. "Resistant" teachers might simply be ones whose immediate networks push against a new behavior, or who cannot access knowledge from colleagues to support new behaviors. Pushing too hard against such norms can place teachers in ambiguous roles, contributing to burnout and compromising the coordinative function of the school.

The overarching implication is that change agents must consider themselves as changing *schools*, not individual *teachers*. The model of identifying an effective practice and then training a few teachers in a given school in an isolated setting does not recognize the social context of the teacher. Instead, change agents should engage the full school. This can be done by requiring a large buy-in of school faculty before implementing reform (e.g., Success for All's requirement of support from 75 percent of a faculty). Or change agents might deliberately attend to how knowledge and support will be circulated throughout a school; for example, by targeting reforms for individuals well integrated into the networks of their schools.[27] Change agents also could cultivate help from subgroups of teachers who have already adopted new practices.[28]

New Trends in Social Network Analysis

We have attended carefully to the models of influence and selection because they are the bedrock of social network analysis and because there is an emerging consensus regarding their specification and estimation. But there are important limitations to these models, which we outline below.

Dynamics of Social Networks

We have presented the models of influence and selection in isolation, when in fact both processes likely occur in most social systems, especially among teachers.[29] For example, a teacher may change her emphasis on phonics practices based on interactions with colleagues, and then change with whom she interacts based on her new emphasis on phonics. The dynamic interplay between influence and selection is shown in figure 12-2.[30] *

At the very least, the potential for dynamic processes creates challenges for causal inference.[31] For example, in modeling behavior as a function of network partners, one must control for prior levels of behavior to account for the possibility of selection of network partners based on prior behavior. Similarly if one models the selection of network ties based on common attributes one must account for prior network ties to identify the *effect* of attributes on the formation of network ties.

A full dynamic conceptualization accounts for actors' behaviors as outcomes influenced by actors' attributes or network (influence model), and actors' networks as outcomes influenced by actors' attributes or behaviors (selection model).[32] Correspondingly, dynamic network models can represent the network processes (e.g., knowledge flow) as both predictor and

---

* Here influence occurs as teachers change behaviors between time 1 and time 2 in response to the relationships in which they engage with other teachers. Selection occurs as teachers change their relations between the 0–1 and 1–2 interval in response to behaviors.

FIGURE 12-2   The interplay between influence of the network and selection of network partners over time

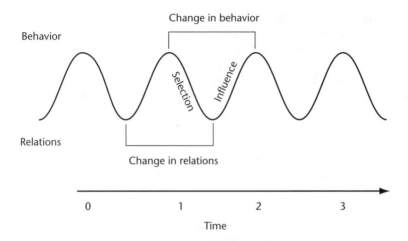

outcome.[33] The advantage of such representations is they can track how resources flow through a network and generate changes in the network as they do so. For example, imagine Ashley learning about how to teach phonics from Kim (Kim → Ashley), but also learning from Sam, who originally learned from Kim (Kim → Sam → Ashley). That is, Ashley learns about phonics directly from Kim and indirectly via Sam. An important question then is the effect of the indirect exposure to knowledge (via Sam) on Ashley's behavior. Frank and Fahrbach posit that indirect exposures represent normative influences as opposed to informational influences; because Ashley receives knowledge directly from Kim, any influence of Sam on Ashley is likely not knowledge based but instead evidence of Ashley conforming to the norm defined by Sam's behavior.[34]

The dynamic models also allow for the possibility that the flow of resources such as knowledge or information can change the network relations. For example, as Ashley receives knowledge of how to teach phonics she may modify her practices (influence). In turn, she may choose to interact with others who use similar practices (selection). The dynamic interplay between influence and selection has implications for outside change agents. For example, consider an outside change agent who recruits volunteers for professional development who are predisposed to the content of the professional development. The training and norms expressed in the professional development may influence the teachers, distancing their practices from others in their school, potentially leading to social isolation. This poses challenges for "train the trainer" types of models.[35]

One particular approach to simultaneously estimating models of influence and selection is Snijders' SIENA models. Parameters are estimated by using simulation to approximate the network and behaviors (or attitudes) at time 2 from the network and behaviors at time 1 based on sets of random sequences of relations and attitudes chosen for reevaluation. Critically, Snijders' conceptualization assumes actors have a utility for interaction partners as well as for changes in behaviors. The approach outlined in this chapter can then be integrated into Snijders' by deriving the separate utilities for influence and selection from the common utility (as in the technical appendix).

While dynamic network models hold great promise, only a few studies have employed these models to date in education settings.[36] Of critical concern is that estimation of more complex models can be unstable if data include only a small number of actors or time points. This highlights the value of obtaining data at more than two more time points and of developing models of influence and selection from a coherent framework.

Agent-Based Models

Utility functions can also be used to inform agent-based models. These models use simulation to explore systemic implications of rules for behavior and interaction assigned to a set of actors. Computational agent-based models are playing an increasing larger role in understanding human–environment interactions.[37] The unique advantage of agent-based modeling comes from being able to simulate the implications of a set of rules applied to a set of actors over a series of discrete time steps in order to explore emergent macro-level properties from individual-level actions.[38] For example, one can use agent-based models to examine the ultimate distribution of teaching practices after diffusion through a network.[39] Graphical representations of such processes can also be found in Moody's creative movies of network processes.[40]

Effects of Subgroups within the Social System

Although our utility models draw on extensive social network theory and findings, our models do not directly incorporate the possibility that social relations are concentrated within subgroups. And yet most social systems consist of subgroups. From the social-psychological perspective, individuals are most strongly influenced by members of their primary groups—people with whom they engage in frequent interactions.[41] In addition, anthropologists have argued that primary groups are integral to understanding people within the contexts of their communities.[42] The corresponding sociological entity is the cohesive subgroup, with boundaries commonly defined across all actors in a system.[43]

Findings among bankers, blue-collar workers, and job seekers suggest that actors will turn to members of their subgroups for support and stability in times of crisis, while they will turn to members of other subgroups to acquire new resources to advance themselves when feeling secure.[44] This has implications for how subgroups structure the diffusion of innovations. For example, figure 12-3 shows a sociogram of close collegial ties among teachers of Westville elementary school.[45] Each number represents a given teacher, with her grade level as indicated by G_. For example, all of the teachers in subgroup B on the right teach second grade, and most of the teachers in group A on the bottom teach third grade. The lines between teachers indicate ties based on teachers' responses to a prompt asking them to list their closest colleagues in the school. The subgroups were identified and drawn by KliqueFinder such that the ties would be concentrated within the non-overlapping subgroup boundaries.[46] The sociogram is called a crystallized sociogram because the concentration of ties within subgroups forms a crystal like structure with the pattern of ties within subgroups nested within the pattern of ties between subgroups.

Frank and Zhao then used 12-4 to represent the diffusion of technology relative to the underlying subgroup structure defined by close collegial ties in 12.3. In figure 12-4 the social space is as determined by figure 12-3. But the lines have been replaced with lines indicating who talked to whom about technology, and the ID numbers have been replaced by dots; the larger the dot the more a teacher indicated having implemented technology in her classroom at time 1 of the study. Ripples around a dot indicate increases in use of technology between time 1 and time 2 (roughly one year apart). Frank and Zhao described use of computer technology as being developed around the early implementer (teacher 2) in subgroup B and then being conveyed to subgroup A via the bridging actor 20 in subgroup C.

Critically, Frank and Zhao confirmed the findings in the case study represented in figures 12-3 and 12-4 by estimating the effect of subgroup membership on the occurrence of talk about technology in a model of selection in nineteen schools. They also found that the subgroups structured talk about curricular innovations in much the same way that they structured talk about technology. Therefore, it may not be necessary to study a unique social structure that pertains to each innovation. Instead, one can study how innovations diffuse through a single stable underlying social structure, such as the crystallized sociogram of close collegial ties as in figure 12-3. Of course, that social structure can be modified, slightly, as innovations diffuse through the system. For example, Frank and Zhao (2005) found that talk about computer technology anticipated the formation of new close collegial ties.[47]

Subgroup effects can be attenuated or accentuated by identity. For example, Levi-Strauss describes a dual organization in which "members of a community . . . are divided into two parts which maintain complex relationships varying from open hostility to very close intimacy, and with which various forms of cooperation and rivalry are associated".[48] This applies, for exam-

FIGURE 12-3 Crystallized sociogram of collegial ties at Westville

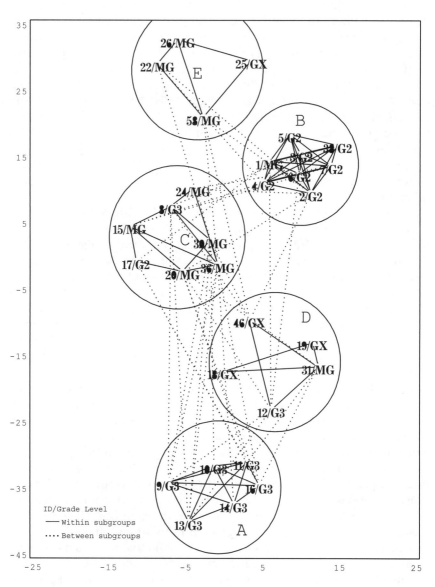

Within subgroup scale expanded by a factor of 9.

FIGURE 12-4 Talk about technology within and between subgroups at Westville, including changes in levels of technology use.

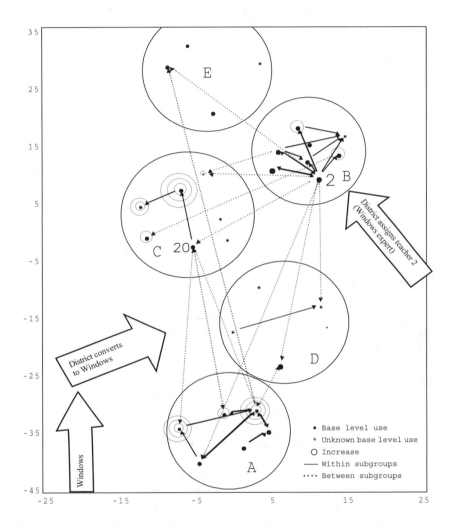

ple, to the Hatfields and McCoys or the fictional Capulets and Montagues in *Romeo and Juliet*. Though Levi-Strauss studied examples from ancient and relatively isolated cultures, he characterized the dual organization as a general structural phenomenon, in which moieties (kin-based subgroups) have the capacity to regulate "relations among members of the community, forming a framework for the numerous mutual obligations between individuals and groups. They strengthen the sense of social unity and at the same time encourage competition, thus stimulating the activities of the system."[49]

Implied in Levi-Strauss's characterization is that moieties define the dual organization to the extent that actors identify with members of their moieties more than other members of their social system. Frank then inverts the identify assumption: if actors identify with members of their system as a collective, they will allocate resources relatively uniformly throughout the collective, overriding tendencies to favor the close direct or indirect relations that occur within subgroups or moieties. Thus, Frank refers to identification with the collective as a *quasi-tie* because it directs the allocation of resources in the absence of direct personal relations.[50] Quasi-ties can facilitate the fluid movement of resources in larger systems than can be sustained by dense direct personal relationships. Thus, we might expect teachers to allocate their knowledge and other resources evenly throughout their school communities to the extent that they identify with members of their community as a collective, overriding the tendency to favor subgroup members. Otherwise, knowledge and other resources can become concentrated within subgroups, creating challenges for those who seek schoolwide coordinated action.

Two-Mode Social Networks

A new trend in social network analysis is the analysis of *two-mode network data*, or *bipartite graphs*.[51] For example, Frank et al. represented high school transcript data in terms of clusters of students and the courses they took, as in figure 12-5.[52] The authors refer to the clusters as *local positions*, consisting of a set of students with the courses as focal points of the position.[53] They reasoned that local positions defined pools of potential friends with common interests (represented by the courses), opportunities to interact with others (during course participation), and with third parties present (the other students in the courses) to enforce norms. They then theorized that because the local positions contained pools of potential friends the local positions anticipated the selection process. Therefore adolescents could be influenced by the potential friends who were members of their local positions. This is consistent with recent findings and theoretical arguments that adolescents are influenced as much by the peers with whom *they would like to be friends* as by their current friends, who accept them for who they are.[54] In fact, Frank et al. found that girls' math course taking was influenced by the prior math levels of other girls in their local positions.

The analysis of two-mode data has important potential in many social contexts, including that of teachers. One can imagine defining local positions of teachers based on committee memberships, participation in professional development, and grade level.[55] These local positions might then

FIGURE 12-5   Local positions of students focused around courses

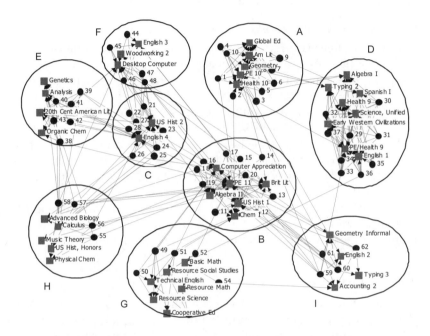

Source: Frank et al., "The Social Dynamics of Mathematics CourseTaking in high school," *American Journal of Sociology* 113, no. 6 (2008):1645–1696.

anticipate the formation of close collegial ties through which knowledge and normative influence can flow.

Local positions also serve as important leverage points for change agents. Administrators or providers of professional development may not be able to mandate specific interactions or practices. But they can provide venues that define focal points for local positions. For example, professional development focused around whole language may not merely serve as an opportunity to deliver content, but also for convening teachers among whom knowledge and influence concerning the teaching of whole language might flow.

Of course, much of current writing on professional development attends to interactions among participants.[56] But the two-mode network approach considers participation in a particular professional development as just one of a set of experiences that knit the social fabric of the school. Thus the sense a teacher makes of the whole-language workshop may well depend on whether she attends with others with whom she is familiar because of participation in other common events, or whether she experiences the professional development as an isolated experience.

Measurement of Social Networks

Marsden has extensively reviewed the measurement of social networks. and examples of network instruments for teachers can be found online..[57] Here we signal a new approach to measurement attending to the nature of teachers' interactions instead of merely the presence or absence of an interaction. Motivated by Coburn's attention to the importance and variability of depth of interactions, new social network instruments used by Penuel and Gallagher and by Cobb and Smith include items concerning the depth of collaborative activities about teaching, including "sharing how to use curricular materials," "discussion of why and how students can learn best," or "demonstrating a lesson or activity." [58] Analyzing the psychometric properties of the measures of depth is challenging because, just as in the model of selection, the observations are *dependent*. One approach is to follow the multilevel models of selection to nest the item analysis within nominators and nominees. [59]

OTHER DISCIPLINES

We have not addressed in any depth the contribution of those who study epidemiology, physics, or economics.[60] While such work is provocative, typically it conceptualizes networks on a larger scale than experienced by the teacher within her school. Of course, one could analyze teacher networks outside of their schools, especially as facilitated by professional development (e.g., National Writing Project) or by "social networking" sites such as *Facebook*. The cautionary note we will sound here derives from the teacher's utility function, which includes the desire to fit into the social organization of *her school*, among members who share *her context*. Networks outside of the school may be valuable sources of information but they may strain against the norms and coordinative functions within the school which should not be taken for granted.

CONCLUSION

In general, we encourage change agents and researchers to focus on the teacher and her decision making. It is the teacher's practices that directly contribute to educational outcomes, but teachers make decisions within the social contexts of their schools. Thus we bring the new tools of utility functions and social networks to bear on the classic challenge of understanding the decision making of the teacher within the social organization of her school.

TECHNICAL APPENDIX

Formalization of Teachers' Utility

In this technical appendix we develop formal models based on Youngs' et al.'s theory of a teacher's utility.[61] Because our theory clearly has origins in labor economics (since teachers are focused on productivity), we could develop standard labor economic models such as those that employ a Cobb-Douglas utility function.[62] But our utility function does not include income and does include the importance of conforming to other teachers in ways that are difficult to explain purely in labor economic terms. Therefore, we build on Akerlof and Kranton's utility function, which incorporates both a conventional trade-off between leisure and work but also gains from conformity to members of a social context.[63] Critically, we emphasize that this function is just one, very specific function allowing for interdependent production.

We present a teacher's utility as a function of productivity, leisure, and social constraints. Individuals achieve their optimal outcome through the choice of individual effort, e_i, made over the return for their effort, w_i, and social constraints, $\bar{e}(C)$:

$$U_i(e_i, w, \bar{e}(C)) = \alpha \left[w_i e_i - \tfrac{1}{2} e_i^2 \right] + \left[-\tfrac{1}{2}(e_i - \bar{e}(C))^2 \right] \qquad \text{(1A)}$$

The term in the first set of brackets, $\left[w_i e_i - \tfrac{1}{2} e_i^2 \right]$, is a conventional if specific utility function. For the hypothetical teacher Ashley, w_i might represent the learning return for unit effort on teaching phonics, and e_i might represent the amount of effort Ashley exerts to teach phonics (e.g., number of times per week she teaches phonics based lessons). Thus $w_i e_i$ represents the return for the phonics lessons Ashley teaches. The term $-\tfrac{1}{2} e_i^2$ represents how effort reduces utility through the loss of leisure time and exhaustion. For example, $-\tfrac{1}{2} e_i^2$ would represent the burnout teachers experience partly as a result of trying to satisfy conflicting demands.[64]

The term $-\tfrac{1}{2}(e_i - \bar{e}(C))^2$ in (1A) represents the cost to a teacher of deviating from the social norms represented by $\bar{e}(C)$, the mean expectations or level of effort of the teacher's peers. For example, if the norm in first grade is to teach four phonics-based lessons a week, a first- grade teacher who teaches two lessons experiences a loss of utility: of $-\tfrac{1}{2}(2-4)^2 = -2$. Furthermore, because the term $-\tfrac{1}{2}(e_i - \bar{e}(C))^2$ is quadratic, the cost of deviating becomes substantially larger with larger deviations from the social norm.

Critically, (1A) shows how the relative trade-offs between pursuing one's own efficacy versus conforming to the social context are governed by α. The larger the value of α, the more a teacher values efficacy versus conformity to her social context. Conversely, small values of α represent how much a teacher is willing to sacrifice for standing in the community by replacing her own judgment or context with that of other members. Thus α is critical in governing teacher behavior, with implications for how much teachers are influenced by others and how they choose interaction partners.

Application to Empirical Models

Maximizing Utility with Respect to Effort and Influence in a Network

Although the expression for utility in (1A) may appear awkward involving squared terms and coefficients of ½, it yields a simple expression when maximized with respect to effort (known as the first-order condition for effort). Assuming a budget constraint in the form of a fixed amount of time/effort, utility is maximized with respect to effort when[65]

$$e_i = \frac{\alpha}{1+\alpha} w_i + \frac{1}{1+\alpha} \overline{e}(C) \tag{2A}$$

Utility is maximized by accounting both for the return to individual effort, $\frac{\alpha}{1+\alpha} w_i$, and the status gained by conforming to a norm: $\frac{1}{1+\alpha} \overline{e}(C)$. As teachers place greater value on their own efficacy, $\alpha \to \infty$, and the w_i term dominates the effort decision; a teacher will emphasize whole language if she prioritizes her own effectiveness. As the individual places greater weight on status, $\alpha \to 0$, and conformity to the norm plays a larger role in the effort decision. Thus in the main text we describe the teacher Ashley, who will emphasize phonics if she prioritizes fitting in with her colleagues.

The expression in (2A) has a regression analog. For example, the extent to which Ashley teaches phonics could be modeled as a function of her perceptions of the value of phonics for student learning as well as the mean prior level of phonics teaching of her colleagues:

Utility Based		Empirical Regression Model	
$e_i =$		teacher's phonics practices$_i = \beta_0 +$	(3A)
$\dfrac{\alpha}{1+\alpha} w_i$		β_1 perceived value of phonics practices$_i$	
$+\dfrac{1}{1+\alpha} \overline{e}(C)$		β_2 mean prior phonics practices of colleagues$_i$	

In translating from the left to the right, w_i corresponds to Ashley's perceived value of phonics practices, and $\overline{e}(C)$ is represented by the prior practices of colleagues. Correspondingly, β_1 represents the effect of perceived efficacy on practice and β_2 the effect of conforming to the norm, with the comparison of β_1 and β_2 representing the relative effects of each, as in the comparison of $\frac{\alpha}{1+\alpha}$ and $\frac{1}{1+\alpha}$. Note that model (3A) is a basic regression model, with β_2 representing the network effect.[66]

Utility and the Model of Selecting Others in a Network

The utility function in (1A) can also help us to represent how teachers choose to whom to allocate resources (e.g., provision of help, sharing of curricular materials, providing emotional support). In particular, teacher i invests in j versus j' if $U[e|(z_{ij}=1)] > U[e|(z_{ij'}=1]$, where z_{ij} takes a value of 1 if teacher i invests in j, 0 otherwise. That is, teacher i invests in j versus j' if the utility of teacher i is greater as a result of investing in j than as a result of investing in j'.

Using the result from (2A), assuming actors maximize utility with respect to effort,

$$U[e|(z_{ij}=1)] > U[e|(z_{ij'}=1] \quad \text{if}$$

$$E\left[\frac{\alpha}{1+\alpha}w\,|\,(z_{ij}=1)_i + \frac{1}{1+\alpha}\overline{e}(C,j)\right] > E\left[\frac{\alpha}{1+\alpha}w\,|\,(z_{ij'}=1)_i + \frac{1}{1+\alpha}\overline{e}(C,j')\right] \quad (4A)$$

If allocating resources to teacher j versus j' will yield both higher efficacy, $w|(z_{ij} = 1)i > w|(z_{ij'} = 1)_i$, and greater status, $e(C,j) > e(C,j')$, then clearly the decision is to allocate to teacher j. More interesting is, if allocating to teacher j yields higher efficacy: $w|(z_{ij} = 1)i > w|(z_{ij'} = 1)_i$, but less status $e(C,j) < e(C,j')$. For example, Ashley might have to choose between helping an isolated teacher who teaches the preceding grade versus a senior teacher leader who teaches a higher grade level. Helping the isolated teacher contributes more to efficacy, but less to status.

Solving (4A) shows Ashley should allocate to j if:

$$\frac{E\left[w\,|\,(z_{ij}=1)-w\,|\,(z_{ij'}=1)\right]}{E\left[\overline{e}(C,j')-\overline{e}(C,j)\right]} > \frac{1}{\alpha} \quad (5A)$$

Equation (5A) shows that teachers will invest in j versus j' to the extent that the return to learning for investing in j, $E[w|z_{ij} = 1) - w|(z_{ij'} = 1)]$, is large relative to the return to status for investing in j', $E[\overline{e}(C,j') - \overline{e}(C,j)]$. These two components are balanced against each other in the ratio $1/\alpha$. If $\alpha \to \infty$, indicating that the individual places high value on efficacy, the right-hand side of (5A) goes to zero, and the choice is to allocate to j for the greater return on efficacy, regardless of the status advantage of allocating to j'. When α goes to 0, signifying the importance of status relative to efficacy, the right-hand side of (5A) goes to ∞ and the choice is to allocate to j' for the greater return on status, regardless of the return on efficacy for allocating to j. Thus equation (5A) expresses a model directing allocation to others in terms of α in the initial utility function in (1A).

Equation (5A) implies a model that can be estimated from data. Choices such as whom to help can be modeled as:

$$\log\left[\frac{p(help_{ij})}{1-p(help_{ij})}\right] = \theta_0 + \theta_1\, j \text{ teaches in lower grade than } i_{ij} \quad (6A)$$

where p(*help*$_{ij}$) represents the probability that teacher i provides help to teacher j and θ_1 represents the effect of teacher j teaching in a lower grade than i on the provision of help. Other terms could be included representing the expected returns on status or levels of knowledge as a result of allocating help.[67] These might include the popularity of j or perceived knowledge differences between i and j.

Estimating models such as (6A) is complicated because the observations are not independent of one another. Whether Ashley helps Kim is not independent of whether Ashley helps Sam, and whether Kim helps Sam. There have been many strategies for estimating selection models such as in (6A).[68] Here we show how Marijtje Van Duijn controls for dependencies associated with the provider and receiver of help."[69] She models θ_0, as a function of provider (u_i) and receiver (v_j) effects in a cross-nested multilevel model:[70]

$$\theta_0 = \gamma_{00} + u_i + v_j \qquad (7A)$$

Thus the selection model includes the effects known as out-degree (associated with u_i) representing the tendency for teacher i to nominate others and in-degree (associated with v_j) representing the tendency for j to be nominated. [71]

CHAPTER 13

Studies of Networks in Education

Methods for Collecting and Managing High-Quality Data

Jorge Ávila de Lima

Over recent decades, networks have become a major focus for educational policy initiatives, as well as an increasingly attractive template for practitioners who seek to organize themselves professionally in a collectively meaningful way.[1] In education, many scholars, policymakers and practitioners believe that networks "provide the opportunity for the environment and the system to become 'recultured' in ways that are more cooperative, interconnected and multiagency".[2]

However, in the educational literature, networks have generally been conceived mostly in instrumental terms, rather than as phenomena to do research on.[3] The need to do more research on these systems confronts us with new methodological challenges for which many of the common approaches traditionally adopted by educational researchers are not particularly adequate.[4] Traditionally, when educational researchers have sought to investigate the characteristics of educational phenomena, their focus has been mostly on individual, statistically independent units. Researchers commonly collect data from individuals through surveys or interviews and then combine data over all participants. Data are regarded cumulatively and often the interconnections between actors are imputed by the researcher rather than tracked down by the actual research methods that are employed. However, as Jackson et al. remind us, social systems are more than the mere sum of their individual members: "Traditional survey methods may identify groups within the population, but tell us little about how individuals within these groups are related to and affect one other".[5]

Social network analysis goes beyond atomistic views of social and educational phenomena.[6] Its main strength is that the kind of data it collects preserves the interconnected nature of the phenomena under study. This specific approach can help illuminate change processes in education in important ways.

However, a major problem with the social network approach is that one often cannot be certain whether or not a respondent-centered network study actually reflects the social interactions that do take place in a given context. This chapter discusses this issue and provides a set of recommendations for collecting and managing high-quality network data.

LEVELS OF ANALYSIS IN NETWORK STUDIES

Like networks in general, educational networks may be analyzed at different levels, depending on the issues of interest to the researcher or practitioner. Each of these levels involves a specific type of data. Most social network analyses focus on one or more of the following kinds of data: personal (egocentric) data, whole or complete (sociocentric) data, and cognitive data.

Egocentric Analysis

Egocentric network analysis views a social network as a particular actor's set of connections. More precisely, this kind of network, referred to as the *ego network* or *personal network*, consists of "a focal actor, termed *ego*, a set of alters who have ties to ego, and measurements on the ties among these alters."[7] Two advantages of the egocentric approach are that it has modest data requirements and that it can be adapted to large-scale survey research.[8] For this reason, most population-level network studies utilize this approach.[9] Within this framework, researchers usually study a sample of ego networks in a given population. This is done under the assumption that each respondent's ego network is independent from other respondents' networks—a reasonable assumption, if the sample of respondents is chosen from a large population.[10]

One of the major contributions of the egocentric approach is that it provides insights into the size of these kinds of networks. Some researchers working within this framework have also attempted to measure *structure* within each actor's network.[11] This requires asking participants not only about their ties to others, but also about their partners' relations to one another (alter-alter relations). However, this is a controversial methodological choice, because, among other reasons, it puts high demands on respondents. Indeed, the addition of alters leads to geometrical growth in the size of networks. McCarty et al. have shown that, for example, in a network of ten alters, this approach requires the respondent to report on forty-five ties; a network of fifty alters would require respondents to provide information on 1,225 ties.[12] The strategy of asking respondents about alter-alter relations also has reliability issues, because it is not reasonable to expect that actors will know a great deal about other members of their network with whom they have, at best, indirect relations.[13] For this reason, it is advisable that when analysts use the alter-alter strategy, they limit themselves strictly to crude and easily available information on those relationships, such as the mere presence or absence of relations.[14]

Whole Network Analysis

The second level at which networks may be analyzed is the *whole network* level. In this case, researchers collect information on relationships from *all* actors to all other actors in a bounded population. The properties of this whole system of relations are then studied, as well as the effects that these properties have on phenomena of interest, such as the diffusion of knowledge or innovations, inefficiency in information flow, loose coupling in educational organizations, or social influence and leadership in subject departments.[15]

Covering a whole network has several advantages.[16] It allows for (1) the identification of the naturally existing peer networks within a given setting or context; (2) the simultaneous collection of data on the units of the system under analysis and on the structures generated by the relations developed among those units; and (3) the identification of indirect ties between and among actors. Since studies of this type allow for the determination of both global and local social properties, they may be regarded as "the 'gold standard' of network analysis."[17] However, the strict data requirements that characterize this approach make it difficult to apply to networks in large populations. Despite its clear advantages, there are costs involved in using this approach, in terms of information demands, logistics, time necessary to collect and analyze the data, and participant effort in responding.

Cognitive Network Analysis

Some researchers underscore the role of cognition, as opposed to mere structure, in social action.[18] For this reason, they have become interested in a third level of network analysis—cognitive networks. In social network analysis, *cognitive social structures* are identified on the basis of self-report data that illustrate actors' *perception* of who is linked to whom and in what ways within a given social system.[19]

A cognitive social structure perspective on social networks emphasizes that actors' perception of the patterns of interaction in their network has consequences for their attitudes and actions, "above and beyond the social structural reality in which social actors are embedded."[20]

As with the designs mentioned previously that use reports on alter-alter relations, a clear drawback of the cognitive social structure approach is that as each informant is asked to report on all pairs of actors within his or her network, the number of items on a data collection instrument increases polynomially. This actually restricts the feasibility of this approach to relatively small networks.[21]

DATA QUALITY IN NETWORK STUDIES

Relationships are not properties of actors, but rather phenomena defined on dyadic interactions that involve pairs of actors (*dyads*) taken together.[22] This implies that, ideally, the complete description of a relationship requires information from all actors involved in it. Also, ideally, to analyze a whole network, researchers would collect data from all its members.[23] However, in practice, incomplete data matrices are common in network analysis.[24] The problem is that "network analysis is especially sensitive to missing data."[25] This problem is often compounded by a lack of confidence in the quality of the data that are actually collected.

There are several possible sources of poor data quality in social network studies. Some of the most relevant are: (1) inadequately specified network boundaries, (2) nonresponse, (3) respondent inaccuracy, and (4) study design factors. Moreover, compound mechanisms are also likely to be encountered.[26]

Definition of System Boundaries

A fundamental task for researchers planning to do studies of networks in education is dealing with the so-called "boundary specification problem."[27] Indeed, when the network boundary is not properly specified, not only are some relevant actors excluded, but also, in Butts's words "all relationships between those actors and others in the population (not to mention all relationships internal to the included/excluded entities). Furthermore, many structural properties of interest (e.g., connectivity) can be affected by the presence or absence of small numbers of relationships in key locations (e.g., bridging between two cohesive subgroups)."[28]

The issue of deciding who are the relevant actors may seem relatively straightforward in the case of closed sets of actors with clearly defined boundaries, such as the teaching staff of schools where complete membership lists are usually available. The matter of boundary specification raises problems particularly in situations where one needs to set the limits of data collection on social networks that in reality have no obvious limits or that have ambiguous boundaries.[29]

Alba has warned that "natural boundaries may at times prove artificial, insofar as individuals within the boundaries may be linked through others outside of them."[30] The consideration of external ties may thus be relevant, because these ties may be important for understanding a network's internal structure. With this caveat in mind, explicit questions should be asked of respondents to investigate this possibility. If the data obtained show that participants interact seldom with actors outside the boundaries that were defined, then there may be good reasons to believe that the "natural" boundaries of the network constructed by the researcher do in fact represent the "true" boundaries of the system under analysis.

Nonresponse

A common problem in network studies is nonresponse from actors who have been correctly identified as members of the population under study. Some actors refuse to answer relational questions because they wish to keep such information private. Others may not be present at the time of data collection or may have left the organization right before the study began and it becomes difficult or impossible to locate them and get them to respond. Typically, the respondents who are missed or refuse to participate in a study are peripheral actors who have few connections to the network under analysis.[31] However, some key informants may also refuse to participate, for instance, because they are simply too busy.[32]

The consequences of nonresponse for network studies are usually more serious than in more traditional methods. Stork and Richards provide an illustration of how many data are actually missing from the data matrix when some actors do not respond in a network study.[33] In a survey of an entire network of sixty people, the authors estimate that, with a 75 percent response rate, there are complete data for only 55 percent of the relationships in the network.

Missing or incomplete data situations pose a particularly serious problem for analyses conducted at the whole-network level, because they create huge empty spaces in the data matrix and may significantly distort research results that refer to whole-system properties.[34]

An alternative to this problem is network sampling. If and how to sample is perhaps *the* major problem currently confronting network analysis methodologists. While sampling may be a reasonable choice in egocentric designs for large populations, in whole network designs the process of sampling may generate the loss of important structural features of social networks. As Alba indicates, there is a "contradiction between the usual need to treat units as independent of each other and the most essential feature of networks: the interdependence of units."[35] For this reason, in whole network designs, whenever possible, the best choice is *not to sample*. This means collecting network data from *all* actors in the system under investigation. Obviously, when sampling is excluded, obtaining a high response rate becomes critical. Concerns with this aim must underlie all methodological decisions made in a study. Alternatively, researchers may opt for egocentric designs and in this case sampling is clearly an option to consider.

Respondent Inaccuracy

Respondent inaccuracy is potentially one of the most serious sources of error and thus of low data quality in network analysis. Since verbal and self-written reports are by far the more commonly used source of information in this kind of research, the problem of informant accuracy is particularly sensitive in the field. The fundamental question is that of knowing whether or not respondent cognition and reports are valid proxies for their and other people's actual relational behavior.[36]

Casciaro, Carley, and Krackhardt broadly define accuracy in social network perception as "the degree of similarity between an individual's perception of the structure of informal relationships in a given social context and the actual structure of those relationships."[37] Alternatively, a cognitive network view of accuracy in social network perception defines it as "the agreement between an individual's perception of the social relationship linking each pair of people in the group and the consensus between the people in each dyad on the social relationship linking them."[38] In the former case, there is the assumption that there exists a criterion (or *actual*) network, which is formed from actual interactions between actors and is in some sense verifiable apart from the reports or perceptions of its members. Then accuracy is measured as the degree to which informant reports match this actual interaction.[39] In the latter case (the cognitive approach), there is no assumption that there is an actual structure and that this structure can be known; the issue is rather one of determining the degree to which an actor's perception of the nature of each dyad in the network agrees with how the members of that dyad perceive and define their relationship.

Krackhardt presents several measures that may be used to assess the degree to which an actor's perceptions of relations between pairs of other actors correspond to those actors' reports of the actual links that exist between them.[40] The author's work shows that informant accuracy may be operationalized in multiple ways.

Accuracy in network perception may be better understood in terms of an actor's ability to accurately perceive specific subsets of their network, rather than the structure of the entire network. Drawing on this idea, Casciaro, Carley, and Krackhardt draw a distinction between *global accuracy* (the perception of the structure of relations between all members of a network to one another) and *local accuracy* (actors' accuracy in reporting with precision the structure of the relations between those who are directly related to them).[41]

Kashy and Kenny proposed several measures of accuracy at both the individual and the dyadic level.[42] The authors hold that informants are able to report interaction frequencies accurately, especially at the dyadic level. They further propose two *internal* measures of accuracy: (1) the *internal individual accuracy correlation*, which measures the extent to which an individual actor's reports of interaction with others in general in his or her network corresponds to what these others say about their interaction with that particular actor; and (2) the *internal dyadic accuracy correlation*, which measures the extent to which an actor's report of his or her interaction with a specific alter is confirmed by that particular alter.

Kashy and Kenny also propose three *external* measures of accuracy, which use as criterion scores the observed interaction data: (1) *response set accuracy* (the extent to which an actor's report of his or her interaction with others corresponds to his or her observed levels of interaction with those others); (2) *external individual accuracy correlation* (the extent to which others' ratings of their interaction with a specific actor correspond to their observed interaction with that actor); and (3) *external dyadic accuracy* (the extent to which an actor's report of his or her interaction with a specific alter corresponds to his or her observed interaction with that other). In their empirical work, the authors found that actors did not display significant levels of internal individual accuracy, but that they did show significant levels of *dyadic* accuracy, both internal and external. The evidence for the *dyadic* component was especially strong. This work suggests that to determine accuracy we need to employ interactive designs and use statistical procedures that model the two-sided nature of social interaction.[43]

Currently there is considerable evidence on the prevalence of informant inaccuracy in the field of network research. The most prominent results have been described in various works conducted by Bernard, Killworth, and Sailer in the 1970s and 1980s, and they are less optimistic than Kashy and Kenny's work.[44]

Bernard and his colleagues conducted a series of studies in which they examined the relationship between network information collected via respondents' verbal reports and information collected through direct observation of their actual interactions. Analysis of their own and other findings led the authors to the conclusion that "on average, about half of what informants report is probably incorrect in some way".[45] The studies conducted by the authors suggest that informants make two kinds of errors: (1) they fail to report relationships that have occurred (omission error); and (2) they claim to have interacted with others with whom they have not (commission error). The former type leads an observer to report present ties as being absent (false negatives), whereas the latter generates reports on absent ties as being present (false positives).[46]

Later studies that extended and critiqued this work generally confirmed this finding, but also suggested that the situation may not be as grim as the original studies suggested.[47] Several authors have criticized Bernard et al.'s approach by arguing that the primary concern of social network researchers should not be with particular interactions but rather with *relatively stable patterns of interaction*—the ones that in their view reveal the "true" structure of a system. These scholars stress that the information contained in respondents' verbal reports is not a detailed de facto description of events, but rather the product of memory and cognition processes that reveal not particular instances, but rather *long-term regularities*. The people forgotten by an informant tend to be those with whom they hold infrequent interactions in the network, and the people falsely recalled are those with whom they have frequent interactions. The reporting bias thus seems to work in the direction of consistency with an actual long-term pattern.[48] This and other findings have led some researchers to the conclusion that the accurate representation of relationships is actually possible with careful study design.[49] More precisely, "informants seem able accurately to report whether a relationship exists or not, and whether a relationship is fairly close or not. In general, finer judgments should probably not be relied on".[50] These arguments should be taken into account in network studies in education, which may preferably ask respondents to report on existent versus nonexistent, and close versus less close *typical* behaviors and relationships, rather than on specific interactions.

Design Factors

The content of informants' reports of network information differs in response to differently formulated questions. While these variations can be seen as generating serious methodological problems, they can also be regarded as an opportunity to select the techniques that elicit the best quality network information.[51] This implies dealing carefully with issues such of question format and the use of name generators in network data collection.

Question Format

There are different forms in which respondents' reports may be elicited, and they have different consequences for the quality of network data. Critical decisions in this respect refer to (1) whether or not to rely merely on respondents' spontaneous recollections, (2) whether or not to limit the number of relations respondents can elicit, and (3) whether or not to measure the intensity of relationships.[52]

Relying on Respondents' Recollections: Free Recall Versus Recognition. An important decision to make prior to gathering network data is whether or not respondents will be presented with a complete list of all the members in their network (when this is available), then asked specific questions about their interaction with those members. When this is the case, the format is called the *roster technique* (also known as the *recognition method*). Respondents are given a list of names and are allowed to nominate as many other actors from the list as they choose. In an alternative method, *free recall* (also called the *free list* or *name generator* technique), respondents are simply asked to indicate, by recall, the people with whom they have established a specific kind of relation. Both format choices have strengths and weaknesses, but the roster technique is a better choice, whenever possible, because it facilitates responses by introducing a reminder for respondents who might otherwise forget about individuals with whom they have interacted.[53] This is especially relevant in systems with large numbers of actors, where faults of recall may be greater.

In contrast to the free-recall technique, the roster approach increases the likelihood that more of the actual ties, and also weaker ties, are reported.[54] This illustrates the extent to which design choice can artificially determine the identification of network properties, namely, network-density levels.[55]

In contrast, the literature provides several empirical examples of the problems associated with free recall designs.[56] These examples show that "the persons recalled in a network elicitation task are only a sample of the possible set of persons who could be named."[57] Additionally, in designs that collect information across multiple waves of measurement, free recall formats pose problems because informants sometimes use different names for the same alter.[58]

Because of these problems, the roster technique is the recommended choice in research on educational networks, whenever possible. For example, if this involves intra- and/or interschool networks, a list of staff in each school, or a list of sites affiliated with a particular organization, can be generated using administrative records. In the network questionnaire, names may be organized by subject department or by some other relevant organizational category and, within each category, by alphabetical order. A blank space may be provided beside each name. In that space, respondents are then asked to indicate their name and to circle or tick off the name of others with who they are or have been in contact for a particular purpose. For reasons of simplicity and expediency, respondents can be asked to leave blank the spaces that refer to people with whom they have had no contact in the specific kind of relation that is being investigated.

The problem with the roster technique is that, despite its advantages, instrument length grows linearly with the number of possible actors a respondent is related to and "generally becomes unwieldy when more than 30–50 names are involved".[59] Also, this type of instrument can only be used where the researcher knows in advance the whole set of potential alters and where it is practical and safe to use it (i.e., when the divulging of the list of names does not create a breach of confidentiality).

When free recall is the only available or feasible option, prompting techniques become critical in the collection of data. In this case, when conducting a network survey, researchers may first use a standard question to generate names of alters and then administer a series of prompts for additional alters with whom respondents share a given relation.[60] A particularly useful prompt is the contexts in which actors interact with others. By encouraging respondents to think of those contexts and to recall people with whom they have interacted in each, researchers are usually able to obtain a more complete list of the alters with whom their participants actually interact.

The Number of Relations Respondents Can Elicit: Fixed Choice Versus Free Choice. *Fixed choice* designs are those in which respondents are given an indication of the number of network members they can nominate in response to a network survey question. The data are *free choice* when respondents are presented with no format constraints as to the maximum number of people they can name.

The limit placed on the number of alters that participants can indicate is usually designed to reduce respondent burden, while still allowing most respondents to list most of the people with whom they interact.[61] However, the number of ties that an actor appears to have can be artificially limited (and therefore distorted) by this type of design. Existing research has demonstrated that adults can name upward of over fifteeen hundred acquaintances.[62] Although this is an extreme value and will be of little interest to most researchers, who focus on more specific ties, it suggests that excluding most of actors' contacts may create gross distortions of the real structural properties of their social networks.[63] Some authors have called this the *fixed choice effect.*[64] The recommended option is thus the free choice format.

Measuring the Intensity of Relationships: Ratings Versus Rankings. In *ratings* network designs, respondents are asked to assign a value to each of their ties to other actors, expressing the strength, frequency, or intensity of their relations with those actors. In *ranking* designs, on the other hand, respondents are expected to rank order all the other members in their network according to the type of tie they have with each. In the case of large systems, rank ordering all actors becomes complex and burdensome and may lead to (or complicate) the problem of missing data.[65] Ratings are easier to administer than rankings and people can give scale ratings on a list of actors quicker than they can rank the same set. Another reason for choosing rating rather than ranking is that rating makes it possible to precisely measure the intensity of relationships, a key characteristic of relationships in network analysis.

Estimates of tie strength are usually preferable to questions that merely focus on the presence or absence of a tie. Merely binary data (presence or absence of links), according to Stork and Richards, "yield weak descriptions of linkages and relationships. This makes it impossible to distinguish between links of varying degrees of significance and reduces the number of options available for handling missing and discrepant descriptions."[66] There are also conceptual reasons for collecting data on the strength, frequency, or intensity of relations—links of different strengths have been shown to perform different structural and instrumental functions in networks—namely, those related to the flow of information and ideas across individuals and groups.[67]

For this reason, nearly all network researchers collect some measure of tie strength.[68] These measures include, for example, the number of distinct types of relationships the respondent shares with the alter (multiplexity), the degree of emotional closeness reported by the members of each dyad, or the duration of their relationship and the frequency with which they interact.[69]

In the measurement of tie strength, explicitly numerical scales are preferable, in order to avoid ambiguity in the interpretation of participants' responses. Indeed, participants sometimes have radically different perceptions of what is means to have "many" or "very few" ties. For instance, in a study, one respondent who said he "knew a lot of people" generated 173 network members while another respondent who claimed to be "a loner" generated 163 names.[70]

Name Generators

As I have mentioned previously, *name generators* are specific types of questions generally used in free recall formats to have informants identify the members of their networks. Several types of constraints can be built into a name generator, resulting in specific kinds of questions.

Once a respondent has produced a list of names, he or she is usually presented with a series of follow-up questions, called *name interpreters*, that yield additional data on the characteristics of each alter, the relationship between ego and alter and the relationships between alters. Besides providing individual profiles of respondents and their alters, the data collected through name generators and interpreters can be aggregated into composite measures of network composition or structure, such as size, density, range, level of homophily, heterogeneity or average tie strength.[71]

There are two ways that name interpreter questions can be asked.[72] The first is *by alters*—taking each alter individually and asking all questions about him/her, going alter by alter until the whole list of alters has been covered. The other way (*by questions*) is to take the first question and ask it for all alters on the list provided by the respondent and then proceed similarly with regard to the remaining questions. Recent methodological work suggests that data collection is more reliable by alters than by questions, because the by-questions technique is more cognitively demanding and time-consuming.[73]

Some important variations across network studies in substantive network traits are actually a consequence of the nature of the questions asked for identifying informants' social ties. Network scholars have thus given some attention to the consequences of the use of specific name generators for the type of data they obtain. The validity and reliability of the data collected depends on decisions about specific wording and the choice of how many generators to include in a survey.[74] Research also suggests that surveys designed to collect network data may be vulnerable to question-order effects.[75]

Wording. One of the best-known and most widely used instruments for the collection of egocentric (personal) network data was first administered in the 1985 General Social Survey (GSS).[76] The instrument uses a name generator that poses the following question to elicit the persons deemed to lie in a survey respondent's network: *From time to time, most people discuss important matters with other people. Looking back over the last six months—who are the people with whom you discussed matters important to you?*

Bailey and Marsden discussed how people comprehend or interpret this name generator, in particular, its reference to "important matters."[77] The authors found that respondents use five distinct interpretive frameworks for this name generator: (1) "literal" interpretations referring to specified topics or matters (43 percent of the respondents), (2) interpretations making vague or general references to discussions with others (28 percent), (3) translations into emotional intimacy/trust, sometimes mixed with role labels (13 percent), (4) translations into frequency of contact, often mixed with role labels (13 percent), and (5) responses expressing confusion or uncertainty (4 percent). The authors also found that what people actually regard as "important" topics may range from recent events in the news to issues of "personal" importance or even to relatively trivial events such as, for example, getting a new haircut or caring for the neighbor's lawn. The main lesson to be learned from this study is that it is important to reduce the variety of interpretive frameworks that respondents use when naming actors with whom they are related.

Single Versus Multiple Name Generators. A critical question with which researchers are often faced is the number of name generators that they can reasonably use. Although asking several name-generating questions provides better coverage of respondents' networks, there are practical considerations of cost, interviewing time, and respondent motivation that often force less ambitious research strategies.[78] The problem is that, as I have pointed out previously, different name generators elicit distinct types of networks.[79] For example, Burt tested nine different name generators and found that, although they asked about similar kinds of relations, there was little overlap in the contacts elicited—over half of the contacts were cited on only one name generator.[80]

There are substantive and methodological reasons for including more than one name generator in a survey.[81] Substantively, name generators create opportunities for analyzing how different kinds of interaction are associated with one another within relationships. This makes it possible to analyze the social structure of network environments in a more subtle way. Methodologically, name generators allow for a more precise specification of the relationships of interest, and they cover a wider range of actors' actual networks, thus helping to improve data validity and reliability.

STRATEGIES FOR DEALING WITH MISSING, INCOMPLETE, OR INACCURATE DATA IN NETWORK STUDIES

There are several approaches available for dealing with missing, incomplete, or inaccurate data in network datasets. Below I consider a set of possibilities for tackling these problems.[82]

Respecification of the Network Boundary

The most straightforward option is simply to analyze the data as is: all links for which there is no or only partial information are discarded and only completely described links are retained in the analysis. This pragmatic approach actually restricts the analysis to the subset of actors for whom network information is available and complete and effectively leads to a respecification of the network boundary.[83] Some authors have used this strategy in defining criteria for the inclusion of relations in a network. For example, Krackhardt defined the "actual" network as the set of ties for which both members of each dyad report the existence of a relationship between them.[84] However, when applied outside the cognitive network framework, the approach has serious validity problems.

Imputation

An imputation approach is operationalized by supplying linkage descriptions where *none* is provided by either member of each pair of actors in the network.[85] Missing values are replaced by estimated values, and the resulting complete data matrix is then analyzed. While some authors hold that imputing relationship descriptions is not a reasonable methodological choice, others disagree.[86]

Authors propose differing decision rules for imputing data when there are missing values for both members of a dyad. For example, if neither actor in a dyad responded, Krackhardt used a "voting scheme" whereby the relation between those two actors was considered as existing as long as the mean of all other nonmissing respondents' reports on that relation was at least 0.5.[87] This criterion leads to what has been called the *central graph* approach, in which the central graph is defined as "the collection of the ties (i,j) where each tie is recorded as existing only if a majority of 0.5 of the actors in the same social system agree on its existence."[88]

Reconstruction

Reconstruction strategies use the value provided by a member of a dyad to impute that value to the other (nonresponding) member.[89] This approach assumes that if one member of a dyad describes a relationship with the other member, then a relationship does exist between them. The relation is thus defined by ascribing the respondent's description of the tie to the non-respondent. The approach seems analogous to imputation, but there is a difference: it does not add links to the data set where there are none; it simply determines the presence or strength of a relationship on the basis of one respondent's report, rather than two.

Dichotomization

When two actors who are members of the same dyad do respond but provide different reports on the nature of their tie, a straightforward way to overcome the discrepancy is to create a matrix where the original scaled data are *dichotomized*. Dichotomizing the data does not require that the respondents accurately confirm the intensity of their relations, and thus allows for working with binary information that indicates only the confirmation (or not) of relationships (0 = no tie, 1 = tie).[90] Although this involves a cost in terms of data complexity, the data does become more reliable.

Symmetrization

In situations where there are two reports on a relationship originating from within a dyad, but they do not converge, an alternative to dichotomization is the *symmetrization* strategy, whereby the researcher treats nonreciprocated responses as being indicative of symmetry in relationships.[91] This strategy is especially relevant for situations in which, when data are collected on what is *logically* a symmetric relation (for instance, "has planned lessons with," "has discussed important matters with"), due to measurement error (e. g., faulty memories), researchers end up with actual data that *are not* symmetric.

How do we handle the situation in which frequency estimates for a single relationship differ? There are several options. One is to use the mean of the frequencies reported by the two parties as the measure of contact frequency or intensity in that dyad.[92] Another option, which emphasizes disconnections in the network, is to set the relation between the two actors as equal to the weakest reported relationship between them. A third alternative, which minimizes disconnections in the network, is to set the relation as equal to the strongest relation reported.[93] When there are no substantive reasons for emphasizing or minimizing disconnections, the best option may be to average relations across actors within each dyad, using unweighted averages. However, we do not have equal confidence in every report: some informants are more knowledgeable of their network and more accurate than others.[94] For this reason, Adams and Moody suggest that "even if the data are found to be largely discordant, researchers could use the reliability estimates to simulate or weight networks by giving [actors] a probability based on the observed reliability."[95]

The literature on social networks indicates that reciprocity rates are often low, even in networks in which relations are logically symmetric.[96] Data of this nature is often "symmetrized" in much current network research, but figures are seldom published on the actual value of these rates in particular studies.[97] It is crucial that we describe the tendency toward mutuality in the networks that we study in order to determine the number of mutual dyads. Unfortunately, only a few works deal with these types of measures.[98] Of course, if the rate of unreciprocated relations is high, there is less reason to be confident that symmetrization will be a valid procedure. On the other hand, if the overall rate of mutuality is high in a network, there is more solid ground to assume that symmetrizing a few ties will not significantly distort overall research findings.[99]

However, whereas symmetrization may sometimes be appropriate in the study of undirected relations (i.e., relations that are logically symmetric), it is inadequate for dealing with *directed* ones, such as friendship ties or exchanges of advice, information, or materials. Ignoring unreciprocated ties of this sort would result in gross distortions and in failing to devote attention to *reciprocated* relationships as *special analytical cases* that stand out for their *strength* and *mutuality* of exchanges and sentiments.[100]

Triangulation

Another strategy is to triangulate methods and information by using alternative data sources (not available in the immediate data set) to supplement and/or validate informants' reports. Instead of looking at confirmation simply as a check to see whether the network members named by a respondent are confirmed as such by data provided by one or more other respondents, this strategy entails using different sources (e.g., records of organizational exchange transactions or systematic observations of actual interactions) to confirm the relationship.[101]

CONCLUSION

A network is not simply a phenomenon that is out there waiting for us to find it; it is fundamentally a conceptual and methodological construction—the types of networks elicited in a given study will depend on the types of questions asked and on the types of data collected. This has significant implications for research design in network studies.

Educational practitioners looking into using social network analysis as a tool for preparing for or analyzing change initiatives and processes need to take into account the specific nature of this research approach and the best practices that are recommended in terms of data collection design and procedures.

The most important implication of this chapter is that researchers and practitioners who seek to study networks in education need to realize the potential that methodological choices in this field have for distorting or enhancing substantive findings, and they should be particularly tentative in drawing conclusions from data that are likely to be affected by nonresponse, data incompleteness, and respondent inaccuracy.

Since no study has yet provided a definitive answer to the question of whether or not sociometric network data collection may dispense with complete network response or at which response rate this is likely to create problems of validity, it is advisable, whenever possible, to collective data on entire networks and to obtain response rates as close as possible to 100 percent.

Despite doubts that the most common form of network data (informant self-reports) can be considered to represent actual interactions and relations between actors, there is reason to believe that the data that respondents provide about their communication and behavior with others can be taken at least as approximately indicative of their actual social behaviors, especially of typical behaviors, of the existence versus nonexistence of ties and of the closeness of those ties.

In the face of the considerable reliability and validity problems that may arise when collecting network information from respondents, a fundamental concern of the interested researcher or practitioner must be to find means of collecting high quality data. In this chapter, I have focused particularly on the design of the data collection instrument as a means of improving the quality of the data and on how this instrument can affect the response rate and the completeness of the data that respondents provide. The recommended choices in this respect are roster designs (whenever feasible), free choice formats, asking respondents to rate the strength of their ties to others, and using—when appropriate—multiple (rather than single) unambiguous name generators. In other words, even though we face challenges in terms of bias in respondent self-reports, we can reduce some of this bias by making the most adequate methodological choices.

As I have shown, there are strategies for overcoming some of the limitations that are sometimes inherent in the network data we collect. It is worth emphasizing, though, that generally the most productive strategy will be triangulation, which will often result in richer information and in a more reliable and valid picture of the network under study. This implies that we do not limit ourselves to a single survey instrument and that we do everything we can to complement this information with at least some other kind of data (e.g., archive records, e-mail flow information) and collect data through alternative means, such as observation, interviews, and document analysis. The key is to collect complete data from and with respect to as many network members as possible, using all possible sources available.

CHAPTER 14

Surveying the Terrain Ahead

Social Network Theory and Educational Change

Alan J. Daly

The foundation of social network theory is the primacy of the relationship and that the ties one has in a network determine the resources to which one has access. These ties represent a complex system of opportunities and constraints. For example, growing up in a working-class family, I had strong ties to people working in skilled trades. These ties afforded me opportunities to ride in big trucks, work with my hands, and operate a printing press—all things I loved. However, as I got older and grew more interested in attending college, I had fewer direct ties to individuals who could help me navigate the path to university. This changed when I began doing yard work for an elderly man in my neighborhood.

On one hot afternoon after losing a battle with a particularly vicious onslaught of weeds, I casually mentioned my desire to go to college. My employer, who had become more of a mentor at this point, insisted I meet some of his friends—one of whom happened to be a college counselor. I drank in the resources that flowed from the tie with the counselor and slowly gained the insider knowledge and information that would enable me to apply and eventually be accepted into a college. I am a beneficiary of the strength of weak ties because I lost a hard-fought war with dandelions and made an offhand comment to a man for whom I did the proud work of labor. Ties matter sometimes in ways of we are not aware.

Despite the normative labels often attached to networks, rarely are ties and their resulting social structures either one thing or another. My network growing up exposed me to things I loved—or I loved those things because of my network. I didn't consider my relations restrictive; rather, I wondered what lay beyond. My ties constrained yet simultaneously offered opportunities I did not fully realize. In this sense, networks are not good or bad in a normative sense; rather they represent a yin and yang of strong and weak, central and peripheral, near and far, connected and disconnected, and opportunities and constraints. Among many other reasons, it is this coexisting duality of relations that draws me to network theory—a characteristic I think is thoughtfully reflected throughout the work in this book.

The number of studies that draw on social network theory and methods is increasing throughout the social sciences, and more recently in education. This approach offers three benefits for educational researchers and those interested in change. First, many studies, ranging from reform policy creation to implementation to teacher learning to change, invoke social network concepts such as relations and brokering. Network theory provides a frame to understand individual and organizational outcomes based in part on position in the network and the overall structure of a social system.

Second, network theory provides a robust and growing methodology to describe and examine the structure of relational networks and their relationship with outcomes. Moreover, more sophisticated network models allow for predicting how patterns of relations form, and also how such patterns, in combination with characteristics of educators and schools/districts, may relate to educational outcomes.

Third, in a practical sense, social network analysis offers value to those who are interested in examining relational ties and the flow of resources within a network by providing specific measures and visualizations. Social Network Analysis (SNA) metrics and maps foreground the intuitive impact of informal ties on the work of educational change and, if facilitated well, provide an opportunity for thoughtful consideration of existing relations. Understanding network structures, as has been noted in many of the chapters, is useful for practitioners in reflecting on, leveraging, and modifying networks in creating, using, and diffusing resources more effectively. In addition, the research pushes the boundary of what social networks can mean for the work of education in better understanding the social processes through which change is supported or constrained.

This volume includes some of the latest developments in the field of network research. These rigorous studies provide detailed results and insights into both network theory and educational change. Therefore, in surveying the terrain of the book, this chapter will focus on some of the meta-themes that arise from the contributions as they relate to these issues. The overarching take-away is that, when considering, enacting, and evaluating change from a network perspective one must:

- Attend to formal and informal structures.
- Access and mine existing expertise .
- Leverage and connect subgroups.
- Invest in human and social capital in reform.

ATTEND TO FORMAL AND INFORMAL STRUCTURES

One of the most common threads woven throughout the chapters is the importance of attending to both the formal and informal structures that exist in an organization/social system. Much of the literature on educational change has focused on the formal structures involved in supporting reform. This work has made a significant contribution to the understanding of how change occurs in educational systems. Thanks in part to the work of a number of thoughtful scholars, we better understand the value of formal structures in change. In addition there is a growing body of literature on the more informal interactions of educators as they go about the work of improving instruction or engaging efforts at reform.[1] This text adds to this line of work and is unique in that it offers a number of studies that explore the intersection of formal and informal structures in change.

Figure 14-1 makes this idea more concrete, presenting a visual example of the intersection between formal and informal systems. The organizational chart on the left-hand side shows the prevailing rational model of how formal systems are typically organized. It represents a school district, with the top box representing the superintendent and the boxes below other administrators. The superintendent's prominent position denotes status and hierarchical superiority, indicating the importance of that role in the formal structure. On the right is a network map of the same district, based on the responses of the leaders represented in the formal organization chart to the question, "Who has the most influence on the district?" The arrow from the formal organizational chart indicates the position of the superintendent in the informal "influence" network. As can be clearly seen, although the superintendent plays an important role in the formal structure, in the informal network of influence this person is marginalized, and other actors play more influential roles. This figure, while fairly simple, graphically represents the complexity and differences between formal and informal systems.

The research in this book examines the dynamic multidirectional interactions between formal structures and informal relations, which have the potential to either support or constrain the flow of resources (knowledge, expertise, advice, attitude, etc.) related to change. In chapter 3, Coburn, Choi, and Mata illustrate that formal structures do in part influence informal relations, suggesting the importance of policy for creating opportunities for informal and potentially productive interactions to occur. For example, creating formal opportunities for collaboration can support interactions related to accessing expertise. Moreover, formal reform efforts can successfully challenge norms around teacher work and actually result in a restructuring of existing relations. Therefore, formal structures matter and thus need to be thoughtfully crafted and enacted in a way that supports opportunities for interaction that enhances the social capital of educators to do

FIGURE 14-1   Comparison of formal and informal system

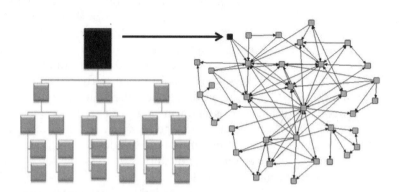

the work of change. The authors further suggest that if these formal structures are removed before enough time has been given to strengthen new
ties, the informal system is likely to return to previous states of interactions.
This chapter highlights the need for those designing change efforts not only
to craft formal structures that create opportunities for interactions, but also
ensure the longevity of these efforts by enabling the building and sustaining
of ties that resist the relational inertia that can exist in networks.[2]

Although research collected here documents how formal structures have
the potential to influence informal relations, these informal ties also affect
the success of formal structures. The work in the chapters 4, by Atteberry and
Bryk, and 5, by Cole and Weinbaum, suggests that formal structures are layered onto existing informal relations, which form a "base state" of interactional patterns. These preexisting networks may either support or constrain
the successful implementation of a change effort. For example, if a district
undertakes a professional learning community reform that includes collaboration, and then layers that effort onto a grade level that lacks the informal
ties necessary for that collaboration, the reform is less likely to be successful. A typical response would be to conclude that the technical elements of
the reform were faulty when in fact failure might be more related to the
quality or lack of ties between teachers.[3] These studies reveal how crucial
understanding of an organization's informal relations prior to enacting formal structures is in any change effort.

In addition to providing training and support around the content of the
reform, capacity building around the "social work" of change may support
efforts. Interpersonal skills such as facilitating, questioning, active listening,
and collaborating are often assumed to be among the capacities of of educators, but that assumption is potentially faulty and can derail efforts. Research

suggests that support and training around these important competencies can support collaborative work.[4] One message for those studying and enacting educational change is that variation in change efforts often has to do with not only the type of intervention and the support provided, but the quality of the informal relations upon which the effort is layered and coevolves.

On the leadership level, although a team approach to leadership is often formally espoused, the informal network may be fragmented and disconnected, as Finnigan and I show in chapter 10. As evidenced in our study, a fragmented network between district and site leaders may inhibit the flow of relational resources between administrators and thus may have direct impact not only on the improvement efforts of individual schools, but also on the district. This idea is supported by recent work on the interdependent nature of district offices and school sites in improvement.[5] In disconnected leadership networks, some leaders may act as brokers who bridge disconnected groups. In doing so these leaders play key roles in moving resources and connecting disconnected others. However, this bridging role is unlikely to be engaged in a systematic way. As a result, some administrators in the system will be unable to access important resources necessary for improvement. This can create a system of "have and have-nots," with some leaders amassing resources and thus having a disproportionate influence over the organization. While the network position of others may constrain them and limit their access to assets, a problem Hite Hite, Mugimu, and Nsubuga address in chapter 11. Intentionally creating formal opportunities for leaders across districts to interact may provide opportunities to influence their informal network and open up conduits for resource flow.

Creating and sustaining school to district and interschool network relations creates the ties through which critical resources related to systemic change can flow.[6] The contribution of Hite and colleagues suggests that the personal connections between leaders often trump geography and distance in supporting the flow of resources related to improving schools. Their analysis also reveals a constraint in network dynamics: if the ties that can bring resources to a school are attached to a single actor, such as a principal, the whole school may be penalized when that leader moves on, taking those ties away. Therefore, leaders must be intentional about not only developing the necessary personal ties to resources; they must also simultaneously create redundant connections between the school and the sources of those resources.

Leadership is not simply attached to formal position, and the contributions of Spillane, Healey and Kim (chapter 8) as well as Penuel, Frank, and Krause (chapter 9) illustrate the significance of informal leaders in reform. These chapters reveal the important ways informal leaders play critical roles in the success of a reform effort. They are often sought for advice and assistance in enacting change, and so play crucial linking roles between teachers. This suggests that beyond individuals in formal leadership roles, the distribution of leadership to informal leaders is important during the enactment of a reform effort. More specifically, when there is less access to professional development necessary for a change in practice, it is important to have more individuals in both formal and informal roles connected to the reform effort to equally disperse and support new practices.

The work in this volume illustrates that variation in reform uptake and outcomes as well as attitude toward the change effort is related to both formal and informal structures that are simultaneously at work in human systems. Simultaneous consideration of the formal structures in change and informal relations upon which reform is layered represents a promising direction in developing, enacting, and evaluating efforts at change. Creating formal, sustained opportunities and supports for intra- and interorganizational interactions appears to hold promise for better outcomes in change efforts. This suggests the interdependent nature of change as it is enacted between and among educators and networks across formal and informal systems. However, in a nod to the yin and yang of relations, further study is required to understand the effects of formalizing informal relations, as that transition may inhibit the work that was initially trying to be accomplished. Attending to the landscape of formal and informal relations when developing, enacting, and evaluating change is clearly an essential lesson of this work.

ACCESS AND MINE EXISTING EXPERTISE

The ability to engage in educational change depends on the capacity of the actors within the system to do the work of the reform. Knowledge, skills, expertise, and attitude represent some of the relational resources required to develop, engage, and sustain change. In chapter 3, Coburn and colleagues demonstrate that access to expertise is a critical element in the ability of a system to engage reform efforts. Common models of change suggest the importance of external (outside a system) expertise in the delivery of professional development as codified through formal trainings and resource materials. As has been suggested, this formal approach at building the explicit capacity of the organization to engage reform is necessary, yet it potentially undervalues the expertise within a system or the co-constructed knowledge of educators. Successful organizations engage in both exploration (accessing resources from outside the system) and exploitation (accessing existing resources from within a system) in order to learn and change.[7] From a network perspective, as exemplified in many of the studies in this volume, existing tacit knowledge within the system varies by degree. Identifying and accessing this expertise is a potentially pivotal function in change efforts. In a network sense, if knowledge resides in a peripheral corner or is disconnected from the network, then accessing and leveraging that expertise to meet goals may be difficult. This suggests that in addition to investments in exploration through external expertise, a systematic effort to transform existing tacit knowledge and practices into explicit expertise is an equally important and often under-utilized approach in supporting reform.

Supportive organizational conditions such as those that provide for teachers to interact around specific tasks related to teaching and learning can provide opportunities for accessing and exchanging expertise both in a school and professional development setting as related in chapters 6, by Moolenaar and Sleegers, and 7, by Baker-Doyle and Yoon. These developing relations around expertise can reconstruct existing network relations and support a deeper level of knowledge exchange. However, in order for this to occur, an intentional and formal approach to connecting expertise is necessary. Making the existing tacit expertise within a system more explicit can have both individual and organizational benefits, since, given the often isolated nature of the education endeavor, expertise is often hidden in plain sight. It should also be noted that while networks can support the transmission of expertise related to reform, they might also move attitudes, as is suggested by Cole and Weinbaum, which may quickly derail efforts. Collaboration can take the form of "contrived congeniality" in which there may be existing ties, but what flows between these actors is counter to efforts at change.[8] Therefore, it may be useful to attend not only to the ties of expertise between actors, but to also acquire a deeper understanding of the content that flows between these individuals and within the network.

Expertise can be exchanged by individual actors within a system but may also exist within small groups. For example, a team of well-connected third-grade teachers may have a group expertise at developing assessments. This grade-level expertise may have been developed and honed through the interactions within this cohesive unit, but unless this team of teachers is connected to others, the expertise remains an attribute of that team. Conceptualizing expertise beyond the individual to a dyadic, group, and network level property expands the traditional focus of expertise as a singular attribute to suggest the importance of the dyadic and collective nature of the construct.

Successful change efforts are a combination of exploring and exploiting existing resources. Providing opportunities to connect, leverage, and make explicit existing expertise is an important activity in support of change efforts. This idea, as addressed by a number of this book's authors, suggests the value of ties between educators at different levels of a system as a rich source of social capital. Moreover, a clearer understanding of existing expertise may also provide insights into the specific targeted capacities that need to be brought into the system from external sources. This targeted approach to learning may better focus resources and maximize the limited time available for development. Being able to access and coordinate knowledge and skills in dynamic environments is particularly critical given the complexities of contemporary educational systems.

LEVERAGE AND CONNECT SUBGROUPS

One of the most consistent findings from across the studies in this collection is the importance of subgroups—three or more actors who are typically more connected to one another than to others in the larger system.[9]

Subgroups can shape the individual experience of their members and in doing so filter group norms, information flow, and influence over attitudes.[10] Strong ties within cliques can assist actors in coordinating systemic action and the movement of resources such as knowledge, because the members have direct access to the resources of the others.[11] On the other hand, strong ties within cliques are also likely to represent redundant information between these actors, which may reduce the overall access to novel information and reinforce existing approaches.

Ties between cliques are likely to play meaningful roles within networks. Some research suggests that increased performance is associated with intensive overlap between cliques.[12] On the other hand, ties between cliques may be sparse, resulting in structural holes and diminishing the opportunity to move novel information between subgroups. Ties between subgroups may be valuable in providing novel information (from outside the clique), but they may not be efficient in moving that resource, as members of different subgroups may not share common language or understanding.[13] For example, grade-level teams may represent groups that readily share curricular resources among themselves, but may share less between levels since they speak a different curricular language. The contributions of Penuel et al., Spillane et al., and Cole and Weinbaum underscore these ideas, describing different aspects of the importance of subgroups as one of the primary relational structures through which critical change-related resources such as expertise, knowledge, and attitude readily flow.[14] A well-connected group that engages in frequent communication with peers can easily influence attitude and the subsequent implementation of reform.

Moreover, as Moolenaar and Sleegers suggest, densely connected groups can also develop the trust and strong ties necessary for supporting risk taking and change-oriented practices that influence the perception of climate. This means that the normative pressure created within subgroups can have an effect on the attitude toward reform as well as the level and depth of engagement with a change effort. Subgroups within an organization, such as departments in a high school, form some of the basic relational structures through which resources may flow and as such may either support or constrain efforts at change.

While densely connected subgroups can promote the exchange of reform-related resources and attitudes, connections between subgroups can also promote access to unique information that may support change efforts. Chapters 8 and 9 posit that ties between subgroups can stimulate the development of novel information as well as create linkages between formal and informal structures. Creating and supporting opportunities for subgroups (e.g., clusters of principals being connected to others, as Finnigan and I suggest) to exchange reform-related resources has the potential to develop novel information that not only benefits the group, but the larger system in which the cluster resides. These lateral connections are important conduits for complex information, knowledge exchange, and innovation. In addition, dense lateral ties may increase a subgroup's *absorptive capacity*—a group's ability to assimilate and replicate new information from external sources.[15]

Previous research has suggested that the ability of a subgroup to absorb information is directly related to its output of information.[16] This input-output relationship creates a reciprocal process that is facilitated by ties within and between subgroups. Therefore, investing in a subgroup's ability to take in information from other subgroups may lead to that group outputting additional new information into the larger organization. At the school level, this indicates the importance of developing ties between subgroups at different levels. For example, within a school, leadership teams comprising grade-level/department heads hold promise in creating such cross-cutting lateral ties, which in turn can support efforts at change.[17] At the district level, the importance of ties between central office and site administrators represent a potential way to build subgroup absorptive capacity in support of overall organizational goals.

Strong ties related to reform resources (expertise, knowledge, skills) between educators in a subgroup (e.g., grade level, school, district) may be instrumental in developing the depth of interaction and trust building necessary for exchanging tacit information and innovation related to improvement. As has been suggested, cohesive subgroups are potentially an important starting point for change efforts, but connections between these groups are also important for the transmission of novel information. Such connections do not have to be of the same level of frequency or strength, just available for the exchange of resources that further support the work of the subgroup and ultimately the larger system. However, because subgroups often have developed specific norms and ways of interacting, the provision of formal opportunities for these subgroups to interact and "learn the language" of the other group is important.

INVEST IN HUMAN AND SOCIAL CAPITAL IN REFORM

Educational institutions are investing heavily on focused training. A narrow range of texts, prescriptive curricula, and standardized measurement systems typify the policy response adopted by underperforming districts and schools.[18] These approaches foreground a more human capital, bureaucratic, resource-management approach to reform, which may have constrained the development of relational linkages between actors and subgroups and thus limited schools' ability to leverage existing expertise and knowledge.[19]

Social capital, as opposed to human capital, is an investment in the social relations within in a system through which the resources of other individuals can be accessed, borrowed, or leveraged[20] The studies presented in chapters 3 and 4 (Coburn Coburn, Choi, and Mata; and Atteberry and Bryk) note the importance of formal human capital approaches to reform, but also highlight the need to create opportunities and structures for networks to flourish and support the exchange of change-related resources. It bears noting that this emphasis on the more relational linkages suggests an equally important *supplementing*, not a supplanting, of the more technical aspects of school improvement that is currently demanded by federal and state policy.[21] The implication of the work is that the interaction of these two important elements may yield positive reform-related outcomes.

In terms of reform policy, a continuing focus on standards and assessments as a common referent point for exchange is important, but the addition of incentives to foster and support the exchange of social capital may also provide additional gains.[22] Examples might include providing the opportunities for daily grade-level meetings, gathering points for faculty, and supports for group-level performance. The studies in this volume also suggest the importance of relational linkages as a means of sharing expertise and important change-related resources. Social capital therefore plays an important role in both individual teacher success and overall school improvement. This idea has implication for the current interest in measuring the "value added" of individual teachers.

A value-added measure, although hotly debated in methodological and policy circles, is a combination of teacher knowledge/training/experience; ability to effectively teach the content; and student demographics. However, equations like this generally do not attend to the effect of the social capital upon which a teacher may draw. For example, a new teacher who enters a disconnected grade level will have limited access to the expertise residing in that subgroup, while a new teacher in that same school entering in a densely connected grade level (assuming the ties are in support of good instruction) has more access to social capital, which may ultimately impact her value added. In this way, the social ties and context both have impact on the ability of a teacher to add value to a student's learning experience, both of which are missing in the current conceptualizations of value-added models. This idea is especially important given the potential high-stakes nature of these measures as well as a growing number of studies indicating the influence of peers and relational trust on instructional practices and outcomes.[23]

Efforts at reform, therefore, rely on a combination of human and social capital. Both are important in the change equation, but until recently the social capital element has played at best a secondary role. The work in this book supports a growing base of literature that suggests the importance of social capital, and the importance of "capital in context"—connecting human and social capital within a specific context—in the work of change.[24]

PROMISING DIRECTIONS

The studies presented in this book provide additional empirical evidence for understanding change through a network theory lens. Although social network theory and methods are becoming more prevalent in educational research, there is still a wide array of educational change phenomena that would benefit from continued and initial exploration. Several promising directions are suggested in these chapters. This nonexhaustive list of promising areas includes:

- Uptake and resistance of change efforts at multiple levels of the system
- Development and implementation of reform policy
- Impact of social influence and contagion around new practices/ideas/ attitudes
- Process of key opinion leaders on improvement efforts
- Influence of leadership network and organizational outcomes;
- Interaction effect of attributes (personality, demographics, attitudes) on network position and overall structure in change efforts
- Intersection between formal and informal systems in reform
- Effect of overall network formation and structure on improvement
- Role of intermediary organizations (governmental agencies, foundations, universities, private consultants, etc.) and flow of resources in change strategies
- Relationship between ego networks, individual outcomes, and organizational reform efforts
- Formation and evolution of networks and association with educational outcomes

In examining the above areas there remains a need for basic mixed-methods empirical work that examines the effect of overall network structure on the access, use, and diffusion of resources related to change. Better understanding of the impact of "local" dyadic, triadic, and subgroup relations as well as the role of strong and weak ties on the exchange of resources within and between actors is a promising area of investigation. Related to this area of inquiry is the impact of those local subgroup interactions on overall network structure and outcomes.

Although there has been work on innovation in education, basic empirical research on how innovation is adopted and diffused through a network would be useful in light of the current focus on innovation. Further empirical work as to how formal and informal opinion leaders are able to influence the process of uptake and diffusion of change efforts in education is critical, given the increasing number of intermediary organizations and hired consultants involved in the change process. Exploring distributed models of leadership and shared governance through a network theory lens is a promising arena in this regard. It should be noted that although the work in this volume has focused primarily on the ties between adults in the system, there remains a rich opportunity in examining the relations between and among student peers as well as between students and adults in the change process.[25]

Ties and Flows

Network theory and analysis provide excellent insight into the ties between actors in a system. Although the relations are specific, such as reform related expertise, the work does not specifically explore what "flows" between ties. As is suggested by Borgatti and Ofem in chapter 2, research that examines both the ties and the flows between actors represent some of the promising directions in both the larger network field as well as in education. Better understanding of the structure of ties, and the specific content and depth of flows within those ties, is an area that is critical in understanding change. Exploring ties and flows suggests the importance of combining theoretical frames and mixed methods to allow for examining not only the structure of relations, but how those ties impact the way in which phenomena are understood. For example, combining network theory and sense-making may yield important insights into the extent to which ties between actors support or constrain the process of making meaning around an experience or phenomena. Another promising theoretical intersection is between network theory and organizational learning as a way to understand the degree to which relations between actors and network structure facilitate or inhibit the process of individual and organizational learning. Both of these examples would also benefit from longitudinal studies that apply quantitative and qualitative methodologies as a way to better "count" the ties and assess the "quality" of exchanges over time.

Practical Application

In addition to further research, another promising area of network theory is the practical application of the methods. Using social network data in efforts at improvement and evaluation can be an extremely useful approach. Social network methods as applied to practice can be used as a tool to: diagnose, evaluate, and as a data point/artifact in change efforts. Baker-Doyle and Yoon used social network analysis as a diagnostic tool to enable the refinement of programs and determine next steps in making the learning experience for teachers even stronger. Using SNA as an effective evaluation instrument, Atteberry and Bryk were able to examine how well an intentional focus on building relationships and connecting to expertise was accomplished over the period of an intervention effort. Another application of social network methods, as Finnigan and I suggest, is as an interactive data point/artifact to support greater awareness of network structures in supporting change.

Researchers across multiple disciplines have been able to successfully use network data and visualizations to illuminate aspects of the informal social system that often remain hidden.[26] The interactive guided processing of the results of network studies has allowed for reflection, dialogue, action planning, and adjusting management arrangements in organizations. Creating opportunities for organizational members to better understand the structure and access to existing expertise is an important activity related to change in systems that can potentially be enhanced through the process of data feedback. A promising extension of this applied approach would be to trace the process through which data is fed back into the system and trace how that data and related planning processes and action steps were enacted and tied to measurable outcomes.

Ethical Considerations

There has been some excellent work on the ethics involved in social networks data collection and use.[27] This section is not meant to substitute in any way for a careful and thorough reading of that literature, but merely to mention the importance of ethics in network research. Network studies differ from traditional social science research in a number of ways, as described in chapter 13, by Ávila de Lima, but one of the most salient differences in data collection, as he mentions, is the lack of anonymity. In traditional survey research the respondent is anonymous, but in the network paradigm the respondents must identify themselves and those with whom they have a tie. This carries extra risk to the respondent if the data is compromised. Therefore, in conducting network research it is crucial to do no harm to the participants by: emphasizing the voluntary nature of the data collection; disclosing how the data will be used; and disguising the data so that respondents are unidentifiable. In addition, if the study data are going to be reported back, it is vital to inform the respondents of the manner in which the this will be done. It is imperative to keep at the forefront the unique ethical considerations involved in network research. Since the field is relatively new, as it continues to develop, further ethical concerns along these lines will arise, and will require thoughtful approaches and responses.

PROMISING METHODS AND MODELS

Random Graph Models

Because network data is interdependent and as such violates the assumptions of independence in most statistical tests, advanced statistics and modeling have been introduced and continue to flourish in the field. Advanced social network models consider hypothesis-driven research questions about how networks form and what effects networks have on outcomes. These models are robust and statistically complex, as they have to handle the interdependence of the data. Two general approaches to modeling social networks include random graph theory and statistical models.[28] Random graph theory focuses on modeling the assumptions about the random emergence of ties leading to a variety of network structures. The second approach involves fitting exponential random graph models, or p* (p star), models to data. These analyses focus on estimating the probability that a given network will form, based on other network variables, or characteristics of the nodes, in comparison to randomly generated graphs. Comparing collected data to randomly generated graphs can provide insight into how different the collected data is from chance.

Agent-Based Models

Agent-based modeling, as described by Frank and collaborators in chapter 12, is used to examine the outcomes of specific preselected rules for behavior and interactions assigned to a set of nodes. Modeling and modifying these rules can provide insight into how behavior and interactions occur over multiple iterations. This provides for the exploration of emergent patterns over the entire system based on the micro-level interactions of agents. These results can then be analyzed and compared against or used to predict activity in a human social system. The use of agent-based modeling is a promising approach for the field of social network theory.

Multilevel Models

The studies collected here span multiple levels of the system, including: individual teacher networks, ties between leaders within a large urban system, schools within one district, and professional development programs. Taken together, they underscore the importance and utility of examining multiple levels and perspectives through a network lens—an emphasis of the Ávila de Lima chapter. As network data is often nested—for example, pairs of teachers within grade levels within schools—models that examine these multiple levels within a system provide a more nuanced examination of the phenomena as well as the interaction between levels. Multilevel analysis, as applied in the Moolenaar and Sleegers chapter, offers a promising approach, providing a method for analyzing both macro and micro perspectives.

Dynamic Longitudinal Models

Another developing area of network research is around the examination of network change over time.[29] Exploring the influence of interpersonal networks on individual preferences and behaviors, as suggested by Frank, Kim, and Belman, is one area that may be particularly rewarding. Understanding behavioral dynamics in a simultaneously evolving social network represents one of the thorniest issues in the social sciences. This difficulty stems from the general interdependence between the group members' individual behavior and attitudes, and the network structure of relations in which they reside. In order to gain a deeper understanding of social selection and structure, it is important to study the dynamics of individual outcomes and network structure and how these impact one another. This requires examining the dynamic elements of the network structure (homophily, centrality, etc.) as well as relevant actor attributes (indicators of performance, attitude, cognitions, behaviors, etc.) as joint dependent variables in a longitudinal time frame where network structure and individual attributes mutually influence one another.[30]

Being able to better understand the differential impact of social selection and social influence is a core questions that requires additional empirical work. This area is particularly ripe, as correlations are often found between the behavior of an individual and the behavior of their peers. Such associations are often attributed to peer influence (social influence effect), the possibility that individuals may choose friends who are similar to themselves in terms of some behavior (social selection effect) is ignored. Better understanding and theorizing about how and why networks evolve, how positions such as brokers change over time, and the cumulative costs/benefits of occupying a central position over time are critical. Applying these analytic modeling tools will enable education researchers to examine network outcomes and better explore and theorize the underlying mechanisms involved in the formation and maintenance of social systems. Moreover, considering how these data may be visualized in a thoughtful manner that makes explicit underlying assumptions is an important related element in dynamic models.[31]

AIMING TOWARD PROMISE

As the work of learning and change is ultimately conducted by and through individuals in formal and informal social systems, social network theory offers a useful and promising lens for understanding and exploring numerous educational phenomena. The perspective and methods offer a way, additional to the more human capital/bureaucratic explanations, to understand the variable success of change efforts. Network theory offers a lens and methods to explore the access, diffusion, modification, control, and potential leverage points of any number of resources that flow through a network. The network perspective is well positioned to provide useful insights into complex phenomena through increasingly sophisticated and predictive methods and models especially related to educational change and reform. In addition, network theory provides a robust and complementary theoretical lens to other approaches such as sense-making and organizational learning. The promise of network theory is in its ability to help us to better understand the social worlds we negotiate every day as we make our way in this increasingly complex world.

Notes

CHAPTER 1

1. Judith W. Little, "Inside Teacher Community: Representations of Classroom Practice," *Teachers College Record* 105, no. 6 (2003): 913–945; Judith W. Little, "Locating Learning in Teachers' Communities of Practice: Opening up Problems of Analysis in Records of Everyday Work, Teaching and Teacher Education, 18 (8) (2002): 917–946; Susan Moore Johnson and the Project on the Next Generation of Teachers, *Finders and Keepers: Helping New Teachers Survive and Thrive in Our Schools*, Jossey-Bass Education Series (San Francisco: Jossey-Bass, 2007); Susan Moore Johnson et al., "The Support Gap: New Teachers' Early Experiences in High-Income and Low-Income Schools," *Education Policy Analysis Archives* 12, no. 61 (2005).

2. Little, "Inside Teacher Community."

3. William R. Penuel, Margaret Riel, Ann E. Krause, and Kenneth A. Frank, "Analyzing Teachers' Professional Interactions in a School as Social Capital: A Social Network Approach," *Teachers College Record* 111, no. 1 (2009): 124-163; Alan J. Daly and Kara Finnigan, "The Ebb and Flow of Social Network Ties Between District Leaders Under High-Stakes Accountability", *American Educational Research Journal* (In press); Stephen P. Borgatti and Rob Cross, "A Relational View of Information Seeking and Learning in Social Networks," *Management Science* 49, no. 4 (2003): 432–445.

4. Martin Kilduff and Wenpin Tsai, *Social Networks and Organizations* (London: Sage, 2003).

5. John Scott, *Social Network Analysis*, 2nd edition (London: Sage, 2000); Stanley Wasserman and Katherine Faust, *Social Network Analysis: Methods and Applications* (New York: Cambridge University Press, 1998).

6. Rob Cross, Stephen Borgatti, and Andrew Parker, "Making Invisible Work Visible: Using Social Network Analysis to Support Strategic Collaboration," California Management Review, 44, no. 2 (2002): 25–46.

7. Alan J. Daly and Kara Finnigan, "Understanding Network Structure to Understand Change Strategy," *Journal of Educational Change* 11, no. 2 (2010): 111–138; Lea, Hubbard., Hugh Mehan, and Mary Kay Stein, *Reform as Learning: School Reform, Organizational Culture, and Community Politics in San Diego* (New York: Routledge, 2006).

8. Susan A. Mohrman, Ramkrishnan V. Tenkasi, and Allan M. Mohrman, "The Role of Networks in Fundamental Organizational Change," *Journal of Applied Behavioral Science* 39, no. 3 (2003): 301–323.

9. Tiziana Casciaro, Kathleen M. Carley, and David Krackhardt, "Positive Affectivity and Accuracy in Social Network Perception," *Motivation and Emotion* 23, no. 4 (1999): 285–306; Rob Cross and Andrew Parker, *The Hidden Power of Social Networks* (Boston: Harvard Business School Press, 2004); Martin. Kilduff and David. Krackhardt, "Bringing the Individual Back In: A Structural Analysis of the Internal Market for Reputation in Organizations," *Academy of Management Journal* 37, no. 1 (1994): 87–108.

10. Stephen P. Borgatti and Pacey C. Foster, "The Network Paradigm in Organizational Research: A Review and Typology," *Journal of Management* 29, no. 6 (2003): 991–1013.
11. Ibid.; Nienke M. Moolenaar, "Ties with Potential: Nature, Antecedents, and Consequences of Social Networks in School Teams" (unpublished doctoral dissertation, 2010).
12. Pierre Bourdieu, "The Forms of Social Capital," in *Handbook of Theory and Research for the Sociology of Education*, eds. John G. Richardson (New York: Greenwood, 1986), 241–258; Nan Lin, *Social Capital: A Theory of Social Structure and Action* (New York: Cambridge University Press, 2001); Janine Nahapiet and Sumantra Ghoshal, "Social Capital, Intellectual Capital, and the Organizational Advantage," *Academy of Management Review* 23, no. 2 (1998): 242–266.
13. Lin, *Social Capital*, 24 ..
14. James S. Coleman, "Social Capital in the Creation of Human Capital," *American Journal of Sociology* 94 (1988): 95–120; Sandra L.Dika and Kusum Singh, "Applications of Social Capital in Educational Literature: A Critical Synthesis," *Review of Educational Research* 72, no. 1 (2002): 31–60.
15. Alejandro Portes, "The Two Meanings of Social Capital," *Sociological Forum* 15, no. 1 (2000): 1–12.
16. Ronald S. Burt, *Structural Holes: The Social Structure of Competition* (Cambridge, MA: Harvard University Press, 1992); Coleman "Social Capital in the Creation of Human Capital"; Mark S. Granovetter, "The Strength of Weak Ties," *American Journal of Sociology* 78, no. 6 (1973); Mark S. Granovetter, "The Strength of Weak Ties: A Network Theory Revisited," in *Social Structure and Network Analysis*, eds. Peter V. Marsden and Nan Lin (Beverly Hills, CA: Sage, 1982), 105–130; Robert D. Putnam, "Bowling Alone: America's Declining Social Capital," *Journal of Democracy* 6 (1995): 65–78; Robert D. Putnam, *Making Democracy Work* (Princeton, NJ: Princeton University Press, 1993).
17. Morten T. Hansen, "The Search-Transfer Problem: The Role of Weak Ties in Sharing Knowledge Across Organization Subunits," *Administrative Science Quarterly* 44, no. 1 (1999): 82–111; Ray Reagans and Bill McEvily, "Network Structure and Knowledge Transfer: The Effects of Cohesion and Range," Administrative Science Quarterly 48, no. 2 (2003): 240–267; Brian Uzzi, "Social Structure and Competition in Interfirm Networks: The Paradox of Embeddedness," Administrative Science Quarterly 42, no. 1 (1997): 35–67.
18. Burt, *Structural Holes*.
19. Stephen P. Borgatti, Martin G. Everett, and Lin Freeman, *UCINET For Windows: Software for Social Network Analysis* (Harvard MA: Analytic Technologies, 2002). For a general list, see the International Network for Social Network Analysis, http://www.insna.org/software/index.html.
20. Ibid.

CHAPTER 2

1. Linton C. Freeman, *The Development of Social Network Analysis: A Study in the Sociology of Science* (Vancouver, Canada: Empirical Press, 2004).
2. R. Duncan Luce and Albert D. Perry, "A Method of Matrix Analysis of Group Structure," *Psychometrika* 14, no. 2 (1949): 95–116.
3. Alex Bavelas, "Communication Patterns in Task-Oriented Groups," *Journal of the Acoustical Society of America* 22 (1950): 725–730.
4. Rob Cross and Andrew Parker, *The Hidden Power of Social Networks* (Boston: Harvard Business School Press, 2004); Judith A. Levy and Bernice A. Pescosolido, eds., *Social Networks and Health* (London: Elsevier, 2002); Marc Sageman, *Understanding Terror Networks* (Philadelphia: University of Pennsylvania Press, 2004).

5. Birger Wernerfelt, "A Resourced-based View of the Firm," *Strategic Management Journal* 4 (1984): 171–180.

6. Martin Kilduff and Wenpin Tsai, *Social Networks and Organizations* (Thousand Oaks, CA: Sage Publications, 2003).

7. Ranjay Gulati, *Managing Network Resources: Alliances, Affiliations, and Other Relational Assets* (New York: Oxford University Press, 2007).

8. Joel Podolny, "Networks as the Pipes and Prisms of the Market," *American Journal of Sociology* 107 (2001): 33–60.

9. Ronald S. Burt, *Structural Holes: The Social Structure of Competition,* (Cambridge, MA: Harvard University Press, 1992).

10. Bavelas, "Communication Patterns in Task-Oriented Groups."

11. Miller McPherson, Lynn Smith-Lovin, and James M. Cook, "Birds of a Feather: Homophily in Social Networks," *Annual Review of Sociology* 27 (2001): 415–444.

12. Peter V. Marsden, "Core Discussion Networks of Americans," *American Sociological Review* 52 (1987): 122–131.

13. Thomas J. Allen, *Managing the Flow of Technology: Technology Transfer and the Dissemination of Technological Information within the R&D Organization,* (Cambridge, MA: MIT Press, 1977).

14. Kilduff and Tsai, *Social Networks and Organizations.*

15. Bonnie Erickson, "The Relational Basis of Attitudes," in *Social Structures: A Network Approach.* eds. Barry Wellman and Stephen D. Berkowitz (New York: Cambridge University Press, 1988), 99–121.

16. Solomon E. Asch, "Opinions and Social Pressure," *Scientific American*, November 1955, 31–35.

17. James S. Coleman, Elihu Katz, and Herbert Menzel, "The Diffusion of Innovation Among Physicians," *Sociometry* 20 (1957): 253–270; Gerald F. Davis, "Agents Without Principles? The Spread of the Poison Pill Through the Inter-corporate Network," *Administrative Science Quarterly* 36 (1991): 583–613; Elizabeth E. Umphress, Giuseppe Labianca, Daniel J. Brass, Edward Kass, and Lotte Scholten, "The Role of Instrumental and Expressive Social Ties in Employees' Perceptions of Organizational Justice," *Organization Science* 14 (2003): 738–753.

18. Ajay Mehra, Martin Kilduff, and Daniel Brass, "The Social Networks of High and Low Self-monitors: Implications for Workplace Performance," *Administrative Science Quarterly* 46, (2001): 121–146.

19. Katherine J. Klein, Beng-Chong Lim, Jessica L. Saltz, and David M. Mayer, "How Do They Get There? An Examination of the Antecedents of Centrality in Team Networks," *Academy of Management Journal* 21 (2004): 952–963.

20. Ajay Mehra, Martin Kilduff, and Daniel Brass, "The Social Networks of High and Low Self-monitors: Implications for Workplace Performance," *Administrative Science Quarterly* 46 (2001): 121–146; Herminia Ibarra and Steven B. Andrews, "Power, Social Influence, and Sense-making: Effects of Network Centrality and Proximity on Employee Perceptions," *Administrative Science Quarterly* 38 (1993): 277–303; Timothy T. Baldwin, Michael D. Bedell and Jonathan L. Johnson, "The Social Fabric of a Team-based MBA Program: Network Effects on Student Satisfaction and Performance," *The Academy of Management Journal* 40 (1997): 1369–1397; Ranjay Gulati, Nitin Nohria and Akbar Zaheer, "Strategic Networks," *Strategic Management Journal* 21 (2001): 203–215.

21. Albert-László Barabási, *Linked: The New Science of Networks* (Cambridge, MA: Perseus Publishing, 2002).

22. Don A. Dillman, Jolene D. Smyth, and Leah M Christian, *Internet, Mail, and Mixed-Mode Surveys: The Tailored Design Method* (Hoboken, NJ: Wiley and Sons, 2009).

23. Not all whole network data need be collected through surveys. Relational data can also be collected through the use of archival data, such as publicly available databases, social media websites, and other electronic sources that provide information on the relations among a given set of actors.

24. Stephen P. Borgatti, Martin G. Everett, and L. C. Freeman, *UCINET 6 for Windows: Software for Social Network Analysis* (Harvard, MA: Analytic Technologies, 2002).

25. Stephen P. Borgatti and Martin G. Everett, "Models of Core/Periphery Structures," *Social Networks* 21 (1999): 375–395.

26. David Krackhardt, "Predicting with Networks: Nonparametric Multiple Regression Analysis of Dyadic Data," *Social Networks* 10 (1988): 359–381.

27. David Krackhardt, "Assessing the Political Landscape: Structure, Cognition, and Power in Organizations," *Administrative Science Quarterly* 35 (1990): 342–369.

CHAPTER 3

1. Paul S. Adler and Seok Woo Kwon, "Social Capital: Prospects for a New Concept," *Academy of Management Journal* 27, no. 1 (2002): 17–40; Marlene E. Burkhardt and Daniel J. Brass, "Changing Patterns or Patterns of Change: The Effects of a Change in Technology on Social Network Structure and Power," *Administrative Science Quarterly* 35, no. 1 (1990): 104–127; James S. Coleman, "Social Capital in the Creation of Human Capital," *American Journal of Sociology* 94 (1988): 95–120; Kenneth A. Frank, Yong Zhao, and Kathryn Borman, "Social Capital and the Diffusion of Innovations Within Organizations: The Case of Computer Technology in Schools," *Sociology of Education* 77, no. 2 (2004): 148–171; Janine Nahapiet and Sumantra Ghoshal, "Social Capital, Intellectual Capital, and the Organizational Advantage," *Academy of Management Review* 23, no. 2, (1998): 242–266; William R. Penuel, Margaret Riel, Ann E. Krause, and Kenneth A. Frank, "Analyzing Teachers' Professional Interactions in a School as Social Capital: A Social Network Approach," *Teachers College Record* 111, no. 1 (2009): 124–163; Brian Uzzi, "Social Structure and Competition in Interfirm Networks: The Paradox of Embeddedness," *Administrative Science Quarterly* 42, no. 1 (1997): 35–67; Brian Uzzi and Ryon Lancaster, "Relational Embeddedness and Learning: The Case of Bank Loan Managers and their Clients," *Management Science* 49, no. 4 (2003): 383–399.

2. Ronald S. Burt, *Structural Holes: The Social Structure of Competition* (Cambridge, MA: Harvard University Press, 1992); Anthony S. Bryk and Barbara Schneider, *Trust in Schools: A Core Resource for Improvement* (New York: Russell Sage Foundation, 2002); Coleman, "Social Capital in the Creation of Human Capital"; Nahapiet and Ghoshal, "Social Capital, Intellectual Capital, and the Organizational Advantage."

3. Mario L. Small, *Unanticipated Gains: Origins of Network Inequality in Everyday Life,* (Oxford: Oxford University Press, 2009); Ronald S. Burt, "Decay Functions," *Social Networks* 22 (2000): 1–28.

4. Stephen P. Borgatti and Rob Cross, "A Relational View of Information Seeking and Learning in Social Networks," *Management Science* 49, no. 4 (2003): 432–445; Peter R. Monge, Lynda White Rothman, Eric M. Eisenberg, Katherine I. Miller, and Kenneth K. Kirste, "The Dynamics of Organizational Proximity," *Management Science* 31, (1985): 1129–1141; Burkhardt and Brass, "Changing Patterns or Patterns of Change"; William R. Penuel, Margaret Riel, Christine Korbak, and Barbara Means, "Investigation of a Social Capital Approach to the Adoption of Reform Practices" (paper presented at the annual meeting of American Educational Research Association, San Diego, CA, April 2004); James P. Spillane, Tim Hallett, and John B. Diamond, "Forms of Capital and the Construction of Leadership: Instructional Leadership in Urban Elementary Schools," *Sociology of Education* 76, no. 1 (2003): 1–17; Charles E. Bidwell and Jeffrey Yasumoto, "The Collegial

Focus: Teaching Fields, Collegial Relationships, and Instructional Practice in American High Schools," *Sociology of Education* 72, no. 4 (1999): 234–256; Burt, "Decay Functions"; Julie M. Hite, Ellen J. Williams and Steven C. Baugh, "Leadership Through Multiple Network Perspectives: An Analysis of the Multiple Administrator Networks in a Public School District," (paper presented at the University Council of Educational Administration, Pittsburgh, PA., November 2002); Frank, Zhao, and Borman, "Social Capital and the Diffusion of Innovations Within Organizations."

5. Small, *Unanticipated Gains*.
6. Burt, *Structural Holes*.
7. Morten T. Hansen, "The Search-Transfer Problem: The Role of Weak Ties in Sharing Knowledge Across Organization Subunits," *Administrative Science Quarterly* 44, no. 1 (1999): 82–111; Ray Reagans and Bill McEvily, "Network Structure and Knowledge Transfer: The Effects of Cohesion and Range," *Administrative Science Quarterly* 48, no. 2 (2003): 240–267; Uzzi, "Social Structure and Competition in Interfirm Networks."
8. Mark S. Granovetter, "The Strength of Weak Ties: A Network Theory Revisited," in *Social Structure and Network Analysis*, eds. Peter V. Marsden and Nan Lin (Beverly Hills, CA: Sage, 1982), 105–130; Everett M. Rogers, *Diffusion of Innovations* 4th ed., (New York: Free Press, 1995); Uzzi and Lancaster, "Relational Embeddedness and Learning."
9. Reagans and McEvily, "Network Structure and Knowledge Transfer," 242; Burt, *Structural Holes*.
10. Coleman, "Social Capital in the Creation of Human Capital."
11. Small, *Unanticipated Gains*.
12. Definition from Miller McPherson, Lynn Smith-Lovin, and James M. Cook, "Birds of a Feather: Homophily in Social Networks," *Annual Review of Sociology* 27, (2001): 415–444.
13. Bidwell and Yasumoto, "The Collegial Focus"; Burt, "Decay Functions"; Hite, Williams, and Baugh, "Leadership Through Multiple Network Perspectives"; Frank, Zhao, and Borman, "Social Capital and the Diffusion of Innovations Within Organizations"; Penuel et al., "Investigation of a Social Capital Approach to the Adoption of Reform Practices."
14. David Krackhardt, "Constraints on the Interactive Organization as an Ideal Type," in *The Post-Bureaucratic Organization: New Perspective on Organizational Change*, eds. C. Heckscher and A. Donnellon, (Thousand Oaks, CA: Sage Publications, 1994), 211–222; Monge et al., "The Dynamics of Organizational Proximity"; G. Lawrence Zahn, "Face-to-Face Communication in an Office Setting: The Effects of Position, Proximity, and Exposure," *Communications Research* 18, no. 6 (1991): 737–775.
15. Monge et al., "The Dynamics of Organizational Proximity."
16. Ibid.
17. Burkhardt and Brass, "Changing Patterns or Patterns of Change"; Penuel et al., "Analyzing Teachers' Professional Interactions in a School as Social Capital"; Spillane, Hallett, and Diamond, "Forms of Capital and the Construction of Leadership."
18. Borgatti and Cross, "A Relational View of Information Seeking and Learning in Social Networks."
19. Small, *Unanticipated Gains*.
20. Bidwell and Yasumoto, "The Collegial Focus"; Cynthia E. Coburn and Joan E. Talbert, "Conceptions of Evidence-based Practice in School Districts: Mapping the Terrain," *American Journal of Education* 112, no. 4 (2006): 469–495; Penuel et al., "Analyzing Teachers' Professional Interactions in a School as Social Capital."
21. Burt, "Decay Functions."
22. Specifically, we asked district leaders to nominate schools where the faculty had, on average, relatively high and low levels of human and social capital, with human capital described as math instructional expertise and social capital described as interaction

about mathematics instruction. We conducted preliminary site visits for each nominated school during which time we interviewed the principal, coaches, and key teachers about the nature of the social interaction in the school as a whole and level of expertise about mathematics. These visits confirmed that the four schools nominated by the district mathematics coach varied in respect to their overall levels of interaction around mathematics and the degree to which there were teachers with instructional expertise in mathematics in the school.

23. Barry Wellman and S.D. Berkowitz, *Social Structures: A Network Approach.* (Cambridge, UK: Cambridge University Press, 1988). The strength of the egocentric approach is that rather than making assumptions about the nature and form of teachers' social networks, we took identification of the networks as an essential first step for empirical study. Because the analyst maps networks from the ground up using nominations solicited from the interviewee themselves, the egocentric approach does not assume the locus of professional community is in formal structures such as grade-level groups or even resides within preexisting boundaries such as the school (Carrasco et al. 2006; Reagans and McEvily 2003). However, the limitation of the egocentric approach is that because we did not do social network analysis with all teachers in the school (as one would with sociocentric approaches to network analysis), we are not able to map the social network structure for the entire school nor can we ascertain the degree to which focal teachers' social networks are representative of other teachers' networks in the school.

24. A *t-test* assesses whether the means of two groups are *statistically* different from each other.

25. Matthew B. Miles and Michael Huberman, *Qualitative Data Analysis: An Expanded Sourcebook*, 2nd edition, (Thousand Oaks, CA: Sage, 1994).

26. An alternative explanation for the increase in expertise in spite of the decrease in size of networks is that existing people in teachers' networks increased their level of expertise from year 2 to year 3. However, upon investigation, we found that only one individual was both in the network across both years *and* had increased expertise from year 2 to year 3.

27. Small, *Unanticipated Gains.*

28. Adler and Kwon, "Social Capital."

29. Small, *Unanticipated Gains*

30. Cynthia E. Coburn and Jennifer L. Russell, "District Policy and Teachers' Social Networks," *Educational Evaluation and Policy Analysis* 30, no. 3 (2008): 203–235.

31. Borgatti and Cross, "A Relational View of Information Seeking and Learning in Social Networks."

32. Dan C. Lortie (1975). *Schoolteacher: A Sociological Study.* (Chicago: University of Chicago Press, 1975); Judith W. Little, "The Persistence of Privacy: Autonomy and Initiative in Teachers' Professional Relations," *Teachers College Record* 91, no. 4 (1990): 509–536; Judith W. Little, "Inside Teacher Community: Representations of Classroom Practice," *Teachers College Record* 105, no. 6 (2003): 913–945.

33. Daniel M. Wegner, "A Contemporary Analysis of the Group Mind," in *Theories of Group Behavior*, eds. B. Mullen and G.R. Goethals, (New York: Springer-Verlag, 1987); Samer Faraj and Lee Sproull, "Coordinating Expertise in Software Development Teams," *Management Science* 46, no. 12 (2000): 1554–1568; Kyle Lewis, Donald Lange, and Lynette Gillis, "Transactive Memory Systems, Learning, and Learning Transfer," *Organization Science* 16, no. 6 (2005): 581–598; Diane Wei Liang, Richard Moreland, and Linda Argote, "Group Versus Individual Training and Group Performance: The Mediating Factor of Transactive Memory," *Personality and Social Psychology Bulletin* 21, no. 4 (1995): 384–393; Richard L. Moreland and Larissa Myaskovsky, "Exploring the Performance Benefits

of Group Training: Transactive Memory or Improved Communication?" *Organizational Behavior and Human Decision Processes* 82, no. 11 (2000): 117–133.

34. Faraj and Sproull, "Coordinating Expertise in Software Development Teams."

35. Yuqing Ren, Kathleen M. Carley, and Linda Argote, "The Contingent Effects of Transactive Memory: When Is It More Beneficial to Know What Others Know?" *Management Science* 55, no. 5 (2006): 671–682.

36. Small, *Unanticipated Gains.*

37. Cynthia E. Coburn, "Collective Sensemaking About Reading: How Teachers Mediate Reading Policy in their Professional Communities," *Educational Evaluation and Policy Analysis* 23, no. 2 (2001): 145–170.

CHAPTER 4

1. Paul Berman and Milbrey W. McLaughlin, "Implementation of Educational Innovation." *Educational Forum* 40, (1976): 345–370; Susan Moore Johnson, *Teachers at Work* (New York: Basic Books, 1990; Victoria Boyd, "School Context: Bridge or Barrier for Change?" *Southwest Educational Development Laboratory*, 1992.

2. Karen S. Louis, Sharon D. Kruse, and Anthony S. Bryk, "Professionalism and Community: What Is It and Why Is It Important in Urban Schools," in *Professionalism and Community: Perspectives on Reforming Urban Schools*, eds. Karen S. Louis and Sharon D. Kruse (Thousand Oaks, CA: Corwin Press, 1995), 3–24; Milbrey W. McLaughlin and Joan Talbert, *Professional Communities and the Work of High School Teaching* (Chicago: University of Chicago Press, 2001).

3. Anthony S. Bryk, Penny B. Sebring, Elaine Allensworth, Stuart Luppescu, and John Q. Easton, *Organizing Schools for Improvement* (Chicago: University of Chicago Press, 2010).

4. Irene Fountas and Gay Su Pinnell, *Guided Reading: Good First Teaching for All Children* (Portsmouth, NH: Heinemann Educational Books, 1996); Irene Fountas and Gay Su Pinnell, *Guiding Readers and Writers, Grades 3–6: Teaching Comprehension, Genre, and Content Literacy* (Portsmouth, NH: Heinemann Educational Books, 2001); Irene Fountas and Gay Su Pinnell, *Teaching for Comprehending and Fluency: Thinking, Talking, and Writing About Reading, K–8* (Portsmouth, NH: Heinemann Educational Books, 2006); Marie M. Clay, *Reading: The Patterning of Complex Behaviour* (Portsmouth, NH: Heinemann Educational Books, 1977); Marie M. Clay, *Change over Time in Children's Literacy Development* (Portsmouth, NH: Heinemann Educational Books, 2001); Literacy Collaborative Web site, http://literacycollaborative.org.

5. Allison C. Atteberry and Anthony S. Bryk, "Analyzing Teacher Engagement in Literacy Coaching Activities," *Elementary School Journal* (forthcoming, 2010).

6. Heather Hough, Anthony S. Bryk, Gay Su Pinnell, David Kerbow, Irene Fountas, and Patricia L. Scharer, "The Effects of School-Based Coaching: Measuring Change in the Practice of Teachers Engaged in Literacy Collaborative Professional Development" (paper presented at the American Educational Research Association conference, New York, 2008).

7. Gina Biancarosa and Anthony S. Bryk, "Assessing the Value-Added Effects of Literacy Collaborative Professional Development on Student Learning." *Elementary School Journal* (forthcoming, 2010).

8. Etienne Wenger, *Communities of Practice: Learning, Meaning, and Identity* (Cambridge, UK: Cambridge University Press, 1999); McLaughlin and Talbert, *Professional Communities and the Work of High School Teaching.*

9. Valerie E. Lee, Julia B. Smith, and Robert G. Croninger, "How High School Organization Influences the Equitable Distribution of Learning in Mathematics and Science." *Sociology of Education* 70, no. 2 (1997): 128–150; Anthony S. Bryk, Eric Camburn, and Karen

S. Louis, "Professional Community in Chicago Elementary Schools: Facilitating Factors and Organizational Consequences," *Educational Administration Quarterly* 35, no. 5 (1999): 751; Anthony S. Bryk and Barbara Schneider, *Trust in Schools: A Core Resource for Improvement* (New York: Russell Sage Foundation Publications, 2002); Judith W. Little, "Locating Learning in Teachers' Communities of Practice: Opening up Problems of Analysis in Records of Everyday Work," *Teaching and Teacher Education* 18, no. 8 (2002): 917–946; Louise Stoll, Ray Bolam, Agnes McMahon, Mike Wallace, and Sally Thomas, "Professional Learning Communities: A Review of the Literature" *Journal of Educational Change* 7, no. 4 (2006): 221–258.

10. Kenneth A. Frank, Yong Zhao, and Kathryn Borman, "Social Capital and the Diffusion of Innovations Within Organizations: The Case of Computer Technology in Schools," *Sociology of Education* 77, no. 2 (2004): 148–171.

11. Elliot H. Weinbaum, Russell P. Cole, Michael J. Weiss, and Jonathan A. Supovitz, "Going with the Flow: Communication and Reform in High Schools," in *The Implementation Gap: Understanding Reform in High Schools*, eds. Jonathan A. Supovitz and Elliot H. Weinbaum (New York: Teachers College Press, 2008): 68–102.

12. Cynthia Coburn and Jennifer L. Russell, "District Policy and Teachers' Social Networks" *Educational Evaluation and Policy Analysis* 30, no. 3 (2008): 203; Alan J. Daly, Nienke M. Moolenaar, Jose M. Bolivar, and Peggy Burke, "Relationships in Reform: The Role of Teachers' Social Networks," *Journal of Educational Administration* 48, no. 3 (2010): 359–391.

13. Daniel C. Lortie, *Schoolteacher: A Sociological Study.* (Chicago/London: University of Chicago Press, 1975); Mary M. Kennedy, "Knowledge and Teaching," *Teachers and Teaching* 8, no. 3 (2002): 355–370.

14. Lortie, *Schoolteacher,* 144.

15. Bryk and Schneider, *Trust in Schools.*

16. Duncan J. Watts and Steven Strogatz, "Small World." *Nature* 393 (1998): 440–442; Brigham S. Anderson, Carter Butts, and Kathleen Carley, "The Interaction of Size and Density with Graph-Level Indices," *Social Networks* 21, no. 3 (1999): 239–268.

17. We posit the following model:

$$Y_{j,k} = \beta_0 + \beta_1 X_{1k} + \beta_2 X_{2k} + \varepsilon_k$$

Where $Y_{j,k}$ is the average cumulative number of coaching sessions received across j teachers from coach k, X_{1k} is the base state valued and normalized centrality of each coach (standardized around the 2005 mean), and X_{2k} is the number of K–3 teachers in the school in spring 2005 (centered around a school with twelve teachers).

18. For a complete description of these four measures, their construction, and the items that relate to these measures, see the Consortium on Chicago School Research Web site, http://ccsr.uchicago.edu/.

19. Biancarosa and Bryk, "Assessing the Value-Added Effects of Literacy Collaborative Professional Development on Student Learning."

20. Albert Bandura, "Self-Efficacy," in *Encyclopedia of Human Behavior*, vol. 4, ed. V. S. Ramachaudran (New York: Academic Press, 1994), 71–81.

CHAPTER 5

1. M. Fullan, *Probing the Depth of Educational Reform.* (London: Falmer Press, 1993); D. Tyack, and L. Cuban, *Tinkering Toward Utopia: A Century of Public School Reform* (Cambridge, MA: Harvard University Press, 1995).

2. K.E. Weick, "Educational Organizations as Loosely Coupled Systems" *Administrative Science Quarterly* 21 no 1 (1976): 1–19; D. C. Lortie, *Schoolteacher* (Chicago: University of

Chicago Press. 2002); L. Siskin, *Realms of Knowledge: Academic Departments in Secondary Schools* (London: Falmer, 1994).

3. T. K. Glennan, S. J. Bodilly, J. Galegher, and K. A. Kerr, *Expanding the Reach of Education Reforms: Perspectives from Leaders in the Scale-Up of Educational Interventions* (Santa Monica, CA: RAND, 2004).

4. J.A., Supovitz and H. M.Turner, "The Effects of Professional Development on Science Teaching Practices And Classroom Culture," *Journal of Research in Science Teaching* 37, no 9 (2000): 963–980.

5. I. Ajzen and T. J. Madden, "Prediction of Goal-Directed Behavior: Attitudes, Intentions, and Perceived Behavioral-Control." *Journal of Experimental Social Psychology* 22 no 5 (1986): 454.

6. R. Elmore. "Getting to Scale with Good Educational Practice" *Harvard Educational Review* 66 (1996): 1–26.; F. M. Hess, *Spinning Wheels: The Politics of Urban School Reform* (Washington, DC: The Brookings Institution Press. 1999); S. J. Bodilly, *Lessons from New American Schools' Scale-Up Phase: Prospects for Bringing Designs to Multiple Schools* (Santa Monica, CA: RAND, 1998).

7. T. Corcoran, M. Hoppe, T. Luhm, and J. A. Supovitz, 'America's Choice Comprehensive School Reform Design: First Year Implementation Evaluation Summary (Philadelphia: Consortium for Policy Research in Education, 2000); M. Berends, S. N. Kirby, S. Naftel, , C. McKelvey, S. Stockly, R. J. Briggs, J. Chun, E. Gill, J. Heilbrunn, "NAS Designs and Academic Achievement," in *Facing the Challenges of Whole School Reform: American Schools After a Decade*, eds. Mark Berends, Susan J. Bodilly, and Sheila Nataraj Kirby (Santa Monica, CA: RAND, 2002); *Comprehensive School Reform Quality Center and American Institutes for Research* (Washington, DC: CSRQ Center, 2006).

8. J. P. Spillane, "A Fifth Grade Teacher's Reconstruction of Mathematics and Literacy Teaching: Exploring Interactions Among Identity, Learning, and Subject Matter," *Elementary School Journal* 100, no 4 (2000): 307–330.; M. F. Pajares, "Teacher Beliefs and Educational Research: Cleaning Up a Messy Construct," *Review of Educational Research* 62, no 3 (1992): 307–332; C. E. Coburn, "Collective Sensemaking about Reading: How Teachers Mediate Reading Policy in Their Professional Communities," *Educational Evaluation and Policy Analysis* 23, no 2 (2001): 145–170.

9. M.S. Garet, A. C. Porter, L. Desimone, B. F. Birman, and K. S. Yoon, "What Makes Professional Development Effective? Results from a National Sample of Teachers"," *American Educational Research Journal* 38, no. 4(2001): 915–945; W. R. Penuel, B. J. Fishman, R. Yamaguchi, L. P. Gallagher, "What Makes Professional Development Effective? Strategies That Foster Curriculum Implementation," *American Educational Research Journal* 44, no 4 (2007): 921–958.

10. Penuel et al., "What Makes Professional Development Effective?"

11. L.R. Glasman and D. Albarracín, "Forming Attitudes That Predict Future Behavior: A Meta-Analysis of the Attitude Behavior Relation," *Psychological Bulletin* 132, no. 5 (2006): 779–822.

12. S. J. Kraus. "Attitudes and the Prediction of Behavior: a Meta-Analysis of the Empirical Literature," *Personality and Social Psychology Bulletin* 21 (1995): 58–75.

13. R. Cooke and P. Sheeran, "Moderation of Cognition Intention and Cognition-Behavior Relations: A Meta-Analysis of Properties of Variables from the Theory of Planned Behavior," *British Journal of Social Psychology* 43 (2004): 159–186.

14. P. V. Marsden and N. E. Friedkin, "Network Studies of Social Influence," *Sociological Methods and Research,* 22 no 1 (1993): 127–151; G. Robbins, P. Pattison, and P. Elliot, "Network Models for Social Influence Processes," *Psychometrika* 66, no. 2 (2001): 161–189.

15. H. Assael and G. S. Day, "Attitudes and Awareness As Predictors of Market Share," *Journal of Advertising Research* 8, no 4 (1968): 3–10.

16. G. J. Blau and R. Katerberg, "Toward Enhancing Research with the Social Information Processing Approach to Job Design," *Academy of Management Review* 7 (1982): 543–550; G. R. Salancik and J. Pfeffer, "Social Information Processing Approach to Job Attitudes and Task Design," *Administrative Science Quarterly* 23, no. 2 (1978): 224–253; M. D. Zalesny and J. K. Ford, "Extending the Social Information Processing Perspective-New Links to Attitudes, Behaviors, and Perceptions"," *Organizational Behavior and Human Decision Processes* 47, no. 2 (1990): 205–246.

17. Ajzen and Madden, "Prediction of Goal Directed Behavior."

18. J. Lave and E. Wenger, *Situated Learning: Legitimate Peripheral Participation* (Cambridge, UK: Cambridge University Press, 1991); C. Abelmann and R. Elmore, *When Accountability Knocks, Will Anyone Answer?* (Philadelphia: Consortium for Policy Research in Education, 1999).

19. Ajzen and Madden, "Prediction of Goal Directed Behavior."

20. L. Festinger, "Informal Social Communication," *Psychological Review* 57, no. 5 (1950): 271–282; S. Schachter, "Deviation, Rejection, and Communication," *Journal of Abnormal and Social Psychology* 46 (1951): 190–207; I. Steiner, "Personality and the Resolution of Interpersonal Disagreements," in *Progress in Experimental Personality Research*, vol. 3, ed. B. Hahler (New York: Academic Press, 1966): 195–239; P. Blau, *Inequality and Heterogeneity* (New York: Macmillan, 1977); F. Heider, *Psychology of Interpersonal Relations* (New York: John Wiley, 1958); P. V. Marsden, "Models and Methods for Characterizing the Structural Parameters of Groups," *Social Networks* 3, no. 1 (1981): 1–27.

21. Ajzen and Madden, "Prediction of Goal Directed Behavior."

22. Ibid.

23. E. H. Weinbaum, R. P.Cole, M. J. Weiss, J. A. and Supovitz, "Going with the Flow: Communication and Reform in High Schools," in *The Implementation Gap: Understanding Reform in High Schools*, eds. J. A. Supovitz and E. H. Weinbaum (New York: Teachers College Press. 2008).

24. R.L. Hartman and J. D. Johnson, "Social Contagion and Multiplexity-Communication Networks as Prdictors of Commitment and Role Ambiguity," *Human Communication Research* 15, no. 4 (1989): 523–548; K. C. Land, G. Deane, and J. R. Blau, "Religious Pluralism and Church Membership—A Spatial Diffusion Model," *American Sociological Review* 56, no. 2 (1991): 237–249; R.E. Rice, A. E. Grant, J. Schmitz, and J. Torobin, "Individual and Network Influences on the Adoption and Perceived Outcomes of Electronic Messaging," *Social Networks* 12, no. 1 (1990): 27–55; R. E. Rice and C. Aydin, "Attitudes toward New Organizational Technology-Network Proximity As a Mechanism for Social Information Processing," *Administrative Science Quarterly* 36, no. 2 (1991): 219–244.

25. Marsden and Friedkin, "Network Studies of Social Influence"; Robbins, Pattison, and Elliot, "Network Models for Social Influence Processes."

26. M. Fishbein, "Attitude and the Prediction of Behavior," in *Readings in Attitude Theory and Measurement*, ed. M. Fishbein (New York: Wiley, 1967) 477–492.; M. Fishbein and I. Ajzen, *Belief, Attitude, Intention and Behavior* (Reading, MA: Addison-Wesley, 1975).

27. J. A. Davis, "Clustering and Structural Balance in Graphs," *Human Relations* 20 (1967): 131–137.

28. C. E. Bidwell, K. A. Frank, and P. A. Quiroz, "Teacher Types, Workplace Controls, and the Organization of Schools," *Sociology of Education* 70, no. 4 (1997): 285–307.

29. H. Ibarra, "Personal Networks of Women and Minorities in Management-a Conceptual Framework," *Academy of Management Review* 18, no. 1 (1993): 56–87.

30. B. H. Erickson, "The Relational Basis of Attitudes," in *Social Structures: a Network Approach*, eds. Barry Wellman and Steven D. Berkowitz (New York: Cambridge University Press, 1998), 99–121.

31. P. V. Marsden, "Homogeneity in Confiding Relations," *Social Networks* 10, no. 1 (1998): 57–76.

32. M. Granovetter, "The Strength of Weak Ties," *American Journal of Sociology* 78, no. 1 (1973): 1360–1380. e

33. Ibarra, "Personal Networks of Women and Minorities in Management"; B. Uzzi, "Social Structure and Competition in Interfirm Networks: the Paradox of Embeddedness," *Administrative Science Quarterly* 42, no. 1 (1997): 35–67.

34. M. Granovetter, "The Strength of Weak Ties: a Network Theory Revisited," in *Social Structure and Network Analysis*, eds. P. V. Marsden and N. Lin (Beverly Hills, CA: Sage, 1982), 105–130; D. Krackhardt, "The Strength of Strong Ties: The Importance of Philos in Organizations," in *Networks and Organization Structure, Form and Action*, eds. Nitin Nohria and Robert G. Eccles (Cambridge, MA: Harvard University Press, 1992), 216–239; E. M. Rogers and L. D. Kincaid, *Communication Networks* (New York: Free Press, 1981).

35. L. Darling-Hammond and M. W. McLaughlin, "Policies That Support Professional Development in an Era of Reform" *Phi Delta Kappan* 76, no. 8 (1995): 597–604; K. A. Frank and K. Fahrbach, "Organizational Culture as a Complex System: Balance and Information in Models of Influence and Selection," *Organization Science* 10, no. 4 (1998), 514–515.

36. J. A. Mueller, and K. Hovde, "Theme and Variation in the Enactment of Reform: Case Studies," in *The Implementation Gap: Understanding Reform in High Schools*, eds. J. A. Supovitz and E. H. Weinbaum (New York: Teachers College Press, 2008).

37. Four of the high schools were using programs that seek to enhance students' literacy skills (Penn Literacy Network and Ramp Up to Literacy). Three of the high schools were using comprehensive school reform programs, First Things First and High Schools That Work. Two of the high schools were using SchoolNet, a company that provides a range of services that are intended to help school staff to access and use data and information. Because the focus of this chapter is on the *transmission* and *change* of attitudes, as opposed to initial perceptions of particular reform elements, the particular program designs are not discussed in depth here.

38. R. L. Gorsuch, *Factor Analysis*, 2nd edition (Hillsdale, NJ: Erlbaum, 1983).

39. L. J. Cronbach, "Coefficient Alpha and the Internal Structure of Tests," *Psychometrika* 16, no. 3 (1951): 297–334.

40. S.W. Raudenbush and A. S. Bryk, *Hierarchical Linear Models: Applicatins and Data Analysis Methods*, 2nd edition (Thousand Oaks, CA: Sage, 2002).

41. Limiting the potential responses to five colleagues may have impacted the data collected. However, few of our respondents provided five names, suggesting that the limit did not constrain the potential information. Only 15 percent of respondents provided either four or five names in the 2005 survey, and fewer than 13 percent of respondents provided either four or five names in the 2006 survey.

42. We loosely refer to the communication patterns that resulted from the survey responses to the three questions as *communication networks* or *social networks*.

43. See Marsden and Friedken ("Network Studies of Social Influence," 135) for more information on the use of the deviation of peer attitudes as predictors of attitude change. This method described in the prose allowed us to utilize attitude and network data from all respondents at a particular time point as contributing to the peer attitude scores for the analysis sample.

44. Similarly, if an individual were three or four links away from a peer, the weight for those paths would be one-third and one-fourth, respectively.

45. In computing the weighted average attitude deviation scores for each network, the contribution of direct peers was excluded, and therefore the attitudes available through direct and indirect peers represent different sources of information.

46. Garet et al., "What Makes Professional Development Effective?"; Penuel et al., "What Makes Professional Development Effective?"; J. A. Supovitz and H. M. Turner, "The Effects of Professional Development on Science Teaching Practices and Classroom Culture," *Journal of Research in Science Teaching* 37, no. 9 (2000): 963–980.

47. Marsden and Friedkin, "Network Studies of Social Influence"; Salancik and Pfeffer, "Social Information Processing Approach to Job Attitudes and Task Design."
48. H. Ibarra and S. B. Andrews, "Power, Social Influence, and Sense Making-Effects of Network Centrality and Proximity on Employee Perceptions," *Administrative Science Quarterly* 38, no. 2 (1993): 277–303.
49. M.W. McLaughlin, "The RAND Change Agent Study Revisited: Macro Perspectives and Micro Realities," *Educational Researcher* 19, no.9 (1990): 11–16.
50. E. M. Rogers. *Diffusion of Innovations* (New York: Free Press, 1995).
51. K. A. Frank, Y. Zhao, and K. Borman, "Social Capital and the Diffusion of Innovations Within Organizations: The Case of Computer Technology in Schools," *Sociology of Education* 77, no.2 (2004): 148–171.
52. A. S. Bryk and B. Schneider, *Trust in Schools: a Core Resource for Improvement* (New York: Russell Sage, 2002).
53. Granovetter, "The Strength of Weak Ties."
54. M. W. McLaughlin and J.E. Talbert. *Professional Communities and the Work of High School Teaching* (Chicago: University of Chicago Press, 1990); P. W. Jackson, *Life in Classrooms* (New York: Teachers College Press, 1968).

CHAPTER 6

1. Martin Kilduff and Wenpin Tsai, *Social Networks and Organizations* (London: Sage, 2003).
2. Vicki Vescio, Dorene Ross and Alyson Adams, "A Review of Research on the Impact of Professional Learning Communities on Teaching Practice and Student Learning," *Teaching and Teacher Education* 24, no. 1 (2008): 80–91.
3. Cynthia E. Coburn and Jennifer Lin Russell, "District Policy and Teachers' Social Networks," *Education Evaluation and Policy Analysis* 30, no. 3 (2008): 203–235; Nienke M. Moolenaar, Alan J. Daly, and Peter J. C. Sleegers, "Ties with Potential: Social Network Structure and Innovation in Dutch Schools," *Teachers College Record* (in press); William R. Penuel, Kenneth A. Frank, and Ann E. Krause, *A Social Network Approach to Examining the Effects of Distributed Leadership in Schoolwide Reform Initiatives,* (paper presented at the Annual Meeting of the American Educational Research Association, Chicago, 2007).
4. G. Ahuja, "Collaboration Networks, Structural Holes, and Innovation: A Longitudinal Study," *Administrative Science Quarterly* 45, no. 3 (2000): 425–455; Wenpin Tsai and Sumantra Ghoshal, "Social Capital and Value Creation: The Role of Intrafirm Networks," *Academy of Management Journal* 41, no. 4 (1998): 464–478.
5. Cathleen McGrath and David Krackhardt, "Network Conditions for Organizational Change," *Journal of Applied Behavioral Science* 39, no. 3 (2003): 324–336.
6. Alain Degenne and Michel Forsé, *Introducing Social Networks* (London: Sage, 1999).
7. Ikujiro Nonaka and Hirotaka Takeuchi, *The Knowledge-creating Company* (New York: Oxford University Press, 1995).
8. Sami Paavola, Lasse Lipponen, and Kai Hakkarainen, "Models of Innovative Knowledge Communities and Three Metaphors of Learning," *Review of Educational Research* 74, no. 4 (2004): 557–576.
9. Gerben S. Van der Vegt, Evert Van de Vliert, and Xu Huang, "Location-Level Links between Diversity and Innovative Climate Depend on National Power Distance," *Academy of Management Journal* 48, no. 6 (2005): 1171–1182.
10. Nienke M. Moolenaar, Alan J. Daly, and Peter J. C. Sleegers, "Ties with Potential: Social Network Structure and Innovation in Dutch Schools," *Teachers College Record* (in press).
11. Corrie Giles and Andy Hargreaves, "The Sustainability of Innovative Schools as Learning Organizations and Professional Learning Communities During Standardized Reform," *Educational Administration Quarterly* 42, no. 1 (2006): 124–156.

12. See, for example, Pierre Bourdieu, "The Forms of Social Capital," in *Handbook of Theory and Research for the Sociology of Education*, ed. John G. Richardson (New York: Greenwood, 1986), 241–258; Nan Lin, *Social Capital: A Theory of Social Structure and Action* (New York: Cambridge University Press, 2001).

13. Janine Nahapiet and Sumantra Ghoshal, "Social Capital, Intellectual Capital, and the Organizational Advantage," *The Academy of Management Review* 23, no. 2 (1998): 242–266.

14. Carrie R. Leana and Harry J. Van Buren III, "Organizational Social Capital and Employment Practices," *Academy of Management Review* 243, no. 3 (1999): 538–555; Wenpin Tsai and Sumantra Ghoshal, "Social Capital and Value Creation: The Role of Intrafirm Networks," *Academy of Management Journal* 41, no. 4 (1998): 464–478.

15. For a review of educational research on social capital, see: Sandra L. Dika and Kusum Singh, "Applications of Social Capital in Educational Literature: A Critical Synthesis," *Review of Educational Research* 72, no. 1 (2002): 31–60.

16. David Halpern, *Social Capital* (Cambridge, MA: Polity Press, 2005).

17. Inge Bakkenes, Cornelis De Brabander, and Jeroen Imants, "Teacher Isolation and Communication Network Analysis in Primary Schools," *Educational Administration Quarterly* 35, no. 2 (1999): 166–202.

18. Mark S. Granovetter, "The Strength of Weak Ties," *American Journal of Sociology* 78, no. 1 (1973): 1360–1380.

19. Ronald S. Burt, *Structural Holes* (Cambridge, MA: Harvard University Press, 1992).

20. Brian Uzzi and Jarrett Spiro, "Collaboration and Creativity: The Small World Problem," *American Journal of Sociology* 111, no. 2 (2005): 447–504.

21. Ray E. Reagans and Bill McEvily, "Network Structure and Knowledge Transfer: The Effects of Cohesion and Range," *Administrative Science Quarterly* 48, no. 2 (2003): 240–267; Reed E. Nelson, "The Strength of Strong Ties: Social Networks and Intergroup Conflict in Organizations," *Academy of Management Journal* 32, no. 2 (1989): 377–401; Alan J. Daly and Kara Finnigan, "Understanding Network Structure to Understand Change Strategy," *Journal of Educational Change* 11, no. 2 (2010): 111–138; Julie M. Hite, Ellen J. Williams, and Steven C. Baugh, "Multiple Networks of Public School Administrators: An Analysis of Network Content and Structure," *International Journal on Leadership in Education* 8, no. 2 (2005): 91–122.

22. Alejandro Portes, "Social Capital: Its Origins and Applications in Modern Sociology," *Annual Review of Sociology* 24, no. 1 (1998): 1–24.

23. Wayne K. Hoy and Megan Tschannen-Moran, "The Conceptualization and Measurement of Faculty Trust in Schools: The Omnibus T-Scale," in *Studies in Leading and Organizing Schools*, eds. Wayne K. Hoy and Cecil G. Miskel (Greenwich, CT: Information Age, 2003), 181–208.

24. Megan Tschannen-Moran, *Trust Matters: Leadership for Successful Schools* (San Francisco: Jossey-Bass, 2004).

25. Megan Tschannen-Moran, "Collaboration and the Need for Trust," *Journal of Educational Administration* 39, no. 4 (2001): 308–331.

26. Anthony S. Bryk and Barbara L. Schneider, *Trust in Schools: A Core Resource for School Improvement* (New York: Russell Sage Foundation, 2002).

27. William R. Penuel, Barry J. Fishman, Ryoko Yamaguchi, and Lawrence P. Gallagher, "What Makes Professional Development Effective? Strategies that Foster Curriculum Implementation," *American Educational Research Journal* 44, no. 4 (2007): 921–958.

28. All names are pseudonyms.

29. All names are pseudonyms.

30. *Public Use Dataset. 2001 Survey of Students and Teachers. User's Manual* (Chicago: The Consortium on Chicago School Research, 2004).

31. Questions were scored using a four-point Likert-type agreement scale, ranging from 1 (*strongly disagree*) to 4 (*strongly agree*). Principal component analysis provided support for a single factor solution that accounted for 60.1 percent of the variance (α = .87). Scale scores were composed using the mean score of all items.

32. Wayne K. Hoy and Megan Tschannen-Moran, "The Conceptualization and Measurement of Faculty Trust in Schools: The Omnibus T-Scale," in *Studies in Leading and Organizing Schools*, eds. Wayne K. Hoy and Cecil G. Miskel (Greenwich, CT: Information Age, 2003), 181–208.

33. The software program UCINET 6.0 was used to calculate and analyze all social network characteristics.

34. Stanley Wasserman and Katherine Faust, *Social Network Analysis* (Cambridge, UK: Cambridge University Press, 1994).

35. Reuben M. Baron and David A. Kenny, "The Moderator-Mediator Variable Distinction in Social Psychological Research: Conceptual, Strategic and Statistical Considerations," *Journal of Personality and Social Psychology* 51, no. 6 (1986): 1173–1182.

36. Addition of the proposed mediator trust to the regression equation reduces the direct effect of density on IC (from Beta$_c$ = .14 p < .01 to Beta$_{c'}$ = .11, p < .01), thus suggesting partial mediation. Examination of Sobel's test confirmed the significance of the reduction (Sobel test statistic = 2.14, p < .05).

37. Meredith I. Honig, "No Small Thing: School District Central Office Bureaucracies and the Implementation of New Small Autonomous Schools Initiatives," *American Educational Research Journal* 46, no. 2 (2009): 387–422.

38. Amanda Datnow and Marisa E. Castellano, "Leadership and Success for All," in *Leadership for School Reform: Lessons from Comprehensive School Reform Designs*, eds. Joseph Murphy and Amanda Datnow (Thousand Oaks, CA: Corwin Press, 2003), 187–208.

39. Alan J. Daly, Nienke M. Moolenaar, Jose M. Bolivar, and Peggy Burke, "Relationships in Reform: The Role of Teachers' Social Networks," *Journal of Educational Administration* 48, no. 3 (2010): 359–391.

CHAPTER 7

1. Linda Darling-Hammond and Milbrey W. McLaughlin, "Policies That Support Professional Development in an Era of Reform," *Phi Delta Kappan* April (1995): 597–604; Judith W. Little, "Professional Development in Pursuit of Reform," in *Teachers Caught in the Action: Professional Development that Matters*, eds. Ann Lieberman and Lynn Miller (New York: Teachers College Press, 2001), 23–44.

2. Ann Lieberman and Lynn Miller, *Teachers: Transforming their World and Their Work* (New York: Teachers College Press, 1999).

3. Cynthia Coburn, "Collective Sensemaking About Reading: How Teachers Mediate Reading Policy in Their Professional Communities," *Educational Evaluation and Policy Analysis* 23, no. 2 (2001): 145–170; Cynthia C. Coburn, "Shaping Teacher Sensemaking: School Leaders and the Enactment of Reading Policy," *Educational Policy* 19, no. 3 (2005): 476–509; Little, "Professional Development in Pursuit of Reform."

4. Darling-Hammond and McLaughlin, "Policies That Support Professional Development in an Era of Reform"; Ann Lieberman, "Networks as Learning Communities: Shaping the Future of Teacher Development," *Journal of Teacher Education* 51, no. 3 (2000): 221–227; Lieberman and Miller, *Teachers*.

5. Anne Burns Thomas, "Supporting New Visions for Social Justice Teaching: The Potential for Professional Development Networks," *Penn GSE Perspectives on Urban Education* 5, no. 1 (2007): 1–18; Lieberman, "Networks As Learning Communities."; James R. Pennell and William A. Firestone, "Changing Classroom Practices through Teacher Networks: Match-

ing Program Features with Teacher Characteristics and Circumstances," *Teachers College Record* 98, no. 1 (1996): 46–76.

6. Michael S. Garet et al., "What Makes Professional Development Effective? Results from a National Sample of Teachers," *American Educational Research Journal* 38, no. 4 (January 1, 2001): 915–945; Christopher Dede et al., *Scaling Up Success: Lessons Learned from Technology-Based Educational Improvement* (San Francisco: Jossey-Bass, 2005); Joan E. Hughs and Ann Ooms, "Content-Focused Technology Inquiry Groups: Preparing Urban Teachers to Integrate Technology to Transform Student Learning," *Journal of Research on Technology in Education* 36, no. 4 (2004): 397–411; Karen Swan et al., "Situated Professional Development and Technology Integration: The Capital Area Technology and Inquiry in Education (CATIE) Mentoring Program," *Journal of Technology and Teacher Education* 10, no. 2 (2002): 169–190.

7. *Cyberinfrastructure Vision for 21st Century Discovery* (Arlington, VA: National Science Foundation, 2007); *The Intellectual and Policy Foundations of the 21st Century Skills Framework* (Tucson, AZ: Partnership for 21st Century Skills, 2007).

8. Carl Bereiter, *Education and Mind in the Knowledge Age* (Mahwah, NJ: Lawrence Erlbaum Associates, 2002); Frank Levy and Richard J. Murnane, "Education and the Changing Job Market," *Educational Leadership* 62, no. 2 (October 2004): 80.

9. Barry Fishman et al., "Creating a Framework for Research on Systemic Technology Innovations," *Journal of the Learning Sciences* 13, no. 1 (2004): 43; Susan A Yoon and Eric Klopfer, "Feedback (F) Fueling Adaptation (A), Network Growth (N), and Self-Organization (S): A Complex Systems Design and Evaluation Approach to Professional Development" *Journal of Science Education and Technology* 15, nos. 5–6 (December 2006): 353–366.

10. Dede et al., *Scaling Up Success*; Yoon and Klopfer, "Feedback (F) Fueling Adaptation (A), Network Growth (N), and Self-Organization (S)"; Susan A Yoon et al., "Understanding Emergent Challenges and Adaptations in the Design of an OST STEM Project Through a Structure, Behavior and Function (SBF) Complexity Lens" (presented at the annual meeting of the National Association for Research in Science Teaching, Orange County, CA, 2009).

11. Amanda Datnow, "The Sustainability of Comprehensive School Reform Models in Changing District and State Contexts," *Educational Administration Quarterly* 41, no. 1 (February 2005): 121–153; Dede et al., *Scaling Up Success*; Andy Hargreaves and Dean Fink, "The Three Dimensions of Reform." *Educational Leadership* 57, no. 7 (2000): 30–33.

12. Richard F. Elmore, "Getting to Scale with Good Educational Practice," *Harvard Educational Review* 66, no. 1 (1996): 21.

13. Fishman et al., "Creating a Framework for Research on Systemic Technology Innovations," *Journal of the Learning Sciences* 13, no. 1 (2004): 43–76.

14. Coburn, "Shaping Teacher Sensemaking."

15. E. Camburn, B. Rowan, and J. Taylor, "Distributed Leadership in Schools: The Case of Elementary Schools Adopting Comprehensive School Reform Models," *Educational Evaluation and Policy Analysis* 25, no. 4 (2003): 347–374; J. P. Spillane, R. Halverson, and J. B. Diamond, "Toward a Theory of Leadership Practice: A Distributed Perspective," *Journal of Curriculum Studies* 36, no. 1 (2004): 3–34; J. Y. Yasumoto, K. Uekawa, and C. E. Bidwell, "The Collegial Focus and High School Students' Acheivement," *Sociology of Education* 74, no. 3 (June 2001): 181–209; C. Bidwell, K. A. Frank and P. A. Quiroz, "Teacher Types, Workplace Controls, and the Organization of Schools," *Sociology of Education* 70, no. 4 (October 1997): 285–307; C. Bidwell and J. Y. Yasumoto, "The Collegial Focus: Teaching Fields, Collegial Relationships, and Instructional Practice in American High Schools," *Sociology of Education* 72, no. 4 (October 1999): 234–256; C. Bidwell, "Analyzing Schools as Organization: Long Term Permanence and Short Term Change," *Sociology of Education* 74, Extra Issue: *Currents of Thought: Sociology of Education at the Dawn of the 21st Century* (2001): 100–114.

16. Peter Youngs, Kenneth A. Frank, and B. Pogodzinsky, "The Role of Person-Organization Fit in Beginning Teacher Commitment" (presented at the Annual Conference of the American Edcuational Research Association, San Diego, CA, 2009); Kira Baker-Doyle, "Social Network Analysis in Research on Teacher Networks: Uncovering Informal Support Networks and Networking Characteristics of Teachers" (presented at the Annual Conference of the American Educational Research Association, New York City, 2008); William R. Penuel et al., "Analyzing Teachers' Professional Interactions in a School as Social Capital: A Social Network Approach," *Teachers College Record* 111, no. 1 (2009): 124–163.

17. Baker-Doyle, "Social Network Analysis in Research on Teacher Networks"; D. Boud and H. Middleton, "Learning from Others at Work: Communities of Practice and Informal Learning," *Journal of Workplace Learning* 15, no. 5 (2003): 194–202; P. J. Hinds et al., "Choosing Work Group Members: Balancing Similarity, Competence, and Familiarity," *Organizational Behavior and Human Decision Processes* 81, no. 2 (2000): 226–251.

18. Baker-Doyle, "Social Network Analysis in Research on Teacher Networks"; A. Mehra, M. Kilduff, and D. J. Brass, "The Social Networks of High and Low Self-Monitors: Implications for Workplace Performance," *Administration Science Quarterly* 46, no. 1 (2001): 121–146; M. Kilduff and D. Krackhardt, "Bringing the Individual Back In: A Structural Analysis of the Internal Market for Reputation in Organizations," *Academy of Management Journal* 37, no. 1 (1994): 87–108; M. Kilduff, "The Friendship Network as a Decision-Making Resource: Dispositional Moderators of Social Influences on Organizational Choice," *Journal of Personality and Social Psychology* 62, no. 1 (1992): 168–180.

19. Morten T. Hansen, "The Search Transfer Problem: The Role of Weak Ties in Sharing Knowledge Across Organizational Subunits," *Administrative Science Quarterly* 44, no. 1 (1999): 82–111; J. P. Spillane and C. L. Thompson, "Reconstructing Conceptions of Local Capacity: The Local Education Agency's Capacity for Ambitious Instructional Reform," *Educational Evaluation and Policy Analysis* 19, no. 2 (1997): 185; D. Z. Levin, R. Cross, and L. C. Abrams, "The Strength of Weak Ties You Can Trust: the Mediating Role of Trust in Effective Knowledge Transfer," *Management Science* 50, no.11 (2004): 1477–1490.

20. Kira Baker-Doyle and Susan A. Yoon, "In Search of Practitioner-Based Social Capital: A Social Network Analysis Tool for Understanding and Facilitating Teacher Collaboration in a Professional Development Program," *Professional Development in Education* (forthcoming).

21. For more information on this index, see Susan A Yoon, Lei Liu, and Sao Ee Goh,, "Convergent Adaptation in Small Groups: Understanding Professional Development Activities Through a Complex Systems Lens," *Journal of Technology and Teacher Education* (forthcoming).

22. When a TCI score was at least 1 SD above the mean (5 or above), it was classified as a "High TCI."

23. Ann Lieberman, "Practices That Support Teacher Development," *Phi Delta Kappan* 76, no. 8 (1995): 592.

24. Kilduff and Krackhardt, "Bringing the Individual Back In."

25. Rob Cross et al., "Knowing What We Know: Supporting Knowledge Creation and Sharing in Social Networks," *Organizational Dynamics* 30, no. 2 (2001): 112.

26. Robert E. Floden, Margaret E. Goertz, and Jennifer O'Day, "Capacity Building in Systemic Reform," *Phi Delta Kappan* 77, no. 1 (September 1995): 19–21; Little, "Professional Development in Pursuit of Reform."

27. Charles Bidwell, "Analyzing Schools as Organization"; J. P. Spillane, "External Reform Initiatives and Teachers' Efforts to Reconstruct Their Practice: The Mediating Role of Teachers' Zones of Enactment," *Journal of Curriculum Studies* 31, no. 2 (1999): 143–175.

CHAPTER 8

1. Lee S. Shulman, "Knowledge and Teaching: Foundation of the New Reform," *Harvard Educational Review* 57 (1987): 1–22.
2. Milbrey W. McLaughlin and Joan E. Talbert, "How the World of Students and Teachers Challenges Policy Coherence," in *Designing Coherent Education Policy: Improving the System*, ed. Susan Fuhrman (San Francisco: Jossey-Bass, 1993); David K. Cohen and Carol A. Barnes, "Pedagogy and Policy," in *Teaching for Understanding: Challenges for Policy and Practice*, eds. David K. Cohen, Milbrey W. McLaughlin, and Joan E. Talbert (San Francisco: Jossey-Bass, 1993).
3. Viviane M. J. Robinson, Claire A. Lloyd, and Kenneth J. Rowe, "The Impact of Leadership on Student Outcomes: An Analysis of the Differential Effects of Leadership Types," *Educational Administration Quarterly* 44, no. 5 (2008): 635–674.
4. Melville Dalton, *Men Who Manage: Fusions of Feeling and Theory in Administration* (New York: John Wiley, 1959); Anthony Downs, *Inside Bureaucracy* (Boston: Little, Brown, 1967); George C. Homans, *The Human Group* (New York: Harcourt, Brace, 1950); John W. Meyer and Brian Rowan, "Institutionalized Organizations: Formal Structure as Myth and Ceremony," *American Journal of Sociology* 83, no. 2 (1977).
5. James P. Spillane, *Distributed Leadership* (San Francisco: Jossey-Bass, 2006); James P. Spillane and John B. Diamond, *Distributed Leadership in Practice* (New York: Teachers College Press, 2007).
6. Eric Camburn, Brian Rowan, and James E. Taylor, "Distributed Leadership in Schools: The Case of Elementary Schools Adopting Comprehensive School Reform Models," *Educational Evaluation and Policy Analysis* 25, no. 4 (2003); M. F. Heller and W. A. Firestone, "Who's in Charge Here? Sources of Leadership for Change in Eight Schools," *Elementary School Journal* 96, no. 1 (1995); Spillane, *Distributed Leadership*; James P. Spillane, Bijou Hunt, and Kaleen Healey, "Managing and Leading Elementary Schools: Attending to the Formal and Informal Organization," *International Studies in Educational Administration* 37, no. 1 (2009); James P. Spillane and Kaleen Healey, "Conceptualizing School Leadership and Management from a Distributed Perspective," *Elementary School Journal* (in press).
7. Virginia Pitts and James P. Spillane, "Using Social Network Methods to Study School Leadership," *International Journal of Research and Method in Education* 32, no. 2 (2009); James Pustejovsky and James P. Spillane, "Question-Order Effects in Social Network Name Generators," *Social Networks* 31, no. 4 (2009).
8. Spillane, *Distributed Leadership*; Spillane and Healey, "Conceptualizing School Leadership and Management from a Distributed Perspective"; Spillane, Hunt, and Healey, "Managing and Leading Elementary Schools."
9. Kenneth A. Frank, "Identifying Cohesive Subgroups," *Social Networks* 17(1995); Kenneth A. Frank, "Mapping Interactions Within and Between Cohesive Subgroups," *Social Networks* 18, no. 2 (1996).
10. David Krackhardt, "Simmelian Ties: Super Strong and Sticky," in *Power and Influence in Organizations*, eds. Roderick M. Kramer and Margaret A. Neale (Thousand Oaks, CA: Sage Publications, 1998); David Krackhardt, "The Ties That Torture: Simmelian Tie Analysis in Organizations," *Research in the Sociology of Organizations* 16 (1999).
11. Not included in the SSQ sample are art, music, and computer teachers, paraprofessionals, administrative secretaries and clerks, social workers, psychologists, and food service workers. Notably, the principal did not complete this survey. However, this did not prevent staff members from naming their principal, or any other colleague not part of the sample, as an individual from whom they seek instructional advice.
12. Krackhardt, "Simmelian Ties"; Krackhardt, "The Ties That Torture."

13. Expressed by the following equation:

$$C_B(n_i) = \frac{\sum_{j<k} g_{jk}(n_i)}{g_{jk}} \qquad \text{(equation 1-1)}$$

14. Expressed by the following equation:

$$C'_B(n_i) = \frac{C_B(n_i)}{(g-1)(g-2)/2} \qquad \text{(equation 1-2)}$$

15. Frank, "Identifying Cohesive Subgroup."; Frank, "Mapping Interactions Within and Between Cohesive Subgroups."; Ann Krause et al., "Compartments Exposed in Food-Web Structure," *Nature* 426 (2003); Kenneth A. Frank and Jeffrey Y. Yasumoto, "Linking Action to Social Structure within a System: Social Capital Within and Between Subgroups," *American Journal of Sociology* 104, no. 3 (1998).

16. One school was excluded from this part of the analysis because cohesive subgroups could not be identified in the school.

17. Dalton, *Men Who Manage*Downs, *Inside Bureaucracy*; Homans, *The Human Group*; Meyer and Rowan, "Institutionalized Organizations."

18. John Seely Brown and Paul Duguid, "Organizational Learning and Communities-of-Practice: Toward a Unified View of Working, Learning, and Innovation," *Organization Science* 2, no. 1 (1991).

19. Peter M. Blau, *The Dynamics of Bureaucracy: A Study of Interpersonal Relations in Two Government Agencies* (Chicago: University of Chicago Press, 1955).

20. Meyer and Rowan, "Institutionalized Organizations."

21. Spillane and Diamond, *Distributed Leadership in Practice*.

22. Spillane, *Distributed Leadership*.

23. Camburn, Rowan, and Taylor, "Distributed Leadership in Schools"; Heller and Firestone, "Who's in Charge Here?"; Spillane, *Distributed Leadership*.

24. Camburn, Rowan, and Taylor, "Distributed Leadership in Schools."

25. As reported in Spillane and Healey, "Conceptualizing School Leadership and Management from a Distributed Perspective", in 2005 there were 4.8 formally designated leaders per school. It is unclear at this time what caused such a sizable jump in the two years between surveys.

26. Ibid.

27. Brown and Duguid, "Organizational Learning and Communities-of-Practice."

28. Spillane, Hunt, and Healey, "Managing and Leading Elementary Schools."; Spillane and Healey, "Conceptualizing School Leadership and Management from a Distributed Perspective."

29. Three schools that did not have a formally designated mathematics coordinator or chair were not included in this analysis.

30. Three schools that did not have a formally designated language arts coordinator or chair were not included in this analysis.

31. Brian Rowan, "Commitment and Control: Alternative Strategies for the Organizational Design of Schools," *Review of Research in Education* 16 (1990); Brian Rowan, "Teachers' Work and Instructional Management, Part II: Does Organic Management Promote Expert Teaching?," in *Theory and Research in Educational Administration*, eds. Wayne K. Hoy and Cecil G. Miskel (Charlotte, NC: Information Age Publishing, 2002).

32. Georg Simmel, *The Sociology of Georg Simmel* (New York: The Free Press, 1950); Krackhardt, "The Ties That Torture"; Krackhardt, "Simmelian Ties."

33. Some individuals were key advice givers in both language arts and math.

34. Some individuals were informal leaders in both language arts and math.

35. Robert A. Hanneman and Mark Riddle, *Introduction to Social Network Methods* (Riverside, CA: University of California Press, 2005).

36. Across the schools in our sample, the average percentage of students meeting or exceeding state standards was 81 percent in language arts and 80 percent in math.

37. Mark S. Granovetter, "The Strength of Weak Ties," *American Journal of Sociology* 78, no. 6 (1973).

38. Morten T. Hansen, "The Search-Transfer Problem: The Role of Weak Ties in Sharing Knowledge Across Organization Subunits," *Administrative Science Quarterly* 44(1999); Ray Reagans and Bill McEvily, "Network Structure and Knowledge Transfer: The Effects of Cohesion and Range," *Administrative Science Quarterly* 48, no. 2 (2003); Brian Uzzi, "Social Structure and Competition in Interfirm Networks: The Paradox of Embeddedness," *Administrative Science Quarterly* 42 (1997).

39. Kenneth A. Frank, Yong Zhao, and Kathryn Borman, "Social Capital and the Diffusion of Innovations Within Organizations: The Case of Computer Technology in Schools," *Sociology of Education* 77, no. 2 (2004).

40. One school was excluded in this part of the analysis because cohesive subgroups could not be identified in the school.

41. Pitts and Spillane, "Using Social Network Methods to Study School Leadership."

42. Pustejovsky and Spillane, "Question-Order Effects in Social Network Name Generators."

43. Charles C. Ragin, *Fuzzy-Set Social Science* (Chicago: University of Chicago Press, 2000).

44. Work on this article is supported by the Distributed Leadership Studies (http://www.distributedleadership.org) funded by reasearch grants from the National Science Foundation (REC—9873583, RETA Grant #EHR—0412510), the Institute for Education Sciences (Grant #R305E040085), The Spencer Foundation (200000039). Northwestern University's School of Education and Social Policy and Institute for Policy Research supported this work. All opinions and conclusions expressed in this article are those of the authors and do not necessarily reflect the views of any funding agency.

CHAPTER 9

1. Roy D. Pea, "Practices of Distributed Intelligence and Designs for Education." in *Distributed Cognitions: Psychological and Educational Considerations*, ed. Gavriel Solomon,. (New York: Cambridge University Press, 1993), 47–87; Edward Hutchins, *Cognition in the Wild* (Cambridge, MA: MIT Press, 1996); Gavriel Salomon, ed. *Distributed Cognitions: Psychological and Educational Considerations* (New York: Cambridge University Press, 1993).

2. James P. Spillane, Richard R. Halverson, and John B. Diamond, "Investigating School Leadership Practice: A Distributed Perspective." *Educational Researcher* 30, no. 3 (2001): 23–27.

3. Michael A. Copland, "Leadership of Inquiry: Building and Sustaining Capacity for School Improvement, "*Educational Evaluation and Policy Analysis* 25, no. 4 (2003): 375–395.

4. Brian Rowan, Delena M. Harrison, and Andrew Hayes, "Using Instructional Logs to Study Mathematics Curriculum and Teaching in the Early Grades," *Elementary School Journal* 105, no. 1 (2004): 103–127; Milbrey W. McLaughlin and Joan E. Talbert, *Professional Communities and the Work of High School Teaching.* (Chicago: University of Chicago Press, 2001); Richard F. Elmore, "Getting to scale with good educational practice," *Harvard Educational Review* 66, (1996): 1–26.

5. Thomas B. Timar, "The Politics of School Restructuring," *Phi Delta Kappan* 71, no. 4 (1989): 165–175; Susan J. Bodilly, *Lessons from New American Schools' Scale-up Phase*

(Santa Monica, CA: RAND, 1998); Amanda Datnow and Sam Stringfield, "Working Together for Reliable School Reform." *Journal of Education for Students Placed at Risk (JESPAR)* 5, no. 1, 2 (2000): 183–204; John A. Nunnery, "Reform Ideology and the Locus of Development Problem in Educational Restructuring," *Education and Urban Society* 30 (1998): 277–295.

6. James P. Spillane, *Distributed Leadership*, (San Francisco: Jossey-Bass, 2006); Kenneth, Leithwood and Doris Jantzi, "The Relative Effects of Principal and Teacher Sources of Leadership on Student Engagement with School," *Educational Administration Quarterly* 35 (2000): 679–706.

7. Eric Camburn, Brian Rowan, and James E. Taylor, "Distributed Leadership in Schools: The Case of Elementary Schools Adopting Comprehensive School Reform Models," *Educational Evaluation and Policy Analysis* 25, no. 4 (2003): 347–373; Penny B. Sebring and Anthony S. Bryk. "School Leadership and the Bottom Line in Chicago". (Chicago: Consortium on Chicago School Research, 2000); Philip Hallinger, Leonard Bickman, and Ken Davis, "School Context, Principal Leadership and Student Achievement," *Elementary School Journal* 96, no. 5 (1996): 498–518; Lawrence D. Brenninkmeyer, Bruce L. Sherin, and James P. Spillane, "Representing a Problem Space: Towards a Deeper Understanding of the Practice of Instructional Leadership," in *Proceedings of the Sixth International Conference of the Learning Sciences*, eds. Yasmin B. Kafai, W. A. Sandoval, N. Enyedy, A. S. Nixon and F. Herrera (Mahwah, NJ: Erlbaum, 2004), 97–104; Mark A. Smylie, Sharon Conley, and Helen Marks, "Exploring New Approaches to Teacher Leadership for School Improvement," in *The Educational Leadership Challenge: Redefining Leadership for the 21st Century*, ed. Joseph. Murphy, (Chicago: University of Chicago Press, 2002), 162–188.

8. Kenneth A. Frank, Yong Zhao, and Kathryn Borman. "Social Capital and the Diffusion of Innovations within Organizations: Application to the Implementation of Computer Technology in Schools," *Sociology of Education* 77, no. 2 (2004): 148–171.

9. Alessandro Portes, "Social Capital: Its Origins and Applications in Modern Sociology," *Annual Review of Sociology* 24 (1998): 1–24; Nan Lin, *Social Capital: A Theory of Social Structure and Action* (New York: Cambridge University Press, 2001).

10. Nan Lin, *Social Capital*.

11. Jennifer Z. Sherer, "Distributed Leadership Practice: The Subject Matters" (paper presented at the Annual Meeting of the American Educational Research Association, San Diego, CA, April 2004).

12. Milbrey W. McLaughlin and Joan E. Talbert, *Professional Communities and the Work of High School Teaching*.

13. Kenneth A. Frank, "Identification with a Collective as a Quasi-Tie" (paper presented at the Annnual Meeting of the American Sociological Association, Washington, DC, August 2000); George Akerlof and Rachel E. Kranton, "Identity and Schooling: Some Lessons for the Economics of Education," *Journal of Economic Literature* 40, no. 4 (2002): 1167–1201.

14. Anthony S. Bryk and Barbara Schneider. *Trust in Schools: A Core Resource for Improvement* (New York: Russell Sage Foundation, 2002).

15. Ion Bogdan Vasi and Michael W. Macy, "The Mobilizer's Dilemma: Crisis, Empowerment, and Collective Action," *Social Forces* 81, no. 3 (2003): 979–998; Brent Simpson and Michael W. Macy, "Power, Identity, and Collective Action in Social Exchange," *Social Forces* 82, no. 4 (2004): 1373–1409; Michael W. Macy, "Chains of Cooperation: Threshold Effects in Collective Action," *American Sociological Review* 56, no. 6 (1991): 730–747.

16. Kenneth A. Frank and Kyle Fahrbach, "Organizational Culture as a Complex System: Balance and Information in Models of Influence and Selection,"*Organization Science* 10, no. 3 (1999): 253–277.

17. Ronald S. Burt, *Structural Holes: The Social Structure of Competition*. (Cambridge, MA: Harvard University Press, 1992); Mark S. Granovetter, "The Strength of Weak Ties: Network Theory Revisited," *American Journal of Sociology* 78, no. 6 (1973): 1360–1380.

18. Kenneth A. Frank, "Identifying Cohesive Subgroups." *Social Networks* 17, (1995): 27–56; Kenneth A. Frank and Yong Zhao. "Subgroups as a Meso-Level Entity in the Social Organization of Schools," in *The Social Organization of Schooling*, ed. L. V. Hedges and B. Schneider, 200–224. New York: Sage, 2005.

19. Datnow and Stringfield, "Working Together for Reliable School Reform."

20. David K. Cohen and Deborah L. Ball, *Instruction, Capacity, and Improvement*. (Philadelphia: Consortium for Policy Research in Education, 1999).

21. Bodilly, *Lessons from New American Schools' Scale-up Phase*.

22. Camburn, Rowan, and Taylor, "Distributed Leadership in Schools."

23. This is expressed in the formula:

$$(\text{help}_{ii' \, t-1 \to t}\text{level of implementation})$$

$$\text{Total access to expertise}_i = \Sigma_{i'} \, \text{help}_{ii' \, t-1 \to t}\text{level of implementation}_{i' \, t-1}$$

24. Bryk and Schneider. *Trust in Schools*

25. See ibid.

26. David K. Cohen and Deborah L. Ball, *Instruction, Capacity, and Improvement*. (Philadelphia: Consortium for Policy Research in Education, 1999).

27. Kenneth A. Frank and Jeffrey Y. Yasumoto. "Embedding Subgroups in a Sociogram: Linking Theory and Image,"*Connections* 19, no. 1 (1996): 43–57; Kenneth A. Frank, Yong Zhao, and Kathryn Borman. "Social Capital and the Diffusion of Innovations Within Organizations: Application to the Implementation of Computer Technology in Schools," *Sociology of Education* 77, no. 2 (2004): 148–171.

28. Stanley Wasserman and Katherine Faust, *Social Network Analysis: Methods and Applications* (New York: Cambridge University Press, 1994); Emmanuel Lazega and Marijtje van Duijn, "Position in Formal Structure, Personal Characteristics and Choices of Advisors in a Law Firm: A Logistic Regression Model for Dyadic Network Data," *Social Networks* 19, (1997): 375–397.

29. Defined in terms of figure 9-1, the odds ratio is:

$$AD/BC = \frac{(\textit{Absence of relationships outside of subgroups})*(\textit{presence of relationships within subgroups})}{(\textit{Presence of relationships outside of subgroups})*(\textit{absence of relationships within subgroups})}$$

30. Stephen W. Raudenbush and Anthony S. Bryk, *Hierarchical Linear Models: Applications and Data Analysis Methods*, 2nd ed.(Thousand Oaks, CA: Sage, 2002).

31. Frank, "Identification with a Collective as a Quasi-Tie"; George Akerlof, and Rachel E. Kranton, "Identity and Schooling: Some Lessons for the Economics of Education," *Journal of Economic Literature* 40, no. 4 (2002): 1167–1201.

32. Frank, "Identification with a Collective as a Quasi-Tie"; Akerlo, and Kranton, "Identity and Schooling."

33. Henry Jay Becker, "Opportunities for Learning Curriculum and Instruction in the Middle Grades." (Baltimore: Center for Research on Elementary and Middle Schools, Johns Hopkins University, 1990); Jeannie Oakes, *Multiplying Inequalities: The Effects of Race, Social Class, and Tracking on Opportunities to Learn Mathematics and Science*, (Santa Monica, CA: RAND, 1990); Jeannie Oakes, "Social Policy and Diversity: Inequality, Stratification, and the Struggle for Just Schooling." (paper presented at the International Conference of the Learning Sciences, Santa Monica, CA, 2004); Gary Orfield, Susan E. Eaton, and Elaine R. Jones, *Dismantling Desegregation: The Quiet Reversal of Brown v. Board of Education* (New York: New Press, 1997).

CHAPTER 10

1. Michael Fullan, *Leadership and Sustainability: Systems Thinkers in Action* (Thousand Oaks, CA: Corwin Press, 2005).
2. See, for example, Amy M. Hightower, Michael S. Knapp, Julie A Marsh, and Milbrey W. McLaughlin, eds., *School Districts and Instructional Renewal* (New York: Teachers College Press, 2002); Meredith Honig, "District Central Offices as Learning Organizations: How Sociocultural and Organizational Learning Theories Elaborate District-Central-Office Administrators' Participation in Teaching and Learning Improvement Efforts," *American Journal of Education*, 114 (2008): 627–664; Milbrey McLaughlin and Joan Talbert, *Reforming Districts: How Districts Support School Reform* (Seattle: University of Washington, 2003); Jon A. Supovitz, *The Case for District-Based Reform: Leading, Building, and Sustaining School Improvement* (Cambridge, MA: Harvard Education Press, 2006); Wendy Togneri and Stephen Anderson, *Beyond Islands of Excellence: What Districts Can Do to Improve Instruction and Achievement in All Schools* (Washington, DC: The Learning First Alliance and the Association for Supervision and Curriculum Development, 2003).
3. Andrea K. Rorrer, Linda Skrla, and James J. Scheurich, "Districts as Institutional Actors in Educational Reform," *Educational Administration Quarterly*, 44 no. 3 (2008): 307–358; Amanda Datnow and Marisa Castellano, "Leadership and Success for All," in *Leadership for School Reform: Lessons from Comprehensive School Reform Designs*, eds. Joseph Murphy and Amanda Datnow (Thousand Oaks. CA: Corwin Press, 2002), 187–208.
4. Kim Agullard and Dolores Goughnour, *Central Office Inquiry: Assessing Organization, Roles, and Actions to Support School Improvement* (San Francisco: WestEd, 2006).
5. Fullan, *Leadership and Sustainability* Andy Hargreaves and Dean Fink, *Sustainable Leadership* (San Francisco: Jossey-Bass, 2005). McLaughlin and Talbert, *Reforming Districts*.
6. Fullan, *Leadership and Sustainability*.
7. See, for example, Chris Argyris, *On Organizational Learning*, 2nd edition (Oxford: Blackwell Publishers, 1999); Chris Argyris and Donald A. Schön, *Organizational Learning II: Theory, Method, and Practice* (Reading, MA: Addison-Wesley, 1996); George P. Huber, "Organizational Learning: The Contributing Processes and the Literatures," *Organization Science 2*, no. 1 (1991): 88–115; Barbara Levitt and James G. March, "Organizational Learning," *Annual Review of Sociology* 14 (1988): 319–340; James G. March, "Exploration and Exploitation in Organizational Learning," *Organization Science 2*, no. 1 (1991): 71–87; Everett M. Rogers, *Diffusion of Innovations*, 5th edition (New York: Free Press, 2003).
8. Honig, "District Central Offices as Learning Organizations."
9. Cathleen McGrath and David Krackhardt, "Network Conditions for Organizational Change," *Journal of Applied Behavioral Science 39*, no. 3 (2003): 324–336; Seokwoo Song, Sridhar Nerur, and James T.C. Teng, "An Exploratory Study on the Roles of Network Structure and Knowledge Processing Orientation in the Work Unit Knowledge Management," *Advances in Information Systems 38*, no. 2 (2007): 8–26; Ramkrishnan V. Tenkasi and Marshall C. Chesmore, "Social Networks and Planned Organizational Change," *Journal of Applied Behavioral Science 39*, no. 3 (2003): 281–300.
10. Nan Lin, *Social Capital: A Theory of Social Structure and Action* (New York: Cambridge University Press, 2001), 24.
11. Ronald S. Burt, *Structural Holes: The Structure of Competition*. (Cambridge, MA: Harvard University Press, 1992); James S. Coleman, "Social Capital in the Creation of Human Capital," *American Journal of Sociology* 94 (1988): 95–120; James S. Coleman, *Foundations of Social Theory* (Cambridge, MA: Harvard University Press, 1990); Mark S. Granovetter, "The Strength of Weak Ties," *American Journal of Sociology* 78 (1973): 1360–1380; Mark S. Granovetter, "The Strength of Weak Ties: A Network Theory Revisited," in *Social Structure and Network Analysis*, eds. Peter V. Marsden and Nan Lin (Beverly Hills, CA: Sage, 1982), 105–130; Nan Lin, "Building a Network Theory of Social Capital," *Connections* 22, no. 1

(1999), 28–51; Nan Lin, *Social Capital: A Theory of Social Structure and Action* (New York: Cambridge University Press, 2001); Alejandro Portes, "The Two Meanings of Social Capital," *Sociological Forum* 15, no. 1 (2000): 1–12; Robert D. Putnam, "Bowling Alone: America's Declining Social Capital," *Journal of Democracy*, 6 (1995): 65–78; Robert D. Putnam, *Making Democracy Work* (Princeton, NJ: Princeton University Press, 1993).

12. John Scott, *Social Network Analysis*, 2nd edition (London: Sage, 2000); Stanley Wasserman and Katherine Faust, *Social Network Analysis: Methods and Applications* (New York: Cambridge University Press, 1998).

13. Morten T. Hansen, "The Search-Transfer Problem: The Role of Weak Ties in Sharing Knowledge Across Organization Subunits," *Administrative Science Quarterly* 44, no. 1 (1999): 82–111.

14. Fullan, *Leadership and Sustainability*; Bruce Kogut and Udo Zander, "What Firms Do? Coordination, Identity, and Learning," *Organization Science* 7, no. 5 (1996): 502–518.

15. Sumantra Ghoshal, Harry Korine, and Gabriel Szulanski, "Interunit Communication in Multinational Corporations, *Management Science* 40, no. 1 (1994): 96–110; Song, Nerur, and Teng, "An Exploratory Study on the Roles of Network Structure and Knowledge Processing Orientation in the Work Unit Knowledge Management."; Wenpin Tsai and Sumantra Ghoshal, "Social Capital and Value Creation: The Role of Intrafirm Networks," *Academy of Management Journal* 41, no. 4 (1998): 464–476.

16. Ray Reagans and Ezra W. Zuckerman, "Networks, Diversity, and Productivity: The Social Capital of R&D Teams," *Organization Science* 12 (2001): 502–517.

17. Rob Cross, Stephen Borgatti, and Andrew Parker, "Making Invisible Work Visible: Using Social Network Analysis to Support Strategic Collaboration," *California Management Review* 44, no. 2 (2002): 25–46; Song, Nerur, and Teng, "An Exploratory Study on the Roles of Network Structure and Knowledge Processing Orientation in the Work Unit Knowledge Management."

18. David Krackhardt, "Network Conditions of Organizational Change" (paper presented at the Academy of Management Annual Meeting, Washington, DC, 2001); Susan A. Mohrman, Ramkrishnan V. Tenkasi, and Allan M. Mohrman, "The Role of Networks in Fundamental Organizational Change," *Journal of Applied Behavioral Science* 39, no. 3 (2003): 301–323; Ramkrishnan V. Tenkasi and Marshall C. Chesmore, "Social Networks and Planned Organizational Change," *Journal of Applied Behavioral Science* 39, no. 3 (2003): 281–300.

19. Lin, "Building a Network Theory of Social Capital"; Scott, *Social Network Analysis*.

20. See, for example, Cynthia E. Coburn and Jennifer L. Russell, "District Policy and Teachers' Social Networks," *Educational Evaluation and Policy Analysis* 30, no. 3 (2008): 203–235; Robert L. Cross and Andrew Parker, *The Hidden Power of Social Networks: Understanding How Work Really Gets Done in Organizations* (Cambridge, MA: Harvard Business School Press, 2004); Cross, Borgatti, and Parker, "Making Invisible Work Visible"; Alan J. Daly and Kara S. Finnigan, "A Bridge Between Worlds: Understanding Network Structure to Understand Change Strategy." *Journal of Educational Change* 11, no. 2 (2010): 111–138; Alan J. Daly and Kara S. Finnigan, "The Ebb and Flow of Social Network Ties Between District Leaders Under High-Stakes Accountability," *American Educational Research Journal* (in press); Julie M. Hite, Ellen Williams, and Steven C. Baugh, "Multiple Networks of Public School Administrators: An Analysis of Network Content and Structure," *International Journal on Leadership in Education* 8, no. 2 (2005): 91–122; Meredith I. Honig, "Street-Level Bureaucracy Revisited: Frontline District Central Office Administrators As Boundary Spanners in Education Policy Implementation," *Educational Evaluation and Policy Analysis* 28(4 (2006), 357–383;. Jon A. Supovitz, *The Case for District-Based Reform: Leading, Building, and Sustaining School Improvement* (Cambridge, MA: Harvard Education Press, 2006); Togneri and Anderson, *Beyond Islands of Excellence*.

21. Stephen P. Borgatti, Martin G. Everett, and Lin Freeman, *UCINET For Windows: Software for Social Network Analysis* (Harvard MA: Analytic Technologies, 2002).
22. Kathleen M. Carley and David Krackhardt, "Cognitive Inconsistencies and Non-Symmetric Friendship," *Social Networks*, 18, no. 1 (1999): 1–27; Krackhardt, "Network Conditions of Organizational Change."
23. Herminia Ibarra, "Personal Networks of Women and Minorities in Management: A Conceptual Framework," *Academy of Management Review* 18, no. 1 (1993), 56–87.
24. Stephen P. Borgatti and Pacey C. Foster, "The Network Paradigm in Organizational Research: A Review and Typology," *Journal of Management* 29, no. 6 (2003): 991–1013; Cross and Parker, *The Hidden Power of Social Networks*.
25. Kathleen M. Carley and Vanessa Hill, "Structural Change and Learning Within Organizations," in *Dynamics of Organizations: Computational Modeling and Organizational Theories*, eds. Alessandro Lomi and Erik R. Larsen (Menlo Park, CA: AAAI Press, 2001), 63–92.
26. Ibid.
27. James G. March, "Exploration and Exploitation in Organizational Learning," *Organization Science*, 2, no. 1 (1991): 71–87.
28. Daly and Finnigan, "A Bridge Between Worlds"; Daly and Finnigan, "The Ebb and Flow of Social Network Ties Between District Leaders Under High-Stakes Accountability."
29. David Krackhardt and Robert Stern, "Informal Networks and Organizational Crises: An Experimental Simulation," *Social Psychology Quarterly* 51, no. 2 (1988): 123–140; McGrath and Krackhardt, "Network Conditions for Organizational Change."
30. Stephen P. Borgatti, "The Key Player Problem," in *Dynamic Social Network Modeling and Analysis: Workshop Summary and Papers*, eds. Ronald Breiger, Kathleen Carley, and Phillipa Pattison (Washington DC: The National Academies Press, 2003), 241–252; Stephen P. Borgatti, "Identifying Sets of Key Players in a Network," *Computational, Mathematical and Organizational Theory* 12, no. 1 (2006): 21–34.
31. For more on professional learning communities see, for example, Richard DuFour, Rebecca DuFour, and Robert Eaker, *Revisiting Professional Learning Communities at Work: New Insights for Improving Schools* (Bloomington, IN: Solution Tree, 2008); Shirley M. Hord, *Professional Learning Communities: Communities of Continuous Inquiry and Practice* (Austin, TX: Southwest Educational Development Laboratory, 1997); Shirley M. Hord and William A. Sommers, *Leading Professional Learning Communities* (Thousand Oaks, CA: Corwin Press, 2008); Milbrey W. McLaughlin and Joan E. Talbert, *Professional Communities and the Work of High School Teaching* (Chicago: University of Chicago Press, 2001). For the application of these district-wide see Michael S. Knapp, Michael A. Copland, Joan E. Talbert, *Leading for Learning: Reflective Tools for School and District Leaders* (Seattle: Center for the Study of Teaching and Policy, University of Washington, 2003).
32. Meredith Honig, "District Central Offices as Learning Organizations" Etienne Wenger, *Communities of Practice: Learning, Meaning and Identity* (Cambridge, UK: Cambridge University Press, 1998).
33. This work supported by the W. T. Grant and Spencer Foundations. All opinions and conclusions expressed in this chapter are those of the authors and do not necessarily reflect the view of any funding agency.

CHAPTER 11

1. David W. Chapman, Lisa Burton, and Jessica Werner, "Universal Secondary Education in Uganda: The Head Teachers' Dilemma," *International Journal of Educational Development* 30, no. 1 (2010): 77–82.
2. UNESCO, *Dakar Framework for Action, Education for All: Meeting Our Collective Committments* (Paris: UNESCO, 2000); WCEFA, *Meeting Basic Learning Needs: A Vision for the*

1990s—Jomtien, Thailand, March 5–9, 1990 (New York: Inter-Agency Commission for the World Conference on Education for All, 1990).

3. Chapman, Burton, and Werner, "Universal Secondary Education in Uganda"; UNESCO, *Education for All: Is the World on Track?* (Paris: UNESCO, 2002).

4. Alan Penny et al., "Education Sector Reform: The Ugandan Experience," *International Journal of Educational Development* 28, no. 3 (2008): 268–285; UMOES, *Guidelines on Policy, Roles and Responsibilities of Stakeholders in the Implementation of Universal Primary Education (UPE)* (Kamapala, Uganda: UMOES, 1998).

5. UNESCO, *Education for All: Is the World on Track?*; UNESCO, *World Education Report—1998* (Paris: UNESCO, 1998); UNESCO, *Education for All Global Monitoring Report 2009: Overcoming Inequality: Why Governance Matters* (Paris: UNESCO, 2009).

6. David W. Chapman and Shirley A. Burchfield, "How Headmasters Perceive Their Role: A Case Study in Botswana," *International Review of Education* 40, no. 6 (1994): 401–419; David W. Chapman and Conrad Wesley Snyder Jr., "Can High Stakes National Testing Improve Instruction: Reexamining Conventional Wisdom," *International Journal of Educational Development* 20, no. 6 (2000): 457–474; Julie M. Hite, Steven J. Hite, W. James Jacob, W. Joshua Rew, Christopher B. Mugimu, Yusuf K. Nsubuga., "Building Bridges for Resource Acquisition: Network Relationships among Headteachers in Ugandan Private Secondary Schools," *International Journal of Educational Development* 26, no. 5 (2006): 495–512.

7. Pamela R. Hallam, Julie M. Hite, and Steven J. Hite, "The Development and Role of Trust in Educational Leadership: A Comparative Study of U. S. And Ugandan School Administrators," in *Educational Leadership: Global Contexts and International Comparisons*, eds. Alexander W. Wiseman and Iveta Silova (Brighton, UK: Emerald Publishing, 2009), 49–80.

8. Stephen P. Heyneman, "Economic Crisis and the Quality of Education," *International Journal of Educational Development* 10, no. 2/3 (1990): 115–129; Joel Samoff, "Education Sector Analysis in Africa: Limited National Control and Even Less National Ownership," *International Journal of Educational Development* 19, no. 4/5 (1999): 249–272; Joel Samoff, "From Funding Projects to Supporting Sectors? Observation on the Aid Relationship in Burkina Faso," *International Journal of Educational Development* 24, no. 4 (2004): 397–427.

9. Penny et al., "Education Sector Reform"; Julie M. Hite et al., "Building Bridges for Resource Acquisition". Paul Bennell and Yusuf Sayed, *Improving the Management and Internal Efficiency of Post-Primary Education and Training in Uganda* (Kampala: Uganda Ministry of Education and Sports, 2002); Mikiko Nishimura, Takashi Yamano, and Yuichi Sasaoka, "Impacts of the Universal Primary Education Policy on Educational Attainment and Private Costs in Rural Uganda," *International Journal of Educational Development* 28, no. 2 (2008): 161–175.

10. Jay B. Barney, "Firm Resources and Sustained Competitive Advantage," *Journal of Management* 17, no. 1 (1991): 99–120; Jay B. Barney, "The Resource-Based View of the Firm," *Organization Science* 7, no. 5 (1996): 469.

11. Julie M. Hite and William S. Hesterly, "The Evolution of Firm Networks: From Emergence to Early Growth of the Firm," *Strategic Management Journal* 22, no. 3 (2001): 275–286; Ha Hoang and Bostjan Antoncic, "Network-Based Research in Entrepreneurship: A Critical Review," *Journal of Business Venturing* 18, no. 2 (2003): 165–187.

12. Adam M. Brandenburger and Barry J. Nalebuff, *Co-Opetition* (New York: Doubleday, 1996); Devi R. Gnyawali, Jinyu He, and Ravindranath Madhavan, "Impact of Co-Opetition on Firm Competitive Behavior: An Empirical Examination," *Journal of Management* 32, no. 4 (2006): 507–530; Devi R. Gnyawali and Ravindranath Madhavan, "Cooperative Networks and Competitive Dynamics: A Structural Embeddedness Perspective," *Academy of Management Review* 26, no. 3 (2001): 431–445.

13. Hallam et al., "The Development and Role of Trust in Educational Leadership."
14. Noshir S. Contractor, Stanley Wasserman, and Katherine Faust, "Testing Multitheoretical, Multilevel Hypotheses About Organizational Networks: An Analytic Framework and Empirical Example," *Academy of Management Review* 31, no. 3 (2006): 681–703; Julie M. Hite, "The Role of Dyadic Multi-Dimensionality in the Evolution of Strategic Network Ties," in *Network Strategy*, eds. Joel C. Baum and Timothy J. Rowley (Oxford: JAI/Elsevier, 2008), 133–170.
15. Stanley Wasserman and Katherine Faust, *Social Network Analysis: Methods and Applications* (Cambridge, UK: Cambridge University Press, 1994).
16. Julie M. Hite et al., "Building Bridges for Resource Acquisition"; Nitin Nohria, "Is a Network Perspective a Useful Way of Studying Organizations?" in *Networks and Organizations: Structure, Form and Action*, eds. Nitin Nohria and Robert G. Eccles (Boston: Harvard Business School Press, 1992), 1–22.
17. Julie M. Hite et al., "Building Bridges for Resource Acquisition"; ; Hoang and Antoncic, "Network-Based Research in Entrepreneurship"; Gnyawali and Madhavan, "Cooperative Networks and Competitive Dynamics"; Nohria, "Is a Network Perspective a Useful Way of Studying Organizations?"; Kenneth King, "Networking as a Knowledge System," in *Crossing Lines: Research and Policy Networks for Developing Country Education,* ed. N. McGinn (London: Praeger Publishers, 1996), 19–21.
18. Mawaya Wa Kitavi and Philip C. Van Der Westhuizen, "Problems Facing Beginning Principals in Developing Countries: A Study of Beginning Principals in Kenya," *International Journal of Educational Development* 17, no. 3 (1997): 251–263; A. Herriot, M. Crossley, M. Juma, J. Waudo, M. Mwirotsi, and A, Kamau, "The Development and Operation of Headteacher Support Groups in Kenya: A Mechanism to Create Pockets of Excellence, Improve the Provision of Quality Education and Target Positive Changes in the Community," *International Journal of Educational Development* 22, no. 5 (2002): 509–526.
19. Jon Lauglo, "Evolution of Networks: Evolution from Networks," in *Crossing Lines: Research and Policy Networks for Developing Country Education,* ed. N. McGinn (London: Praeger Publishers, 1996), 7–8.
20. Julie M. Hite and Hesterly, "The Evolution of Firm Networks"; Hoang and Antoncic, "Network-Based Research in Entrepreneurship"; Julie M. Hite, "Patterns of Multi-Dimensionality Among Embedded Network Ties: A Typology of Relational Embeddedness in Emerging Entrepreneurial Firms," *Strategic Organization* 1, no. 1 (2003): 9–49.
21. Miller McPherson, Lynn Smith-Lovin, and James M. Cook, "Birds of a Feather: Homophily in Social Networks," *Annual Review of Sociology* 27(2001): 416.
22. Keith Barney, "Re-Encountering Resistance: Plantation Activism and Smallholder Production in Thailand and Sarawak, Malaysia," *Asia Pacific Viewpoint* 45, no. 3 (2004): 337.
23. Steven J. Hite et al., "Geographic Space and Social Space: A Statistical Analysis of Euclidean, Actual, and Least-Cost Distance and Network Ties of Headteachers in Uganda," in *Proceedings of the International Workshop on Social Space and Geographic Space—SGS'07* (Victoria, Australia: Melbourne Business School, 2007), 77.
24. Julie M. Hite, "Patterns of Multi-Dimensionality Among Embedded Network Ties"; Stephen P. Borgatti and Rob Cross, "A Relational View of Information Seeking and Learning in Social Networks," *Management Science* 49, no. 4 (2003): 432–445.
25. Steven J. Hite et al., "Geographic Space and Social Space."
26. Ibid.
27. Julie M. Hite and Hesterly, "The Evolution of Firm Networks."
28. Gnyawali and Madhavan, "Cooperative Networks and Competitive Dynamics"; James Samuel Coleman, "Social Capital in the Creation of Human Capital," *American Journal of Sociology* 94, no. Supplemental (1988): 95–120.

29. Gnyawali and Madhavan, "Cooperative Networks and Competitive Dynamics"; Matthew S. Kraatz, "Learning by Association? Interorganizational Networks and Adaptation to Environmental Change.," *Academy of Management Journal* 41, no. 6 (1998): 621–643.

30. Gnyawali, He, and Madhavan, "Impact of Co-Opetition on Firm Competitive Behavior"; Joel A. C. Baum and Jane E. Dutton, "The Embeddedness of Strategy," in *Advances in Strategic Management*, ed. Jane E. Dutton (Greenwich, CT: JAI Press, 1996), 3–40; Mark S. Granovetter, "Economic Action and Social Structure: The Problem of Embeddedness," *American Journal of Sociology* 91, no. 3 (1985): 481–510.

31. Gnyawali and Madhavan, "Cooperative Networks and Competitive Dynamics."

32. Ibid.; Wasserman and Faust, *Social Network Analysis*.

33. Ranjay Gulati, Nitin Nohria, and Akbar Zaheer, "Strategic Networks," *Strategic Management Journal* 21, no. 3 (2000): 203–215.

34. Gnyawali and Madhavan, "Cooperative Networks and Competitive Dynamics"; Wasserman and Faust, *Social Network Analysis*; Walter W. Powell, Kenneth W. Kogut, and Laurel Smith-Doerr, "Interorganizational Collaboration and the Locus of Innovation: Networks of Learning in Biotechnology," *Administrative Science Quarterly* 41, no. 1 (1996): 116–145.

35. David Knoke and Song Yang, *Social Network Analysis* (Thousand Oaks, CA: Sage Publications, 2008).

36. Stephen P. Borgatti, Martin G. Everett, and Lin C. Freeman, *UCINET for Windows: Softare for Social Network Analysis* (Natick, MA: Analytic Technologies, 1999).

37. Stephen P. Borgatti, *NetDraw* (Natick, MA: Analytic Technologies, 2003).

38. George Tita and Katherine Faust, *Spaced Out: The Spatial Dimensions of Social Networks*, (paper presented at the Sunbelt XXV International Social Network Conference, Redondo Beach, CA, February 17, 2005).

39. The following algorithm used the O-level summary score assigned to each student (1, 2, 3, 4, 7 or 9, with 1 being the highest passing mark, 4 being the lowest, and 7 or 9 a failing score) to compute a school performance average:

*[(# students @ 1 x 1) + (# students @ 2 x 2) + (# students @ 3 x 3) + (# students @ 4 x 4) +
(# students @ 7 x 5) + (# students @ 9 x 5)]/ (total # students) = School average*

40. Steven J. Hite et al., "Geographic Space and Social Space."

41. Julie M. Hite and Hesterly, "The Evolution of Firm Networks."

42. Chapman, Burton, and Werner, "Universal Secondary Education in Uganda".

43. David Schaefer, "Resource Variation and the Development of Cohesion in Exchange Networks," *American Sociological Review* 74, no. 4 (2009): 551–572.

44. Julie M. Hite, "The Role of Dyadic Multi-Dimensionality."

45. Julie M. Hite, "Patterns of Multi-Dimensionality."

46. Kraatz, "Learning by Association?"

47. Julie M. Hite and Hesterly, "The Evolution of Firm Networks."

48. Paul J. DiMaggio and Walter W. Powell, "The Iron Cage Revisited: Institutional Isomorphism and Collective Rationality in Organizational Fields," *American Sociological Review* 48, no. 1 (1983): 147–160.

49. Hallam et al., "The Development and Role of Trust in Educational Leadership."

50. Akbar Zaheer, Bill McEvily, and Vincenzo Perrone, "Does Trust Matter? Exploring the Effects of Interorganizational and Interpersonal Trust on Performance," *Organization Science* 9, no. 2 (1998): 141–159.

CHAPTER 12

1. http://orgtheory.wordpress.com/2008/11/14/why-social-networks-are-overrated-a-3-when-they-are-at-best-a-2/
2. Ronald L. Breiger, "The Analysis of Social Networks," in *Handbook of Data Analysis*, eds. Melissa Hardy and Alan Bryman (London: Sage Publications, 2004), 505–526; Barry Wellman, "Structural Analysis," in *Social Structures*, eds. Barry Wellman and Stephen D. Berkowitz (Cambridge: Cambridge University Press, 1988), 19–61.
3. Kenneth A. Frank, "Identifying Cohesive Subgroups" (PhD diss., University of Chicago, 1993); Kenneth A. Frank, "Identifying Cohesive Subgroups," *Social Networks* 17, (1995): 27–56; Kenneth A. Frank, "Mapping Interactions Within and Between Cohesive Subgroups," *Social Networks* 18 (1996): 93–119; Kenneth A. Frank and Jeffrey Y. Yasumoto, "Embedding Subgroups in the Sociogram: Linking Theory and Image," *Connections* 19, no. 1 (1996): 43–57; see https://www.msu.edu/~kenfrank/resources.htm#KliqueFinder.
4. See, for example, Patrick Doreian, "Causality in Social Network Analysis," *Sociological Methods and Research* 30, no. 1 (2001): 81–114.
5. Examples of such research include: Barry Wellman, "Structural Analysis"; Peter J. Carrington, John Scott, and Stanley Wasserman, *Models and Methods in Social Network Analysis* (Cambridge, UK: Cambridge University Press, 2005); Stanley Wasserman and Katherine Faust, *Social Network Analysis: Methods and Applications* (Cambridge, UK: Cambridge University Press, 1994); John Scott, *Social Network Analysis*, 2nd edition (London: Sage Publications, 2000); Ronald L. Breiger, "Ethical Dilemmas in Social Network Research: Introduction to Special Issue," *Social Networks* 27, (2005): 89–93.
6. David K, Cohen, Stephen W. Raudenbush, and Deborah Loewenberg Ball, "Resources, Instruction, and Research," *Educational Evaluationand Policy Analysis* 25, no. 2 (2003): 1–24.
7. Orley Ashenfelter and Richard Layard, *Handbook of Labor Economics* (Amsterdam: North Holland, 1986).
8. Angus Deaton and John Muellbauer, *Economics and Consumer Behavior* (Cambridge, UK: Cambridge University Press, 1980).
9. See ibid. for relevant assumptions.
10. Peter Youngs, Kenneth A. Frank, Yeow Meng Thum, and Mark Low, "The Motivation of Teachers to Produce Human Capital and Conform to Their Social Contexts," in *Yearbook of the National Society for the Study of Education*, vol. 110, *Organization and Effectiveness of High-Intensity Induction Programs for New Teachers* (Malden, MA: Blackwell Publishing, in press).
11. Charles E. Bidwell, "The School as a Formal Organization," in *Handbook of Organizations*, ed. James G. March (Chicago: Rand-McNally, 1965), 972–1022; Charles E. Bidwell, "School as Context and Construction: A Social Psychological Approach to the Study of Schooling," in *Handbook of the Sociology of Education*. ed. Maureen T. Hallinan (New York: Kluwer Academic/Plenum Publishers, 2000), 13–37; Charles E. Bidwell, "Analyzing Schools as Organizations: Long Term Permanence and Short Term Change," *Sociology of Education*, (2001): 100–114; Oliver E. Williamson, "The Economics of Organization: The Transaction Cost Approach," *American Journal of Sociology* 87, no. 3 (1981): 548–575.
12. See https://www.msu.edu/~kenfrank/resources.htm > influence models, for SPSS and SAS modules and PowerPoint demonstration that calculate a network effect and include it in a regression model.
13. Kenneth A. Frank, Yong Zhao, and Kathryn Borman, "Social Capital and the Diffusion of Innovations Within Organizations: The Case of Computer Technology in Schools," *Sociology of Education* 77, no. 2 (2004): 148–171.
14. Min Sun, Kenneth A. Frank, William R. Penuel, and Chong Min Kim, *Formal Leadership versus Informal Leadership: How Institutions Penetrate Schools*, (paper presented at the

annual meeting of the American Educational Research Association, Denver, CO, May, 2010).

15. See William R. Penuel, Kenneth A. Frank, and Ann Krause, "Between Leaders and Teachers: Using Social Network Analysis to Examine the Effectiveness of Distributed Leadership," chapter 9 in this volume. Reference is to Frank, "Identifying Cohesive Subgroups."

16. See Russell P. Cole and Elliot H. Weinbaum, "Changes in Attitude: Varieties of Peer Influence in High School Reform," chapter 5 in this volume.

17. Noting that Cole and Weinbaum's dependent variable (defined by change in attitude) and the independent variable (defined by deviance of attitude from a norm) are both functions of the prior attitude of teacher i.

18. Their covariates also included residualized school effects, controlling for school membership in an alternate way from the multilevel modeling approach.

19. Frank, Zhao, and Borman, "Social Capital and the Diffusion of Innovations Within Organizations."

20. Jesse Rothstein, "Student Sorting and Bias in Value Added Estimation: Selection on Observables and Unobservables." *Education Finance and Policy* 4, no. 4 (2009): 537–571.

21. Julie M. Hite, Steven J. Hite, Christopher B. Mugimu, and Yusuf K. Nsubuga, "Strategic 'Co-opetition': Headteacher Networking in Uganda's Secondary Schools," chapter 11 in this volume. Their model might look like this:

$$\log\left[\frac{p\,(\text{interact frequently}_{ij})}{1-p\,(\text{interact frequently}_{ij})}\right] = \theta_0$$
$$+\,\theta_1 \quad \text{same gender}_{ij} \qquad\qquad (2)$$
$$+\,\theta_2 \quad \text{same tribe}_{ij}$$
$$+\,\theta_3 \quad \text{membership in MHTPA}_{ij}$$
$$+\,\theta_4 \quad \text{similarity of school size}_{ij}$$
$$+\,\theta_5 \quad \text{similarity of sector (private vs government)}_{ij}$$
$$+\,\theta_6 \quad \text{similarity of performance}_{ij},$$

where p($help_{ij}$) represents the probability that teacher i provides help to teacher j; θ_0 represents the base or intercept level of help; and the other parameters (θ_1 through θ_6) represent the effects of characteristics of the pair of teachers on the likelihood that teacher i helps teacher j. Note that Hite et al., did not specify their model as a logistic regression.

22. James P. Spillane, Kaleen Healey, and Chong Min Kim, "Leading and Managing Instruction: Formal and Informal Aspects of the Elementary School Organization," chapter 8 in this volume.

23. Peter M. Blau, *Exchange and Power in Social Life* (New York: Wiley, 1967); John C. Glidewell, Sharon Tucker, Michael Todt, and Sharon Cox, "Professional Support Systems: The Teaching Profession," in *New Directions in Helping: Applied Perspectives on Help-Seeking and Receiving*, eds. Arie Nadler, Jeffrey D. Fisher, and Bella M. DePaulo (New York: Academic Press, 1983): 189–212; Judith Warren Little, "The Persistence of Privacy: Autonomy and Initiative in Teachers' Professional Relations," *Teachers College Record* 91 (1990): 129–151; Kip Tellez, "Mentors by Choice, Not Design: Help-Seeking by Beginning Teachers," *Journal of Teacher Education* 43, no. 3 (1992): 214–221.

24. Cole and Weinbaum, "Changes in Attitude"; Frank, Zhao, and Borman, "Social Capital and the Diffusion of Innovations Within Organizations."

25. Kenneth A. Frank and Kyle Fahrbach, "Organizational Culture as a Complex System: Balance and Information in Models of Influence and Selection," *Organization Science* 10, no. 3 (1999): 253–277.

26. Scholastic,   2010,   http://www.scholastic.com/primarysources/pdfs/Scholastic_Gates_0310.pdf.

27. Frank and Fahrbach, "Organizational Culture as a Complex System."

28. Kenneth A. Frank, Ann E. Krause, and William R. Penuel, "Knowledge Flow and Organizational Change," (under review).

29. See *Social Networks* 32, Special Issue, no.1 (2010) for background on which this section draws.

30. Adapted from Roger Th. A. J. Leenders, "Structure and Influence: Statistical Models for the Dynamics of Actor Attributes, Network Structure and Their Interdependence." (Thesis, Amsterdam, 1995).

31. See Frank, "Identifying Cohesive Subgroups," and "Mapping Interactions Within and Between Cohesive Subgroups"; and Frank and Yasumoto, "Embedding Subgroups in the Sociogram: Linking Theory and Image."

32. Frank and Fahrbach, "Organizational Culture as a Complex System."

33. Ibid.

34. Ibid.

35. Ibid.

36. See, for example, Alan J. Daly and Kara S. Finnigan, "The Ebb and Flow of Social Network Ties Between District Leaders Under High Stakes Accountability," *American Education Research Journal* (in press); Chong Min Kim and Kenneth A. Frank, *Dynamics of Teachers' Mathematics Networks and Mathematics Instruction* (paper presented at the International Network for Social Network Analysis Annual Conference: Sunbelt XXX, Trento, Italy, July, 2010); Enrique C. Orlina, "Informatin Seeking, Trust, and Turnover: Three Essays Examining Middle School Instructional Advice Networks" (PhD diss., Northwestern University, 2010).

37. Spiro Maroulis, Roger Guimera, Hisham Petry, Louis Gomez, Luis, A. N. Amaral, Uri Wilensky, U. "A Complex Systems View of Educational Policy Research." Forthcoming in *Science*. Daniel G. Brown, Scott Page, Rick Riolo, Moira Zellner, and William Rand, "Path Dependence and the Validation of Agent-Based Spatial Models of Land Use." *International Journal of Geographical Information Science* 19, no. 2 (2005): 153–174; Lim et al.,"Agent-Based Simulations of Household Decision-Making a Land Use Change Near Altamira, Brazil," in *Integrating Geographic Information Systems and Agent-Based Techniques for Simulating Social and Ecological Processes*, ed. H. Randy Gimblett (New York: Oxford University Press, 2002): 277–308; Parker et al., "Multi-Agent Systems for the Simulation of Land-Use and Land- Cover Change: A Review," *Annals of the Association of American Geographers* 93 (2003): 314–337.

38. Agent-based models are usually comprised of three components: agents, environment, and rules (See Joshua M. Epstein and Robert Axtell, *Growing Artificial Societies* (Cambridge, MA: MIT Press, 1996), introduction; Uri Wilensky, *Modeling Nature's Emergent Patterns with Multi-Agent Languages* (paper presented at the EuroULogo, Linz, Austria, 2001). In the context of a social system, *agents* are usually people with heterogeneous attributes. The attributes can be fixed characteristics (e.g., race, gender) or attributes that can change over time (e.g., knowledge, wealth, preferences). The *environment* often takes the form of a lattice of sites or "patches" that themselves can be viewed as agents with attributes. For example, a patch might represent a plot of land on a farm and have an attribute that captures the fertility of that geographic location. Importantly for social systems, the environment can additionally, and more broadly, be conceived as including a network of social relations taking the form of "links" between the agents. Similar to patches, the links themselves can be thought of agents with attributes (e.g., strength of tie). *Rules* govern the behavior of the agents, the patches, and the links. An example of an agent rule might be something like "always allocate resources to maximize your util-

ity." For patches or links, a rule might govern some underlying rate of growth or decay of the resources at a site or the strength of a relation. Rules can also govern the inter-action between agents and their environment ("cultivate the most fertile patch"), the interaction between agents and agents ("transfer knowledge only to my closest social relations"), and the dynamic formation of the network topology ("you are more likely to help a friend of a friend than a stranger").

39. See, for example, Frank and Fahrbach, "Organizational Culture as a Complex System."
40. James Moody, Daniel A. McFarland and Skye Bender-DeMoll, "Dynamic Network Visu-alization: Methods for Meaning with Longitudinal Network Movies," *American Journal of Sociology* 110 (2005): 1206–1241.
41. Charles Horton Cooley, *Social Organization* (New York: Schocken, 1909); Arnold L. Epstein, *The Network and Urban Social Organization* (London: H.M. Stationary Office, 1961); Leon Festinger, Stanley Schachter, and Kurt Back, *Social Pressures in Informal Groups* (Stanford, CA: Stanford University Press, 1950); Charles Kadushin, "The Friends and Supporters of Psychotherapy: On Social Circles in Urban Life," *American Sociological Review* 31 (1966): 786–802.
42. John Barnes, "Social Networks," in *Addison-Wesley Module in Anthropology Module 26*, (Reading, MA: Addison-Wesley, 1972), 1–29; Elizabeth Bott, *Family and Social Network: Roles, Norms and External Relations* (London: Tavistock,1971).
43. Peter M. Blau, *Inequality and Heterogeneity* (New York: Macmillian, 1977); George C. Homans, *The Human Group* (New York: Harcourt Brace and Company, 1950); George Simmel, *Conflict and the Web of Group Affiliations* (Glencoe, IL: Free Press, 1955); Herbert A. Simon, "The Architecture of Complexity," in *General Systems: Yearbook of the Society for General Systems* 10 (1965): 63–76; for a review, see Linton C. Freeman, "The Sociological Concept of 'Group': An Empirical Test of Two Models." *American Journal of Sociology* 98, no. 1 (1992): 152–166.
44. Ronald S. Burt, *Brokerage and Closure: An Introduction to Social Capital* (Oxford: Oxford University Press, 2005); Kenneth A. Frank and Jeffrey Y. Yasumoto, "Linking Action to Social Structure within a System: Social Capital Within and Between Subgroups," *American Journal of Sociology* 104, no. 3 (1998): 642–686; Mark Granovetter, "The Strength of Weak Ties," *American Journal of Sociology* 78 (1973): 1360–1380; Nan Lin, "Building a Network Theory of Social Capital. Sunbelt Keynote Address." *Connections* 22, no. 1 (1999): 28–51.
45. Kenneth A. Frank and Yong Zhao, "Subgroups as a Meso-level Entity in the Social Orga-nization of Schools," in *Social Organization of Schools*, eds. L. Hedges and B. Schneider (New York: Sage Publications, 2005): 279–318.
46. Frank and Zhao also used Frank's (1995) sampling distribution simulations to determine that the ties were concentrated within subgroup boundaries at a rate that was unlikely to have occurred by chance alone, $p \leq .01$.
47. Frank and Zhao, "Subgroups as a Meso-level Entity in the Social Organization of Schools."
48. Claude Levi-Strauss, *The Elementary Structures of Kinship* (Boston: Beacon Press, 1969), 69.
49. Paraphrase, ibid., 78, citing von-Fürer-Haimendorf, 1938.
50. Kenneth A. Frank, "Quasi-Ties: Directing Resources to Members of a Collective," *American Behavioral Scientist* 52, (2009): 1613–1645.
51. See upcoming special issue of *Social Networks*: http://www.elsevier.com/framework_prod-ucts/promis_misc/cfp_socnet_2mode.pdf).
52. References throughout this paragraph are to Frank et al., "The Social Dynamics of Math-ematics CourseTaking in High School," *American Journal of Sociology* 113, no. 6 (2008): 1645–1696.

53. See Scott L. Feld, "The Focused Organization of School Ties," *American Journal of Sociology* 86, no. 5, (1981): 1015–1035.

54. Kathleen T. Call and Jeylan T. Mortimer, *Arenas of Comfort in Adolescence: A Study of Adjustment in Context.* (Mahwah, NJ: Lawrence Erlbaum, 2001); R. Cronsoe et.al., "Peer Group Contexts of Girls' and Boys' Academic Experiences," *Child Development* 79, no. 1 (2008): 139–155; Peggy C. Giordano, "Relationships in Adolescence," *Annual Review of Sociology* 29 (2003): 257–281; Susan Harter and Kurt W. Fischer, *The Construction of the Self: A Developmental Perspective* (New York: Guilford Press, 1999); Dana L. Haynie, "Delinquent Peers Revisited: Does Network Structure Matter?" *American Journal of Sociology* 106, no. 4 (2001): 1013–1057.

55. H. Alix Gallagher, William R. Penuel, Robert F. Murphy, Kristin R. Bosetti, and Patrick M. Shields, *National Evaluation of Writing Project Professional Development: Year 1 report* (Menlo Park, CA: SRI International, 2009).

56. See, for example, Ann Lieberman and Lynne Miller, *Teachers in Professional Communities: Improving Teaching and Learning* (New York: Teachers College Press, 2008); Milbrey W. McLaughlin and Joan E. Talbert, *Professional Communities and the Work of High School Teaching* (Chicago: University of Chicago Press, 2001).

57. Peter Marsden, "Recent developments in network measurement," in *Models and Methods in Social Network Analysis*, eds. Peter J. Carrington, John Scott, Stanley Wasserman (Cambridge: Cambridge University Press, 2005); for online examples, see file:///C:/Documents%20and%20Settings/kenfrank/My%20Documents/MyFiles/my%20web%20page/resources.htm#survey

58. See, for example, Cynthia E. Coburn and Jennifer Lin Russell, "District Policy and Teachers' Social Networks," *Educational Evaluation and Policy Analysis* 30, no. 3 (2008): 203–235.

59. Min Sun, "Shaping Professional Development to Promote the Diffusion of Instructional Expertise Among Teachers" (PhD diss., Michigan State University, 2010).

60. For some of this research, see Thomas Valente, *Network Models of the Diffusion of Innovations* (Cresskill, NJ: Hampton Press, 1995); Alberto-Laszlo L. Barabasi, *Linked: How Everything Is Connected to Everything Else and What It Means* (London: Penguin Books, A. L. 2003); Duncan J. Watts, *Six Degrees: The Science of a Connected Age* (New York: Norton, 2003); Duncan J. Watts, *Small Worlds: The Dynamics of Networks Between Order and Randomness (Princeton Studies in Complexity)* (Princeton, NJ: Princeton University Press, (2003); Matthew O. Jackson,*Social and Economic Networks* (Princeton, NJ: Princeton University Press, 2008).

61. Youngs et al., "The Motivation of Teachers to Produce Human Capital and Conform to Their Social Contexts."

62. James S. Coleman, *Foundations of Social Theory* (Cambridge, MA: Harvard University Press, 1990).

63. George A. Akerlof and Rachel E. Kranton, "Identity and and Schooling: Some Lessons for the Economics of Education," *Journal of Economic Literature* 40, no. 4 (2002): 1167–1201.

64. Richard L. Schwab and Richard L. Iwanicki, "Perceived Role Conflict, Role Ambiguity, and Teacher Burnout," *Educational Administration Quarterly* 18, no. 1 (1982): 60–74; It would be more conventional to write the utility function it terms of the gain to leisure rather than the cost of additional effort. If l stands for leisure, then our gain from leisure might be $\frac{1}{2}l^2 \frac{1}{2}l^2$. Using the constraint that leisure and effort must add up to all time available, say twenty-four hours, we could then rewrite the equation as $\left(\frac{1}{2}\right)(24-e)^2\left(\frac{1}{2}\right)(24-e)^2$. When simplified, this would give us equation (1) with the additional of 288, a constant that will not affect the maximization of the utility function.

65. Obtained by taking the first derivative of (2) with respect to e_i, setting it equal to zero and solving for e_i.

66. Noah E. Friedkin and Peter V. Marsden, "Network Studies of Social Influence," in *Advances in Social Network Analysis*, eds. Stanley Wasserman and Joseph Galaskiewicz (Thousand Oaks, CA: Sage Publications, 1994), 1–25.

67. See, for example, Frank, "Quasi-Ties"; Frank and Zhao, "Subgroups as a Meso-level Entity in the Social Organization of Schools."

68. See, for example, Robins et al., " Recent Developments in exponential random graph (p*) models for social networks," *Social Networks* 29 (2007): 192–215; Snijders et al., "New Specifications for Exponential Random Graph Models," *Sociological Methodology* (2006): 99–153.

69. Marijtje Van Duijn,"Estimation of a Random Effects Model for Directed Graphs," in *Symposium Statistische Software, nr. 7. Toeval Zit Overal: Programmatuur voor Random-Coefficient Modellen [Chance Is Omnipresent: Software for Random Coefficient Models]*, ed. Tom A. B. Snijders (Groningen, The Netherlands: ProGaMMA, 1995): 113–131; Emmanuel Lazega and Marijtje Van Duijn, "Position in Formal Structure, Personal Characteristics and Choices of Advisors in a Law Firm: A Logistic Regression Model for Dyadic Network Data," *Social Networks* 19 (1997): 375–397.

70. The u_i are assumed normally distributed with variance $\tau(u)$ and the v_i are normally distributed with variance $\tau(v)$.

71. Linton C. Freeman, "Centrality in Social Networks: Conceptual Clarification," *Social Networks* 1 (1978): 215–239.

CHAPTER 13

1. Christopher Day and Mark Hadfield, "Learning Through Networks: Trust, Partnerships and the Power of Action Research," *Educational Action Research* 12 (2004): 575–586; Wiel Veugelers and Mary John O'Hair, *Network Learning for Educational Change* (Maidenhead, UK: Open University, 2005).

2. Judith Chapman and David Aspin, "Networks of Learning: A New Construct for Educational Provision and a New Strategy for Reform," in *Handbook of Educational Leadership and Management*, ed. Brent Davies and John West-Burnham (London: Pearson/Longman, 2003), 654.

3. Jorge Ávila de Lima, "Thinking More Deeply About Networks in Education," *Journal of Educational Change* 11, no. 1 (2010): 1–21.

4. Stephen D. Berkowitz, *An Introduction to Structural Analysis: The Network Approach to Social Research* (Toronto: Butterworths, 1982); Everett M. Rogers and D. Lawrence Kincaid, *Communication Networks: Toward a New Paradigm for Research* (New York: Free Press, 1981); Barry Wellman, "Network Analysis: Some Basic Principles," in *Sociological Theory 1983*, ed. Randall Collins (San Francisco: Jossey-Bass, 1983), 155–186; Barry Wellman, "Structural Analysis: From Method and Metaphor to Theory and Substance," in *Social Structures: A Network Approach*, eds. Barry Wellman and Stephen D. Berkowitz (Cambridge, UK: Cambridge University Press, 1988), 19–61.

5. Daniel Jackson, John Kirkland, Barry Jackson, and David Bimler, "Social Network Analysis and Estimating the Size of Hard-to-Count Subpopulations," *Connections* 26 (2005): 49.

6. Thomas Mathien, "Network Analysis and Methodological Individualism," *Philosophy of the Social Sciences* 18, no. 1 (1988): 1–20.

7. Stanley Wasserman and Katherine Faust, *Social Network Analysis: Methods and Applications* (Cambridge, UK: Cambridge University Press, 1994), 42.

8. Carter T. Butts, "Social Network Analysis: A Methodological Introduction," *Asian Journal of Social Psychology* 11 (2008): 13–41.

9. See, for example, Ronald S. Burt, "Network Items and the General Social Survey," *Social Networks* 6 (1984): 293–339; Claude S. Fischer, *To Dwell Among Friends* (Chicago: University of Chicago Press, 1982); Peter V. Marsden, "Core Discussion Networks of Americans," *American Sociological Review* 52, no. 1 (1987): 122–131; Barry Wellman, "The Community Question: The Intimate Networks of East Yorkers," *American Journal of Sociology* 84, no. 5 (1979): 1201–1231.

10. Barry Wellman, "Challenges in Collecting Personal Network Data: The Nature of Personal Network Analysis," *Field Methods* 19, no. 2 (2007): 111–115.

11. Christopher McCarty, "Measuring Structure in Personal Networks," *Journal of Social Structure* 3, no. 1 (2002), http://www.cmu.edu/joss/content/articles/volume3/McCarty.html.

12. Christopher McCarty, José Luis Molina, Claudia Aguilar, and Laura Rota, "A Comparison of Social Network Mapping and Personal Network Visualization," *Field Methods* 19, no. 2 (2007): 145–162.

13. jimi adams and James Moody, "To Tell the Truth: Measuring Concordance in Multiply Reported Network Data," *Social Networks* 29 (2007): 44–58; Butts, "Social Network Analysis"; Kevin White and Susan Cotts Watkins, "Accuracy, Stability and Reciprocity in Informal Conversational Networks in Rural Kenya," *Social Networks* 22 (2000): 337–355.

14. McCarty, "Measuring Structure in Personal Networks"; Wellman, "Challenges in Collecting Personal Network Data."

15. On the diffusion of knowledge or innovations, Everett M. Rogers, *Diffusion of Innovations*, 5th edition (New York: Free Press, 2003); Thomas W. Valente, *Network Models of the Diffusion of Innovations* (Cresskill, NJ: Hampton Press, 1995); on inefficiency in information flow: Kazuo Yamaguchi, "The Flow of Information Through Social Networks: Diagonal-free Measures of Inefficiency and the Structural Determinants of Inefficiency," *Social Networks* 16 (1994): 57–86; on loose coupling in educational organizations: Jorge Ávila de Lima, "Teachers' Professional Development in Departmentalised, Loosely Coupled Organisations: Lessons for School Improvement From a Case Study of Two Curriculum Departments," *School Effectiveness and School Improvement* 18, no. 3 (2007): 273–301; on social influence and leadership in subject departments: Jorge Ávila de Lima, "Department Networks and Distributed Leadership in Schools," *School Leadership and Management* 28, no. 2 (2008): 159–187.

16. Deirdre M. Kirke, "Collecting Peer Data and Delineating Peer Networks in a Complete Network," *Social Networks* 18 (1996): 333–346.

17. Butts, "Social Network Analysis," 18.

18. Tiziana Casciaro, Kathleen M. Carley and David Krackhardt, "Positive Affectivity and Accuracy in Social Network Perception," *Motivation and Emotion* 23, no. 4 (1999): 285–306.

19. David Krackhardt, "Cognitive Social Structures," *Social Networks* 9 (1987): 109–134; Ece Batchelder, "Comparing Three Simultaneous Measurements of a Sociocognitive Network," *Social Networks* 24 (2002): 261–277; Tiziana Casciaro, "Seeing Things Clearly: Social Structure, Personality, and Accuracy in Social Network Perception," *Social Networks* 20 (1998): 331–351.

20. Casciaro, Carley, and Krackhardt, "Positive Affectivity and Accuracy in Social Network Perception," 285–286; see also Martin Kilduff and David Krackhardt, "Bringing the Individual Back In: A Structural Analysis of the Internal Market for Reputation," *Academy of Management Journal* 37, no. 1 (1994): 87–108.

21. Carter T. Butts, "Network Inference, Error, and Informant (In)accuracy: A Bayesian Approach," *Social Networks* 25 (2003): 135–136.

22. Peter R. Monge, "The Network Level of Analysis," in *Handbook of Communication Science*, eds. Charles R. Berger and Steven H. Chaffee (Newbury Park, CA: Sage, 1987), 239–270.

23. Peter R. Monge and Noshir S. Contractor, "Communication Networks: Measurement Techniques," in *Handbook for the Study of Human Communication*, ed. Charles H. Tardy (Norwood, NJ: Ablex, 1988), 107–138.

24. Diana Stork and William D. Richards, "Nonrespondents in Communication Network Studies: Problems and Possibilities," *Group and Organization Management* 17, No. 2 (1992): 193–210.

25. Ronald S. Burt, "A Note on Missing Network Data in the General Social Survey," *Social Networks* 9 (1987): 63.

26. Gueorgi Kossinets, "Effects of Missing Data in Social Networks," *Social Networks* 28 (2006): 247–268.

27. Edward O. Laumann, Peter V. Marsden, and David Prensky, "The Boundary Specification Problem in Network Analysis," in *Applied Network Analysis: A Methodological Introduction*, eds. Ronald S. Burt and Michael J. Minor (Beverly Hills, CA: Sage, 1983), 18–34.

28. Butts, "Social Network Analysis."

29. David Knoke and James H. Kuklinski, *Network Analysis* (Newbury Park, CA: Sage, 1982); Garry Robins, Philippa Pattison, and Jodie Woolcock, "Missing Data in Networks: Exponential Random Graph (p*) Models for Networks with Non-respondents," *Social Networks* 26 (2004): 257–283.

30. Richard D. Alba, "Taking Stock of Network Analysis: A Decade"s Results," *Research in the Sociology of Organizations* 1 (1982): 43.

31. Elizabeth Costenbader and Thomas W. Valente, "The Stability of Centrality Measures When Networks Are Sampled," *Social Networks* 25 (2003): 283–307.

32. Robins, Pattison, and Woolcock, "Missing Data in Networks."

33. Stork and Richards, "Nonrespondents in Communication Network Studies."

34. See, for example, Devon D. Brewer, "Forgetting in the Recall-based Elicitation of Personal and Social Networks," *Social Networks* 22 (2000): 29–43; Devon D. Brewer and Cynthia M. Webster, "Forgetting of Friends and Its Effects on Measuring Friendship Networks," *Social Networks* 21 (1999): 361–373; Butts, "Network Inference, Error, and Informant (In)accuracy"; Costenbader and Valente, "The Stability of Centrality Measures When Networks Are Sampled"; Scott L. Feld and William C. Carter, "Detecting Measurement Bias in Respondent Reports of Personal Networks," *Social Networks* 24 (2002): 365–383; Kossinets, "Effects of Missing Data in Social Networks"; Alexandra Marin, "Are Respondents More Likely to List Alters with Certain Characteristics? Implications for Name Generator Data," *Social Networks* 26 (2004): 289–307; Peter V. Marsden, "The Reliability of Network Density and Composition Measures," *Social Networks* 15 (1993): 399–421.

35. Richard D. Alba, "From Small Groups to Social Networks: Mathematical Approaches to the Study of Group Structure," *American Behavioral Scientist* 24, no. 5 (1981): 692; see also Mark Granovetter, "The Theory-gap in Social Network Analysis," *Perspectives on Social Network Research*, eds. Paul W. Holland and Samuel Leinhardt (New York: Academic Press, 1979), 504.

36. H. Russell Bernard and Peter D. Killworth, "Informant Accuracy in Social Network Data II," *Human Communication Research* 4 (1977): 3–18.

37. Casciaro, Carley, and Krackhardt, "Positive Affectivity and Accuracy in Social Network Perception"."

38. Casciaro, "Seeing Things Clearly."

39. H. Russell Bernard, Peter D. Killworth, and Lee Sailer, "Informant Accuracy in Social Network Data IV: A Comparison of Clique-level Structure in Behavioral and Cognitive Network Data," *Social Networks* 2 (1979): 191–218; Butts, "Network Inference, Error, and Informant (In)accuracy."

40. David Krackhardt, "Assessing the Political Landscape: Structure, Cognition, and Power in Organizations," *Administrative Science Quarterly* 35 (1990): 342–369.

41. Casciaro, Carley, and Krackhardt, "Positive Affectivity and Accuracy in Social Network Perception."

42. Deborah A. Kashy and David A. Kenny "Do You Know Whom You Were With a Week Ago Friday? A Re-Analysis of the Bernard, Killworth, and Sailer Studies," *Social Psychology Quarterly* 53, no. 1 (1990): 55–61.

43. David A. Kenny and Linda Albright, "Accuracy in Interpersonal Perception: A Social Relations Analysis," *Psychological Bulletin* 102, no. 3 (1987): 390–402.

44. Peter D. Killworth and H. Russell Bernard, "Informant Accuracy in Social Network Data," *Human Organization* 35 (1976): 269–286; Peter D. Killworth and H. Russell Bernard, "Informant Accuracy in Social Network Data III: A Comparison of Triadic Structure in Behavioral and Cognitive Data," *Social Networks* (1979/1980): 19–46; Bernard and Killworth, "Informant Accuracy in Social Network Data II"; Bernard, Killworth, and Sailer, "Informant Accuracy in Social Network Data IV"; H. Russell Bernard, Peter D. Killworth, and Lee Sailer, "Summary of Research on Informant Accuracy in Network Data, and on the Reverse Small World Problem," *Connections* 4 (1981): 11–25; H. Russell Bernard, Peter D. Killworth, and Lee Sailer, "Informant Accuracy in Social Network Data V: An Experimental Attempt to Predict Actual Communication from Recall Data", *Social Science Research 11* (1982): 30–66; H. Russell Bernard, Peter D. Killworth, David Kronenfeld, and Lee Sailer, "The Problem of Informant Accuracy: The Validity of Retrospective Data," *Annual Review of Anthropology* 13 (1984): 495–517.

45. Bernard et al., "The Problem of Informant Accuracy"."

46. Butts, "Network Inference, Error, and Informant (In)accuracy."

47. See, for example, Steven R. Corman and Lisa Bradford, "Situational Eeffects on the Accuracy of Self-reported Organizational Communication Behavior," *Communication Research* 20, no. 6 (1993): 822–840; Linton C. Freeman and A. Kimball Romney, "Words, Deeds and Social Structure: A Preliminary Study of the Reliability of Informants," *Human Organization* 46 (1987): 330–334; Linton C. Freeman, A. Kimball Romney, and Sue C. Freeman, "Cognitive Structure and Informant Accuracy," *American Anthropologist (New Series)* 89, no. 2 (1987): 310–325; Muriel Hammer, "Reply to Killworth and Bernard," *Connections* 3 (1980): 14–15; A. Kimball Romney and Susan C. Weller, "Predicting Informant Accuracy from Patterns of Recall Among Individuals," *Social Networks* 6 (1984): 59–77.

48. Freeman, Romney, and Freeman, "Cognitive Structure and Informant Accuracy."

49. adams and Moody, "To Tell the Truth""; for other findings, see David C. Bell, Isaac D. Montoya, and John S. Atkinson, "Partner Concordance in Reports of Joint Risk Behaviors," *Journal of Acquired Immune Deficiency Syndromes* 25, no. 2 (2000): 173–181; Michael Calloway, Joseph P. Morrissey, and Robert I. Paulson, "Accuracy and Reliability of Self-Reported Data in Interorganizational Networks," *Social Networks* 15 (1993): 377–398; Peter V. Marsden, "Network Data and Measurement," *Annual Review of Sociology* 16 (1990): 435–463.

50. Muriel Hammer, "Reply to Killworth and Bernard."

51. Ibid.

52. Alba, "Taking Stock of Network Analysis"; Wasserman and Faust, *Social Network Analysis*.

53. Anuska Ferligoj and Valentina Hlebec, "Evaluation of Social Network Measurement Instruments," *Social Networks* 21 (1999): 111–130; Alba, "Taking Stock of Network Analysis."

54. Valentina Hlebec and Anuska Ferligoj, "Reliability of Social Network Measurement Instruments," *Field Methods* 14, no. 3 (2002): 288–306; Stork and Richards, "Nonrespondents in Communication Network Studies."

55. Costenbader and Valente, "The Stability of Centrality Measures When Networks are Sampled."

56. See, for example, H. P. Bahrick, P. O. Bahrick, and R. P. Wittlinger, "Fifty Years of Memory for Names and Faces: A Cross-Sectional Approach," *Journal of Experimental Psychology: General* 104, no. 1 (1975): 54–75; Brewer, "Forgetting in the Recall-based Elicitation of Personal and Social Networks"; Brewer and Webster, "Forgetting of Friends and Its Effects on Measuring Friendship Networks"; Muriel Hammer, "Explorations into the Meaning of Social Network Interview Data," *Social Networks* 6 (1984): 341–371; Seymour Sudman, "Experiments in the Measurement of the Size of Social Networks," *Social Networks* 7 (1985): 127–151.

57. Jackson et al., "Social Network Analysis and Estimating the Size of Hard-to-Count Subpopulations."

58. Alayne M. Adams, Sangeetha Madhavan, and Dominique Simon, "Measuring Social Networks Cross-culturally," *Social Networks* 28 (2006): 363–376; David C. Bell, Benedetta Belli-McQueen, and Ali Haider, "Partner Naming and Forgetting: Recall of Network Members," *Social Networks* 29 (2007): 279–299; Mark Granovetter, "Network Sampling: Some First Steps," *American Journal of Sociology* 81, no. 6 (1976): 1287–1303.

59. Butts, "Social Network Analysis."

60. Brewer, "Forgetting in the Recall-based Elicitation of Personal and Social Networks"; Marin, "Are Respondents More Likely to List Alters with Certain Characteristics?"

61. Burt, "Network Items and the General Social Survey"; Alexandra Marin and Keith N. Hampton, "Simplifying the Personal Network Name Generator: Alternatives to Traditional Multiple and Single Name Generators," *Field Methods* 19, no. 2 (2007): 163–193.

62. H. Russell Bernard, Eugene C. Johnsen, Peter D. Killworth, Christopher McCarty, Gene A. Shelley, and Scott Robinson, "Comparing Four Different Methods for Measuring Personal Social Networks," *Social Networks* 12 (1990): 179–215.

63. Alba, "Taking Stock of Network Analysis"; Costenbader and Valente, "The Stability of Centrality Measures When Networks Are Sampled."

64. Paul W. Holland and Samuel Leinhardt, "The Structural Implications of Measurement Error in Sociometry," *Journal of Mathematical Sociology* 3, no. 1 (1973): 85–111.

65. Batchelder, "Comparing Three Simultaneous Measurements of a Sociocognitive Network."

66. Stork and Richards, "Nonrespondents in Communication Network Studies."

67. Noah Friedkin, "A Test of Structural Features of Granovetter's Strength of Weak Ties Theory," *Social Networks* 2 (1980): 411–422; Mark Granovetter, "The Strength of Weak Ties," *American Journal of Sociology* 78, no. 6 (1973): 1366–1380; Gabriel Weimann, "The Strength of Weak Conversational Ties in the Flow of Information and Influence," *Social Networks* 5 (1983): 245–267.

68. Peter V. Marsden and Karen E. Campbell, "Measuring Tie Strength," *Social Forces* 63 (1984): 482–501; McCarty, "Measuring Structure in Personal Networks."

69. Marin, "Are Respondents More Likely to List Alters with Certain Characteristics?"

70. Bernard et al., "Comparing Four Different Methods for Measuring Personal Social Networks."

71. Marin and Hampton, "Simplifying the Personal Network Name Generator"; Peter V. Marsden, "Interviewer Effects in Measuring Network Size using a Single Name Generator," *Social Networks* 25 (2003): 1–16; Marsden, "Network Data and Measurement."

72. Tina Kogovšek, Anuska Ferligoj, Germa Coenders, and Willem E. Saris, "Estimating the Reliability and Validity of Personal Support Measures: Full Information ML Estimation with Planned Incomplete Data," *Social Networks* 24 (2002): 1–20; Tina Kogovšek and Anuska Ferligoj, "Effects on Reliability and Validity of Egocentered Network Measurements," *Social Networks* 27 (2005): 205–229.

73. Kogovšek and Ferligoj, "Effects on Reliability and Validity of Egocentered Network Measurements"; Kogovšek et al., "Estimating the Reliability and Validity of Personal Support Measures."

74. Marin and Hampton, "Simplifying the Personal Network Name Generator."
75. James E. Pustejosvsky and James P. Spillane, "Question-order Effects in Social Network Name Generators," *Social Networks* 31 (2009): 221–229.
76. For a description, see Burt, "Network Items and the General Social Survey."
77. Stefanie Bailey and Peter V. Marsden, "Interpretation and Interview Context: Examining the General Social Survey Name Generator Using Cognitive Methods," *Social Networks* 21(1999): 287–309.
78. Mart G. M. Van der Poel, "Delineating Personal Support Networks," *Social Networks* 15 (1993): 49–70; Bruce C. Straits, "Ego's Important Discussants or Significant People: An Experiment in Varying the Wording of Personal Network Name Generators," *Social Networks* 22 (2000): 123–140.
79. Eric van Sonderen, Johan Ormel, Els I. Brilman, and G. F. E. Chiquit van Linden van den Heuvell, "Personal Network Delineation: A Comparison of the Exchange, Affective, and Role-relation Approach," in *Social Network Research: Substantive Issues and Methodological Questions*, eds. Kees C. P. M. Knipscheer and Toni C. Antonucci (Amsterdam: Swets and Zeitlinger, 1990), 101–120; Karen E. Campbell and Barren A. Lee, "Name Generators in Surveys of Personal Networks," *Social Networks* 13 (1991): 203–221; Van der Poel, "Delineating Personal Support Networks"; Marin and Hampton, "Simplifying the Personal Network Name Generator."
80. Ronald S. Burt, "A Note on Social Capital and Network Content," *Social Networks* 19 (1997): 355–373.
81. Burt, "Network Items and the General Social Survey."
82. For a discussion of this issue in longitudinal studies of networks, see Mark Huisman and Christian Steglich, "Treatment of Non-Response in Longitudinal Network Studies," *Social Networks* 30 (2008): 297–308.
83. Robins, Pattison, and Woolcock, "Missing Data in Networks."
84. Krackhardt, "Cognitive Social Structures; see also Casciaro, Carley, and Krackhardt, "Positive Affectivity and Accuracy in Social Network Perception," and Daniele Bondonio, "Predictors of Accuracy in Perceiving Informal Social Networks," *Social Networks* 20 (1998): 301–330.
85. Ibid.
86. On the use of the imputation approach, see Stork and Richards, "Nonrespondents in Communication Network Studies"; Burt, "A Note on Missing Network Data in the General Social Survey"; Krackhardt, "Assessing the Political Landscape." For a critique of simple imputation procedures, see Mark Huisman, "Imputation of Missing Network Data: Some Simple Procedures," *Journal of Social Structure*, 10 (February 4, 2009). http://www.cmu.edu/joss/.
87. Krackhardt, "Assessing the Political Landscape."
88. Bondonio, "Predictors of Accuracy in Perceiving Informal Social Networks"."; see also David Banks and Kathleen Carley, "Metric Inference for Social Networks," *Journal of Classification* 11 (1994): 121–149.
89. Stork and Richards, "Nonrespondents in Communication Network Studies."
90. Calloway, Morrissey, and Paulson, "Accuracy and Reliability of Self-Reported Data in Interorganizational Networks."
91. Forrest A. Deseran and Lisa Black, "Problems with Using Self-Reports in Network Analysis: Some Empirical Findings in Rural Counties," *Rural Sociology* 46, no. 2 (1981): 310–318; Forrest A. Deseran and Lisa Black, "Problems with Using Self-Reports in Network Analysis: Further Considerations," *Rural Sociology* 46, no. 3 (1981): 518–520.
92. Stork and Richards, "Nonrespondents in Communication Network Studies."
93. Ronald S. Burt and Don Ronchi, "Measuring a Large Network Quickly," *Social Networks* 16 (1994): 91–135.

94. Ibid.

95. adams and Moody, "To Tell the Truth."

96. See, for example, Burt and Ronchi, "Measuring a Large Network Quickly"; Deseran and Black, "Problems with Using Self Reports in Network Analysis: Some Empirical Findings in Rural Counties"; Feld and Carter, "Detecting Measurement Bias in Respondent Reports of Personal Networks"; Hammer, "Explorations into the Meaning of Social Network Interview Data"; White and Watkins, "Accuracy, Stability and Reciprocity in Informal Conversational Networks in Rural Kenya."

97. Deseran and Black, "Problems with Using Self Reports in Network Analysis: Some Empirical Findings in Rural Counties."

98. Micha Mandel, "Measuring Tendency Towards Mutuality in a Social Network," *Social Networks* 22 (2000): 285–298; A. Ramachandra Rao and Suraj Bandyopadhyay, "Measures of Reciprocity in a Social Network," *Sankhya: The Indian Journal of Statistics* 49, Series A, pt. 2 (1987): 141–188.

99. Several currently available software packages specifically designed for social network analysis can assist in the process of performing tasks such as reconstruction, dichotomization, or symmetrization.

100. Alba, "Taking Stock of Network Analysis"; Kathleen M. Carley and David Krackhardt, "Cognitive Inconsistencies and Non-symmetric Friendship," *Social Networks* 18 (1996): 1–27.

101. Joseph Galaskiewikz, "The Structure of Community Organizational Networks," *Social Forces* 57, no. 4 (1979): 1346–1364; Bernard et al., "Comparing Four Different Methods for Measuring Personal Social Networks."

CHAPTER 14

1. Ilana Horn and Judith W. Little, "Attending to Problems of Practice: Routines and Resources for Professional Learning in Teachers' Workplace Interactions," *American Educational Research Journal* 47, no. 1 (2010): 181–217; Judith W. Little and Ilana Horn, "'Normalizing' Problems of Practice: Converting Routine Conversation into a Resource for Learning in Professional Communities," in *Professional Learning Communities: Divergence, Detail and Difficulties*, eds. Louise Stoll and Karen Seashore-Louis (Maidenhead, UK: Open University Press, 2007), 79–92; Robert McCormick, Alison Fox, and Patrick Carmichael, *Researching and Understanding Educational Networks* (New York: Routledge, 2010)

2. See also Alan J. Daly and Kara Finnigan, "The Ebb and Flow of Social Network Ties between District Leaders Under High Stakes Accountability," *American Educational Research Journal* (in press) for a case of relational inertia.

3. See also Alan J. Daly, Nienke M. Moolenaar, Jose M. Bolivar, and Peggy Burke, "Relationships in Reform: The Role of Teachers' Social Networks," *Journal of Educational Administration* 48, no. 3 (2010): 359–391.

4. Janet Chrispeels, *Learning to Lead Together: The Promise and Challenge of Sharing Leadership* (Thousand Oaks, CA: Sage Publications, 2004).

5. Meredith Honig, "District Central Offices as Learning Organizations: How Sociocultural and Organizational Learning Theories Elaborate District-Central-Office Administrators' Participation in Teaching and Learning Improvement Efforts," *American Journal of Education* 114, no. 4 (2008): 627–664; Meredith I. Honig, "No Small Thing: School District Central Office Bureaucracies and the Implementation of New Small Autonomous Schools Initiatives," *American Educational Research Journal* 46, no. 2 (2009): 387–422.

6. Judith W. Little, "Professional Learning and School-Network Ties: Prospects for School Improvement," *Journal of Educational Change* 6 (2005): 277–283.

7. Meredith I. Honig, "Street-Level Bureaucracy Revisited: Frontline District Central Office Administrators As Boundary Spanners in Education Policy Implementation," Educational Evaluation and Policy Analysis 28(4 (2006), 357–383; James G. March, "Exploration and Exploitation in Organizational Learning," Organization Science, 2, no. 1 (1991): 71–87.

8. Andrew Hargeaves, Changing Teachers, Changing Times. Teacher's Work and Culture in the Postmodern Age (New York: Teachers College Press, 1994).

9. John Scott, Social Network Analysis, 2nd edition (London: Sage, 2000); Stanley Wasserman and Katherine Faust, Social Network Analysis: Methods and Applications (New York: Cambridge University Press, 1998).

10. Frank and Zhao, "Subgroups as a Meso-level Entity in the Social Organization of Schools."

11. Ray Reagans and Bill McEvily, "Network Structure and Knowledge Transfer: The Effects of Cohesion and Range," Administrative Science Quarterly 48, no. 2 (2003): 240–267; Kenneth A. Frank, "Identifying Cohesive Subgroups," Social Networks 17 (1995), 27–56; Kenneth A. Frank, "Mapping Interactions Within and Between Cohesive Subgroups," Social Networks 18 (1996): 93–119; Sai Yayavaram and Gautham Ahuja,"Decomposability in Knowledge Structures and Its Impact on the Usefulness of Inventions and Knowledge-Base Malleability," Administrative Science Quarterly 53 (2008): 333–362.

12. Frank, "Mapping Interactions Within and Between Cohesive Subgroups."

13. Wenpin Tsai and Sumantra Ghoshal, "Social Capital and Value Creation: The Role of Intrafirm Networks," Academy of Management Journal 41, no. 4 (1998): 464–78.

14. Jon Supovitz and Elliot Weinbaum, The Implementation Gap: Understanding Reform in High Schools (New York: Teachers College Press, 2008).

15. Wesley Cohen and David Levinthal, "Absorptive Capacity: A New Perspective on Learning and Innovation," Administrative Science Quarterly 35: (1990): 128–152.

16. Prasad Balkundi and David Harrison, "Ties, Leaders, and Time in Teams: Strong Inference About Network Structure's Effects on Team Viability and Performance," Academy of Management Journal 49: (2006): 49–68; Sumantra Ghoshal, Harry Korine, and Gabriel Szulanski, "Interunit Communication in Multinational Corporations," Management Science 40, no. 1 (1994): 96–110; Gabriel Szulanski, "Exploring Stickiness: Impediments to the Transfer of Best Practice Within the Firm," Strategic Management Journal 17 (1996) 27–43.

17. Janet Chrispeels, Peggy Burke, Peggy Johnson, and Alan J. Daly, "Aligning Mental Models of District and School Leadership Teams for Reform Coherence," Education and Urban Society 40, no. 6 (2008): 730–750.

18. Alan J. Daly, "Rigid Response in an Age of Accountability," Educational Administration Quarterly 45 no. 2 (2009): 168–216; Heinrich Mintrop, Schools on Probation: How Accountability Works (And Doesn't Work) (New York: Teachers College Press, 2004).

19. Mark Smylie and Andrea Evans, "Social Capital and the Problem of Implementation," in New Directions in Education Policy: Confronting Complexity, ed. Meredith. Honig (Albany, NY: State University of New York Press, 2006): 187–208.

20. James S. Coleman, "Social Capital in the Creation of Human Capital," American Journal of Sociology 94 (1988): 95–120; Sandra L. Dika and Kusum Singh, "Applications of Social Capital in Educational Literature: A Critical Synthesis," Review of Educational Research 72, no. 1 (2002): 31–60; Nan Lin, Social Capital: A Theory of Social Structure and Action (New York: Cambridge University Press, 2001).

21. James Spillane, Brian Reiser, and Louis Gomez, "Policy Implementation and Cognition: The Role of Human, Social, and Distributed Cognition in Framing Policy Implementation" (Albany, NY: State University of New York Press, 2006), 47–64.

22. Frits Pil and Carrie Leana, "Applying Organizational Research to Public School Reform: The Effects of Teacher Human and Social Capital on Student Performance," Academy

of Management Journal 52, no. 6 (2009): 1101–1124; Jon Supovitz, Phillip Sirinides and Henry May, "How Principals and Peers Influence Teaching and Learning," *Educational Administration Quarterly* 46, no. 1 (2010): 31–57.

23. Anthony S. Bryk and Barbara Schneider, *Trust in Schools: A Core Resource for Improvement* (New York: Russell Sage Foundation, 2002); Alan J. Daly and Janet Chrispeels, "A Question of Trust: Predictors of Adaptive and Technical Leadership," *Leadership and Policy in the Schools* 71, no. 1, (2008): 30–63; Pil and Leana, "Applying Organizational Research to Public School Reform"; Megan Tschannen-Moran, *Trust Matters: Leadership for Successful Schools* (San Francisco: Jossey-Bass, 2004).

24. Spillane, Reiser, and Gomez, "Policy Implementation and Cognition."

25. See work by Daniel McFarland in this area.

26. A seminal piece is Linton Freeman, "Visualizing Social Networks," *Journal of Social Structure* 1, no 1: (2000).

27. Steve Borgatti and José-Luis Molina, "Toward Ethical Guidelines for Network Research in Organizations," *Social Networks* 27, no. 2 (2005): 107–118; Charles Kadushin, "Who Benefits from Network Analysis: Ethics of Social Network Research," *Social Networks* 27, no. 2 (2005): 139–154.

28. Béla Bollobás, *Random Graphs*, 2nd Edition. (Cambridge, UK: Cambridge University Press, 2001); Gary Robins, Pip Pattison, Yuval Kalish, and Dean Lusher, "An Introduction to Exponential Random Graph (p*) Models for Social Networks," *Social Networks* 29 (2007): 173–191; Gary Robins and Martina Morris, "Advances in Exponential Random Graph (p*) Models," *Social Networks* 29 (2007): 169–172.

29. Alan J. Daly and Kara Finnigan, "The Ebb and Flow of Social Network Ties Between District Leaders Under High Stakes Accountability," *American Educational Research Journal* (in press); Thomas Snijders, Christian Steglich and Gerhard Van de Bunt, "Introduction to Actor-Based Models for Network Dynamics," *Social Networks* 32, no. 1 (2010): 44–60.

30. Christian Steglich, Thomas Snijders, and Michael Pearson, "Networks and Behavior: Separating Selection from Influence," *Sociological Methodology* (in press); Thomas Snijders, "Models for Longitudinal Network Data," in *Models and Methods in Social Network Analysis*, eds. Peter Carrington, John Scott, and Stanley Wasserman (New York: Cambridge University Press, 2005).

31. Skye Bender-deMoll and Daniel A. McFarland, "The Art and Science of Dynamic Network Visualization," *Journal of Social Structure* 7, no 2: (2006).

About the Editor

Alan J. Daly, PhD, is an assistant professor of education at the University of California, San Diego. He earned his PhD in education from the University of California, Santa Barbara. In addition to fifteen years' experience in public education as a teacher, psychologist, and administrator, Daly has also been the program director for the Center for Educational Leadership and Effective Schools at the University of California, Santa Barbara. In this position he collaboratively supported the delivery of high-quality services and research to five school districts, focusing on social networks, trust, and potential of systems for change. Daly has presented and published work in the areas of social network theory and impact of current accountability structures as well as on educational reform and organizational learning.

About the Contributors

Allison Atteberry is a PhD candidate in the Administration and Policy Analysis program at the Stanford School of Education. Her research interests include school intervention strategies to improve learning opportunities, especially for children in disadvantaged settings. Allison's dissertation work focuses on issues related to the estimation of causal effects of teachers and schools and implications for accountability systems. She is also interested policies designed to improve teacher self-efficacy and effectiveness.

Kira J. Baker-Doyle, PhD, is an assistant professor of education at Pennsylvania State University-Berks. Her work focuses on teachers' social networks and professional support. She is the author of a forthcoming book on new teachers' social networks, to be published by Teachers College Press in 2011.

Dale Belman, PhD, is a professor in the School of Human Resources and Labor Relations at Michigan State University. His interests include the regulation of labor markets, the effect of collective bargaining and education on labor market outcomes, and the employment relationship in construction and trucking. His publications include quantitative and theoretic analysis of the effect of the minimum wage on employment and hours, the effect of prevailing wages on the employment of minority workers in construction, and how unions affect firm performance. He has published a book on the employment relationship in the trucking industry and is currently working on a book on the "new" minimum wage literature.

Stephen P. Borgatti, PhD, is the Paul Chellgren Endowed Chair of Management at the University of Kentucky. His research interests include social networks, knowledge management, and research methods.

Anthony S. Bryk, PhD, is the ninth president of The Carnegie Foundation for the Advancement of Teaching. He held the Spencer Chair in Organizational Studies in the School of Education and the Graduate School of Business at Stanford University from 2004 until assuming Carnegie's presidency in September 2008. Before coming to Stanford, he held the Marshall Field IV Professor of Education post in the sociology department at the University of Chicago, where he founded the Center for Urban School Improvement which supports reform efforts in the Chicago Public Schools. Bryk also founded the Consortium on Chicago School Research, which has produced a range of studies to advance and assess urban school reform.

Linda Choi is a PhD candidate in education policy at University of California, Berkeley's Graduate School of Education. She studies the ways school-level actors interpret and enact policies. Specifically, her research looks at the way teachers interpret and act on institutionalized categories and labels under current accountability conditions.

Cynthia E. Coburn, PhD, is an associate professor in policy, organization, measurement, and evaluation at the University of California, Berkeley's Graduate School of Education. Her research brings the tools of organizational sociology to the understanding of the relationship between instructional policy and teachers' classroom practices in urban schools. She has studied these issues in the context of state and national reading policy, attempts to scale up innovative school reform programs, and districtwide professional development initiatives.

Russell P. Cole, PhD, (Policy Research, Evaluation, and Measurement, University of Pennsylvania), is a researcher at Mathematica Policy Research. His interests include using social network data to understand how individual and organizational social structures influence behavior. He is currently using network methodology to describe the partnership structures of organizations providing evidence-based home visitation services to prevent child maltreatment.

Jorge Ávila de Lima, PhD, is associate professor of education in the Department of Education of the University of the Azores, Portugal. He is strongly involved in teacher education, both at the primary and secondary school levels. He also has several years of experience as a school board member in a large secondary school. De Lima's PhD thesis used network concepts and tools to study the personal and professional relationships among teachers in two Portuguese secondary schools. Since then, he has published nationally and internationally, including several methodological, conceptual, and empirical works on networks, teacher collaboration, and school development.

Kara S. Finnigan, PhD, is an associate professor of educational policy at the University of Rochester's Warner School of Education. Her research, which focuses on urban school districts, blends perspectives in education, sociology, and political science, employing both qualitative and quantitative methods. Her substantive interests include accountability policies, choice policies, organizational learning, district reform, and social network analysis.

Kenneth A. Frank, PhD, is a professor in counseling, educational psychology and special education as well as in fisheries and wildlife at Michigan State University. His substantive interests include the diffusion of innovations; the study of schools as organizations; social structures of students and teachers; and school decision making, social capital, and resource flow, especially concerning natural resource usage.

Kaleen Healey is a graduate student in the Human Development and Social Policy program at Northwestern University. She holds a bachelor's degree from the University of Notre Dame and a master's degree from Loyola University Chicago.

Julie M. Hite, PhD, is an associate professor of organizational leadership and strategy in the Department of Educational Leadership and Foundations, Brigham Young University. Her research focuses on strategic organizational networks, resource acquisition, and performance of U.S. and Ugandan schools, using qualitative and network methods.

Steven J. Hite, EdD, is a professor of educational research theory and methodology at Brigham Young University. His work focuses on applying the full range of quantitative and qualitative research and evaluation systems to improve the quality, efficiency, effectiveness, and equality of educational opportunities for disadvantaged individuals, families, and communities globally. Dr. Hite works extensively with UNESCO on projects in developing countries throughout the world.

Chong Min Kim is a PhD candidate in the Measurement and Quantitative Methods program at the College of Education at Michigan State University and a research analyst for the Distributed Leadership Study at Northwestern University's School of Education and Social Policy. His areas of interest include social network analysis, distributed leadership, hierarchical linear modeling, and school reform.

Ann Krause, PhD, is assistant professor of ecology in the Department of Environmental Sciences at the University of Toledo. Her research interests include systems ecology, network theory and methodology, and coupling of human and natural systems for sustainable ecosystems.

Willow Mata is a doctoral candidate in education policy at University of California, Berkeley's Graduate School of Education. She studies the relationship between social policy and informal interaction in schools, especially under conditions of diversity and demographic change. Her dissertation research focuses on school and policy responses to new immigrants in Barcelona, Spain.

Nienke M. Moolenaar, PhD, is a postdoctoral researcher at the Department of Educational Sciences at the University of Twente, the Netherlands. Her research interests include social capital theory, social network analysis, school leadership, organizational behavior, and students' citizenship competences in elementary education. In the course of her PhD project, she received various grants and scholarships to present her work at international conferences. She attended the University of California, San Diego as a visiting scholar.

Christopher B. Mugimu, PhD, received his doctorate in educational leadership from Brigham Young University. He is currently a senior lecturer and head of the Department of Curriculum, Teaching, and Media of Makerere University, Kampala, Uganda. His research interests are on comparative international development education, higher education, contemporary curriculum issues (e.g., HIV curriculum integration), assessment of learning and evaluation, teacher education, and open education resources.

Yusuf K. Nsubuga, PhD, is the director of basic and secondary education in Uganda's Ministry of Education and Sports. He is also the Coordinator of HIV/AIDS in the entire education sector. His research interests are in education leadership and management. He is also very much interested in research in the areas of HIV/AIDS and education, human rights, and law and ethics in relation to HIV/AIDS. He is participating in research on quality of education, particularly in developing countries.

Brandon Ofem is a PhD student in management at the University of Kentucky. His research interests include theory of social networks, top management teams, and competitive dynamics. He is the winner of the Barry Armandi Award for Best Student Paper in Management Education Research at the 2010 Academy of Management Annual Meeting.

William R. Penuel, PhD, is director of evaluation research at the Center for Technology in Learning at SRI International. His research interests focus on teacher professional development, technology to support classroom assessment, and the implementation of ambitious curricular reforms in mathematics and science education.

Peter J. C. Sleegers, PhD, is professor of educational organization and management at the University of Twente, The Netherlands. Dr. Sleegers has published extensively on leadership, innovation. and educational policy in more than forty refereed journal articles and several edited books. Current research projects include studies of the effects of educational leadership on student motivation for school, longitudinal research on the sustainability of reforms, and design studies of professional learning communities.

James P. Spillane, PhD, is the Spencer T. and Ann W. Olin Professor in Learning and Organizational Change at the School of Education and Social Policy at Northwestern University. He is also chair of the Human Development and Social Policy program, professor of management and organizations, and a faculty associate at Northwestern's Institute for Policy Research. Spillane has published extensively on issues of education policy, policy implementation, school reform, and school leadership.

Elliot H. Weinbaum, PhD, is a research assistant professor at the University of Pennsylvania's Graduate School of Education and a senior researcher at the Consortium for Policy Research in Education. His work focuses on the development of education policy and its impact on professional practice and improvement at the school and central office levels. Elliot is coeditor of *The Implementation Gap: Understanding Reform in High Schools* (Teachers College Press, 2008). He holds a PhD in education policy from the University of Pennsylvania and a BA from Yale University.

Susan A. Yoon, PhD, is assistant professor of education at University of Pennsylvania Graduate School of Education. Her research spans the disciplines of science and technology education and the learning sciences. She is pursuing several lines of research, including investigating curricular applications and learning outcomes of using social network analysis in decision making about socioscientific issues with students.

Index